Religious Zionism
and the Settlement Project

Religious Zionism and the Settlement Project

Ideology, Politics, and Civil Disobedience

Moshe Hellinger, Isaac Hershkowitz,
and Bernard Susser

SUNY
PRESS

Published by State University of New York Press, Albany

For information, contact State University of New York Press, Albany, NY
www.sunypress.edu

Library of Congress Cataloging-in-Publication Data

Names: Hellinger, Moshe, author. | Hershkowitz, Isaac, author. | Susser,
   Bernard, 1942– author.
Title: Religious Zionism and the settlement project : ideology, politics, and
   civil disobedience / Moshe Hellinger, Isaac Hershkowitz, and Bernard
   Susser.
Description: Albany : State University of New York Press, [2018] | Includes
   bibliographical references and index.
Identifiers: LCCN 2017013952 (print) | LCCN 2017015234 (ebook) | ISBN
   9781438468402 (ebook) | ISBN 9781438468396 (hardcover   ) |
   ISBN 9781438468389 (pbk.   )
Subjects: LCSH: Religious Zionism—Israel—History. | Religious Zionists—Israel—
   Attitudes. | Land settlement—Political aspects—Gaza Strip. | Land settlement—
   Political aspects—West Bank. | Israelis—Colonization—Gaza Strip. | Israelis—
   Colonization—West Bank. | Democracy—Religious aspects—Judaism. | Gaza
   Strip—Ethnic relations. | West Bank—Ethnic relations.
Classification: LCC DS150.R32 (ebook) | LCC DS150.R32 H44 2018 (print) | DDC
   331.3/15694—dc23
LC record available at https://lccn.loc.gov/2017013952

*Moshe Hellinger dedicates this book to the blessed memory
of his late parents and sister, Shlomo and Hava Hellinger
and their daughter Rachel Hellinger.*

*Isaac Herskowitz dedicates this book to the blessed memories
of his grandparents, Hayyim and Sarah Harel,
and David and Naomi Hershkowitz,
who believed their whole life in the Religious-Zionist vision
and educated their offspring in its spirit.*

Bernard Susser dedicates this book to Eli Chapnick, his cousin/brother.

Contents

Acknowledgments

We would like to thank the three anonymous readers whose comments and suggestions contributed to the quality of the book. The production manager, Eileen Nizer, patiently navigated our way through the various tasks in involved in turning a manuscript into a book. Our special thanks goes to our editor, Rafael Chaiken, for his unstinting assistance and encouragement. We also thank Bar llan University for its support in this project.

Acknowledgments

We would like to thank ...

Introduction

For nearly two millennia, the Jews were a stateless people. No wonder then that issues like religion and state, the temporal and the sacerdotal, war and peace, faith and the rule of secular law, Halacha and the proper form of government were usually glossed over or relegated to scholarly, theoretical discourse. While the Christian Middle Ages raged with debate and conflict between the church and the secular sovereign powers, there was little in the way of a parallel Jewish discourse. When such discussions did take place, they were largely philosophical in character, often limited to legal discussions of community versus individual rights or treated in the context of the messianic era when Jewish sovereignty in the Land of Israel would be restored.

The founding of a Jewish state in 1948 transformed this muted, relatively moribund discourse into a new, frequently tumultuous necessity. Unprecedented issues were faced for which the tradition had only incomplete answers. Rabbis confronted governments with halachic demands just as the newly constituted secular state staked out its claim to authority over issues that intruded upon Jewish religious law. Issues related to the Sabbath, marriage and divorce, dietary laws, army service, and conversion pitted the newly established state against entrenched rabbinic authorities. These issues have been exhaustively treated in a burgeoning scholarly literature.

No group in Israeli society has been so profoundly embroiled in the religion-state impasse than the religious Zionists. (We use the lowercase "religious" to emphasize that religious Zionism is not one movement—it is composed of many.) In the past forty years the central flashpoint of this struggle has been the "settlement project" that religious Zionists have championed and spearheaded. This project and the group that constitutes its driving force have been the object of very different attitudes—ranging from admiration to rebuke.

Not surprisingly, there is a deep gulf between the settler's self-image and the one presented by its opponents and by most of the research until

the last decade. In the eyes of its spokespersons, religious Zionism is nothing less than the pioneering movement that leads toward the providential
redemption of the Jewish people. Theirs is the authentically patriotic
movement of Zionist renewal that seeks to energize what has increasingly
become a lethargic, ideologically jaded public. In the secular, liberal, left-
leaning camp, however, their image tends to be badly tarnished. They are
frequently portrayed as religious fanatics who threaten to destroy the State of
Israel in its present democratic form and to transform it into an apartheid,
pariah state cut off from the enlightened Western countries. It is often
argued by the settler camp that the greater part of the media shares this
negative view. These dissonant images convulse Israeli public life. For its
supporters, the struggle is over preserving the religious, moral, and national
character of the Jewish state. For its opponents, the settlement project is
nothing short of catastrophic—both in regard to its messianic goals and to
the democracy-defying policies it not infrequently promotes.

Religious Zionism, at least in its activist *Gush Emunim* (Bloc of the
Faithful) settlement movement version, has forcefully struggled to realize its
central goal: the Jewish people settling and controlling the Greater Land of
Israel. It fought to establish the first settlements in the 1970s in the eastern
Samarian ridge, continued in its battle against vacating settlements first in
Yamit (Sinai Peninsula) and then in Gush Katif (Gaza Strip), persisted in
its zealous opposition to the Oslo Process and the Rabin government, and,
as these lines are being written, has given rise to (at least at its margins)
the anarcho-fanatical youths who go by the name "Price Tag" (*Tag Mechir*).
There are those for whom these ongoing struggles to "liberate" the Land
of Israel need to be seen as expressions of moral purity, of unstinting self-
sacrifice for the sake of Jewish people's deepest interests. Indeed, the settlers
have been described as the unsung biblical heroes of the modern era. Not
surprisingly, where some see morality and sacrifice, others see immorality,
brutality, and ideological gangsterism—what some have called the "great
tragedy" of the Zionist movement.

Whether the settlement project deserves approbation or opprobrium,
in our view both of these positions tend to be one-dimensional and fail
to grasp the totality of a very complex movement. In the last decade, a
new generation of scholars such as Shlomo Fischer (2007), Michael Feige
(2009), and Motti Inbari (2012) have presented a more nuanced analysis
of the settler's rabbinic and intellectual discourse. Our research follows
this approach.

The book's objective is to enrich the debate surrounding this fraught
subject by analyzing the political theology, halachic and intellectual discourse as it impinges upon the settlement project. More specifically, we

take up the obligation that many (if not most) religious Zionists feel to obey the laws regarding Jewish settlements passed by a democratically elected government—however distasteful they may be—against their claim that following these laws deals irremediable harm to Judaism, the Zionist movement, and the Jewish people. Beyond presenting the historical-factual evolution of the settlement project, our main focus is on the ideological, halachic, and political justifications that lie at the heart of the settlement agenda. This study offers a panoramic view of the religion/state, obedience/disobedience, Halacha/democracy divides in regard to the struggle for the Land of Israel—from the rise of Gush Emunim to the present.

The rise of Gush Emunim in 1974 and its subsequent repercussions on Israeli society constitutes a critical turning point in the relationship between religion and state in the Jewish state's public life. By contrast to the internal tensions arising from the Haredi-secular confrontation on issues like conscription of Yeshiva students into the IDF, the Gush Emunim-driven settlement project has become an international issue that sometimes impugns the legitimacy of Israel's public policy—if not, in certain quarters, its status among the nations. Moreover, settlement activity has presented a critical obstacle to a two-state solution to the Israel-Palestine conflict—a solution supported by virtually the entire Western world. It renders the improvement of relations with other Arab states that are ostensibly prone to improve relations with the Jewish state (such as Saudi Arabia and the United Arab Emirates) unlikely to bear fruit anytime in the near future. There are also critical national/moral questions that military occupation of a subject people produces for Israel internally, for the Jewish people internationally and for international community as a whole.

For many observers, the Greater Land of Israel movement and its settlement activity have already rendered a two-state solution impractical if not impossible. The movement's élan and its fervent on-the-ground activities have, arguably, made it the most dynamic and influential presence in Israeli political life over the last few decades. In certain areas, religious Zionism is in the process of replacing center-left Ashkenazi secularism as the leading elite group in Israeli society. A growing cohort of traditionalists and Haredim indentify with the values and goals of the religious Zionist Right even if they do not consider themselves a part of the religious Zionist community. Beyond the *HaBayit Hayehudi* (Jewish Home) party which is the religious Zionists main political representative, the community and its ideological agenda have struck deep roots in the long-ruling Likud party. Many religious Zionists have achieved positions of leadership in the Likud elite. As of this writing, the ministers of education, justice, agriculture (whose role in settlement activity is central) and for Jerusalem, the Speaker of the Knesset, the Attorney General, the Deputy Foreign Minister, the Chief of Police and the head of the Mossad all travel in religious Zionist circles. This has no precedent in Israeli public life.

The IDF has felt this evolving change as well. The spectacular growth in the percentage of religious Zionist soldiers and officers who today comprise—in some critical fighting units—roughly a third of the army's manpower makes it entirely possible that were the army to receive an order to evacuate settlements which religious Zionist rabbis would declare prohibited by Jewish law, its implementation would be alarmingly problematic. It cannot be emphasized too strongly that a reluctant army is a problem the Jewish state has never faced. To be sure, there are, on the humanist Left, perhaps a few dozens of soldiers who refuse to serve beyond the Green Line, but they are marginal and receive only scant media attention. Religious right-wing insubordination is an entirely different matter. Not only because of their numbers and the indispensable combat positions they fill, but also because religious prohibitions, at least in the way that many religious Zionist rabbinic authorities have articulated them in the past, leave no room for doubt, no room for halfway measures. Israeli democracy and the solidarity of Israeli society might well suffer a mortal blow if large-scale disobedience were to become a realistic option.

Although it belongs to a different category, the tensions between Haredim and secular Jews should not be underestimated. The number of Haredim who were not drafted into the IDF reached some 12 percent of the yearly conscription quota and the days of intense bitterness during the Ehud Barak's tenure as Prime Minister will not soon be forgotten. But in recent years what has become noteworthy is the significant rise in Haredim who do serve—estimated to be in the thousands. In any event, this is a local issue with few consequences for Israel in the international arena. Even internally, it is unlikely to threaten the character of Israel as a democratic state. We present a comprehensive and systematic study of the religious Zionist settlement project because of the unprecedented challenge it poses to the relationship between religion and state, its unique challenge the Jewish state's democratic character and, not least, to Israel's standing in the international community.

Religious Zionists experience the religion-state conflict more intensely than other Israeli communities. The position of the secular Right is far less nuanced and complex. Cultural, national, and security-oriented in character, secular right-wing Zionists do not face dilemmas of split religious-civilian personalities. For their part, ultra-Orthodox (Haredi) Jews express profound animosity to the secular Zionist State and their attitude to the Land of Israel is neither ideologically sharp nor especially aggressive. There are, to be sure, a number of ultra-Orthodox settlements in Judea and Samaria, but they were established more in order to ease severe housing pressures in the traditional ultra-Orthodox neighborhoods than because of a commitment to the Greater Land of Israel. The ultra-Orthodox do not—mildly stated—accept the religious status accorded to the State of Israel by the religious Zionists. If anything, the secular state is an offence to their religious sensibilities, an abomination. Some Haredim unashamedly see the state as an instrument to advance the interests of the Haredi community. Although some among them have turned sharply rightward in recent years, their hawkishness has nothing to do with the sanctification of the state.

Uniquely, the religious Zionist worldview is riven with profound inner pressures and is sometimes divided against itself. Two different legal systems—the halachic and the civil—vie for their loyalty. Accepting the state as God-given and as part of the drama of messianic deliverance (as many religious Zionists do), means opposing government actions that thwart Israel's millenarian role. Bound to the state by both civil and religious loyalties, religious Zionist politics tend to be—especially since the 1970s—conflicted, discordant, tense, and sometimes violent. It is this tension that our study sets out to explore.

The controversies in which the religious Zionists and the state confront each other go beyond the question of which territories occupied in 1967 ought to be settled. The struggle over the settlements and the territories has triggered the most basic of political questions: where does the sovereign state's authority to impose its will upon recalcitrant citizens end and the civilian right to resist what it perceives as intolerable decrees begin?

Moreover, as opposed to issues like "Who is a Jew?," Sabbath observance and dietary laws whose impact is largely local, that is, focused on Israeli society itself, policies in regard to Judea and Samaria/the West Bank are charged with international consequences of the highest order—the Israeli-Palestinian conflict is perhaps the most explosive, media-covered struggle of the last generation. Furthermore, by contrast with Sabbath and dietary laws that rarely pose threats of major civil disobedience or mass defiance of state laws, the settlement project has triggered a heated halachic-ideological debate over obeying laws and orders that sometimes spills over into violence. Nor is this theopolitical crisis likely to disappear any time soon; indeed, it gives every sign of intensifying, of becoming increasingly intractable.

The Six Day War of 1967 and even more so the Yom Kippur War of 1973 brought about tectonic changes in the religious Zionist movement. The "historic pact" between the secular labor movement and the moderate, accommodating religious Zionists that persevered from the beginning of the twentieth century, was ruptured beyond repair. A young, ardently religious, and nationalist generation turned sharply rightward, leading in short order to the founding of Gush Emunim in 1974. The graduates of the *Mercaz HaRav* yeshiva in Jerusalem, who often rose to positions of leadership in Gush Emunim, orchestrated efforts to intensify religious faith and to promote the vision of a Greater Land of Israel. Indeed, religious renewal and settlement activity are the obverse sides of each other; their union infuses the settler movement with its typical blend of pious, high-minded spirituality and aggressive, on-the ground politics. It is, in fact, this convergence between national/territorial aspirations on the one hand and the sense of a religious mission on the other that makes Gush Emunim and its subsequent incarnations such imposing and singular phenomena.

This radical change of direction among religious Zionists underlies the growing confrontations between the state's institutions and the radicalized settler youth. In countless different incidents (many of them far from the camera's eye) the religious-political agenda of the militant religious Zionist youth triggered conflicts with state authorities in which disobedience to the law became a real option for advocates of the Greater Land of Israel. To be sure, a chronology of settler activity is not our subject. We mainly follow their ideas—halachic, ideological, and political—as they evolved from one crisis to the next, from one evacuation to the next, often becoming more radical with passing time.

Our research has led us to one central conclusion: despite the severe traumas that the religious Zionist community has undergone in the past decades—experiences that profoundly tested it ideologically, religiously, and politically—it has *for the most part* not been drawn to violent mass defiance. Vigilante style behavior has remained peripheral to the movement. It is surely true that violent behavior has taken place. But what has *not happened* can easily be overlooked. What has not happened is a community-wide revolt that challenged the legitimacy of the state and its institutions. There may well be a certain degree of covert sympathy and understanding for some of the violent acts committed by a minority of militants but the undeniable historical fact is that the religious Zionist community has not risen up against state authority. As a whole—and this includes most of the settler community—it has remained tense, restrained, ambivalent, often embittered. Despite prophesies of doom forecasting that religious Zionists in general and religious Zionist settlers in particular would collectively defy, resist, and disobey orders when their backs were up against the wall—this has not happened. The level of violence at charged historical junctures, even when an undeniable trauma was involved (e.g., the evacuation from Gush-Katif/Gaza Strip), has been theatrical, symbolic, and telegenic but not life-endangering. Attempts to inflict serious bodily harm were few and far between.

Herein lies the paradox. While the settler leadership was prepared to clash with the elected government and its laws in day-to-day activities, it was unwilling to delegitimize the sanctified state and its institutions in the traumatic cases of major settlement evacuations. In our view there is a basic structural principle that explains religious Zionism's flouting the sovereign state's institutions while stopping at the brink. In different incarnations, this "balance" has persevered since the 1970s. There was mostly individual violence in the establishing of illegal settlement in the mid-1970s; in calls for disobedience during the Yamit evacuation, in the terrorist activities of the Jewish Underground; in the struggle that went far beyond legitimate disobedience in the period of the Oslo Process; in the Gush Katif/Gaza Strip evacuation; in the clashes with state security forces in establishing illegal "outposts" in Judea and Samaria/West Bank and last, and perhaps most ominous, the vigilante violence and terrorism of *Tag Mechir* (Price Tag).

Emphatically, there *was* violence in some/many of these cases, but it was the violence of individuals and not that of the consolidated religious Zionist community. Just when one would most expect collective mutiny and mass life-threatening violence, it did not take place.

When the "earth trembled" beneath the feet of religious Zionists during the Yamit and especially during the Gush Katif/Gaza Strip evacuations when thousands of settlers were expelled from their homes; when pundits of all ideological stripes spoke of the all-out battle to come—restraint trumped violence. Although histrionic violence was present, it did not go much beyond political theater. The state was not rejected or spurned by religious Zionism; neither did mass, organized resistance occur. Rather, the faith that the State of Israel was endowed with religious sanctity—the "beginning of salvation"—prevented the community from delegitimizing the state or venturing much beyond civil disobedience even if it was, at times, questionable in democratic terms. The partnership between the religious and the secular did not fall apart and although there was some fraying of the social fabric, Jewish Israel remained mostly united.

What can explain this unexpected restraint? Surely it is not that the traumas experienced by the religious Zionist settler community were not, for them, traumatic enough to elicit a more forceful reaction. We suggest that a "theological-normative balance" is at play. A dynamic balance has developed between the holiness attributed to the state on the one hand and its patently secular character on the other. Ideally, religious commitment to the State of Israel is overriding but at the same time, realistically, the state frequently acts in ways that violate religious values and precepts. This clash between two poles of loyalty creates an intra-religious tension that has dogged religious Zionism since its origin more than a century ago. Balancing the two has been the movement's core dilemma. Even when government decisions violated Torah commandments, religious Zionism has been by turns cautious, inclusive, flexible, pragmatic, and at times highly adamant.

In a word: bestowing religious status on the secular state inoculates against the growth of de-legitimation and anti-system politics. The state's religious aura acts to undermine calls for civil, political and military disobedience because reverence for and deference to the state are conceived of as religious duties. Consequently, the religious Zionist discourse of loyalty is primary and paradigmatic while the discourse of disobedience faces serious intellectual obstacles. The theological-normative safety net prevents the descent into a dangerous spiral of secular-religious conflict. We believe that without appreciating this key countervailing power within religious Zionism's worldview, its reaction to the evacuation of settlements cannot be fully understood.

For the most part, the theological-normative balance has held until fairly recently. But of late threatening fissures are opening up within religious Zionist community itself. Although violence is still largely the exception to the rule, when it does occur it is more audacious, more unbridled, and more often sanctioned by rabbis—even though they often wish to retain their anonymity. Of late (summer 2015) this violence turned into outright terrorism. So that while the center continues to hold and the religious Zionist community remains largely law-abiding and loyal to the state, justifications for disobedience—and worse—are growing. Even if pitched battles and mass disobedience are very rare, it is difficult to miss the escalation that has taken place in the discourse and practice of disobedience. This has occurred with varying degrees of severity: conscientious democratic disobedience of individuals, nonviolent public ideological insubordination that falls into the category of "civil disobedience," attempts to establish illegal settlements that are at times accompanied by low-level, symbolic violence, a readiness to disobey military orders when they violate a soldier's religious principles and violent vigilante actions against Palestinians and Christians—their mosques churches, properties, and persons. At the margins, the state's legitimacy has been called into question.

Needless to say, upsetting the heretofore sturdy theological-normative balance carries with it potentially perilous consequences for the relationship between the religious Zionist community and the Israeli government. We turn to this threatening phenomenon in the last part of the book.

It must be said at the outset that most of what has been written up until the last decade by publicists and academics on the subject of the settlement project has been anything but value-neutral. Most writers do not even make the attempt to rise above their political biases and enter into the intellectual universe of the religious settlers, that is, present their internal world without prejudice or preconception. But a new generation of scholars has arisen of late that emphasizes the complexity of the religious Zionist-settler worldview and attempts to see it from within (Fischer, 2007; Feige, 2009; Dalsheim, 2011; Inbari, 2012; Shachor, 2015). We adopt this position. Although we recognize the pitfalls involved in adopting a neutral attitude toward such a fraught subject, it is precisely this that we attempt to do. Consequently, we refrain, at least in this study, from making judgments about the legitimacy, morality, and legality of the settlement project. We attempt to allow the various ideological spokespersons to speak for themselves.

This is a book about the settlers, the religious Right, and the political theology of its intellectual and rabbinic leadership. The views of those unsympathetic to the settlement project although often mentioned are not the subject of our study. There is, of course, much that could be said about Palestinian suffering and the injustices done to them. There is also a great deal that might be said about international law and its condemnatory attitude toward the settlement project, but, once again, this falls outside the scope of our concerns. The settlers, of course, see their actions as exemplary and noble. Critics see these same actions as brutal and inexcusable. For the purpose of this text, we suspend judgment.

Although the standard academic literature is extensively dealt with, most of the book is based on primary Hebrew sources. Moreover, even these sources are often inaccessible to readers of Hebrew. Many of them are in the form of pamphlets, synagogue hand-outs, yeshiva Internet sites, halachic discourse, one-time brochures, Responsa, lectures, interviews, etc., that are unavailable in standard library catalogues. Our intention, therefore, is to present a broad but detailed view of a discourse that is normally difficult to get at. For this reason we have sometimes allowed citations that are longer than what is normally acceptable. Our study then has a dual purpose: first, to analyze the religious-secular discourse surrounding the Land of Israel issue; and second to present an abbreviated "compendium" of sources that offers the reader a record of a decades-long, passionate, and often highly sophisticated debate.

The book begins with a theoretical chapter and the ones that follow take up the religiopolitical discourse at a number of critical junctures since the 1970s. The first theoretical chapter is comprised of two parts. To begin with, we trace a number of contemporary liberal approaches to the issue of disobedience in a democratic society. The second half of this first chapter presents a number of intellectual approaches to disobedience that are typical of religious Zionism and which lead to a presentation of our "theological-normative" thesis. Chapters 2, 3, 4, and 5 take up *seriatim* critical historical

moments in the development of the discourse of obedience vs. disobedience in regard to the Land of Israel. Chapter 2 deals with Gush Emunim's
struggle to establish settlements in opposition to the decisions of Rabin's
first government (1974–1977). It continues with a description and analysis
of the Yamit evacuation (1982) and the religiopolitical debates it triggered.
Finally, it takes up the revelation that a terrorist Jewish Underground had
been actively involved in anti-Palestinian violence (1981–1984). The
third chapter is devoted to religious Zionism's policy and practice during
the Oslo Process. It deals with this community's aggressive actions against
the Rabin Government (1993–1995) ending in Rabin's tragic assassination
by a religious Zionist in November 1995. The unilateral evacuation from
Gush Katif/Gaza Strip orchestrated by Prime Minister Ariel Sharon (2005)
and the bitter polemics it occasioned are the subject of the fourth chapter.
The fifth and final chapter studies a number of the important struggles over
settlement activities that have taken place from the Gaza evacuation up
until the present.

                                    ∾

We cannot close this introduction without mentioning, if only in passing,
how strikingly reminiscent the arguments raised by the settler intellectuals
and rabbis on the one side and representatives of the sovereign state on the
other are to those that rocked Europe from the time of Saint Augustine
to the Wars of Religion. Secular-religious debate regarding the settlement
project rehearses many of the same ideas that were wrangled over by kings
and clerics centuries ago. One could at times take medieval texts and place
them alongside their contemporary Jewish analogs and find noteworthy
correspondences between them. Although there are, of course, no direct
influences involved, it is not difficult to hear echoes from the Christian
medieval past. Again, this is not our subject, but at times one cannot help
but feel a remarkable sense of déjà vu in this discourse—familiar arguments
written from right to left.

   The same might also be said of the discourse on civil disobedience
and passive resistance so prominent in the nineteenth and twentieth
centuries: from Henry David Thoreau, through Lev Tolstoy, to Mahatma
Gandhi and Martin Luther King. In the Israeli case, a remarkably rich use
of these arguments is evident throughout the struggles over settlements
and their evacuation. What are the limits of obedience? Can a majority
impose deeply inimical policies on a defiant minority? Once again: familiar
arguments written from right to left.

Full disclosure: the three authors of this study come from different poles of the religious and ideological spectrum. One of the authors, a political theorist, belongs to the secular Left and has an adversarial relationship to religious Zionism. Another is a religious Zionist, conversant with Halacha, who defines his ideological position as center-Left. The third, a student of Jewish philosophy, belongs to the religious Right and is broadly sympathetic to the settlement project. We often found ourselves embroiled in debates over content, style, interpretation, even the use of specific words. These debates were heated, lengthy, and frequent. Nevertheless, they were salutary inasmuch as they filtered out the inevitable proclivity to formulate issues in prejudicial ideological terms. What seemed to one overly critical appeared to the other two as insufficiently derogatory. At times we confronted a three-way split. This attempt at neutrality will not satisfy many of our readers whether on the Left, the Center or the Right. Still, we believe that the result is not an ecumenical, toothless mélange; it was written to be challenging and provocative. Although none of the authors is entirely satisfied with the final version of the text, we did try to argue the issues until we arrived at formulations that we could each live with. Complexity of perspective is the result. In short, we kept each other honest.

All three of the authors are deeply concerned about the future of Israel as a Jewish and democratic state. These two characteristics (in whichever order) are understood to be critical for the health, indeed for the very existence of the state. Although our discussion will surely not close the debate on the highly controversial settlement project, it is our hope that it will render it more knowledgeable and informed.

Disobedience

Liberal and Religious Zionist

Liberal-Democratic Disobedience:
A Theoretical Perspective

We begin with a definition of disobedience and explore its various forms. The most central contemporary treatment of the subject is that of John Rawls (Rawls, 1971: chapter 6). He distinguishes between two forms of disobedience: civil disobedience and conscientious objection. He defines civil disobedience as follows:

> I shall begin by defining civil disobedience as a public, nonviolent, conscientious yet political act contrary to law usually done with the aim of bringing about a change in the law or policies of the government. By acting in this way one addresses the sense of justice of the majority of the community and declares that in one's considered opinion the principles of social cooperation among free and equal men are not being respected. (Rawls, 1971: 364)

Hence, civil disobedience rests upon principles broadly common to a society that are felt to be violated, in a specific case, by a dissident group.

As opposed to civil disobedience, conscientious objection need not be public; it often takes place in the personal sphere. It is not necessarily directed at a prevailing social-political sense of justice or policy; neither is always directed at public ideological norms accepted by the majority. It can be based on a personal religious faith that is opposed to that of the majority: for example, the disobedience of the early Christians to the laws of the pagan Roman Empire. Conscientious objection does not aim at changing society, its laws, decisions, and operational authority. Indeed, pacifist conscientious objection is the personal repudiation of carrying weapons and being involved in violent actions—it is not an attempt to prevent society as a whole from using violence when it is convinced that such violence is necessary for self-protection (Rawls, 1971: 368–71). Nevertheless, Rawls is aware that at times objectors may simultaneously base themselves on a mixture of conscientious objection and civil disobedience (Rawls, 1971: 371).

A term that various Israeli thinkers use in parallel with civil disobedience is *Meri Ezrachi* that can perhaps be rendered as "civil insubordination." In the same general spirit as Rawls, the legal philosopher Chaim Gans argues that civil disobedience: "'is disobedience intended to attain a change in the policy or the principle served or expressed by the law being disobeyed or by another law" (Gans, 1992: 138).

As opposed to Rawls, different liberal thinkers believe that civil disobedience is not necessarily limited to cases in which public norms are accepted by both the disobeyer and the political community. In their view, there are instances in which individuals who refuse to comply with the law rest their case on principles that are not accepted by the majority (or a large part) of society; it is not only a specific political policy to which they object but something much broader and more basic—a whole system of life that is rejected as was the case with slavery in the American south (Singer, 1973: 84–92; Smart, 1978: 249–60; Greenawalt, 1987: 226–43).

Another variant on this position accepts the general argument that civil disobedience objects to a law or policy conceived of as profoundly unjust but adds that it can also be a simple protest against such a law with no further objectives. Disobedience may be direct as when it struggles against a law or policy (such as the refusal to take part in the evacuation of settlements or the refusal to serve in Vietnam). But it may also be more indirect (such as the refusal to pay taxes so long as slavery persisted—evidenced by the refusal of Henry David Thoreau in the 1850s). In this last view, civil disobedience expresses the unwillingness to continue taking part—even indirectly—in support of laws and decisions that are seen as unjust (Bedau, 1991: 49–67).

Ronald Dworkin's approach is broadly similar to that of Rawls although he utilizes different terminology. Dworkin distinguishes between "defensive" disobedience and "active" disobedience. The first does not attempt to convince others while the latter aims at persuading society of the unjustness of its ways (Dworkin, 1985: chapter 4). Despite the difference in terminology, Dworkin's defensive disobedience is close to conscientious objection while active disobedience is similar to civil disobedience (in Rawls's terminology).

The Israeli philosopher Avi Sagi contends that the conscientious-personal objector bases himself on the freedom society owes him which permits his acting according to his deep moral beliefs. Moral values are the most personal of values since they lie at the basis of our ability to live a fully human life. (Sagi, 2010b: 372–73). In this sense, it appears that a "person who refuses on the basis of morality, believes that the moral blow is a blow to his self-respect, his value and his identity" (Sagi, 2010b: 373–74).

As opposed to Rawls, Joseph Raz claims that there are three forms of disobedience. In addition to conscientious objection and civil disobedience (or civil insubordination) there is yet a third form that is broader in scope and can be called "revolutionary insubordination," that is, activity whose object is the revision of the constitution in its entirety and even a replacement of the regime (Raz, 1979: 262–65). This is not a struggle against a law that is seen as unjust, or even against a broad policy in a specific field—as in the struggle against the war in Vietnam or the prejudicial treatment of African Americans. According to Raz, the third variant of disobedience is the call for a basic and general change in political institutions such as the struggle to cancel the apartheid regime in South Africa and its replacement with a democratic regime in which power would be transferred to the black majority. The recent uprisings in the "Arab Spring"—however they may have soured—could perhaps be included in this category.

No less important is the question of violence: what place does violence have in acts of disobedience? Some thinkers, under certain extreme circumstances, justify violent action against a repressive regime. But two of the greatest cultural heroes of the twentieth century disagreed. Mahatma Gandhi in the India of the 1930s and 1940s and Martin Luther King in the United States during the 1950s and 1960s were convinced that nonviolent resistance was both more effective and more moral in that it did not poison human relations after victory was achieved. Notably, John Rawls as well—although he was not an unconditional supporter of nonviolence—in his aforementioned definition of civil disobedience, expressly conditions it upon nonviolence.

Joseph Raz demurs. He argues that it is impossible to claim that under no circumstances is violence justified as part of civil disobedience. It depends, he declares, on the type of injustice against which the disobeyers are struggling and the degree of violence utilized by reigning powers. The more the injustice is egregious and violent, to that degree is there justification for the use of violence against it (Raz, 1979: 267–68).

Struggles against dictatorial, repressive regimes belong to this category. But for some, even in the context of a democratic regime that is not generally dictatorial or repressive, occasions may arise in which the injustice committed is so essential and violent that it is permitted to act against it with violence as well. This was the position of the Israeli polymath Isaiah Leibowitz, the most outstanding of those who advocated civil disobedience against the Israeli occupation of Lebanon and of the West Bank/Judea and Samaria. Leibowitz did not hesitate to call explicitly not only for civil disobedience—and in so doing he clashed with leaders of the Zionist left like Shulamit Aloni and Yossi Sarid—but expressly called for a revolt against the existing regime and even for civil war. It is hard to escape the literal interpretation of his words (Rotenberg, 2007; Rosen-Zvi, 2007).

A somewhat different categorization of the forms of disobedience is presented by Yossi Ziv (Ziv, 1995). In his view there are four kinds of disobedience: A. conscientious objection; B. civil disobedience or civil insubordination; C. Ideological disobedience; D. ideological insubordination or revolt. Briefly summarizing his position:

A. Conscientious objection: An individual act, not public or political or violent; usually well within the framework of democracy.

B. Civil disobedience or insubordination: It too is nonviolent but as opposed to conscientious objection it is public and political in character. It derives the justifications for its actions from democracy itself. Herein lies the difference between it and the two categories below. The struggles of the early feminists and of Martin Luther King fall into this category.

C. Ideological disobedience: It is normally nonviolent and strives to effect a constitutional or political change. Although not anti-democratic in nature, its disobedience does not draw on democratic principles to justify its actions.

D. Ideological insubordination or revolt: This is ideological disobedience that, in opposition to the foregoing, is not loyal to democratic principles. This form of disobedience does not expressly or necessarily choose violence to advance its ideological commitments. It exploits the means offered by democracy but is not deeply committed to its objectives or its spirit. Hence, it does not recoil from undermining the basis of democracy. Ziv classifies the disobedience of the religious right as belonging to this category.

For our purposes, the more multifaceted the classification, the more useful it is. As we shall see, many acts of disobedience do not fall into binary violent vs. nonviolent classes. Raz and Ziv's richer categorizations provide a wider canvas on which to map the phenomenon of disobedience. In the context of religious Zionist disobedience, four categories present themselves.

A. Conscientious objection based on religious, national or democratic principles.

B. Public-ideological disobedience which at its most activist involves collective insubordination that aims at resetting the public agenda and transforming the public sphere. Religious Zionists, for the very most part, seek to sway the character of the Israeli regime in a more "Jewish" direction and to support the settlement project.

C. Activity that does not respect the rule of law but that normally does not resort to violence. Borderline illegality and exploiting the political maneuvering room provided by democracy is common to this form of disobedience. Attempts to establish illegal settlements fall into this category.

D. At the violent pole of disobedience there are vigilante actions against the property of Palestinians in Judea and Samaria/ West Bank, against Israeli Arabs, and in extreme cases physical attacks against the persons of Arabs and against the Israeli security forces—including outright terrorism.

We shall return to this theoretical introduction regularly throughout the text.

Before concluding this section, three key figures who shaped the discourse of disobedience need to be mentioned if only briefly. Notably, disobedient settlers occasionally referred to them as "proof texts" justifying their actions. They present the most influential versions of the doctrine of nonviolent disobedience and have served as models for resistance to governments whose activities are seen morally deplorable.

Henry David Thoreau (1872–1862) refused to pay taxes to the United States government for so long as slavery existed. His protest continued with the war against Mexico (1846–1848) which he saw as unjustifiable. He was jailed for a single night. In his seminal essay *Civil Disobedience* Thoreau argued for disobeying state law nonviolently in cases of gross miscarriages of justice. Disobedience, he contended, can be of two kinds: first, direct disobedience against those who commit evil acts and, second, more indirect disobedience where it is not only the evildoer who is resisted but, as in the case of not paying taxes, by refusing to be part of a system that acts unjustly (Thoreau, 1993; Bedau, 1991; Ben-Noon, 2015: 88–90).

Two twentieth-century figures, far better known than Thoreau are, of course, Mahatma Gandhi (1869–1948) and Martin Luther King (1929–1968). The first was the leader and symbol of Indian resistance to the British Raj, the second, Martin Luther King, was the central moral, spiritual figure who led the struggle for African-American civil rights in the United States. Gandhi, after a period in South Africa in which he championed the cause of nonviolent resistance to human and civil rights abuses, returned to India and under the slogan, *satyagraha* (truth force), launched a movement of nonviolent resistance against the British. Tragically, both Ghandi and King were assassinated just as their goals were being achieved. To repeat, when resisting government orders to evacuate settlements right-wing activists at times justified their actions by referring to (especially) Gandhi and King (Ben-Noon, 2015).

Disobedience in Israel: A General Survey

Civil disobedience in Israel has taken a different trajectory than what has been common in the West. Western disobedience has generally taken the form of conscientious and ideological resistance to participation in wars, whether for pacifistic reasons or because of left-wing motivated refusal to participate in wars—Vietnam is of course the most prominent example—that were seen as ethically and democratically unjust. Similarly, the struggle for African-American civil rights in the 1960s and 1970s derived from universalistic liberal sources. The mostly marginal (and sometimes quite daft) resistance of whites to what was seen as unwarranted government intervention also relied on arguments that resonated with individualistic liberal antecedents.

Israeli defiance to public law has usually worn a different face. To be sure, there has been left-wing inspired disobedience. Through the years, conscientious objection to serving in the West Bank/Judea and Samaria has been adopted by a relatively small number of soldiers, although it has remained quite far from the political mainstream. They have usually been jailed for relatively short periods and then released. Somewhat more significant was the resistance to serving in the First Lebanese War that was seen as unnecessary and unjust. Although the media did notice this phenomenon, in the end it was more vocal than effective.

By contrast, the more serious and widespread forms of resistance have derived from the Right. Our focus in this study is the disobedience of the religious Zionist movement—the driving force behind the settlement movement—motivated by the nationalistic, often messianic ideal of the

Greater Land of Israel. Nevertheless, over the years the religious Right has also utilized justifications of disobedience on civil and democratic grounds, to wit, that evacuations violated the democratic and property rights of the settlers. Still, it must be made clear that the democratic legitimation of insubordination was always ancillary to the main claim: the land belonged to the Jewish people by Divine, biblical decree.

Although, as we have been arguing, right-wing disobedience has far outweighed that of the Left in past generations, during the pre-state era and the early decades of statehood the picture was far more complex. Perhaps the most dramatic case of disobeying orders took place when the leadership of the *Haganah* commanded Jewish soldiers to volunteer for service in the British army during the Second World War. For a variety of reasons—economic, ideological, security-related—many Haganah members refused. Especially problematic for many of these holdouts was the British "White Paper" that prevented Jewish immigration to Palestine (Stern, 2009).

After the state was founded, the first major case of disobedience was the highly explosive *Altalena* affair. Not a few IDF soldiers, officers, and air force pilots refused to fire upon the ship *Altalena*, which was manned and stocked by the right-wing Etzel (or Irgun) political faction, and was carrying about a thousand fighters and a substantial arms cache from France to Israel in violation of the provisional government's orders. With some loss of life, the ship was sunk by the IDF. The affair, the Irgun's policy, the government's orders, and the military insubordination involved has remained a "hot button" issue in Israeli historiography (Nakdimon, 1978: chapters 10–12).

The first organization promoting disobedience was the Israeli League of War Resistors (*sarbanei milchama*) founded (1947) by Natan Chofshi a long-time *Brit Shalom* member. He drew upon pacifist ideas, especially those of Tolstoy. The movement grew and, in 1951, it began publishing manifestos calling for the right of conscientious objectors to do national service rather than being conscripted into the army. The first conscientious objector—who later became a leading attorney and public figure—was Amon Zichroni. He was arrested a number of times for refusing to be drafted into the IDF and after a hunger strike served briefly in a Civil Defense position. Others followed Zichroni—indeed, after the Six Day War, the group underwent a process of radicalization. But it was not a substantial presence in Israeli public life until the Lebanese War (Epstein, 1999: 328–44).

Alongside general conscientious objection, civil disobedience also had a selective ideological side: refusing to serve in the occupied territories/ Judea, Samaria and Gaza. In 1971, the radical Left group *Matzpen* (compass) dispatched a letter to Defense Minister Moshe Dayan in which they announced their unwillingness to be conscripted into a conquering army. And, indeed, in some cases the army compromised and did not insist that they serve beyond the Green Line. But this conciliatory spirit ended in 1979 when twenty-seven students who were about to enter their last year of high school notified the Minister of Defense that they would refuse to serve in the occupied territories as their part in advancing a Palestinian-Israeli peace accord. Many among them were sentenced to a number of terms of incarceration—their leader Gadi Elgazi was jailed five times. The head of the IDF's Manpower Division explained that the toughening stance was a reaction to the increasing number of resistors and to their becoming an organized force. Nevertheless, civil disobedience from the Left remained more attention grabbing than effective (Epstein, 1999: 337–44).

It was only with the First Lebanese War (1982) that civil disobedience became a significant public issue in Israel. The war's lengthy duration, the army's advancing beyond the 40-kilometer limit that had been announced at the start of the conflict and reaching the Beirut-Damascus highway, provoked not a few soldiers to disobey orders. Most prominent was Colonel Eli Geva, a highly regarded tank brigade commander, who gave up his post rather than enter Beirut with his soldiers. After a discussion with the Chief of Staff (Rafael Eitan), he was dismissed from the army. In the course of the war the *Yesh Gvul* (there is a limit) movement was created in the context of which some 3,000 soldiers lent their signatures to documents stating their intention to disobey orders. About 150 were prosecuted. Disobedience was now a significant component of the political equation and it became one of the weighty considerations that motivated the army to end the war (Epstein, 1999: 344–50; Unger, 2010: 6).

Left-wing disobedience once again proliferated during the First Intifada that began in 1987. About 2,500 soldiers refused to serve in the occupied territories; some 180 were sentenced to different periods of incarceration. Among those who refused to serve, about 1,500 were from Yesh Gvul. Here too, arguably, disobedience had some degree of influence: the manner in which the army related to the Palestinians moderated and, thereafter, led the then Minister of Defense Yitzhak Rabin to search for a political solution to the Palestinian issue—leading ultimately to his policies when he became Prime Minister in 1992 (Lebel, 2011: 240–41).

With Binyamin Netanyahu's rise to power in 1996, the option of refusing to serve in the territories spread among IDF soldiers; it appeared more legitimate because of the collapse of Rabin's peace plan. A great deal of pressure fell upon the courts to deal with cases of disobeying orders on conscientious grounds. Similarly, the government resolved to employ fewer reserve units for policing and security functions in Judea and Samaria and decided to establish a special, permanent company tasked with maintaining day-to-day security in the territories. At this same time, what was called the "Four Mother's Movement" that promoted withdrawing IDF forces from south Lebanon was active: again cases of disobedience were reported (Lebel, 2011: 241–44). A major burgeoning of insubordination—with a clear ideological agenda—took place against the background of the explosive flare-up of the Second Intifada in 2000. On the one hand, Palestinian suicide terrorist attacks were unprecedented in their scope and severity; on the other, Israeli counter-activities became increasingly violent, ending with the recapture (under the leadership of Ariel Sharon) of Judea and Samaria in 2002 in the "Defensive Shield" campaign. Terrorism abated dramatically. A number of collective letters of officers and pilots announcing disobedience were published and, in their wake (December 2003), a new military "profile" was established that recognized the phenomenon of disobedient soldiers. At the height of the "Defensive Shied" campaign in April 2003, some seventy insubordinate soldiers were jailed. In the summer of 2003, the "defiant community" numbered more than a thousand individuals but it was well understood that behind them—even if they had not publicly announced their intentions—there were many more (Lebel, 2011: 244–49).

The mentor and spiritual father of left-wing ideological refusal—first in the Lebanese War and, thereafter, against serving beyond the Green Line—was the well-known religious Israeli philosopher and polymath, Yeshayahu Leibowitz, to whom we presently return. Interviews with left-wing disobedient soldiers conducted by Erika Weiss reveal that refusal to obey orders developed over the years because of a growing disappointment with the consequences of patriotism and because the appeals for military sacrifice appeared hollow and incongruous. Confronting, in the flesh, the injustices inflicted by the occupation, was a major determinant of their decisions to flout orders.

This disappointment led at times to disenchantment with Zionism itself. Left-wing refusal was usually associated with the Ashkenazi well-off strata of Israel's population and many of them had initially volunteered for service in elite combat units out of a sense of national duty that waned over time (Weiss, 2014). Weiss reports that her discussions with the objectors from the religious Right and from the Left led her to the conclusion that on both sides of the political spectrum, questions of conscience were at the heart of the dilemmas soldiers felt regarding the weighty question: to obey or not. Not surprisingly, the difference between the Left and the religious Right was that the former based their actions on universal, humanistic considerations while the latter focused on particularistic Jewish identity (Weiss, 2014: Conclusion).

Yeshayahu Liebowitz, as noted above, was the central intellectual figure who justified disobedience to serve in the occupied territories. Initially,
Liebowitz accepted a mainstream religious Zionist position. From the 1920s
to the mid-1950s, his views were not especially unique in the national
religious community. Israel's founding, he felt, was a critical, even a constitutive religious moment in Jewish history. However, his views underwent
a radical change in the 1950s. It appears that the Kfar Kibiyeh incident
was a major trigger prompting this transformation. In 1953, IDF soldiers
used (what for Liebowitz was) indefensible violence in a retaliation attack
against the population of the Kibiyeh village in which tens of innocent
Arabs were killed. In the late 1950s, Liebowitz already had perceived the
state as merely instrumental, dissevering Zionism from any religious significance (Hellinger, 2008).

In his article "After Kibiyeh," published originally in 1953, Leibowitz
penned a groundbreaking essay that spoke as few had spoken before him—
certainly not in religious Zionist circles. His prose rages; it speaks volumes
about his disappointment with "religious politics."

> What produced this generation of youth, which felt no inhibition
> or inner compunction in performing the atrocity when given the
> inner urge and external occasion for retaliation? . . . The answer
> is that the events at Kibiyeh were a consequence of applying
> the religious category of holiness to social, national, and politi-
> cal values and interests . . . From a religious standpoint only
> God is holy, and only His imperative is absolute. All human
> values and all obligations and undertakings derived from them
> are profane and have no absolute validity. Country, state, and
> nation impose pressing obligations and tasks that are sometimes
> very difficult. They do not, on that account, acquire sanctity.
> They are always subject to judgment and criticism from a higher
> standpoint . . . The original sin of our education appears already
> in our Declaration of Independence. Its use of the expression
> "the Rock of Israel" in the concluding sentence reflects a
> fraudulent agreement between two sectors of the public . . . The
> secular nation and state adjusted the sense of this term at its
> convenience, and used it to bribe the religious minority . . . If
> the nation and its welfare and the country and its security are
> holy, and if the sword is the "Rock of Israel"—then Kibiyeh
> is possible and permissible. This is the terrible punishment for
> transgressing the stringent prohibition, "Thou shall not take
> the name of the Lord thy God in vain." The transgression may

cause our third commonwealth to incur the curse of our father Jacob. (Leibowitz, 1995: 189–90)

In the euphoria following the Six Day War (1967), Leibowitz was one of the few who strenuously objected to Israeli control of the territories and the peoples residing beyond the Green Line. For Leibowitz, the occupation constitutes a real threat to the Jewish and democratic identity of the State of Israel.

> The problem is not the territory; rather it is the population of 1.25 million Arabs who live on the land and upon whom we will need to impose our rule. Including these Arabs (aside from the 300,000 who are citizens of the state) under our jurisdiction entails the annihilation of Israel as the state of the Jewish people, the destruction of the entire Jewish people, the collapse of the social structure we have established in the state and the moral corruption of both Jews and Arabs. A state that rules over 1.5–2 million hostile aliens will, perforce, be a Shabak state with all that this entails for the spirit of education, for the freedom of speech and thought, and for democracy. The corruption that is characteristic of colonial regimes will infect the State of Israel. The administration will need to deal with the repression of Arab resistance on the one hand and with buying Arab Quislings on the other. There is the fear that the IDF, which has been to this point a popular army, will degenerate into a conquering army with its commanders serving as military rulers like their counterparts in other nations . . . and let the astute understand. Therefore, we have no choice, out of concern for the Jewish people and its state, to leave the territories settled with 1.25 million Arabs and this without any connection to the issue of peace. (Leibowitz, 1975: 419–20)

Nevertheless, until the First Lebanese War, Leibowitz did not expressly call for disobedience. It is important to note that Leibowitz consistently rejected anarchism and believed that the rule of law is mandatory for sustaining any human society (Leibowitz, 1987: 147). However, for Leibowitz an exception to this rule exists: the justification of public ideological disobedience to Israel's occupation beyond the Green Line. He distinguishes between "civil disobedience," and "conscientious disobedience." Civil disobedience does not merely express (in the manner of conscientious disobedience) the inability of an individual to execute orders that violate his core beliefs. By his action, the citizen disobeyer strives to change the character of society. It is patently public and political rather than personal and abstractly idealistic and expresses, for Leibowitz, the struggle to prevent nationalism from turning into bestiality. He does not mince words: "I wish to note that I do not see disobedience as the result of a personal conscientious decision but rather as a public-political struggle aimed at ending the movement that leads from 'humanity, via nationalism to bestiality.' The effective means in this struggle is disobedience" (Leibowitz, 1999: 420–21).

Leibowitz's justifications for civil disobedience are reminiscent of those liberal thinkers such as John Rawls and Ronald Dworkin whom we have mentioned above. For them, disobedience is a form of democratic struggle seeking to prevent a society that prides itself on being democratic from degenerating into one that acts immorally and undemocratically. As noted above, Rawls contends that the objective of disobedience is to appeal to the public based on agreed upon principles that govern their social life. By contrast, other liberal thinkers (Singer, 1973: 84–92; Smart, 1978: 249–60; Greenawalt, 1987: 226–43) do not believe that such common principles are required in order to resort to disobedience. In their view, as noted, cases can surely arise when one who disobeys rests upon principles that run against the grain of the public consensus. Their being consensual does not protect them from moral strictures and from disobedience. Leibowitz clearly belongs to the second category

Leibowitz often cites the well-known saying of Ralph Waldo Emerson: "Good men must not obey the laws too well." He understands this to mean:

> A legal order is one promulgated by an institution authorized to give such an order in an existing regime recognized by the "good man" (of whom Emerson spoke) who is with all his heart a citizen of the state. Yet, should the approach of such a man to all orders be like that of trained dog who heeds the orders of his trainer? Or, perhaps, even the laws of a person's state—of the state that he recognizes as his state—are to be judged by the 'good man' who is cognizant that his values are above the values of the state? (Leibowitz, 1990: 7–8)

Like Rawls (1973: para. 59), Leibowitz argues that disobedience does not harm a democratic state and is not tantamount to anarchism because the citizen recognizes the authority of the democratic state. Still, he accepts its authority just so long as it is rooted in its democratic character. On the one hand, it is his state, but on the other, it remains his state and worthy of obedience because it rests upon worthy principles of justice which each individual has a right to judge autonomously. Indeed, disobedience can be seen as contributing to a vibrant democratic government.

There are, Leibowitz regularly contends, two kinds of government: first, the totalitarian-fascist type that sanctifies the state as the highest of values, and, second the liberal democratic type that instills in its citizens the understanding that the state is not the highest of values. The consequences of this dichotomy are crucial:

> Therefore, in specific cases and situations the 'good man' . . . will recognize that a certain legal order ordained by the legal authority is not compatible with what he recognizes to be the highest value that obliges him absolutely. In such a case—from both a mandatory and a *conscientious* point of view—his obligation to obey this law is invalidated; there is even an obligation to violate the law. I am aware of the great danger bound up with accepting this principle, but it is necessary in order to prevent the degeneration into fascism and even into Nazism. (Leibowitz, 1990: 13–14) [Emphasis added]

As Yossi Ziv and Yishai Rosen Tzvi note, Leibowitz's express appeal for civil disobedience appears only in the course of the Lebanese War after it became clear that the occupation was becoming a permanent reality as a direct consequence of the war initiated by Israel in Lebanon. Leibowitz feared that Israel would be transformed from a democratic into a fascist state. The way to struggle against this approaching tragic outcome was, in his view, to call for civil disobedience that would drastically alter the political-legal direction Israel was taking (Ziv, 1995: 228–38, esp, 235; Rosen Zvi, 2007: 348–53).

Both in his Yesh Gvul publications and in recommendations he made to soldiers who turned to him for advice he preached civil disobedience against service in the IDF for so long as it was an anti-democratic conquering army (Leibowitz, 1987: 20). The right to civil disobedience derives, Leibowitz insists, from liberal democratic norms and from Jewish ideas of justice. The State of Israel as a conquering state both annihilates democracy and violates basic Jewish principles:

> Those who refuse to follow the government's and the military authority's orders—both of which are recognized as [formally] lawful—when these orders are directed toward transforming Israel from an independent state of the Jewish people into an apparatus of violent Jewish domination of another people, when

these orders lead to the annihilation of democracy by negating the political rights of 1.5 million people (and together with our puppet state—south Lebanon—2.5 million). This refusal, if it becomes a group phenomenon of even a minority, is likely to undermine the national-fascist consensus within the entire public and become the first step in turning us back from the bestiality that has overtaken the human and Jewish content of our national existence. (Cited in Ziv, 2005: 235–36)

At times Leibowitz appears to be even more radical. He goes beyond nonviolent disobedience and touches upon the resort to violence. In this, he is closer to the position of Joseph Raz than to that of John Rawls as they were explicated in an earlier section of this study. Leibowitz testifies that he told an officer who came to him with a profound sense of frustration regarding his service in Ramallah: "If you are committed to the political independence of the Jewish people—so I told him—then remain here and try to organize a revolt against the existing government" (Leibowitz, 1987: 20). Elsewhere he comments that "you will find in all the nations and cultures cases in which the best of the citizens violated state laws including even violent disobedience" (Leibowitz, 1999: 419).

The question cannot be avoided: Did Leibowitz actually justify violent disobedience? Yishai Rosen Zvi (Rosen Zvi, 2007: 348–53) and Naftali Rotenberg (Rotenberg, 2007: 366–87) argue that this interpretation cannot be dismissed out of hand. However, neither can we write off the possibility that Leibowitz, in his deliberately provocative style, was indulging in impassioned, exaggerated rhetoric.

The worthy religious model of civil disobedience in Leibowitz's thought derives from the prophets of Israel who are clear representatives of a value-based struggle of non-institutionalized religion against the state. For him "all the prophets of Israel were 'traitors' to their wicked states and to their legal kings" (Leibowitz, 1999: 419). Only the liberal democratic position has it in its power to justify a worthy doctrine of disobedience that, in Leibowitz's eyes, is the critical difference between those who refuse to serve in Lebanon and the Gush Emunim activists. "The former violate the state's laws for the sake of humanity while the latter do not violate its laws at all but act under the aegis of the state and with its support for the sake of bestiality" (Leibowitz, 1999: 149). Broadly, this view follows Rawls's idea that justified disobedience rests on a universalistic, Kantian perspective that does not require a belief in God. However, we should not forget that Leibowitz's critique contains another critical aspect: a profound drawing upon Jewish sources. He calls attention to the patriarch Jacob's curse of his sons Simon and Levi who murdered the residents of an entire village without distinguishing between the guilty and the innocent: "I shall disperse them in Jacob; I shall scatter them through Israel" (Genesis, 49:7).

The Fundamentals of Religious Zionism

The religious Zionist community has been, arguably, the most dynamic group in Israeli society over the course of the past decades. It is considerably more compositionally varied than is normally thought. Not only does it include traditional, long-term religious Zionists—some 600,000 to 700,000 individuals—but also, according to a recent study of the Israel Democracy Institute, it comprises two other population groups that flank it on either side: the traditional-religious on the one hand and the Hardelim (messianic Zionists who observe Halacha in a Haredi manner) on the other. As opposed to the prevalent view that religious Zionists number about 10 percent of the Israeli population, this most up-to-date survey argues that the realistic number is more than double: some 22 percent of the Israeli population (Hermann et al., 2014). Religious Zionists most often belong to the middle and upper classes. Its core is more Ashkenazi than Mizrachi although, because of a growing trend to "mixed marriages," the Ashkenazi-Mizrachi divide promises to fade considerably. (This contrasts with the Haredi community where the divide remains sharp and unchanging.)

An integral part of the Zionist movement from its origins onward, religious Zionists have broadly integrated into Israeli public life and see themselves as a "bridge" between tradition and modernity, between the Haredim and the secular. This synthesis between influential Torah authorities on the one side and a substantial presence in fields like medicine, law, the academy, commerce, and the media on the other, underscores the wide range of religious Zionism that is gradually but steadily spreading from the periphery toward the center. Indeed, in its own self-image it sees itself as having taken over from the Labor movement as the spearhead, the dynamic center of the Zionist project. The simultaneous dialogue and struggle between the veteran secular Ashkenazi elite, which is mostly Centrist and left-wing in worldview, and the religious Zionist camp which is identified with the Right, even the hard Right, lies at the heart of many critical political, cultural, and religious processes that have informed Israeli public life for some four decades.

Politically, the settlement project largely driven by religious Zionist youth has become the *cause célèbre* of the Israeli public sphere. It has changed the character of the Jewish state, perhaps irrevocably. The National

Religious Party (NRP) that lost its electoral foothold—decreasing from roughly twelve Knesset seats to five to seven in the past generation—has become invigorated and energized in recent years. Its successor party (the Jewish Home) rose to twelve seats in the 2013 election. Although it lost ground in the 2015 election (falling to eight seats), this does not reflect a diminution in its ideological constituency. Rather, having become so central to the political process and to Israel's mainstream, many attempted to capture the reigning party, the Likud, by joining its ranks, some even becoming members of the Likud's Central Committee. (A September 2016 poll conducted by Israel's Second Television channel reports that the Jewish Home's current strength stands at fourteen seats (Ynet, September 7, 2016).

Religious Zionists have captured key positions in the country's political elite as we noted in the book's opening pages. Of late, the presence of religious Zionists in fields like the media and general culture—traditionally secular redoubts—has become quite common.

The religious Zionist message has spread beyond its sectorial borders. Those spoken of as "traditionalists," a certain cohort of Haredim, even an assemblage of secular Jews who identify with its nationalist, particularistic ideology have broadened religious Zionism's demographic base (Hermann et al., 2014: 225). Especially important is the dramatic rise in the percentage of religious Zionists in the IDF's lower and middle-level officer corps—replacing the secular Ashkenazim as the military's up-and-coming leadership. In a word, religious Zionism has never been more influential than it is at present. To balance the picture it must be noted that certain fields nevertheless remain dominated by the old secular Ashkenazi elite; these include the economy, law, the academy, science, culture, and art. But changes are in the air.

Religious Zionism and Disobedience

Almost certainly the most traumatic political crisis (and crisis of faith) experienced by the religious Zionist community was the evacuation from Gush Katif/Gaza Strip (2005) in which thousands of residents, overwhelmingly religious Zionist, were expelled from their homes by Israeli security forces. Although, as noted, there was violence, it was for the most part symbolic and telegenic. Whence this restraint? Why was the expulsion met with relative forbearance? On its face, the retreat from Gush Katif/Gaza Strip was a true *casus belli* for the religious Zionist community. Not only were long-time residents ejected by force, it also flew in the face of their belief that settling the Land of Israel was the harbinger of messianic salvation.

One attempt to account for the muted reactions of the religious Zionist community was offered by Peter Herriot. In his view, Gush Emunim represents a pure case of an activist fundamentalist movement committed to an absolutist ideology. And yet, at times Gush Emunim (like many other fundamentalist movements) chose dialogue over disobedience, compromise over confrontation because, Herriot claims, in the larger strategic picture they believed that restraint served their deeper interests. Sensing that it could achieve more of its agenda through negotiations—especially when the ruling coalition was sympathetic to its aims—Gush Emunim often preferred to pursue what we might call "balanced pragmatism" rather than to engage in unconditional religious militancy (Herriot, 2009: 104–08).

The anthropologist Joyce Dalsheim spent a year in the Gush Katif settlements just prior to their evacuation. The settlers saw themselves as successors to the classic strategy of the Zionist movement—mostly left wing—to settle the land piece by piece. Interestingly, left-wing kibbutz members living inside the Green Line near the Gaza Strip border rejected this argument, root and branch. Although perhaps counter-intuitive, Dalsheim found that left-leaning kibbutz members were frequently more closed-minded on the subject than their religiously absolutist adversaries. The settlers, she reported, were more interested in dialogue with liberal secular Israelis than vice versa. They felt themselves more bound up with the Jewish national movement than what veteran Zionists were willing to accept. Implicit in Dalsheim's account of the settler's sense of belonging to the Zionist project and of their persistent concern for those who rejected their ideological policies rendered the option of violent resistance an unacceptable one (Dalsheim, 2011).

Another research effort studying the sentiments of the settlers toward the regime during the evacuation period found that there was significant willingness among the settler organizations and their followers to preserve ties, coordinate activities, and set down the ground rules for legitimate forms of resistance against the army and the police. Beyond contributing to moderating resistance, this readiness to cooperate with the security forces demonstrates how deeply the settlers felt themselves a part of the Jewish Israeli collective (Alimi, 2013).

These three studies (Herriot, Dalsheim, and Alimi) point to the pragmatic and Zionist reasons that prevented measured resistance from degenerating into life-endangering battles. But beyond pragmatism, there were deeper reasons without which it is difficult to understand the full significance of settler restraint: why, in spite of their sense of outrage, they mostly preserved the peace.

We come closer to the heart of the matter in David Weisburd and Chagit Lernau's study that examined the alleged vigilante tendencies of the

Gush Katif settlers in the course of the Gaza evacuation. Their research reveals that the oft-repeated prediction that the evacuation would end in bloody pitched battles was not borne out in fact. The resistance to the evacuation was, to be sure, highly charged, but it remained mostly within the bounds of normative passive resistance. We cite their words at length:

> We began with the question of why there was so little violence by settlers in the August 2005 withdrawal from the Gaza Strip. Our conclusion, based on scores of interviews and a survey of settlers, is that the lack of violence in the Gaza Strip was not surprising. This was not because the Gaza settlers were moderate in their beliefs. On the contrary, we have much evidence that settlers there were committed to ideas that could easily have led to violence. As we illustrated earlier, most settlers believed that uprooting settlements would prevent the messianic redemption of Israel. Most argued that those who planned the withdrawal would be judged as traitors. And most thought that evacuating settlements constituted a sin so great that a Jew should be willing to be killed rather than comply with it. For them, settlement evacuation was tantamount to murder or apostasy.
>
> In this sense, the settlers in Gaza were radicals whose beliefs clearly created a potential for violence. But we also found that balancing norms were strongly held values in the settlements. Almost two-thirds of the settlers we surveyed told us that they believed that the unity of the Jewish people and the existence of Israel were more important than the territories. The settlers also showed strong respect for democratic principles. A similar majority said that Israel as a democratic state must be toler-ant of a wide range of opinions, and agreed that they should respect government decisions even if they disagree with them. In this context, it is not hard to understand the lack of violent resistance to the security forces during the withdrawal from the Gaza strip. (Weisburd and Lernau, 2006: 78)

Alongside the deep messianic convictions of the settlers, there existed a powerful belief in a morally united Israel. This belief generated a counter-vailing force that prevented the settlers from indulging in vigilante violence. They argue that this balance was created because the settlers internalized democratic values. These values were expressed in the recognition that a stable Israel is of paramount importance, that a tolerant approach to other opinions is essential, and that civic responsibility is necessary for a healthy society.

As important as it may be, Weisburd and Lernau's research fails to touch upon the profound theological conception that is, in our view, the central pillar upon which settler moderation rests. In her comprehensive study of the evacuation, Anat Roth takes a further step in the direction of appreciating settler restraint in theological terms. In her PhD dissertation (2011) which later appeared as a book (Roth, 2014), she emphasizes the critical importance of *Mamlachtiut* in the sense the concept had for Mercaz HaRav students. In the religious Zionist Mamlachti view, the State of Israel possesses religious sanctity. It is not merely the Jewish homeland; it is infused with holiness and serves as the vehicle for Divine deliverance. Hence, violence against the sovereign State of Israel involves a revolt against God's presence in the world. Restraint, however bitter, was their most acceptable option.

Roth's work concentrates on the evacuation from Gush Katif. It is our intention to broaden the focus to include all the significant confrontations between religious Zionism and the state concerning the settlement project. The evolving (and generally radicalizing) discourse of the settlers and their rabbinical leadership in regard to the rule of law, the legitimacy of democratic government, civil disobedience, soldiers disobeying orders, etc., will be analyzed beginning with the founding of Gush Emunim and proceeding up to the present day. Only a panoramic view of this kind can present settler political theology in its many (quite different) contexts and offer a composite picture of an often sophisticated and complex form of religious discourse.

Moreover, we go beyond the simple Mamlachtiut position as presented by Mercaz HaRav circles and attempt to enter more deeply and specifically into the inner world of settler thinking. Let us focus upon the Israel-centered political theology as taught by Rabbi Avraham Isaac Kook (1865–1935) and his son Rabbi Tzvi Yehuda Kook (1891–1982), that has become the new mainstream, the new orthodoxy in various religious Zionist circles and especially in the settler community. In this religious-political creed, the State of Israel, its institutions, and its army are more than mundane, humanly constructed structures; they are to be understood in sacred, messianic terms.

Although this attribution of theological significance to Israel was present from the very origins of the religious Zionist movement and became even more powerful with the founding of the state, it reached its peak only in the aftermath of the Six Day War. Over the course of the past half-century, these ideas of the Rabbis Kook have struck deep roots in the religious Zionist educational system. The Land of Israel has become the touchstone of religious Zionism. Indeed, some critics complain that it has displaced virtually all the other aspects of Judaism, transcending and overshadowing other classical *loci* of Jewish religious practice.

Merkaz HaRav yeshiva, which was founded by Rabbi Kook the elder, became during the last years of his son's life the center of the revolution in political theology that swept religious Zionism after the Six Days War and the conquest of the West Bank (1967) and even more so after the Yom Kippur War (1974). According to the elder Rabbi Kook, the secular Zionist movement founded by Theodore Herzl in 1896 was only the first step of the redemption of Israel. In order to accomplish the second, approaching stage in Israel's redemption, it is necessary to create a deep synthesis between the holy and the secular, between the spiritual and the earthly political dimensions of reality—a synthesis that would take into account the uniqueness of the Jewish people and its land. Under the influence of the religious-Zionist movement and Merkaz HaRav yeshiva in particular, the State of Israel is destined to fulfill that goal.

Rabbi Kook's political theology begins with a critique of Western society and culture. Although in his view the sacred and the profane are clearly distinguishable from each other, as opposed to the Christian and the Western view, Judaism calls for a consolidation of the mundane as a precondition for the emergence of the sacred: "The sacral should be grounded in the mundane. The mundane is the substance of the sacral, while the sacral serves as its form. The more solid the substance, the more solid the form" (Kook, 1990: part I: 155). On the other hand, in a deeper sense, Kabbalah teaches us that the profane is only the external manifestation of the inner holy foundations that vitalize it (Kook, 1990, part 1: 143; Yaron, 1992: chapter: 6; Ben-Shlomo, 1990: chapters 7–8).

From his earliest writing and activities, Rabbi Kook carried on a fierce polemic against secular Zionism that adopted practical, mundane nationalism and separated nationality from religion. This separation originates in the Christian dichotomy between the sacred and the profane and is alien to the Jewish tradition (Kook, 1982: 21). By contrast, the connection between the sacred and the profane, Rabbi Kook argues, will be realized in the course of future Israeli politics. On this point, there is great similarity between Rabbi Kook's thought and the political, messianic teaching of certain spiritual, national non-Jewish European thinkers who strove to transform the citadel of man into a basis of human redemption in the sense of creating a new man and a worthy moral society (Talmon, 1985; Philipott, 2007). In Rabbi Kook's millenarianism, the renewal of the Jewish nation will bring along with it the renewal of all the world's civilizations (Kook, 1982: 17). The messianic Jewish state ("Jerusalem") will spread its influence around the world spiritually rather than through warfare (Kook, 1982: 17).

The messianic-political image of the state finds its quintessential expression in Rabbi Kook's well-known statements of 1920, in which he distinguishes between a polity based on a mundane social contract and one that operates on a divine ontological level. For Rabbi Kook, emphasis should be placed upon the idealistic-Utopian visions of Plato, Rousseau, and Hegel (without mentioning them explicitly) rather than on the political pragmatism that runs through Western thought from Aristotle up to the founding fathers of the American constitution:

> The state is not the supreme happiness of man. This is true of an ordinary state that amounts to no more than a large insurance company, where the myriad ideas that are the crown of human vitality remain hovering above, not touching it. [But] this is not the case regarding a state that is ideal in its foundation, in whose being is engraved the supreme ideal content that is, truly, the greatest happiness of the individual. This state is truly supreme in the scale of happiness, and this state is our state, the State of Israel, the foundation of God's throne in the world. Its entire aim is that "God be one and His Name one" (Zech. 14:9). For this is, truly, the supreme happiness. (Kook, 1993, part III: 191. We use the translation in Michael Walzer et al., 2000, vol. 1: 480.)

Rabbi Kook constructs a hierarchy of three types of states: (1) the inferior state, based on fraudulent idealism; (2) the ordinary Western state based upon a Hobbesian or Lockean (as opposed to a Rousseauian) social contract between individuals ("a big insurance company"); (3) the Jewish state, based upon genuine, spiritual idealism. Loyal to his theological-ideological method, Rabbi Kook projects onto the future State of Israel his teaching that the worthy national idea originates in the divine idea (Kook, 1982: 102–18). Indeed, one can detect echoes of Rousseau that distinguish between a social contract as representing the *volonté de tous*, the will of all, and a social contract that embodies the *volonté générale*, the general will. For Rabbi Kook, however, the general will ("its entire wish") is *unitary* not only in the popular sense but in a cosmic sense. Hence, this new politics derives from divine unity and gives voice to a restored world, cleansed of the sins of separation that had led to disputes and wars.

Interestingly, it is in this text that Rabbi Kook uses a term not yet current at that time: "the State of Israel" (Ravitzky, 1996: 4–5). Only, this State of Israel, once it is actually established, will be "the foundation of God's throne." There, the mundane—the secular—will indeed serve as the basis for the sacred, which nourishes it. This conceptual world is wide apart—as far as the (spiritual) east is from the (material) west—from the minimalist state in the liberal democratic world, where the individual is central and the state is merely instrumental. These attitudes of Rabbi Kook have had an enormous influence on the anti-liberal positions that struck roots among his followers in the Merkaz HaRav yeshiva and in the expanding circles influenced by the Merkaz.

The model of political theology that emerges from Rabbi Kook's writings is a combination of a number of approaches that are well known in the research literature. According to William Cavanaugh and Peter Scott, one can distinguish between different conceptions of political theology:

> For some, politics is seen as a "given" with its own secular autonomy . . . The task of political theology might be to relate religious beliefs to larger social issues while not confusing the proper autonomy of each. For others, theology is critical reflection on the political. Theology is related as superstructure to the material politico-economic base . . . For still others, theology and politics are essentially similar activities, and both are constituted in the production of metaphysical images around which communities are organized. (Cavanaugh and Scott, 2007: 3)

In Rabbi Kook's political theology, the material political-economic reality serves as a base for theology that functions as the superstructure. This view accords with the second model presented by Cavanaugh and Scott mentioned above. As opposed to the problematic views of Carl Schmitt who emphasized the secular aspect of political theology, for Rabbi Kook, theology consummates the political-economic material, raises it to its full stature (Schmitt, 1985: 36).

Rabbi Kook seems to go back to what Alistair Kee (Kee, 1974: ix) defines as a classical traditional Jewish concept: "Whole areas of the old Testament are given over to theological reflection on the political life of Israel." And yet Rabbi Kook is a modern thinker who, like Schmitt—at least in this aspect—is not satisfied with what he sees as a superficial liberal understanding of politics. Like Schmitt, he too seeks a more profound alternative, but unlike Schmitt he strives to mend the world in an idealistic way that is the entirely opposite to the anti-humanist, power-centered understanding of politics of Schmitt.

In any case, like other religious political theologians he totally disapproves of the separation of religion and state that lies at the heart of mainstream liberal theories of politics from Locke up to Rawls—a separation that creates what Neuhaus calls: "The naked public sphere" of liberal societies (Neuhaus, 1986; Philipott, 2007).

Rabbi Kook's son, Rabbi Tzvi Yehuda Kook and his Gush Emunim acolytes, interpreted Rabbi Abraham Isaac Kook's political theology as both the spiritual basis for Mamlachtiut as well as the legitimacy of the State of Israel as a secular state with sacred roots. But at the same time, this theologized state rejected any parliamentary decision that violated the spirit of the religiously conceived nation and the supra-historic community of Israel. It was no historical accident that when, in the 1970s, the political leaders of Israel acted against the inner convictions of his son and spiritual heir, Rabbi Tzvi Yehuda Kook, by ordering the withdrawal from parts of the Sinai, Rabbi Tzvi Yehuda introduced the notion of *klal Yisrael*, "the entire nation of Israel," which includes Jews outside of Israel and, mystically understood, the entire Jewish nation from its inception to its salvation. This conception, whatever may be its religious standing, is hardly consistent with the liberal democratic, election-based, parliamentary government in the State of Israel.

The spread of Rabbi Kook's ideas in various Yeshiva circles and in pre-army religious seminars (*Mechinot*) in the last generation has made Israel's sanctity essential to the religious Zionist vision. Being drafted into the IDF has become quasi-religious activity, a consecrated rite of passage. Not only conscription is sanctified; serving in front-line combat units entails performing the mitzvah at an even higher level. As noted above, Religious Zionist youth are presently more heavily represented among front-line combat troops, in officer training courses, and in national service programs than any other comparable communal cohort.

More broadly speaking, a united Israel flourishing in Zion, settling in all parts of the Land of Israel and identifying with the symbols of the state have become core elements in the credo of virtually every religious Zionist community in Israel. Similarly, official national holidays like Independence Day and Memorial Day for fallen soldiers are celebrated with much prayer and study. The Jewish nation is not perceived merely as an ethnic, cultural, and linguistic collective any more than the state is seen as a network of sovereign institutions. Both are spiritual presences; they incorporate the covenant binding the Jewish people to God, the forerunner of the messiah.

In every yeshiva high school for both boys and girls, in every Zionist yeshiva for advanced learning, in every pre-army seminar and religious college, an intensive educational effort is made to inculcate the idea that the State of Israel is the instrument of Divine deliverance and that the Land of Israel is unrivalled in its holiness. (Indeed, citing the medieval scholar Nachmanides, it is often claimed that the Mitzvah of settling the Land of Israel is equal in importance to that of all the other Mitzvot combined).

Almost unavoidably, a dynamic balance has developed between the holiness attributed to the state on the one hand, and its patently secular character on the other. Ideally, religious commitment to the State of Israel is overriding but at the same time, realistically, the state frequently acts in ways that violate religious values and precepts. This clash between two poles of loyalty—the legally binding decisions of an elected government and the call of religious duty—creates an intra-religious tension that has dogged religious Zionism since its origin more than a century ago. Balancing the two has been the movement's core dilemma. Even when government decisions violated Torah commandments, religious Zionism has vacillated: it has been by turns rigid, conciliatory, flexible, pragmatic, and at times highly adamant.

Here is where the "theological-normative balance" comes into play. It goes beyond simple Mamlachtiut in that it understands religious Zionist behavior as resting upon a shifting equilibrium, one which attempts to preserve a balance between militancy and restraint, between disobedience and Mamlachtiut. In other words, Mamlachtiut does not stand alone; it is buffeted by rage against government's "anti-religious" behavior—especially when thousands of settlers are expelled from their homes. As already noted in the introduction, to this point (Winter 2017) restraint, for the most part, has had the upper hand. Bestowing religious status on the secular state inoculates against the growth of de-legitimation and anti-system politics. It internalizes deference. The state's religious aura acts to undermine calls for civil, political, and military disobedience because reverence for the state is conceived of as a religious imperative. Consequently, the religious Zionist discourse of loyalty is primary and paradigmatic while the discourse of disobedience faces serious intellectual obstacles. In a word: the "theological-normative" safety net prevents descent into unbridled violence. We believe that without appreciating the "balancing act" played out over and again since the rise of Gush Emunim, religious Zionism's actions and policies in regard to the Land of Israel cannot be fully understood.

Nevertheless, since the evacuation of Gaza strip in 2005 different voices have been heard. The chorus of state-affirming declarations has been joined by a dissonant discourse of disobedience. And this discourse has been translated into aggressive actions.

Clearly, upsetting the heretofore-sturdy "theological-normative balance" carries with it potentially perilous consequences for the partnership between the religious Zionist community and the Israeli government.

The Discourse of Disobedience in Religious Zionism

From Gush Emunim to the Jewish Underground (1974–1984)

Religious Zionism's Historical Setting

From its origins onward, religious Zionism was part of the loosely aggregated *Hibat Zion* (Love of Zion) movement which was formed in the late nineteenth century and included both secular and religious members. From its earliest stirrings, religious Zionism was willing to make substantial compromises on religious issues in order to preserve a single institutional framework for both religious and secular Zionists. With the founding of the Zionist movement by Theodore Herzl, this pragmatic flexibility only grew more pronounced. In 1902, Rabbi Yitzchak Yaacov Reines established the religious Zionist *Mizrahi* (Hebrew acronym for "spiritual center"—also the "East") party with the objective of fostering religious participation in the Zionist movement's proliferating activities. Whether Rabbi Reines did so out of pragmatic motivations or because of esoteric messianic yearnings (Schwartz, 2009; Hellinger, 2005), he, like his admired friend Herzl, emphasized the urgency of responding to the "Jewish distress" of his time.

The ultra-Orthodox (henceforth *Haredim*) rejected Zionism as a detestable secularizing movement whose basic objective was to undermine Jewish commitment to the Torah. Nor can their fears be dismissed: the Zionist movement's secular agenda was explicit, even zealous. From the very first *Aliya* (immigration to the land of Israel) in 1880s led by the *Bilu* (Hebrew acronym for "House of Jacob, let us get up and go") group, secularism was the dominant force. Nevertheless, for religious Zionists like Rabbi Reines and his ally Rabbi Shmuel Mohilever, concerted action to encourage Aliya overrode other considerations. Even though they fully recognized that as a minority in the dominantly secular Zionist movement, religious dilemmas were inevitable, they remained—sometimes with gritted teeth—committed to the cause. Despite the often rocky road, the alliance between religious and secular Zionists—at first the secular Left and of late the secular Right—endured through the early years and has persevered well into the twenty-first century (Luz, 1988: chapter 3; Shalmon, 1990).

Religious dilemmas arose almost at once. For example, what was called the "cultural question" strained relations right from the start. Zionist cultural activities, most often secular in character, posed a difficult challenge for religious Zionists. After much wrangling, a compromise solution was hammered out in 1911: henceforth the Zionist movement would operate both secular and religious cultural programs. And yet, despite the tendency toward conciliation, it was clear who was the leader and who was the follower. The commitment to remain partnered with secular Zionism did not work in the Mizrahi's favor; it was not an association of equals. Pronounced, often aggressively secularizing tendencies characterized the bulk of Zionist activities. And yet the Mizrahi remained within the Zionist fold. But there were important exceptions. Indignant at the non- and anti-religious ideology and programs of mainstream Zionism, many members of the Mizrahi chose (1912) to renounce their Zionist affiliations. A year later some of these dissidents founded *Agudat Yisrael* (Union of Israel), the Haredi, anti-Zionist party. For his part, Rabbi Reines accepted the decisions of the democratic majority in spite of the religious and personal compromises they entailed (Luz, 1988: chapters 7–9).

Cooperation between the religious and the secular continued to flourish during the years of the "Second Aliya" (1904–1914) evolving eventually into a "historic pact" between *Mapai* (the Israeli Labor Party)—Zionism's leading political force—and the national religious camp embodied in the *Hapoel HaMizrahi* (the Religious Worker's Party), the central political and intellectual home of religious Zionism (Horowitz and Lissak, 1989: chapter 2; Don Yehiya, 1997). Although mainstream Zionism had its "spiritualist," quasi-religious circles, it was for the very most part adamantly secular in its central credos (Cenaani, 1977; Liebman and Don Yehiya, 1983: chapter 2). More often than not it championed an outright revolt against Jewish religious traditions and promoted the secularization of the *Yishuv* (the pre-state organized Jewish community in Palestine). The "historic pact" constituted a centerpiece of Mapai and Mizrahi policy during the Yishuv period—a form of "consociational democracy" between the secular majority and the religious minority (Lijphart, 1968; Lijphart, 1977; Cohen and Susser, 2000). This "politics of accommodation" characterized not only the Yishuv's public life; it retained its momentum well into the period of statehood, morphing into what was later called the "status quo" agreement in religious matters.

Few examples better illustrate the cultural discord that prevailed between the secular majority and the religious minority than the controversy over the children of the *Olim* (newly arrived immigrants) from North Africa and the Middle East in the early years of statehood. This very bitter controversy makes clear just how far the Mizrahi was prepared to go in order to preserve its alliance with the secular labor movement. Religiously observant Jews constituted a significant majority among the new Olim. And yet their children were most often sent to secular educational institutions where they were "re-socialized" in the secular mold which included eating non-Kosher food and the non-observance of the Sabbath. Many of them emerged from this experience as fully secular Jews, even learning in not a few cases to ridicule the religious cultural heritage they had brought from their natal lands. They often perceived the secular Ashkenazi *sabra* (native-born Israeli) as the model individual by comparison to whom their own cultural personas were distinctly inferior. Relationships between the two parties were sorely strained but the Mizrahi expressed its displeasure in little more than heated rhetoric and in negotiating with the secular Zionist leadership over the percentage of these children who would be enrolled in religious educational institutions (Don Yehiya, 2008). How to account for this unlikely behavior? As we shall see, the tendency of religious Zionism to conceive of Israel in messianic terms, as the embryo of deliverance, rendered abandoning the driving force behind the county's struggle for security and stability—socialist and secular though it might be—an unacceptable prospect.

Returning to Zionism's early years, the predisposition of religious Zionism to follow Herzl's lead made for some strange alliances. Herzl presented the Sixth Zionist Congress (1903) with what was called the "Uganda plan"—an initiative to set up settlements in Uganda as an interim measure aimed at saving Russian Jews from impending disaster. Despite the unrivalled centrality of the Land of Israel in religious Zionism's vision ("the Land of Israel for the People of Israel according to the Torah of Israel") Rabbi Reines and his followers set aside their convictions and, supporting Herzl's leadership, voted for the proposal. Paradoxically, the parts of the secular Zionist movement for whom the Land of Israel had no religious significance, opposed the plan. Led by *Ahad Ha'am* (pen name for Asher Ginzburghh, a major Zionist essayist and moralist), the secularists refused to set aside their loyalty to the Land even though Jews were in distress (Luz, 1985: chapter 10). In light of the Greater Land of Israel militancy that has overtaken the religious Zionist movement in recent decades, this unity-seeking behavior is nothing less than stunning. It is worth noting as well that when the United Nations partition plan was proposed (1947), many of the rabbis and leaders of religious Zionism were fiercely opposed because much of the historic Land of Israel was excluded from territories allotted to the Jewish population. Nevertheless, the historic pact with Mapai did not unravel; if anything, in the following years it only intensified.

After the merger of the Mizrahi and the Hapoel Hamizrahi into a single party—the Mafdal (Hebrew acronym for the National Religious Party)—the pact with Mapai reached its peak. Under the leadership of Chaim-Moshe Shapira during the 1950s and 1960s, the Mafdal adopted moderate and centrist positions that made it an ideal ally for Mapai. Indeed, at times it was even more dovish than the Labor Party itself. Such was the case in regard to the occupation of the West Bank/Judea and Samaria during the Six Day War (1967), which the Mafdal opposed. Indeed, after the war Shapira and his followers were prepared to retreat from the newly occupied territories for the sake of a peace agreement with the Arabs. Notwithstanding this official moderate policy, it must be noted that even prior to the Six Day War there was a vocal hawkish minority in the Mafdal that opposed Shapira's pacific politics (Don Yehiya, 2004).

In the wake of the Six Day War and even more so following the Yom Kippur War (1973) tectonic changes took place in the religious camp. A "young guard" led by Zvulun Hammer and Yehuda Ben-Meir revolted against the party's established authorities and championed the cause of the Greater Land of Israel. Far more right wing and territorially maximalist than the traditional leadership, these young militants recoiled from the conciliatory, "bourgeois" (that is docile and lukewarm) positions of the Mafdal's historic elite.

Beyond the mutiny against their parents' generation dovish politics, the young guard also shifted rightward on religious issues, rejecting what they saw as the old leadership's tepid piety. Notably, the established Mafdal leadership resisted this transformation only weakly. Rapidly, and eventually entirely, the party's agenda was taken over by the more radical young political activists (Don Yehiya, 2000).

Doubtless, the most important step in the Mafdal's transformation into a right-wing party was the founding of *Gush Emunim* (Block of the Faithful) in 1974 and its bonding with the young guard faction within party's Knesset representation. The messianic passion awakened by the remarkable victory in the Six Day War and the deep frustrations occasioned by the Yom Kippur War transformed the Mafdal into a millenarian party. There were earlier signs of this transformation. As Yoni Garb notes, important figures in the future leadership of Gush Emunim acted in concert with the youthful wing of the Mafdal as early as the 1960s. They were naturally drawn to one another by their common commitment to the teachings of Rabbi Avraham Isaac Kook (1865–1935) that stressed the imminence of the messianic era, the holiness of the Land of Israel, and the centrality of Torah learning (Garb, 2004a).

Just as the victory in the Six Day War was exhilarating, so the humiliation of the Yom Kippur War was bitter. The feelings of rage and frustration expressed by various protest movements produced a new generation of leaders in the Labor Party and would, in a matter of years, bring about the dramatic electoral reversal of 1977. This great political and emotional fracture convinced a generation of young religious Zionists that it was their time to take over the ideological leadership of the limping Zionist movement. Theirs was a compounded revolt: first, against the older religious generation whom they deemed submissive and compromising and, second, against the Labor movement elites who had, they felt, disgraced themselves and were no longer worthy of leading the nation (Don Yehiya, 1980). Without understanding the great convulsion created by the Six Day War and, subsequently, by the Yom Kippur War, it is impossible to grasp the impetus behind the settlement project. It is also critical for understanding how the religious Zionist camp, previously law-abiding to a fault, was taken over by a militant leadership for which civil disobedience became a realistic option.

Gush Emunim and the Settlement Project during the 1970s

Settling the land was always an integral part of the Zionist ethos. From the very first stirrings of the movement in the 1880s "redeeming the land" (*Ge'ulat hakarka'ot*) was a primary Zionist objective. Yehoshua Chankin (1864–1945), the most famous of those who purchased lands from Arabs in order to settle Jews, "redeemed" close to 175,000 acres of land between 1880 and 1945. (It must be cautioned however that a substantial part of the land was purchased from absentee landlords hundreds of whose Arab tenant farmers were uprooted from their lands). Chankin is a national hero honored by a postage stamp (2003) carrying his portrait. Other national figures instrumental in acquiring Arab lands for Jewish settlement included Arthur Ruppin, Menachem Usishkin, and Levi Eshkol.

But not all land "redemption" was as legal as Chankin's. Establishing settlements in the face of British (not to speak of Arab) opposition was common enough during the Yishuv era. Facing waves of immigration, illegal settlements were regularly founded in areas proscribed by the British. Even the prohibitory rules of the Yishuv itself were not infrequently flouted. Apart from housing the immigrants and refugees from Europe, the settlements were meant to help in determining the country's borders when Israel would finally be established as a sovereign state.

Thus, after the Six Day War when settlements were once again founded in Yamit/Sinai, in Judea and Samaria/West Bank and Gush Katif/Gaza Strip, they were not an ex nehilo phenomenon. The settlers saw themselves as the direct successors of a pioneering tradition of settlement even when they violated official policy and even though the settlements they founded lay outside the Green Line that separated pre-1967 Israel from the occupied territories. Relying on the long-standing ethos of settlement, the settlers in *Yesha* (Hebrew acronym for Judea, Samaria, and Gaza) cast themselves as genuine Zionists who were once again raising the enfeebled banner of pioneering. Indeed, acting illegally vindicated the proposition that Zionism had not lost its ideological élan. Not surprisingly many of these illegal settlements were related to by the government forgivingly—as often as not receiving post facto approval and recognition.

Furthermore, noncompliance with the law in the early years of the settlement project was not perceived by the settlers as true civil disobedience. In their eyes they were the agents of the Jewish nation's essential mission; they were certainly not criminals. They admitted, of course, that there was a shallow veneer of illegality present in their actions but even the official political leadership in its heart of hearts recognized that there was something epoch-making and heroic about their actions. Even if the state could not formally underwrite their deeds, in effect, settlement projects that began illegally were retroactively ratified.

Much has been written about Gush Emunim, the settlement project, its stages, its motives and its objectives both by the participants themselves—usually ideologically supportive (Harnoi, 1994; Segal, 1987; Shafat, 1995) and by academic researchers (like the mainstream attitude in the media)—usually ideologically critical (a partial list: Aran, 1987; Aran, 2013; Don Yehiya, 1987; Gorenberg, 2006; Herriot, 2009: chapter 3; Lustick, 1988; Lustick, 1993; Na'or, 2001; Peleg, 1997; Ra'anan, 1981; Rubinstein, 1982; Rubinstein, 2000: chapter 7; Sivan, 1995; Sprinzak, 1981; Sprinzak, 1986: chapter 8; Sprinzak, 1993; Taub, 2010; Tal, 1987; Zertal and Eldar 2007).

According to Dalsheim and Harel the negative attitude toward the settlers both in the media and academia helps to: "construct hegemonic categories of difference, marginalizing religiously motivated settlers while creating a sense of moral legitimacy for broader state projects. . . ." (Dalsheim and Harel, 2009: 219). In other words, these selective condemnations of the settlers do not tell the whole story. The sharp opposition between the actions of the State of Israel within the Green Line and its policies in the occupied territories ignores a more complex reality. In truth, the contrast between what the State of Israel has done within the Green Line—the expropriation of Palestinian lands and the forcible relocation of the Bedouins throughout the years—is not categorically opposed to what is taking place in the West Bank. Settling is in the DNA of the Zionist project—the settlement project since the 1970s, even though clearly unique, cannot be dissociated from Israeli history (Dalsheim and Harel, 2009: 221).

The contradictory narratives presented by Gush Emunim stalwarts and their academic adversaries are close to being Manichean in character. Not surprisingly, what is lost in these simplified binary presentations is complexity and diversity. Critics often focus single-mindedly on the actions of extremists and militants just as supporters tend to record their inner convictions in a breathless, confessional style that leaves little room for critique.

But in the last decade or so a new breed of academic analyst has arisen, one who attempts to comprehend the settlement phenomenon rather than lionize or deprecate it. Balance, complexity, and heterogeneity are the marks of this approach. (Among them are Fischer, 2007; Feige, 2009; Dalsheim, 2011; Inbari, 2012; Roth, 2014; Shahor, 2015.) We count our work as belonging to the last category.

As early as 1968, months after the Six Day War ended, the settlement movement began. *Kfar Etzion* was (re)founded, the Jewish appropriation of the Hebron's Park Hotel took place and, a bit later, the neighboring town of *Kiryat Arba* was established. Eshkol's national unity government gave its blessing to these actions. The driving force behind these early settlements was Yigal Alon, the celebrated leader of the *Palmach*, a hero of the War of Independence and one of the Labor Party's most influential leaders (Segal, 1987: chapter 2; Zertal and Eldar, 2007: chapter1). Other key ministers such as Yisrael Galili and Moshe Dayan also expressed support for settling some of the areas Israel had captured in the Six Day War (Bin-Nun, 2001: 66–67). To put it simply: parts of the Labor Party were invested in the settlements beyond the Green Line. No wonder then that the settlers were convinced that their disobedience reflected the deeper will of the government in spite of the sometimes fierce opposition voiced by their critics.

Despite the enormous emotional power of these early settlements in 1968 and although for many they came after the miraculous "liberation" of Judea and Samaria/West Bank which brought deliverance an important step closer, no organized settling group emerged until after the Yom Kippur War some five years later. It was only after the trauma of the 1973 war that profoundly unnerved Israel's Jewish population and discredited the Labor Party's leadership that an activist, well-organized settling body arouse: Gush Emunim.

One can distinguish between two quite different interpretations of the Gush Emunim phenomenon. Aviezer Ravitzky sees Gush Emunim (much in the same way as he perceives the Chabad movement) as representing a "messianism of success." As opposed to the intuitive view that dominates the research literature on messianism, not only distress can serve as a hot-house for the eruption of millenarian movements—as was the case after the expulsion from Spain. Messianism can also grow out of events that give rise to surges of exhilaration and hope. Gush Emunim and the Mercaz HaRav yeshiva saw the Six Day War as an undeniable act of God. After a Holocaust unparalleled in its devastation, after the founding of a Jewish state after two millennia of Exile, after the miraculous victory of 1967, who could doubt that the "end of days" was upon us? (Ravitsky, 1999).

As opposed to Ravitsky, Motti Inbari points to the traumatic events that preceded the settlement project as the trigger for Gush Emunim's rise. The almost-tragic, fiasco-cum-victory of the Yom Kippur War created a sense of "cognitive dissonance" that demanded resolution, and only activist messianism was suited to the task. Against the national depression that followed the war, Rabbi Tzvi Yehuda Kook and students of the Mercaz HaRav yeshiva felt impelled to counter these feelings of dejection and defeatism by creating settlements in the Greater Land of Israel. As Inbari writes:

> Gush Emunim was founded under the leadership of Mercaz HaRav yeshiva graduates following the crisis created by concern over the possible division of the Land of Israel. The movement was forged at a stage of cognitive dissonance in which the founders of the movement believed that enormous messianic progress had occurred following the conquest of the whole Land of Israel in 1967, although doubts also emerged due to the authorities' willing to make territorial compromises following the Yom Kippur War. The sense of crisis sparked a process of messianic radicalization that led the rabbi and his students to move beyond activity in the world of Torah and become public figures—spiritual leaders of a mass movement that changed the face of Israeli society. The solution the rabbi found to his messianic distress lay in a process of radicalization leading to aggressive action in the public arena. (Inbari, 2012: 35)

A number of loose congeries of settler groups merged early in 1974 to found Gush Emunim. These included: the Elon Moreh *gar'in* (a small "seed" group planning to establish a settlement) the majority of whom came from the Mercaz HaRav yeshiva in Jerusalem and were students of Rabbi Tzvi

Yehuda Kook (1891–1982). A second group, the Western Sharon gar'in, was composed of residents of the greater Tel Aviv area. These two were joined by the "young guard" of the Mafdal led by Zvulun Hammer and Yehuda Ben-Meir (Shafat, 1995: chapter 1; Harnoi, 1995: chapters 1–2).

But beyond Gush Emunim's organizational origins lies the much larger issue of political theology. To understand Gush Emunim's position both concerning the general issue of religion and state and to the more specific problems of civil disobedience. it is critical to undertake an exploration of the intellectual-religious worldview underlying the settlement project. Research into Gush Emunim's ideological sources divides into two broad schools.

The first is perhaps best expressed in the work of Gideon Aran. In a series of studies focusing on the settler movement, he emphasizes the profound association—intellectually, socially, and personally—between Gush Emunim and the *Mercaz HaRav* yeshiva with its charismatic leader Rabbi Tzvi Yehuda Kook: indeed, he labels it "Kookism." In Aran's view, Gush Emunim transformed religious Zionism into a Zionist religion. He argues that for its adherents, the messianic redemption of the Land of Israel became the core element of both Judaism and Zionism, replacing a rich religious tradition and an intellectually heterogeneous national liberation movement with the narrowly focused territorial imperative to settle the Land.

Aran points out that most of the Gush's leadership underwent a similar process of education and socialization. The earliest source of the movement was in the zealous *Gahelet* (ember) group initiated by a few religious Zionist teenagers of the *Bnei Akiva* youth movement in the early 1950s. They studied with Rabbi Moshe Tzvi Neria in the *Kfar Haro'eh* yeshiva high school and then proceeded onto the Mercaz HaRav yeshiva in Jerusalem where they became ardent disciples of Rabbi Tzvi Yehuda Kook. More than just a sage and a teacher, Rabbi Kook was for them the generation's spiritual giant, the trailblazer of a new form of religiosity. The roster of his students includes many of those who went on to become leading figures in religious Zionism and Gush Emunim: Tzefania Drori, Yaacov Filber, Zalman Melamed, Chaim Druckman, Moshe Levinger, and Eliezer Waldman. For them, redeeming the Land of Israel by establishing settlements to its length and to its breadth was the manifest, public aspect of the inner spiritual redemption that had begun with the return of Jews to the Holy Land. Israel—both the land and the people—was in the midst of an eschatological drama that began with the founding of Zionism and reached its peak with the Six Day War when Judea, Samaria, Gaza, and the Sinai were "liberated" from Arab control.

Gush Emunim saw itself as the instrument of deliverance that bonded the nation, the land, and the Torah into a single messianic whole (Aran,

1987; Aran 2003; Aran, 2013). Basing itself on the teachings of Rabbi Tzvi Yehuda Kook, and perhaps even more so on those of his father Rabbi Avraham Isaac Kook, Gush Emunum's political theology centered on the belief that terrestrial, temporal activities (especially settling the land) are the external manifestations of spiritual transcendence (Hellinger, 2008). As we shall see, this conviction had direct consequences for Gush Emunim's settlement activities, for its attitudes toward religion and state, and, most specifically, to its view of disobedience to the elected authorities. The opposition between Divine, redemption-enhancing settlement activities on the one side, and the prohibitory directives of a democratically elected government on the other, created intense inner tensions and highly spirited debate.

The straight line that Aran draws between Gush Emunim and the Mercaz HaRav yeshiva necessarily brings the issue of "fundamentalism" into play. In the terminology of Almond, Appleby, and Sivan, the Gush clearly represents an instance of "a strong religion" (Almond, Appleby, and Sivan, 2003). Not surprisingly, the Fundamentalism Project of the University of Chicago includes a number of research articles devoted to Gush Emunim. Although fundamentalist movements in different religious contexts and various geographic locales are clearly distinct from one another, they do nevertheless possess a "family resemblance." Essentially, fundamentalist movements strive to keep eschatological yearnings alive, to preserve religion in its pure state while drawing a sharp line between themselves and their adversaries (Marty and Appleby, 1993: 1–9). Aran places Gush Emunim in the fundamentalist category because of its messianic character, its emphasis on strict observance of *Halacha* (Jewish law) and its exclusivist and totalizing perspective in which holiness and sin are omnipresent (Aran, 1991).

Fundamentalist movements create enclavic cultures that erect either physical or intellectual barriers to protect themselves from their external surroundings. A clear dichotomy divides in-group religious purity from the "polluted" external cultural wasteland. "Decadent" Western practices like sexual permissiveness and freethinking often head the list of contaminating practices. Persons within the cultural enclave believe they possess a spiritual map that reveals the shape of the future to which they alone are privy (Almond, Appleby, and Sivan, 2003: chapter 2). Hence, fundamentalist movements are often in a state of confrontation with their surrounding world. This confrontation can either be reclusive or militant; Gush Emunim belongs to the latter category.

Like Aran, Lustick consigns Gush Emunim to the fundamentalist camp because of the ideological-messianic fervor upon which it is based. This religious zeal stresses the uniqueness of the Jewish people, the repudiation of the non-Jewish world, and the perception of all historical events as reflections of God's will. Lustick sees Gush Emunim as fundamentalist because it strives toward a form of ideal, pure, and authentic Judaism unsullied by worldly corruptions (Lustick, 1993). Similarly, Uriel Tal identifies Gush Emunim as a fundamentalist, messianic political movement. He argues that in Gush Emunim's self-perception, it represents a vehicle of deliverance. Mundane, quotidian time as it evolves is, they believe, the refraction of mystical-metaphysical revelation in temporal form (Tal, 1987: 114–98).

Another scholar who stresses the fundamentalist character of the movement is Michael Feige. He states: "Gush Emunim is a religious-fundamentalist movement with a certain brand of messianism and an ultra-rightist political outlook" (Feige, 2009: 5). Motti Inbari, whom we cited above, also identifies Gush Emunim's messianic fundamentalism with the Mercaz HaRav yeshiva (Inbari, 2012: 35). Still he insists on the diversity of the movement, its radical vs. its moderate wing, and the evolving discourse of its rabbis from the Yamit evacuation, to the exposure of the Jewish Underground, to the disengagement from Gush Katif/Gaza Strip (Inbari, 2012).

This messianic, fundamentalist, Mercaz HaRav-based narrative is surely the dominant one. There is, however, a second and opposing view that calls attention to the more multidimensional characteristics of the Gush Emunim phenomenon. Charles Liebman and Asher Cohen point to three central fundamentalist features—totality, exclusivity, and certainty—that are present among the students of Rabbi Tzvi Yehuda Kook but are noticeably absent from other parts of the religious Zionist camp. So, although Mercaz HaRav's messianic fundamentalism is critical, it does not apply to many who identify as religious Zionists (Liebman with Cohen, 1997: chapter 3).

Shlomo Fischer claims that even concerning the messianists themselves, the fundamentalist rubric is simplistic and exaggerated. Indeed, Mercaz HaRav's worldview provides a good example of a radical religious movement with modernist elements. It was at times cooperative, conciliatory and pragmatic. As opposed to classic fundamentalists (like the Haredim), it was sympathetic to such themes as human autonomy and the right of women to participate in politics (Fischer, 2007: ch.1). Naomi Shahor testifies—from intimate familiarity with the settler's rabbinic leadership—that there were deep divisions over the legitimacy and limits of disobedience and regarding the religious status of the State of Israel. Although militant, the rabbis did not comprise a one-voiced, authoritarian body (Shahor, 2015).

In sharp contra-distinction to Emanuel Sivan's position that sees the settlers as occupying a fundamentalist "enclaved culture," Dalsheim and Harel argue that the settlers are an integral part of Israeli society: they serve in the army, are part of many cultural activities, and are a critical and variegated part of the Israeli workforce. The first generation of academic students of the settlers reveal how easily research can flatten out the complex and blur the uniqueness of heterogeneous phenomenon (Dalsheim and Harel, 2009: 223).

Avi Sagi and Dov Schwartz dispute the simple and facile identification that Aran and others make between Gush Emunim and the Mercaz HaRav yeshiva. As they rightly point out, a sizeable group of those who headed the settlement project emerged from (what was called) the "middle class" or "bourgeois" center of the "old" religious Zionist community. They did not study in the Mercaz HaRav yeshiva; neither did they ever develop theological-messianic political views. This group understood itself as the successor to earlier secular settlement movements like the second and third *aliyot*. Their project rested on the mainstream Zionist program of "liberating" the land through settling it (Sagi and Schwartz, 2003). Moreover, it was not Rabbi Tzvi Yehuda who singularly created religious Zionism's political theology. High regard for secular Zionist pioneering, for example, was expressed by his father Rabbi Avraham Yitzchak Kook years earlier. The attribution of holiness to the Land of Israel and the belief that Israel was a key element in the process of redemption had long histories. So did the emphasis on the unity of nation, land, and Torah. They did not arise suddenly in the Mercaz HaRav yeshiva following the Six Day War. What Gush Emunim succeeded in doing was to reclaim, resuscitate, and radicalize beliefs that were already decades old (Schwartz, 2000). Nonetheless, Sagi concedes that the Mercaz HaRav-based "Elon Moreh" gar'in became the driving force behind Gush Emunim. Its triumph lay not only in spearheading the settlement agenda but also in essentially transforming religious Zionist discourse, the introduction of messianic mysticism as well as the empowerment of rabbinical authority (Sagi, 2010a).

In much the same spirit, Yoni Garb points to the affinity between Gush Emunim and the young guard of the Mafdal. Although many of the founders of Gush Emunim were students of the Mercaz HaRav yeshiva, in practice the mantle of leadership rapidly passed onto the activists in the field who were charged with implementing the movement's programs. This group included Benny Katzover, Yisrael Harel, Pinchas Wallerstein, Uri Elizur, and others. If it was the long-time students of Rabbi Tzvi Yehuda who created the movement's unique style of ideological discourse, it was the on-the-ground organizers and campaigners who held the central positions in the new settlements and, somewhat later, dominated the Yesha Council. Garb objects to the overstated emphasis on Gush Emunim's messianic character which, he feels, derives from the exaggerated identity of the movement with Mercaz HaRav (Garb, 2004b: 336; Garb, 2004a).

The approach of Rabbi Yoel Bin-Nun, one of the central personalities of Gush Emunim, has a certain affinity to that of Garb's but it places emphases on different elements within the movement. There surely was a division between Mercaz HaRav students and the practical policy makers who tended to derive from the "old" religious Zionist establishment. Moreover, the field-activists and the intellectual leaders were for the most part distinct from one another. In the first category he places the media icons of the movement—figures like Chanan Porat and Rabbi Moshe Levinger—who became the public face of Gush Emunim (Bin-Nun, 2001: 74). Moreover, after many interviews with the Gush's founders, Hoch concluded that although it was the members of the Bnei Akiva *gahelet* gar'in who later became students of Rabbi Tzvi Yehuda that led the movement, they shared this leadership with other non-yeshiva personalities. And yet, it was they who shaped it goals, at least at the outset (Hoch, 1994: 236).

Where the roots of Gush Emunim lie is not merely an esoteric historical question. To the degree that Gush leaders of "middle-class" Zionist origins are seen as the dominant force behind the settlement project, questions of religion-state relationships in general and of disobedience to law in particular take on a different coloration. Although there are exceptions, their motives tended to be less messianic and theological in character and more closely associated with broader Zionist-national objectives. Hence, theirs was a less confrontational politics than those who were convinced that deliverance was at stake. More pragmatic and flexible, they tended to shy away from clashes with the authorities. For example, a 1975 memorandum issued by the West Samaria gar'in formulated by Elyakim Rubenstein (later Attorney General and Supreme Court Justice) surveys the gar'in's activities since its founding in 1973 and goes out of his way to emphasize the groups respect for law:

> Let it be emphasized that to this point the gar'in has insisted on synchronization with the government and has not been active in illegal settlements that have not been authorized . . . All the ministers and government offices with which we dealt expressed their sympathy for the gar'in's ideas and its positions. (Harnoi 1995: 34–35)

Even a Gush Emunim member like Chagai Segal, later apprehended as a member of the terrorist "Jewish Underground," was initially in favor of obeying the law. Gush Emunim, he wrote, "did not have doubts about the legitimacy of the existing government and consistently spoke of the respect that should be accorded to the sovereign Israeli State (*Mamlachtiut*), despite its many defects" (Segal, 1987: 27).

On the other side, lies the more widely publicized "illegalist" character of the movement. Many Gush Emunim campaigns to seize different locations in Judea and Samaria during the first Rabin government (1974–1977) were done in the face of explicit government interdictions. There were those who saw these occupations as attempts to leverage the government into accepting the settler's agenda. Others simply justified their illegal actions by pointing to what they saw as the wicked norms of a recalcitrant government. Notably, the Gush's leaders claimed that even though their actions may have been illegal, they were not illegitimate. In the end, they believed that it was the reality of Jewish history and of Zionism that justified the project of settlement despite its illegal character (Sprinzak, 1986: 124). Moreover, even if their actions were formally illegal, they did not represent a breach of norms currently acceptable in Western democracies. After all, the expression of protest in the form of civil disobedience is common enough in Western democracies when citizens feel that a law is unjust. Disobedience is a right given to adult, autonomous, morally engaged citizens. They refer, for example, to the American Civil Rights Movement of the 1960s and the struggle against Apartheid from the late 1940s until 1994. It is no accident that the right wing think-tank, the Shalem Institute, published a collection of essays that dealt with the great champions of nonviolent civil disobedience such as Mahatma Gandhi and Martin Luther King (Weinstein, 1998).

In their justifications of disobedience, Gush Emunim argued that they were, in fact, the perpetuators of secular Zionism's settlement agenda during the British Mandate period. In their drive to establish new Jewish settlements, these early settlers did not hesitate to defy the British authorities; indeed, they often contravened the policies of the established Yishuv itself. Most especially, the Gush Emunim leadership saw itself as the latter-day incarnation of the Palmach whose very agenda was rife with illegal activities (Sprinzak, 1986: 125). In the eyes of the Gush's organizers and ideologues, there was no difference between the prohibition of settlements by the Mandate government and the proscription of settlement activity by the Israeli government. The government's prevention of settlement activity needed to be resisted for essentially moral reasons and because it violated a basic Jewish entitlement. Settlements should continue to be founded, even without government authorizations because settling in all of the Land of Israel is a religious and Zionist imperative. This view is well expressed in an explanatory pamphlet of Gush Emunim entitled "We Struggle for the Settlement of Israel":

In the entire history of the settlement project when we violated law and order for the sake of aliya and settlement, we
said that these rights possess the validity of a Zionist constitution and every command that prevents or limits them is illegal
and immoral. Our right to settle everywhere in the land is an
elementary Jewish right. This right has not expired with the
establishment of the state and every directive that limits it is
neither legal nor moral—it is imperative to revoke it. (Cited
by Sprinzak, 1986: 125.)

Similarly, Avraham Minz, among the earliest Gush Emunim leaders,
claimed in "A Symposium with Gush Emunim," (*Yediot Achronot* 3 October
1976) that:

We respect the law and the legal institutions of the State, but
we have reservations in regard to the actions that deal with the
most precious thing of all: the Land of Israel. In this field, we
are prepared to stage a struggle even when the struggle does no
accord precisely with the law. Those who control the law can, in
the name of the law, stymie and imprison the spirit. This action
is not legal. At the very least, it is not democratic. Therefore,
in regard to the soul of the Jewish people, the Land of Israel,
we struggle even when the government says that we break the
law. (Cited by Gal Or, 1990: 279.)

Another long-time Gush Emunim stalwart, Gershon Shafat, makes clear how
little those who carried out the settlement project in Judea and Samaria
accepted the criticism that they violated the law. They were, in fact, a
vanguard expressing the deep inner feelings of the nation.

Public opinion awakened into a synchronized chorus to uncom-
promisingly criticize 'the fanatical' violators of the law, those
who challenge 'the rule of democracy in the state.' Despite the
venom leveled at us, there was no doubt in our hearts that we
were acting in the service of the original Zionist idea. . . . This
was always the revolutionary nature of Zionism that was formed
in the unfinished struggle against opponents whose names and
faces no one any longer remembers. (Shafat, 1995: 71)

Shafat leaves no room for doubt:

We attempted to enter Judea and Samaria while observing the law, but we failed; we were convinced that the law of settlements is stronger than an administrative order that prohibits remaining in the area for more than 48 hours. Settlement in the Land of Israel is the pillar of Zionism no less than aliya. If a decision to stop aliya because of the economic situation in Israel were taken, we would bring illegal olim in ships, just as Israel did during the mandate period. (Shafat, 1995: 115)

What stands out in Shafat's argument is that essential Jewish-Zionist interests (as perceived by Gush Emunim) do indeed, override government law. Nevertheless, he insists, the Gush's actions are no more than a marginal violation of rules set down by the authorities. There is here no principled rebellion against the rule of law and there are no legal violations that are exceptional by comparison to what other groups do to advance their causes in public struggles. Wildcat strikers break the law, groups that block traffic to defend their interests break the law, protesters without official permits break the law (not to speak of tax evaders, those who build without authorization, and those who regularly flout traffic rules). Indeed, these lawbreakers are far more objectionable than Gush Emunim because they act illegally to promote narrow group (or individual) interests while Gush Emunim struggles not for personal gain but for the most basic of Jewish rights. As opposed to the run-of-the-mill lawbreakers, they sacrifice for the national good.

In a Gush Emunim pamphlet entitled "What Stands above the Law" (1976), Yoel Bin-Nun—among the more moderate of Gush Emunim leaders—claims that in some exceptional cases disobedience is an integral part of the democratic process. In principle, he recognizes the authority of the state and its laws. But settling the Land of Israel, the heart of the Jewish-Zionist enterprise, transcends legal bounds. Indeed, this is true not only for Israel; it is the prevailing norm in Western democracies. There are some laws that ought not to be obeyed. When a group feels that a severe injustice has been committed by the government, they are within their rights—under certain circumstances—to resist. In itself, such insubordination does not involve rebellion against democratic government or the rule of law. If a law is iniquitous and immoral, disobedience to it—coupled with the willingness of the dissident to pay the price and accept the punishment—is a legitimate political course of action as is clear from the behavior of Gandhi, King, and Mandela. In this sense, disobedience is understood not only as a vital instrument of democracy but also as an educational tool for furthering worthy democratic values. The following contentions of Bin-Nun integrate both Zionist and democratic reasoning:

> Each of us has values that are above the law; the question is which values . . . The injunction limiting settlements is an insulting, humiliating, unjust and immoral directive. It is not worse than limiting political information in order to undermine the struggle against submission to the government. This law contradicts the foundations of Judaism and the principles of Zionism at once. Under these conditions it is mandatory to fight this law until it is totally abolished. This struggle will not be deterred by arrests and trials. If two activists are put on trial, the prosecution will need to press charges against hundreds more. Jail is an energizing drug for this kind of struggle and never a deterrent. (Cited by Segal, 1987: 32.)

Bin-Nun concludes: "It is not against the rule of law that we struggle—only against one part of it that disgraces the State of Israel and its entire legal system" (cited by Segal, 1987: 32).

Many have cast doubt on this argument. They contend that the sense of expressing a kind of Rousseauist "general will" that the government was blind to poses a greater threat to liberal Western democratic norms than the common egoistic lawbreaker who recognizes his wrongdoing and indulges in it nonetheless for short-term gains. For those who level this kind of critique, the fact that Gush Emunim did not attempt to cover up its illegal behavior, that its members presented themselves as model citizens, renders their actions more rather than less inimical to democracy. Their denial, as a matter of principle that the state lacked the right to limit their activities because they represented the genuine popular will, is, for these detractors, a profound blow to the rule of law; indeed it was a claim that they were above the law, outside of state sovereignty. And yet, even the most vocal critics concede that the number of settlers who actually broke the law was relatively small. Indeed, some supporters of the Gush point out that when compared to the numbers of scofflaws in other groups (the Haredim and Arabs for example) the settlers as a whole were quite law-abiding.

And yet, despite their limited numbers, the real issue—critics insist—lies at the level of principle. A relatively small minority broke the law deliberately and habitually in order to further programs of the greatest national magnitude for the sake of views they believed were beyond criticism. This is not, the Gush's adversaries contend, in the same class as cheating on income tax or even protesting without a permit. The "in-your-face" forms of settler disobedience in a central strategic issue place it in a different category than the grayer, less conspicuous disobedience of other groups. They identified their ideological convictions with the national good although a very substantial majority had rejected their views at the ballot box. Critics conclude that there are few greater risks for democracy than when self-appointed guardians of the good put themselves in place of popularly elected governments.

Despite the importance of Gush Emunim's Zionist and democratic justifications of disobedience, it was their theological-Halachic arguments that constituted the most crucial legitimation for their illegal activity. A great deal of the research on Gush Emunim supports this conclusion. For example, Tzvi Ra'anan in his pioneering book on Gush Emunim claims that the worldview of the Gush's leadership was based on the extremely particularistic religious-Halachic belief that Israel is "a people that dwells alone." Gush leaders insisted that in its religious life Israel is different from all other nations of the world (Ra'anan, 1981: chapters 3–4). He cites the argument of an early spokesman of Gush Emunim, Rabbi Yochanan Fried, taken from an interview conducted in April 1975:

> The conception of democracy is not so sacred for me . . . We have a different sort of democracy, a different sort of idea about how to regulate the relationship between majorities and minorities; there are matters that are so principled that they may transcend all the considerations of majority and minority. The State of Israel in its very foundation is not built on the principle of majorities and minorities but rather on principled agreement that it is to be called a state of the Jews. (Cited in Ra'anan, 1981: 187–88.)

The priorities of a Jewish state are different:

> In my view, on the subject of settling the Land of Israel, it is inconceivable that the state's authority can prohibit it. It is an elementary right of every Jew to settle in all parts of Israel. On the other hand, I would not apply this principle to every action that has been taken. There certainly exists state authority but I believe that settling lies outside its bounds. (Cited in Ra'anan, 1981: 187–88.)

Not that Rabbi Fried and his sympathizers in 1975 supported changing Israel from a democratic into a dictatorial state. Gush Emunim never spoke in terms of regime change. Disobedience was justified only in regard to settling the Land of Israel. What they supported was a "different kind of democracy" (what came to be known as "Jewish democracy") that suited Israel's unique Jewish character. In a Jewish state, they asserted, certain issues of high principle transcend the will of transient majorities. In these constitutive issues, state sovereignty is conditional and limited. (And yet, it must be added that when political realities reversed themselves a few decades later, many religious Zionists became ardent supporters of thin "majority rules" democracy). Ra'anan's pithy conclusion is that "the most problematic side-effect of Gush Emunim's actions, the one that raises the most serious controversy in the Israeli public sphere, is its questioning of the state's legal authority. Gush Emunim rejects this authority time and again" (Ra'anan, 1981: 111).

Settling the land, for Gush followers, is the Jewish analog to the "inalienable rights": the "natural rights" championed by liberal democracy. The state cannot revoke them because they precede the state's existence. Only that in the case of liberalism, these rights are universal and generally anchored in a constitutive constitutional document. Rabbi Fried, by contrast, rests his claims on particularistic Jewish rights that do not apply—indeed, some believe that they cause harm—to others. Democratic principles play no role in his justification of disobedience. Clearly, religious imperatives supersede democratic decisions.

Ehud Sprinzak in his seminal research on "illegalism" in Israeli society devotes a substantial chapter to disobedience as an integral part of Gush Emunim's approach to law. He rejects the parallel drawn by the leaders of Gush Emunim between their form of illegalism and the illegalism that characterized the labor movement during the British Mandate period:

> While Gush Emunim likes to draw the parallel between their illegalism and the illegalism of the 'founding fathers' of the labor movement it is not difficult to see that the confrontation in regard to the 'rule of law' in [contemporary] Israel is far more profound in that its essential power draws upon Jewish Orthodox sources . . . What is at stake is not only the practice of illegalism that characterized the founders of the Yishuv but rather a deep conflict between two different legal systems, the positive laws of the state on the one hand and the halachic legal system on the other. (Sprinzak, 1986: 126)

Sprinzak summarizes the differences between the labor movement's disobedience during the British Mandate and that of Gush Emunim during the 1970s under two main headings: 1. The former rose up against a foreign mandate government while the latter violated the democratic rule of law to which they, as citizens of the sovereign State of Israel, were bound; 2. Despite the claims of Gush Emunim, their ultimate justification was not based on Zionism and certainly not on their idiosyncratic view of "true" democracy. Their deepest motives were the transcendent authority of Halacha and the messianic mission of the State of Israel. In Sprinzak's words:

> Gush Emunim is a special case because it is difficult to deny its idealism, pioneering spirit and willingness to sacrifice. It should be said in defense of the Gush that by contrast to many illegalist movements, its leaders always bestowed formal respect upon the independence and sovereignty of the State of Israel . . . Nevertheless, it is here that the trap lies: It is not difficult to censure criminal illegalism or deviations lacking saving graces. It is much more difficult to fight ideological and behavioral illegalism when it is prestigious. If it is not stopped in time, illegalism receives public recognition and enters the 'repertoire' of political activities that are recognized as legitimate. (Sprinzak, 1986: 142)

For Sprinzak, the leaders of Gush Emunim, some of whom later became politically recognized figures in the Yesha council, were ethical individuals whose very ethics led them to act illegally. They did not deny that they were obligated to the State of Israel and to its laws. Indeed, their personal integrity compares favorably with the not-infrequently-corrupt behavior of self-seeking public officials inside the Green Line. Although their political theology certainly justified disobedience, their loyalty to the state may well have prevented them from acting in ways they believed were harmful to the state's interests. Whatever one's views of their activities—and Sprinzak's are negative—it cannot be said that they acted out of avarice, malice, or the desire for personal gain. As opposed to the more complex view of Sprinzak, Aran is unimpressed by their personal integrity. They were calculated lawbreakers who rent the fabric of Israel's democratic regime. "For the purposes of Gush Emunim," he writes, "there is only one law: the commands of God and His will . . . The right to the land is not subject to the laws of nations, for this is a right given to us by God and the Torah. And tactically, if the state's laws do not accord with Divine commandments, there is no obligation to obey them" (Aran, 1987: 137).

A similar critical judgment is found in Røislien's description of the radical Jewish settlement in Hebron. She argues that in their understanding, the commandment to settle the land incorporates elements of violence. Even if the many of the Hebron settlers did not indulge in violence themselves, they understand violence as part of the project to encourage and promote the coming of the Messiah. If God's law overrides all other law, violence against those who would traduce it or subvert it, is justified—certainly when no other options are available. If the Hebron settlers, as members of the Jewish nation, are obliged to bond with God on His holy land in order to expedite the messianic era, mysticism—which is so often intimate and personal—becomes a fighting creed with violent strains. Standing in the way of salvation is a cardinal crime; it should be met with an equally severe response (Røislien, 2007: 183).

Returning to Aran's approach: he presents the settler's movement as driven almost exclusively by theological-messianic motives. Other students of the settlement project see this position as hyperbolic. Focusing too narrowly on Mercaz HaRav halachic-messianic doctrines, Aran emphasizes settler illegalism at the expense of other causal factors. (For an alternate approach that emphasizes the nationalistic, sociological, and anthropological aspects of Gush Emunim more than its religious character, see Feige, 2009). Nevertheless, in the end, whichever side is chosen, illegal is illegal.

The figure who dominated the discourse on the Greater Land of Israel was Rabbi Tzvi Yehuda Kook, the spiritual leader and mentor to many of Gush Emunim's leaders. We will deal systematically with his views on democracy and disobedience below but, at this point, we present preliminarily and without comment, a number of his most striking declarations. In 1974 the settlers refused to leave Chawara, an outpost they had set up in the vicinity of Shechem (Nablus). The IDF was compelled to evacuate them by force. At the time of the evacuation Rabbi Tzvi Yehuda, who was present at the site, declared: "Just as it is impossible to coerce me to eat pork and to profane the Sabbath, you will not coerce me to move from this place." Over time, this parallelism between eating pork, in which case many Jews historically chose martyrdom rather than partake of the forbidden meat, and disobeying laws prohibiting settlements, became common coin among many rabbis, especially Rabbi Avraham Shapira (later Chief Rabbi of Israel and head of the Mercaz HaRav yeshiva) (Segal, 1987, 29).

Not infrequently, analogies of this kind led to the defense of disobedience as rooted in the democratic right to freedom of religion. Religious obligations and resistance to religious coercion are, in this view, protected by the fundamental right to religious liberty, one of the most sacrosanct of liberal democratic rights. For adversaries of the Gush, however, this analogy fails because the two cases are sharply different. First of all, what is called for in regard to settlement prohibition is not an "act of commission" but rather the prevention of changing the political status quo. Notably, they add, Halacha itself distinguishes between the two: doing (*Kum ve'aseh*) and remaining passive (*Shev ve'al ta'aseh*). The latter involves a considerably less severe prohibition than committing the sin of, e.g., eating pork. Second and more critical, Gush opponents ask: would any democratic state in the modern world force an individual to eat pork? Manifestly, democracies do not compel citizens to violate cardinal religious commandments; it is unthinkable that they would. On the other hand, prohibiting settlements in a specific state-held territory, especially when it is under military rule, is a patently legitimate government policy. Even when religious issues are involved, critics insist, settling in areas the government explicitly outlaws—areas in which settlements are likely to have acute political and strategic repercussions—cannot be set aside in the name of religious freedom. If the state is not sovereign to decide in such matters, what can political sovereignty possibly mean?

Indeed, scholars of Jewish law point out that the tradition itself recognizes the distinction between religious rituals in which authority rests with the rabbis and halachic adjudicators, and the management of public affairs, the promulgation of reforms for the communal good, etc. in which political leaders have the last word. In some cases, in fact, the community and its leaders may even act against Halacha for the sake of the public good and nevertheless receive the support of dominant halachic authorities (Elon, 199, chapter 19).

In the Chawara incident, Rabbi Kook turned to the regional IDF commander, Yonah Efrat, and requested that he take off his uniform rather than execute orders that would expel Jews from the Land of Israel. But Rabbi Kook went further still in denying the legitimacy of an elected government in matters related to the Greater Land of Israel. At the time of the first settlement of the Elon Moreh gar'in in June 1974, when IDF soldiers came to evacuate the settlers, Rabbi Tzvi Yehuda said defiantly: "This entire Knesset only has power in regard to financial, economic, money matters—if the public agrees. But in the matter of uprooting us from land, we, WE are commanded by the Creator of the Universe not by the Knesset. Wasted words; there is no substance to all of this talk" (Kook, 1995: 175).

In Rabbi Tzvi Yehuda's eyes, it was not the settlements that were illegal; it was the prevention of settlements:

> He who hinders Jews from settling in the land commits an illegal action . . . These lands belong to us from the days of Abraham, Isaac and Jacob; they are also the patrimony of millions of our brothers all over the world . . . May the names of all those with twisted minds who delay the settlements be shamed and disgraced for all eternity. But, thank God, there are still powers

within the people of Israel, great powers, strong and solid with Jewish awareness that are prepared to sacrifice themselves, and with their help we will endure these difficult moments. All these settlements are legal both from a Torah standpoint and from the standpoint of the state's laws. It is true that here and there fleeting clashes and some unpleasantness occurred but it is absolutely impossible, for any length of time, to delay the settling of the land. (Kook, 1995: 73–74)

These combative words make clear that Rabbi Kook's struggle against the first Rabin government involved not only what he saw as an obligation to obey a Divine imperative; they also reflected his deep conviction that he and his followers—although they struggled against a democratically elected government—were the true representatives of popular will.

Interestingly, Rabbi Kook's views are unique even when compared to the ostensibly similar ideas that were common during the French Revolution and in various socialist movements in the nineteenth and twentieth centuries. The latter based themselves on the idea of a "vanguard," a group that understood the true interests of the people even though they had not yet matured to grasp their authentic will. By contrast, Rabbi Tzvi Yehuda was convinced (or, perhaps, deluded himself) that the people in their heart of hearts actually supported the settlement project, that the settlers represented what the people genuinely wanted and that it was the obstructive government that was acting undemocratically. In a public appeal entitled "Clarified and clear-cut matters," Rabbi Tzvi Yehuda (summer 1974) declared:

First of all: this government is for the people rather than the people being for the government. And when the government betrays the people and its homeland and its life then it is *a fortiori* true that the living, feeling people have no connection to the government at all . . . And we are commanded to settle and we shall settle, to the length and breadth of our homeland. (Kook, 1995: 29)

Rabbi Tzvi Yehuda did not hesitate to use even harsher, more confrontational words. In a letter to the army's Chief of Staff, General Mordechai Gur (May 1975) he threatens:

Thereof I warned Moshe Dayan in the past, I must reiterate once again. On the subject of our absolute control of the full breadth of the land, that is, Judea and Samaria there will certainly be a war among us . . . The teachings of the Torah sages and our faithful rabbis deal with the war between the people of Israel and the nations of the world and let us hope that we are not forced to come to a war between the people of Israel and its failing government. Your faithful devotee blesses you from the depth of his heart. (Kook, 1995: 35)

The position of Mercaz HaRav's spiritual master percolated down to his students. Rabbi Shlomo Aviner, one of Rabbi Tzvi Yehuda's most dedicated disciples and one of religious Zionism's most prominent spokesmen in the post-Rabbi Kook generation makes a sharp distinction between, on the one hand, a democratic government that expresses the majority's will but makes reprehensible decisions and, on the other, the obligation to obey the Torah's laws. His words are especially trenchant because, as we shall see in the following sections, Rabbi Aviner is one of the most outstanding figures in the *anti*-disobedience camp. For him—as for Rabbi Tzvi Yehuda—*Mamlachtiut* (respect for the religious status of the state that ought to be above the political fray) entails deference to legal authorities. And yet, despite his reservations regarding disobedience, it is difficult to miss the illegalist thrust of his words. The Mitzvah of settling the Land of Israel, whose weight is equal to that of the entire Torah, he believes, cannot be abrogated because of "some pact with the nations of the world." Rabbi Aviner insists that:

Any decision of a government body to transfer parts of the Land of Israel to the Gentiles is illegal and in violation of the laws of the Torah and of the land . . . The Torah is the constitution of the Jewish State, its people and its land. As our great teacher Maimonides, the principle adjudicator on the subject of state and kingship writes: 'It is obvious that if the king orders that a Mitzvah be annulled, he is not to be obeyed. And so the leadership of our democracy that stands in place of the Kingdom of Israel and derives it[s] authority from 'majority rules' [Exodus, 23:2] such [majority] decisions become emptiness and falsehoods when they entail 'following the majority for evil purposes,' in opposition to the Torah—when a government comes to uproot and destroy it violates its mission, on which point it is said 'I sent you to improve not to damage'—therefore all those who plan to violate the Torah's command to settle the land, their plan is invalid and illegal. (Aviner, 1983: 38–39)

Nevertheless, there is a marked difference between rhetoric and practice. However heated their oratory, there are controversies about whether Rabbi Kook or Rabbi Aviner truly advocated physical violence. Some of his later disciples believe that Rabbi Kook did advocate violence in practice. And yet, taking all of his statements and actions into account, we are drawn to the conclusion that neither of them promoted a policy of violent confrontation when settlements were being evacuated. Indeed, when the moment of truth arrived just a few years later in the form of the Yamit evacuation, Rabbi Aviner rejected both active resistance to the authorities and soldiers disobeying orders. Still, it must be cautioned that dramatizing the potential conflict between state law and the laws of God—which both Rabbis Kook and Aviner surely did—inevitably creates a dynamic that threatens the functioning of an elected government.

In the mind of Prime Minister Rabin there was no doubt that Gush Emunim posed a very real threat to Israeli democracy. When its leaders contrasted the rule of law with the superior law of the Torah, they undermined the legitimacy of Israel as a democratic state. "I see [this doctrine] as one of the most serious problems that have confronted us. The group that calls itself Gush Emunim, as a group, an outlook, and an approach, is threatening the democratic way of life in the State of Israel, and confronting it must be done on all levels" (cited in Zertal and Eldar, 2007). Even more harshly, Rabin, in his autobiography writes that Gush Emunim is "a grave phenomenon—a cancer in the body of Israeli democracy" (Rabin, 1996).

Rabin's position was not that of his entire government; a number of government members actively aided the Gush. The Mafdal (National Religious Party) in whose political womb Gush Emunim gestated was part of Rabin's coalition and they supported the settlers from within the government. There were even senior cabinet figures such as Foreign Minister Yigal Alon and the Minister of Defense Shimon Peres who were far more favorably disposed toward Gush Emunim than was Rabin. Moreover, highly placed officers among whom the Chief of Staff Mordechai Gurr stands out were more sympathetic than Rabin to Gush Emunim leadership—although they refrained from lending them on-the-ground support. All of this contributed to the feeling, prevalent among the Gush Emunim leaders, that they were not common lawbreakers, that there was substantial institutional support for them and their agenda—even if it was only with a wink and a nod. The leadership of Gush Emunim—Moshe Levinger, Chanan Porat, Benny Katzover, Menachem Felix, Gershon Shafat, Nissan Slomiansky, Yochanan Fried, and Uri Elitzur—was united in its belief that they represented a broad public that went well beyond the borders of religious Zionist camp.

(Indeed, the *Ein Vered* circle established by members of Yitzchak Tabenkin's family—one of the labor movement's founders—contributed to the sense of fraternity the Gush's leaders felt toward the Labor Party). The establishment of settlements like *Ma'aleh Adumim* and *Elkanah* which the government backed also proved to the Gush's leaders that without official sanction the settler movement would not have gotten off the ground. It was widely believed among Gush leaders that in breaking the law they were only doing what the government would have done were it not so weak. Dan Be'eri (later revealed as one of the leaders of the Jewish Underground) wrote:

> And what shall we do when the government does not go in the right direction . . . for this there is a ready answer: 'We are strengthening the government' . . . creating facts on the ground, on the border of coercing the political system . . . while the basic conception of non-intervention in politics remains intact. The action on the ground, even when it was characterized by a clash with the authorities, was perceived by the activists, in all sincerity, as the carrying out of the secret wishes of the government that only 'weakness' prevents it from fulfilling. (Cited by Aran, 1987: 553.)

The conviction that they were advancing the "true" agenda of the government energized Gush Emunim's leadership. In his study of political violence in Israel, Ehud Sprinzak notes that Gush Emunim was careful to avoid being drawn into violent confrontations with the state and its institutions because they were convinced that the government was "really" on their side. Sprinzak argues that as opposed to other protest movements that were born in bitterness and pessimism, Gush Emunim's dynamism grew out of hope and elation (Sprinzak, 1995: 64). As was stated earlier, Aviezer Ravitsky defines the Zionist-religious-messianic ideas of Rabbi Tzvi Yehuda Kook and his disciples as a "messianism of success" that is an exception to the general rule that messianism grows out of misery and oppression (Ravitsky, 1999). The Gush's leaders understood that in order to advance their cause they needed to retain open channels of communication with the establishment. This need for official recognition and support led them to moderate the means they employed in their struggle to establish settlements (Sprinzak, 1995: 64). But the most important reason for their restraint was the ideational-theological one. Sprinzak writes:

> From an ideational-theological point of view, Gush Emunim was never a movement of de-legitimization. And even in its most intense confrontations with the Rabin government, it did not

cast doubt on the theological lawfulness and authority of the secular government. The Gush, which always based itself on the legitimacy that the rabbis of the Kook dynasty bestowed upon the Zionist movement and the State of Israel—the emergent Kingdom of Israel—sanctified sovereign Israeli institutions, the Knesset, the government and most especially the army and the security apparatus. Its confrontations with the government appeared to them less as frontal confrontations and more as an effort to fortify the heart of the people and the government in a difficult hour, as a didactic effort of the highest importance. (Sprinzak, 1995: 63–64)

Perhaps the event that best exemplifies Gush Emunim's complex mix of ideas and behavior was their repeated attempts to establish a settlement in Sebastia so as to bolster the Jewish presence in Samaria. In this effort, the Gush's tendency to disobey the law and simultaneously seek alliances with the government was manifest and unmistakable. In this protracted saga, the Gush again and again deferred to the security forces that prevented the establishment of a settlement. Over the course of three years, there were six attempts to settle in Sebastia. In its seventh attempt (Winter-Chanuka 1975) Gush Emunim no longer played by the rules. On their way to Sebastia, the Gush's activists illegally detoured around an army checkpoint and succeeded in setting down the rudiments of a settlement. One of the group's stalwarts defined this moment as the "great revolution in the settlement project and in the status of Gush Emunim," and as the "breakthrough in renewing Jewish settlement in Samaria" (Harnoi, 1995: 43). With all the importance rightly due to security considerations, Gershon Shaffat makes it clear that pressing ahead with the settlement project in Judea and Samaria/ the West Bank was far more urgent and essential.

For us, Yesha and the Golan were and are a part of the Land of Israel, our forefather's homeland. The Divine promise, the religious faith and the historical bond with the Land of Israel that has not been severed; it is they that form the basis of our right to this land. The bond of the people of Israel to its land was born in Shiloh, Beit-El, Alon Moreh, Gamla and Masada and not in Tel Aviv, Herzliah and Nahariah. Not for reasons of security did the nations of the world recognize our right to the Land of Israel and not for reasons of security did they give Britain the Mandate to establish a Jewish national home in all of Israel, including eastern Trans-Jordan. (Shaffat, 1995: 70)

Speaking about one of the earlier attempts at settling in Sebastia, Shaffat declared:

> In Sebastia, on the ninth day of the month of Av, the Zionist enthusiasm that everyone thought no longer existed, burst forth once again. It was clear to us that the new movement to settle the land forced Israeli society to examine its set of priorities: what came first and what followed; what was the husk and what was the heart of the law. (Shaffat, 1995: 88)

Shaffat reminds his readers that on that very day the veteran kibbutz *Beit Alpha* was also founded despite the opposition of Yishuv's settlement institutions. Only post facto was it recognized as an accredited settlement. The same happened in *Ein Harod*. The Zionist Congress which was the supreme and authorized body of the Zionist movement opposed the initiatives. The settlers simply presented the Yishuv's official institutions with a fait accompli. Shaffat summarizes:

> We were convinced that we were the answer to the crisis of Zionist fulfillment (*Hagshama*); there was no arrogance here, quite the contrary, it was a sense of heavy responsibility in regard to the need and obligation to awaken and renew the momentum of fulfillment, of just those qualities and Jewish spiritual values that constitute the basis of Zionism from its origins onward: immigration and absorption, settling and building, independence and complete sovereignty in the Land of Israel. (Shaffat, 1995: 89)

In the Gush's eyes, the labor movement was spent and jaded, bureaucratically ossified and politically flaccid. It could no longer provide the *élan* that was the secret of Zionist success. Moreover, it had failed the country in the Yom Kippur War. Gush Emunim, by contrast, was young, passionate, and visionary. For the Gush, a change of leadership from moribund left-wing socialism to religious, nationalist, Land of Israel pioneering was the inevitable future of the Zionist saga. The old elite must give way to a new revitalized leadership. Shafat expresses the epic sense that in Sebastia this new generation of leaders was born. Notably, some veteran Labor Party figures were drawn into this Gush Emunim narrative. Nevertheless, it must be kept in mind that the majority among the labor movement's leadership—Yitzhak Rabin above all—saw the Gush activists as false prophets who were leading the country into a future of occupation and repression that would tragically compromise the humanistic values of the Zionist movement.

Whatever their deeper intentions, Gush Emunim did not shrink from dramatizing the threat that they would turn to violence, even it meant bloodshed. The Gush's leadership exploited the threat of disobedience and repeatedly raised the specter of civil war. The testimony of Gershon Shaffat reveals the manipulative tactics adopted by the Gush in its dealings with the Rabin government. Because of the importance of the ideas he expresses, we cite his words at length:

> If the fear of bloodshed was very great, it is thanks to the extremists on the left who worked diligently, conscientiously and indefatigably to present Gush Emunim as an unhinged group that threatens democracy . . . The left wing extremists needed to blacken our image in order to justify the extreme means they demanded should be used against us. The influence of the picture they drew in the end worked—only not in the direction they anticipated. Now everyone was trapped in the fear of the apocalyptic prophesies about revolution and anarchy that they themselves disseminated. It was clear to us that the government at long last and after a considerable delay was taking Gush Emunim with complete seriousness.
>
> Even though we, substantially, deliberately and without the knowledge of the government encouraged the fear of a civil war, for all of this time Gush Emunim had a red line which we would not cross: we would not do anything that would harm a soldier and we would not come into conflict with soldiers. To be sure, we did think of ways to deceive the army in order to infiltrate the territory through its many checkpoints, but we did not intend to come into conflict with the army and we did not conceive of the possibility that even one soldier would be harmed. We were convinced that the soldiers on the ground understood that we had no such intention. If we did not make an effort to refute the threats of a civil war, it was in order to exploit the atmosphere that they created in order to reach a compromise.
>
> Nonetheless, we too were not entirely free of the fear of escalation and violent confrontation between us and the IDF forces. The limits we set from the beginning were well known to the leadership of Gush Emunim and in profound talks well into the night on the question of how to present the issues, we made clear political decisions. But these did not always reach our public that also received many messages in the spirit of 'we will defend the place as a person defends his home.' This was

the formula that captivated our people and awakened a readiness to sacrifice oneself; yet it was understood by many as giving
legitimacy to frontal confrontations. And so, without instructing
anyone to raise his hand in response to a soldier raising his hand,
the spirit that passed through the camp was that we were going
to the very end, which forced us to be particularly careful in
our decisions. (Shaffat, 1995: 202–03)

The Sebastia affair prompted antithetical reactions. On the one side,
Zvulun Hammer, the Minister of Welfare, who was from the 'youth wing'
of the National Religious Party and one of the founders of Gush Emunim
said that vacating the settlers would be a black day for Israel. Completely
opposed to this verdict was that of Minister of Justice Chaim Zadok who
declared that not evicting them would be a black day for Israel. Zadok
went so far as to compare the Sebastia settlement with the 1948 *Altalena*
affair (in which, during the War of Independence, a ship carrying arms
and commanded by the Etzel underground was fired upon by IDF forces in
order to avoid a split in military and political authority). Indeed, Zadok
believed that the Sebastia affair was even more serious "because while the
Altalena intended to undermine the government internally, Sebastia intended
to undermine the government's authority both internally and externally"
(cited in Shaffat, 1995: 203).

As opposed to Zadok, there were members in the Labor Party who
spoke glowingly of settler idealism. The Chief of Staff, Mordechai Gurr,
supported reaching a compromise between the government and the settlers. He saw Gush Emunim as a serious, morally high-minded political
movement with which the government ought to negotiate. Beyond such
considerations, Gurr felt that settlements on the eastern Shomron mountain
ridge were important for security reasons. In the end, Prime Minister Rabin
and Minister of Defense Peres, fearing violent clashes with the settlers,
adopted the compromise resolution proposed by the poet Chaim Guri and
formulated by Minister Yisrael Galilee. According to this compromise, it
was decided that thirty families would reside in the army base at *Kadum*,
which, in the course of time would become the settlement *Kedumim* (Shaffat, 1995: 210–17).

This compromise decision was greeted by the settlers with much jubila-
tion and dancing; leaders of Gush Emunim, like Chanan Porat and Moshe
Levinger, were carried triumphantly on the shoulders of the celebrants. As
was later chronicled by Meir Harnoi, the settlers understood that:

Here in this place and in this hour, the first stake in the change
of attitude toward settlement in the Land of Israel was driven

into the ground. Here, in my opinion, the stake driven into the ground led to the great reversal of 1977, in which the Likud came to power, for the first time since the establishment of the state. (Harnoi, 1995: 51)

This view—that the victory in Sebastia led to the downfall of Labor Party hegemony—is common to many Gush Emunim leaders (Segal, 1987: 33).

Rabin himself, in his autobiography of 1979, justified his capitulation to the Gush by saying that it came after the United Nations vote that Zionism was racism. This vote caused many Jews, at home and abroad, to rally round the flag and to express solidarity for the settler movement. At a time such as this, Rabin writes, he did not want to aggravate the disagreement among the Jews in Israel and give the enemies of Israel cause for joy (Rabin, 1996). Whether this was his real motive or a self-justification after the fact, there can be little doubt that Rabin's hesitations as well as Peres's disingenuousness contributed to the image of the Labor government as weak. The rise of the right wing and of religious groups in Israel's public sphere set the stage for the great fault line in Israeli politics: the rise of the Likud to power in 1977.

The political reversal of 1977 thoroughly changed the relations between Gush Emunim and the Israeli government. Gush Emunim was now a partner to the policies of the Likud that committed itself to settling in all parts of the Land of Israel. There are, to be sure, significant differences between the conception of the Greater Land of Israel in the worldviews of Gush Emunim and the Likud: the Likud championed the Greater land of Israel for national-historic as well as security reasons while Gush Emunim based its return to the land mostly on religious-messianic grounds that drew upon religious Zionism's political theology in general and upon the teachings of Mercaz HaRav in particular (Na'or, 2001). Still, despite these differences, the ideological common denominator between them created a real partnership between the Likud and the religious Zionist camp that persists to this day.

A central figure in this Likud-Gush Emunim collaboration was Ariel Sharon who served as Minister of Agriculture and was responsible for settling Judea and Samaria in the Begin government. His nickname, the "bulldozer," was well earned; his motives were clearly historical and security-related rather than religious, and yet, with the help of Gush Emunim, he worked to realize his vision of Judea and Samaria dominated by Jewish settlements. While there were twenty settlements with about 6,000 settlers set up between 1967 and 1977, in the course of four years after the rise of the Likud to power, another thirty-five settlements were set up with about 17,000 residents. Until 1992 when the second Rabin government rose to power, there were already more than 100,000 settlers in Yesha/the West Bank (Taub, 2007: 73).

As a result of this active collaboration between the political establishment and the settlers in Yesha, the leadership of Gush Emunim underwent a process of institutionalization that transformed it from a fighting ideological force to one whose character was practical, preservative, and bureaucratic. Gush Emunim activists became salaried office holders. Central to this institutionalization was the formation of the Yesha Council that represented the settlements to the relevant government agencies and created umbrella municipal and administrative organizations to advance the interests of the settlements. A great many of the Yesha Council's members were former Gush Emunim activists. Beginning with the ninth Knesset (1977), Gush followers became Knesset members who represented various right-wing parties. One consequence of this institutionalization was the decline in its debates over disobedience. Instead, Gush Emunim in its various incarnations became an organization (or rather organizations) dealing with the policies and logistics of settlement in tandem with a sympathetic government.

To be sure, even after the rise of the Likud to power there were the episodic clashes with the legal authorities. The most prominent was the unwillingness of Gush Emunim to accept the ruling of the Supreme Court in the summer of 1979 that prohibited housing construction for the *Alon Moreh* settlement on privately owned Arab land. Prime Minister Menachem Begin dutifully accepted the court's decision out of respect for the rule of law. He famously declared: "There are judges in Jerusalem." By contrast, Gush activists once again flirted with the idea of disobedience and ignored the court's verdict. Tension abated after Rabbi Tzvi Yehuda Kook ruled that in principle theft of Arab lands was forbidden even if the justification was the desire to establish a Jewish settlement. Moreover, Gush Emunim was compensated for its loss. Only following a deal that was hammered out between the government and the settlers, in which the latter were promised alternative lands on which they could set up the settlement, did they agree to evacuate (Sprinzak, 1986: 131–32). It should be noted that many of Rabbi Kook's disciples adopted his position against theft of privately owned Palestinian lands—although of late this compliance has become attenuated.

After the *Alon Moreh* decision, a rift opened within the ranks of Gush Emunim. Faced with a hostile judiciary, two different strategies developed: on the one side there was the radical messianic faction that stridently distanced itself from the need to accept the state's hegemony. Out of this dissident branch of the movement there arouse, in short order, the Jewish Underground with which we will deal below. On the other side, the majority of the Gush's members understood that it was time to mute the vocabulary of messianic redemption and to move on to a discourse based on state sovereignty, that is, to draw nearer to the Likud's position. Consequently, the more dynamic and ideologically activist Gush Emunim lost its centrality and was replaced by the Yesha Council as the dominant force within the settler community (Taub, 2007: 78–85). (Some scholars disagree: they believe that it was the original militant voice of Gush Emunim that remained the authentic expression of settler Zionism (Wilcox, 2011)). What is certain is that Gush Emunim did not disappear. Its tendency toward disobedience became dramatically visible in the resistance it mounted against evacuating the Yamit settlement (in the Sinai Peninsula) as part of the peace agreements with Egypt in 1981–1982.

As mentor to many of the Yamit activists, Rabbi Tzvi Yehuda Kook's worldview must now be systematically analyzed.

Rabbi Tzvi Yehuda's Struggle against Territorial Concessions in the First Rabin Government (1974–1977)

Gush Emunim's resistance to the retreat from the Sinai originated in the tangled tale of Henry Kissinger's efforts to conclude an interim agreement between Israel and Egypt. In the wake of the Yom Kippur War, an accord was signed (January 1974) that set down the conditions for a disengagement of forces between Israel and Egypt. In his "shuttle diplomacy" between March and August 1975, Kissinger, with considerable persistence and skill, succeeded in bringing about such an interim agreement in September 1975. Israel agreed to retreat 30 to 40 kilometers to the east of the Mitleh and Gidi passes (which were 35 to 50 kilometers east of the Suez Canal) and to evacuate a large part of the Sinai's oil fields. In return, the area was largely demilitarized and Egypt agreed to allow passage of Israeli civilian cargo through the Suez Canal.

While Kissinger was shuttling from capital to capital, there were outbreaks of public protest against the concessions to Egypt in which Gush Emunim was visibly active. In the course of these protests many derogatory remarks about Kissinger were made, going so far as calling him a "Jew boy." Rabbi Tzvi Yehuda took a vigorous part in these protests and his comments, recorded by a number of his followers, had significant influence on the religious Zionist camp, especially on its rabbis. Rabbi Kook developed a systematic doctrine according to which Rabin's elected government did not have the right to make concessions in all the territories under Israeli control, especially not in Judea and Samaria. Rabbi Tzvi Yehuda conflated the two issues in which the government of Israel had taken reprehensible decisions: preventing settlements in Judea and Samaria and accepting the interim agreement with Egypt. In his eyes, both were illegitimate.

Because of his unparalleled eminence in the religious Zionist community in general and Gush Emunim in particular, Rabbi Tzvi Yehuda's teaching deserve careful, in-depth treatment. Above all, Rabbi Tzvi Yehuda was an ardent defender of the doctrine of *Mamlachtiut* that attributes great value—for him holiness—to the State of Israel, its public officials and institutions, most especially to its army. Ravitsky, like many others, attributes. Rabbi Tzvi Yehuda's view that the Jewish people are ontologically unique to the teachings of his father Rabbi Abraham Isaac Kook. Even though the state was not founded in his lifetime, Rabbi Kook the father projected this holiness onto the actual, concrete Jewish Yishuv and the state that would issue from it. Although its emergent institutions did not conduct themselves according to religious law and were not led by religious leaders, its holiness was metaphysically inherent (Ravitsky, 1996: chapter 3). Rabbi Abraham Isaac Kook's utopian dream anticipated the creation of "a State of Israel, the essential throne of God in the world, whose sole desire is that God and His Name be one; this constitutes supreme happiness" (Kook, 1985: vol. 3: 191). Rabbi Tzvi Yehuda followed his father's doctrine, convinced that *Mamlachtiut* obligates the religious Zionist community to base its relation to the State of Israel on the recognition that Israel is, in practice, the throne of God in the world.

In Rabbi Tzvi Yehuda's conception of *Mamlachtiut,* the trappings of statehood (flag, anthem, tanks, airplanes, etc.) are inherently holy—in sharp opposition to the prevailing liberal-instrumental understanding of the state. Rabbi Kook rejected the secular "republican" outlook for which the state's moral standing rests upon the obligations that individual citizens—setting aside their private interests—have for the country's general welfare. This republican outlook—that dominated Ben Gurion's thinking in the 1950s—emphasizes a state-centered "civil religion." Rabbi Tzvi Yehuda's outlook went far beyond republican sacrifice for the general good: it sanctified the very status of Israel's government apparatus. His disciple Rabbi Shlomo Aviner writes unequivocally: "The government of Israel is the representative of the Israeli people, a representative of *Knesset Yisrael* (a Kabbalistic term expressing the holiness, continuity and organic unity of the Jewish people), a representative of the kingdom of heaven that appears in the world in the attire of the Kingdom of Israel—whether this is acknowledged or not" (Aviner, 1996: 6).

Despite Rabbi Tzvi Yehuda's steadfast attribution of holiness to the State of Israel throughout his life, the doctrine of Mamlachtiut after the Yom Kippur War (1973) came to include internal tensions and dissonances.

Inbari is surely right in his claim that Rabbi Kook's political theology must be divided into two historical periods. Until 1973, his identification with the Zionist project was unconditional; for example he bitterly critiqued Haredi anti-Zionism. But after 1973 and the founding of Gush Emunim, a shift of perspective takes place. Against the background of the struggle to establish settlements despite government opposition and the crisis over the evacuation of Yamit, he introduced a conditional element in his heretofore unreserved Zionist commitments. Whatever its supreme religious status, the state had no right to relinquish any part of Judea and Samaria and to transfer it to Arab rule. Were such a retreat decided upon, defiance was the proper response. The inner strains and pressures that characterized Rabbi Kook's post-1973 creed continue to bedevil the ideologues of the settlement project. His followers tend to be drawn to different aspects of his thought: those who emphasize the state's unconditional holiness and those who justify active disobedience to objectionable government decisions (Inbari, 2012: 16).

Shortly before the Six Day War on the 19th anniversary of Israel's independence (May 1967) Rabbi Tzvi Yehuda gave a much publicized lecture to the students of the Mercaz HaRav yeshiva. For his disciples, its contents were prophetic, a portent hinting at the stunning triumph that was to come. When the magnitude of the victory sank in, many, if not most religious Zionists joined Rabbi Tzvi Yehuda in seeing it as nothing short of a miracle, the hand of God intervening in history. In this lecture, Rabbi Kook presented the essentials of his political theology and his views on the Greater Land of Israel. The rabbi described his deep feelings of disquiet on the 29th of November 1947 when the United Nations decided on the establishment of a Jewish state alongside a Palestinian state. While the general atmosphere among Jews was euphoric, Rabbi Tzvi Yehuda told his listeners that he then felt the full impact of the prophesy of Joel that God in the end of days would punish the nations of the world for dispersing Israel and for dividing the Land of Israel ("and my land they divided" (Joel 3:2)). Oddly, just when the United Nations decided to grant Jews, for the first time in two millennia, sovereignty over a part of the Land of Israel, Rabbi Tzvi Yehuda spoke of experiencing dark feelings and cited a despondent verse that speaks of the destruction and dispersal of Israel. This striking dissonance expresses Rabbi Kook's deep commitment to the Greater Land of Israel months before the actual declaration of statehood. In the course of this talk Rabbi Tzvi Yehuda described his pain he felt:

> Where is our Hebron—can we forget this?! And where our
> Shechem, can we forget this?! And where is our Jericho—can we

forget this?! . . . In that condition, wracked in my entire body, all of me injured and cut to pieces—I could not then rejoice. Such was my condition nineteen years ago, in that night, and in that hour. The next day the eminent Rabbi Yaakov Moshe Charlap of blessed memory came to our house—he had the need to come . . . We sat silently and in shock. In the end we recovered and in one voice we said: "This is the Lord's doing, it is marvelous in our eyes." The seal was set! (Kook, 1995: 5)

It was, he said, the messianic vision of a Greater Israel that restored his spirit. The day would come when all of the Land of Israel would be liberated. He proclaimed that anyone with eyes in his head could not miss the process of redemption that was taking place. His hopes were fulfilled by the Six Day War when, as Ravitsky put it, the "revealed end of days" came to pass (Ravitsky, 1996: chapter 3).

Rabbi Tzvi Yehuda relies heavily on the oft-cited words of the medieval sage Nachmanides (in his 4th Critique of Maimonides's *Book of Mitzvot*) in regard to the verse "Take possession of the land and settle in it, for I have given you the land to possess" (Numbers, 33:53). Maimonides, in his numbering of the Torah's commandments, does not count conquering and settling the land as a positive commandment of the Torah. By contrast, Nachmanides claims that we "are commanded to take possession of the land and not leave it in the hands of other peoples or allow it to become a wasteland." When the rabbis spoke of "a commanded war" (*Milchemet mitzvah* as opposed to a *Milchemet reshut* or an "initiated war"), it was precisely this liberating of the land that they had in mind.

Nachmanides's position is novel because it insists that the commandment to take possession of the land referred not only to biblical times but was valid for all future generations and obliges every person of Israel up until the present day. From its origins in the late nineteenth century, religious Zionism regularly argued that this unequivocal statement of Nachmanides provided support for their national-religious objectives. Similarly, Nachmanides's commandment is the essential basis and central proof text for authorizing Rabbi Tzvi Yehuda's position on the Greater Land of Israel (Kook, 1995: 7–9). Rabbi Kook contrasts sharply between, on the one hand, obedience to God's commandment to conquer all of the land and not to transfer any part of it to Gentiles, and on the other, the illegitimate surrendering of Jewish settlements by the Israeli government. His conclusion is unambiguous: the Torah's commandments (as interpreted by Rabbi Tzvi Yehuda), take precedence over obeying contrary decisions of an elected, democratic government.

In a speech given a few weeks later at a festive banquet celebrating the victory in the Six Day War and the capture of Jerusalem, Judea, Samaria, Gaza, and the Golan, he argues unequivocally that one must sacrifice one's life (*Mesirat nefesh*) for every single part of the Land of Israel without taking resident Gentiles into account. Moreover, he makes it clear that the Torah strictly forbids giving non-Jews any permanent standing (*Chanaya kavu'ah*) in the land and if a wrong-headed Jewish leadership nevertheless decides to allow non-Jews any form of sovereignty in the land, this decision has no validity (Kook, 1995: 13–15). Rabbi Kook summarizes his position:

> It should not even be contemplated, whether internally within the people of Israel, whether among the nations of the world, that there is any reality, any power, any value, any condition that will retard this Divine process as part of which we have returned to our ancestral homeland. There is no conquering here. As opposed to their formulations: 'Arab land,' 'Arab foothold'—there *is no Arab land*, there is only God's land. (Kook, 1995: 16–17) [Emphasis in the original]

A short time after the Six Day War, discussions were held in Levi Eshkol's government about the possibility of giving back the territories captured in the war in return for a peace agreement with the Arab world—notably with the support of Chaim Moshe Shapira leader of the National Religious party. In this context, Rabbi Kook, a few months after the war made his "Do not be afraid" proclamation that became the ideological paradigm for the Greater Land of Israel supporters—especially those from Mercaz HaRav. In no uncertain terms he writes:

> Transferring our lands to Gentiles is a sin and a crime . . . It is nothing but weakness, lack of intelligence and faith, nothing more, not for the good of Israel but for their detriment and failure forbid it . . . There is absolutely no right to violate this Torah prohibition of transferring land to the Gentiles, forbid it, certainly not permanently. Therefore, it is incumbent on each person of Israel, on every Torah sage, on every military man in Israel to prevent and hinder this with all might and courage. (Kook, edited by Melamed, 1995: 19)

In another ringing declaration at the same time entitled "For sake of reason," he develops his doctrine prohibiting any territorial concession at length:

This entire land is absolutely ours and cannot be given over to others as God proclaims . . . therefore it must be made absolutely clear once and for all that there are no Arab territories and Arab lands, only the lands of Israel, the eternal patrimony of our fathers to which others came and built upon without our permission or our presence. We have never left nor severed our ties with our patrimony and always, always continued our conscious ties with it and hence we protest against their brutal and artificial possession of it . . . Moreover, these matters are confirmed by the League of Nations at the end of the 1914 war [World War I].

. . . Moreover, even in verbal Arab doctrine it is known that we shall return in end of days to our land, the patrimony of our fathers and also in their Koran. They are known in the League of Nations at the end of WWI. This was the view of Lloyd George [under whose reign as Prime Minister, Lord Balfour made his famous declaration] which I possess and which says that this entire land in its full biblical boundaries belongs to the Israeli regime . . . We did not take [the land] from the Arabs who resided in it, in its desolation, not having set up any governing body. Rather we returned when the foreign regime that temporarily ruled collapsed [the British Mandate], with the approval of the nations of the world, that because of this [collapse] the land was in their hands; they announced in their cultural high-mindedness the justice of the belonging of this land to our government . . . It is also known that we did not expel them from their residence here even though it is our ancestral patrimony . . . but that they themselves, whether from exaggerated fear and panic escaped and left behind some of their places of residence or because of the invention of political programs that inflated things and the creation of 'refugee camps' [to win the sympathy of] the surrounding and distant world. (Kook, 1995: 20–22)

In short, the land taken in 1967 was "liberated" not "conquered." Not only the Bible makes this clear; it is present in Moslem sources and was supported by the nations of the world in the earlier part of the twentieth century. That international public opinion had changed is morally and Jewishly irrelevant. It remains incumbent upon every Jew to settle the land to its length and breadth.

Two aspects of Rabbi Kook's militant position rest upon unapologetic Jewish "exclusivism." Both are grounded in Rabbi Tzvi Yehuda's conception of what he calls "Jewish democracy" and both derive from Jewish enclavic particularism, that is, the essential difference between Jews and Gentiles. First, Rabbi Kook takes up the relationship of Israel to the *external* world of non-Jews—whether they are Arabs or the international community or the United States. Second, he focuses on the character of a Jewish democracy in its *internal* aspect, that is, to the standing Israel's secular elected government in general and, more specifically, to its illegitimacy when it relies upon the support of Arab parties to sustain its ruling coalition. What the rabbi intends by Jewish democracy requires elucidation because its meaning differs so dramatically from what is commonly accepted in the Western liberal tradition. Without understanding these deeply held beliefs, his opposition to withdrawing from any and all territories belonging to the Land of Israel cannot be fully understood.

Rabbi Kook regards concessions to the American government as a deplorable submission to the Gentiles. The Rabbi's position relies on the doctrine—prevalent in the Zionist movement at least since the Holocaust—of the "negation of the Diaspora" (the view that life in the Diaspora is Jewishly wanting and spiritually corrupt) and upon the familiar argument that there exists an essential, qualitative difference between Jews and non-Jews.

As early as 1946 these ideas appear in an article entitled "Not reckoned among the nations," in which Rabbi Tzvi Yehuda declares that Israel is "a singular people" essentially severed from the Gentile world. Jewish life in the Diaspora shattered the united Jewish body into fragmented limbs. In the period of redemption realized through the liberation of the Land of Israel and the return of the Jews from the exile, they would once again become whole, freed from the disjointed world of life among the Gentiles. They would return to their singularity and fullness. In the holy land, once the people's unique inner Jewishness matures, Israel may well become a model for humanity. Noteworthy in Rabbi Kook's article are the clear parallels to nineteenth-century romantic European nationalism that emphasizes the collective, organic, and territorial aspects of nationhood—even if direct lines of intellectual influence are difficult draw:

> In truth, the essence of Israel's uniqueness lies in the difference between Israel and the nations. The king of the world . . . created a nation to recite his praises . . . in our time of the 'revealed end.' (*Ketz hameguleh*) . . . in the encircling public reality of the settlement of our land with the return of its sons and its builders

from the dispersal of the Diaspora, it is more and more revealed, prominent and perfected the form of our nation . . . From dispersal and division to the ingathering and unity, from individual shattering to the kingdom of its priesthood. (Kook, 1967: 73–74)

The mystical motifs that abound in Rabbi Kook's later writings are already foreshadowed in an early essay penned after World War II. Here, his intense nationalism is tied, on the one hand, to a singular Holocaust theodicy that we take up below and, on the other, to an explanation of the national revival of the Jewish people. As Ravitsky notes, Rabbi Tzvi Yehuda's determinist, messianic theology that attempts to give meaning to the Holocaust, repositioned his father's complex ideas and directed them in a far more "particularistic" direction—a direction not necessarily consistent with the original. Although Rabbi Tzvi Yehuda arrogated to himself the role of definitive expounder of his father's views (Ravitsky, 1996 chapter 3), not a few researchers have cast doubt on this claim. They call attention to the profound influence of the Holocaust on his radical doctrine of the "negation of the Diaspora" and on his intensely adversarial views of the non-Jewish world (Don Yehiya, 1987; Don Yehiya, 1992; Schwartz, 2001a: chapter 1).

The Diaspora mentality destroys Jewish pride and hobbles Jewish redemption. In this context, Rabbi Tzvi Yehuda expressed fierce antagonism to all requests made by the Gentile world that Israel withdraw from the land taken in the Six Day War—especially toward those Israeli politicians who were willing to even consider such a possibility. Conceding any part of the Land of Israel, regardless of who demanded it, was simply out of the question. It was precisely this kind of Jewish capitulation that the Zionist movement was meant to overcome. He directs his bluntest and most insulting barbs toward the "Diaspora mentality" of assimilated Jews—the American Secretary of State Henry Kissinger is the target of his greatest vehemence—who attempt to undermine the holy birthright of the people of Israel. In an essay written in 1976 entitled "And to the apostates and informers let there be no reprieve," Rabbi Kook identifies the American pressure for territorial concessions with the Jewish "apostate" Henry Kissinger:

Thank God we have come home . . . and we are an independent, whole, unique and powerful state, not at all dependent upon or beholden to the benevolence of the nations with their sins . . . The obsequious deceit of the apostate and destroyer of Israel together with the weakness of the government that is at present drawn by him, they are transient and will pass. The health of the nation and our land will spit him out as it has all the apostates in all the generations of the Diaspora . . . And the eternity of Israel and its rebuilding will rise up and become lofty in the glory of its power. (Kook, 1995: 43–44)

Rabbi Kook rains down denunciations on Kissinger: "The apostate husband of a Gentile woman" and "a traitor to the nation into which he was born" and the like (Kook, 1987: 68–72). Moreover he continues, even the Jewish Israeli government—whose members are, admittedly not "apostates"—is ready to concede territories of the Greater Land of Israel and, he insists, it must not be obeyed for it does not display sovereignty but rather flaccidity and weakness. These themes, which Rabbi Tzvi Yehuda initiated in the 1970s, only became more intense in the future when his disciples, believing they were honoring his heritage, called for outright defiance during the Oslo Process.

Rabbi Tzvi Yehuda's support for elected democratic government is, as we noted, highly restricted and conditional. Two broad traditions regarding the synthesis between Judaism and democracy have developed in the modern era. The first emphasizes the sui generis character of "Jewish democracy" whose authority rests upon the decisions of a "Jewish majority" as well as upon the unique spiritual character of the people of Israel. It is only weakly obligated to liberal democratic principles such as citizen equality, the rights of the minority, pluralism and the like. By contrast, what might be called "democratic Judaism" reads the Jewish halachic tradition through a prism of liberal democracy and pursues a deeper synthesis between them (Hellinger, 2002).

Rabbi Tzvi Yehuda Kook clearly belongs to the first category and is one of its most influential representatives. His position is already apparent in the very first essay he wrote: "On the agenda" that was published in 1913 when he was in his early twenties: He writes:

> In its usual meaning, politics is not among the concepts that govern our lives. The organized state as a 'large responsible society' [a term he took from his father's *Orot Hakodesh*, 3: 191] has never been our ideal nor the core of our statehood . . . The ideal of a 'kingdom of priests and a holy nation' (Exodus, 19:6) has never been abandoned. It has already registered its deep mark upon us in the course of our general history. (Kook, 1967: 17)

The clear imprint of his father's teachings is visible here. Rabbi Kook the father had much earlier pursued a political theology in which the Jewish state, when it arises, will be unique among the nations. It will rest on spiritual foundations that foster a different kind of politics—neither violent nor belligerent as has been the common practice in human history. What makes Rabbi Tzvi Yehudah's views unique is that he propounded the doctrine of Jewish uniqueness after the State of Israel had taken its place among the nations, that is, when complex and difficult political questions were at stake (Hellinger, 2008; Ravitsky, 1996: chapter 3).

Such was the case concerning the charged concept of Mamlachtiut that lies at the heart of Rabbi Tzvi Yehuda's political theology. Notably, both Ben-Gurion (who coined the term) and Rabbi Kook used the term frequently but the differences between their respective usages are profound. Rabbi Kook's religious sense of the term entails viewing Israeli public life in sacred, redemptive terms. The state is the Divine vehicle of salvation and hence loyalty to it must transcend mundane political differences. On the other side, there is the civil, republican version of Mamlachtiut advocated by Ben Gurion in which the state's legitimacy rises above the fray of partisan politics. To act in a "Mamlachti" fashion is to internalize the dignity of the state and behave—despite political differences—with the good of the whole in mind. Notably, Rabbi Kook used his religious Mamlachtiut to delegitimize civil Mamlachti decisions to which he objected. In a talk entitled "A chapter in the *Halachot* of honoring the Kingdom of Israel" delivered while Rabin was attempting to form a minority government in 1974, Rabbi Tzvi Yehuda states that the essence of the Torah is sanctifying God's name (*Kiddush hashem*) and that Israel is the bearer of this obligation in the world. But when

> there is no proper public and there is no kingdom in Israel, this is the most grievous profanation of God's name. When the public sphere and Mamlachtiut are healthy and in good order, when the *Malchut* (kingdom) prevails toward the outside world, then God's great honor is also revealed inwardly. The honor of Israel that lies in the Kingdom of Israel and the honor of God that is revealed in the Divine domain—these are one thing. (Kook, 1995: 73)

Israeli *Malchut* is possible, Rabbi Tzvi Yehuda contends, only when the state is a truly Jewish state. In the Israeli system of representative government this entails ruling with an absolute Jewish majority, i.e., not being dependent on Arab support. When Gentiles are needed to govern the Jewish state, Mamlachtiut is subverted and dishonored:

> There is room for democratic arrangements in which the majority decides, that is, a majority of Jews. A minority government is a form of sectarian arrogance. The audacity to decide on the basis

of a minority. But here there is an even more terrible dysfunction: the desecration of God's name. There are Gentiles who are here as minorities under the protection of our government but now an opposite reality has been created: a government that is composed by adding the voices of Arabs. A glorious government!? The debasement of the honor of Israel! A minority government is not normal, without parallel in the entire world, creating a situation in which 'the stranger who lives among you will rise up over you, higher and higher.' (Kook, 1995: 74)

For Rabbi Kook, popular sovereignty and majority rules are relevant only when the government represents a Jewish majority. A Jewish state means a state in which politically only Jews count. This is the heart of Rabbi Kook's doctrine of a "Jewish democracy." He clearly rejects the egalitarian image of the state expressed in Israel's Declaration of Independence. He views a government requiring Arab minority support as subversive of the state's Jewish character. This view remains quite common on the Israeli Right. (They defend their position by claiming that when it comes to existential national decisions, such as those regarding the state's borders, Israel's Arab minority will always vote in favor of specifically Arab interests rather than in favor of those that advance the interests of Israel as a Jewish state).

It is true, he concedes, that Western democracies relying on ethnic minorities may be legitimate but that is because they fall into the category of mundane politics-as-usual. Jewish politics is quite the antithesis: it is Divine politics. "We are dealing here not with politics in its narrow sense but rather with the Laws of the Divine Kingdom." Divine politics cannot rest upon a non-Jewish public because its very essence is the expression of Jewish national uniqueness that links heaven and earth. "Jewish democracy" is inherent in genuine "Jewish politics." Neither of them belongs in the same category as "normal" politics as it is practiced among the Gentiles. The latter are transient human activities than cannot transcend their secular instrumental character.

A further implication of Rabbi Tzvi Yehuda's religiopolitical ideal is that rabbis are obligated to intervene in politics. He writes:

There are those who claim that rabbis should not interfere in politics. We are not dealing here with politics in the narrow sense but rather with the laws of the sanctification of God's name, with the Divine that is concretely revealed in the establishment of the Kingdom of Israel. The moment the kingdom dwindles, desecration of God's name erupts. The attitude that rabbis should not intervene in politics is a Christian attitude.

Israeli Mamlachtiut receives its true value and its true content
from this very source of holiness. For the Kingdom of Israel is
bound up with the kingdom of all worlds. These are simple and
clear matters. They remain unclear to those who live in the
fractured world. (Kook, 1995: 73)

Here, at least, Rabbi Tzvi Yehuda treads on solid ground. The separation
of religion from politics is a relatively recent phenomenon in the Christian
West that grew out of specific historical events such as the Protestant Ref-
ormation, the Wars of Religion, the Enlightenment, the French Revolution
and so on. The classical Jewish tradition by contrast makes no such sharp
division. (To be sure, it is nowhere near the unity of religion and politics
preached by Islam but neither is radical separation or *laïcité* consonant with
the Jewish tradition). Political issues often have religious dimensions and
rabbis (until the Jewish Enlightenment of the nineteenth century at least)
could not accept the contention that the two occupied entirely different
domains of human endeavor. Nevertheless, within Jewish discourse itself,
there are many different voices some of which defend the right of political leaders to make public decisions without the interference of religious
authorities. Rabbi Kook is not one of them.

For Rabbi Kook and his Mercaz HaRav disciples, Jewish politics,
with its Divine dimension, necessitates the intervention of rabbis in public
affairs. This religious-political bond includes three basic elements: First, the
Jewish national idea derives from the conception of a unifying, indivisible
God. Second, the concord awaiting us in the era of redemption is radically opposed to the Jewish dissonance and fragmentation present in the
Gentile-dominated Diaspora. And third, the Kook school identifies Jewish spiritual nationalism with Mamlachtiut. In Rabbi Tzvi Yehuda's view,
Israeli government, whatever its formal organizational structure may be, is
essentially theocratic because important political decisions on existential
matters touch upon the Kingdom of God and are religious in character.
Hence, rabbis are especially adept at comprehending and judging issues
arising in the public sphere (Belfer, 2004: chapter 7).

As we noted above, Rabbi Tzvi Yehuda relies heavily on Nachmanides
who argued for the centrality of settling the Land of Israel even before the
coming of the Messiah. Rabbi Kook takes Nachmanides's teaching one critical
step further: he creates an opposition between, on the one hand the need
to obey God's commandment to conquer the land and not transfer parts of
it to Gentiles, and, on the other, the obligation to disobey a government
that is prepared to take such actions. His conclusion is unambiguous: the
commands of the Torah are binding; they override whatever responsibility

a citizen has to comply with an elected but wrong-headed government. It would be facile, however, to contend that this choice—even for Mercaz HaRav stalwarts—is an easy one to make. Recall that the state's sacredness demands loyalty, even submission on the part of the righteous individual. Not lightly is the vehicle of redemption sabotaged. Consequently, two halachic imperatives can find themselves at odds with each other: obey the laws of the Torah and obey the laws of the sacred state.

Rabbi Tzvi Yehuda proposes an argument that many of his disciples would later adopt. He attempts to synthesize Nachmanides's argument that settling the land is mandatory for all times, with Maimonides's injunction against obeying a government whose laws contradict Halacha. Here, for example, are Rabbi Kook's belligerent and uncompromising remarks made at the Mercaz HaRav yeshiva on Independence Day 1974 entitled "Nation of Israel, rise up and live":

> When a coercive situation arises, whether from the Gentiles or perhaps, forbid it, from Jews because of political distortions or distortions of thought, we are all obliged to give up our lives rather than transgress. On Judea and Samaria, on the Golan Heights—it will not be without war! Someone asked me if I wanted to start a 'civil war'; I will not enter the question of terminology and I will not call it by name but this is a fact: it [withdrawal from the land] will not happen, it will not pass without war! Over our bodies and our limbs! All of us! The Gentiles will not succeed in this nor will our own political complications, not by any means in the world! The borders, the kilometers are ours, made holy by Godly holiness, and we cannot, in any shape or form, relinquish them. Beyond this, it is important to remember the simple fact that these kilometers in which we find ourselves now, are not only ours; we are small representatives, representatives of the Jewish people, of Israel as a whole. This land belongs not only to the three million Jews who are here but rather, and no less, to all the Jews in Russia and America and the entire world. We have no right to even raise the idea—we do not have the legal power of attorney to give up these lands. In no shape or form! This is a positive commandment from the Torah itself—die but do not transgress—and no political considerations or complications, no governmental arrangements and no declarations of our ministers will change or effect this. (Kook, 1995: 25–26)

This speech of Rabbi Tzvi Yehuda became one of the most widely cited and influential texts during the period of the Oslo Accords and the evacuation of Gush Katif/Gaza. Because of its centrality, and at the risk of some repetition, we need to carefully analyze the text:

1. There is a clear superiority of religious commandments over the decisions of a democratic, elected government. There is no place in a Jewish state for a government that acts against religious principles. Settling the Land of Israel is one of these most crucial religious principles and therefore the government has no right to evacuate territories that are under the control of the State of Israel.

2. It is forbidden to submit to international pressure in regard to these issues. *Realpolitik* is irrelevant as well. We are obliged only by the Torah's principles.

3. If a government voluntarily agrees to give up territories, it expresses thereby that it has lost its mind ("distortions of politics" and "distortions of mind") and must be condemned and disobeyed.

4. Any decision on the future of the State of Israel's borders needs to be made by the entire *immemorial* Jewish people or, in other words by *Knesset Yisrael*, which includes both the all the living and the dead; hence such a vote is impossible. Clearly Arabs, who are not part of Jewish sovereignty, would not participate. Referenda are irrelevant because (as he writes in November 1967):

   > This land to the breadth of its borders belongs to the entire people of Israel wherever they may find themselves . . . We, the millions of Jews who are here, are representatives and agents of this people, an important part of it but not a majority. The government of the territories of this land and of we who reside in them is not the government of all the people of Israel, . . . [We] have no right or legal historical authority in the name of the people of Israel to make permanent arrangements about sovereignty over parts of our land. (Kook, 1995: 44–45)

   It is of special interest that Rabbi Kook applies this sweeping rejection of liberal democracy only to settling the Land of Israel. Other public areas of potential conflict between Halacha and state such as the state conducting its business morally, or more narrowly religious issues like Sabbath observance, Kashrut etc., are not included.

5. Most basically and most radically: If a government acts in a way that constitutes a revolt against the Jewish religious tradition, against its Holy of Holies, Mamlachtiut, it loses its right to exist. In such cases, the religious community, a minority though it may be, is permitted to rise up against the government and struggle against it. Rabbi Kook, of course, is not basing his call for insubordination on universal democratic principles but on the unique standing of the Jewish people and its eternal sovereignty over the Land of Israel.

Reading these words raises the inevitable question we briefly dealt with above and will deal with in greater detail in chapter 4: does Rabbi Kook really support violent revolution and civil war? Taken at face value, the rabbi's words themselves seem to point clearly in that direction ("on Judea and Samaria and on the Golan Heights—it will not be without war!" . . . "It will not pass without war"). His closest disciples however were not convinced that he meant these words literally and a broad familiarity with the writings and deeds may well prove them right. It should be recalled that Rabbi Tzvi Yehuda himself, when forced by security forces to vacate Sebastia, left without a fight. Many believed that his deeper intention was for broad-based peaceful disobedience. Only a few took Rabbi Kook's call for war in its plain sense. At this point it should be noted briefly that the question of disobedience divides the rabbis of Bet-El A and Bet-El B, that is, Rabbis Shlomo Aviner and Zalman Melamed. While Rabbi Aviner opposes even nonviolent disobedience, Rabbi Melamed understands his teacher's declaration as justifying disobedience to state law when it contravenes the commandment to settle the land. Rabbi Melamed writes:

What kind of war was the Rabbi intending when he said 'on Judea and Samaria there will be a war'? In my humble view and out of familiarity with Rabbi's general ideas, it seems to me that he . . . did in fact intend to prohibit, in any shape or form, collaboration with retreat from the territories, cooperation with any order to withdraw or evacuate settlements—these are manifestly illegal commands because they oppose the Torah, morality and justice. It is forbidden to obey them and one must struggle against them in all public ways including the adoption of non-violent civil disobedience . . . But if you say: This path involves a danger for the existence of the Israel Defense Forces, a danger to the proper functioning of government in Israel—which is our heart of hearts? Not so . . . in regard to manifestly illegal commands, not only is it permitted to transgress, it is obligatory to transgress. Disobeying orders when they contravene the Torah, values, conscience, integrity—preserves the army from moral corruption, from turning into a blind institution, lacking in content and values. (Melamed, in Kook, 1995: 72)

Note that even the radical Rabbi Melamed softens Rabbi Kook's talk of war to mean active civil disobedience. And, as we shall see below, Rabbi Zalman Melamed and his son Rabbi Eliezer Melamed were, in fact, among the leaders of the "disobedience camp" in the period of the Oslo agreements and the Gaza evacuation. Their views have been central to the radical wing of the settler's movement.

The Struggle against Evacuating Yamit (1978–1982)

A new stage in the struggle against the government began after the signing of the Camp David agreements that included the retreat from all of the Sinai Peninsula and the evacuation of the entire Yamit area. In January 1978, in the wake of President Anwar Sadat's visit to Israel as well as Begin's plan to conclude a peace treaty which would include the return of the Sinai to Egypt, Rabbi Tzvi Yehuda asserted—referring to the verse "May God give his people strength, may God bless his people with peace" (Psalms, 29:11) that strength needed to be the basis of peace:

Only out of giving strength to His people will they be blessed with peace. Therefore, talk of peace that does not derive from the strength given to His people, out of authentic inner power, faith, knowledge, and holy wisdom, is a crippled peace neither complete nor real. And they are not governments that will be preserved for generations; but rather they will be disgraced for generations. We have therefore been commanded not to follow the majority into evil—and the greatest evil is weakness of mind in the consciousness of eternal belongingness to the entire congregations of Israel and the Land in its fullness in the spirit of Torah and Halacha. (Kook, edited by Melamed, 1995: 49)

A few days later he writes:

> Sinai and everything in it, is the Land of Israel. And there is a
> severe and absolute Torah prohibition against abandoning even
> a tiny fragment of it to Gentiles, forbid it. An 'autonomy' to
> Gentiles who are resident of lands in Judea and Samaria, that are
> as much the Land of Israel as Tel Aviv, is an anatomy within our
> bodies, within our vitality, within the land of our lives. And may
> the Guardian of Israel protect us and save us from this disgrace
> for generations, from the verbal confusion of 'peace' based on a
> lie and may He shield us with the gift of a true peace that lasts
> forever in His eternal land. (Kook, 1987: para. 140)

The Camp David Accords signed in September of 1978 and the peace
agreement with Egypt in March 1979 included a full retreat from all of
the Sinai—sixteen settlements in all, most notably the town of Yamit. The
agreements declared that the retreat would be completed by April 1982. In
the elections that took place at the end of 1981, the Tehiya (Renaissance)
party that ran on a platform of stopping the retreat won only three seats.
Tehiya's constituency was comprised of ex-Likud members and devotees of
Gush Emunim. Understandably, the government spokesman claimed that
the people had overwhelmingly expressed support for the agreements. It is
difficult to exaggerate the devastating impact of these elections on Rabbi
Tzvi Yehuda and his students. The results were for them a rejection of
Mamlachtiut and the abandonment of the Sinai that was an integral part
of the Greater Land of Israel. This sense of shock accounts for the paucity
of Rabbi Kook's statements in the wake of the Camp David Accords. At
the time of the struggle over Yamit, Rabbi Tzvi Yehuda sadly admitted,
"The people are not with us" (Segal, 5747: 40). According to Shlomo
Fischer, Rabbi Tzvi Yehuda felt crushed by the revelation that, contrary
to his belief, people in the depth of their hearts did *not* support settling in
the Greater Land of Israel. After the elections, his delusion was patently
exposed (Fisher, 2007: 322–25).

Here, for the first time, the intricate balances and tensions that comprise the multifaceted concept of Mamlachtiut become clearly visible. It is
this balance between "reprehensible" state policies and the sacredness of
the state that prevented a turn to violence even among the most ardent
opponents of the retreat from Sinai, a turn that one might have expected
given that messianic promises were being thwarted. Indeed, the imperative
to resist the state became all the more problematic when such a sweeping

majority of *Jewish* Israelis supported the retreat from Yamit/Sinai. In the end, Rabbi Kook came down on the side of a continued mutual relationship with the Mamlachti state. And yet, in future Torah-state confrontations some of the rabbi's students would find it difficult to accept capitulation. In the clash over Yamit, however, Rabbi Kook refused to discredit the Mamlachti state; rather, he advocated deference and submission because the State of Israel was intrinsic to the Divine scheme of things.

At the end of 1981, the Movement to Stop the Retreat from Sinai was established. Although it was composed of both secular and religious Jews, Uri Elizur stood at its head flanked by other central figures of Gush Emunim. Members of the movement stressed the nationalist aspect of their struggle, but in fact most of its active participants were religious Zionists with a religious agenda. Gush Emunim played a pivotal role in the activities of the movement even though the larger part of the Sinai settlers were secular and held views that were very different from those of the national religious camp. The movement worked in different ways: lobbying members of Knesset, courting public opinion in the media, even by defiantly founding a new settlement in the Yamit region. Much of the struggle was accompanied by religious trappings such as giving Torah classes and holding public prayers. Indeed, a number of yeshivot became active in the Yamit region during different stages of the struggle against withdrawal.

The Sinai retreat exposed the deep rifts between the secular discourse of the Likud led by Menachem Begin on the one hand, and that of the religious Zionists supported by Gush Emunim on the other. As might be expected, the nature of commitment to the Land of Israel was at the heart of the dispute: while the secular Likud militants emphasized history, security and sovereignty, the religious camp rested its case primarily on a messianic political theology (Na'or, 2001: 285).

In the last stages of the drama, the Stop the Retreat movement numbered perhaps a thousand individuals who barricaded themselves in the Yamit region while enjoying some passive sympathy from hundreds of supporters outside the area. The movement's members saw themselves as a vanguard struggling for the Israeli people even though their support among the general public was weak (Aran, 1985). According to Aran, as the protests grew more intense, the religious-mystical justifications for the struggle became more evident and more dominant. Not only was the Yamit region conceived of as a part of Greater Land of Israel (a controversial claim), but even was "sanctified by the movement's religious activists to the point that it lost its concrete substantiality. The territory was transformed from an earthly reality into a high spiritual essence" (Aran, 1985: 42). Eschatological motives were so prevalent that Aran dubs it simply as a "religious movement" (Aran, 1985: 9).

For the resistors, the struggle against the government and the army was seen as a sanctification of God's name that would precipitate a cosmic transformation (Aran, 1985: 46–47). But there was dissension in the ranks of the resistors. The chasm that divided the religious Zionist activists from the secular settlers of Yamit (about 5,300 people) grew wider and wider. Despite the great number of secular settlers, only seventy adults expressed willingness to fight against the evacuation (Segal, 1999: 23). The dominant tendency among the secular settlers was to cut a deal and receive reparations—as it turned out very generous. Many Israelis concluded that the Sinai settlers were shrewd dealers who exploited the situation; not surprisingly, this view pained the settlers who, in many cases, underwent serious and long-lasting traumas as a result of being forced out of their homes. As opposed to the original settlers, Aran writes:

> The Movement to Stop the Retreat was fighting for the definition of Israeli identity—which swings between a Jewish religious and traditional pole on the one end and a Zionist secular modern pole at the other. [The religious pole] is an offshoot of an original theological consciousness nurtured by the experience of a genuine religious awakening. The faith-based essence of the Movement to Stop the Retreat is visible in all aspects of its structure and functioning which makes it unique as a social movement. In a certain sense, we are dealing with a religious movement. (Aran, 1985: 9)

Some have seen the Yamit affair in less mystical terms. The struggle for Sinai, they believe, had strategic objectives; it aimed at impeding and discouraging any future attempt to evacuate parts of Yesha. (Notably, this genre of justification repeated itself during the evacuation of Gush Katif in the Gaza Strip). Disobeying the law was quite common. It often took the form of illegal penetration by activists and yeshiva students into the Yamit area even though it had been officially sealed off by the IDF. For example, starting from the nearby *Kfar Maimon*, a group of activists reached Yamit under the cover of night (Wiessman, 1990: 271–72). Awaiting the order to vacate, many determined, confrontational voices called for government orders to be disobeyed. This was an unprecedented mutiny against the sovereign decisions of the elected Knesset. Indeed, Knesset support for the evacuation was overwhelming; it included MKs from almost all parts of the political spectrum. But simple disobedience was not the end of the story. Many of the militants began hoarding food in preparation for a long siege. Strategies about how to resist the soldiers were prepared. At the margins, even talk of collective suicide was heard.

In the course of 1981, many discussions among the leaders of Gush Emunim were held over the question of what was to be done to resist the government. Chanan Porat proclaimed: "the decision to uproot settlements has no moral validity at all. We will oppose its implementation with all our might. I hereby begin a campaign of signatures on a petition that will obligate its signatories to protect the Sinai settlements when they will be called upon to do so" (Segal, 1987: 41). As the time of evacuation drew near, these militant themes became more radical both among the activists on the ground as well as among some of the movement's intellectual and political leadership. The head of the movement, Uri Elizur, later confessed that he asked himself whether it was appropriate to give up one's life (*Mesirat nefesh*) in order to prevent the evacuation. Rabbi Moshe Levinger expressed outright support for the suicide of individuals, himself included although, in the end, he deferred to the authority of Rabbis Shapiro and Eliyahu (both later to be elected as Israel's chief rabbis) who rejected the idea. There were also those who advocated the use of force against the army, but they were overruled by Rabbis Tau and Zuckerman, senior rabbis at the Mercaz HaRav yeshiva who forbad all violence (Segal, 1987: 121–32).

At a conference convened in February 1982, a fundamental ideological divide between the supporters and opponents of disobedience became dramatically apparent. Not surprisingly, both sides saw their views as deriving from Rabbi Tzvi Yehuda's teachings. Support for disobedience was led by the communal rabbi of Yamit, Rabbi Yisrael Ariel and his followers. They called for establishing a large settlement in the Sinai composed of hundreds of protesters who would come to Yamit in violation of the government's decision. By contrast, Rabbi Yehoshua Zuckerman of the Mercaz HaRav yeshiva rejected this activist strategy denying that any benefit would come of disobeying the law. Other rabbis from Mercaz HaRav, like Rabbis Kaminetsky and Bleicher—who also served as rabbis in the Yamit area— and Rabbi Yaacov Ariel, the head of the Yamit yeshiva, all supported the moderate position (Weissman, 1990: 266–69).

In a conference of rabbis that took place in Yamit (April 1982), a "Torah judgment" (*Da'at Torah*) was promulgated by many of the prominent rabbis and leaders of religious Zionism; among them were Rabbis Tzvi Neriah, Chaim Druckman, Eliezer Waldman, Dov Lior, Yaacov Ariel, Yisrael Ariel, Danny Shiloh, Benny Katzover, Dov Bigun, Chanan Porat, and Yitzchak Levy. It declared:

Severing a part of the Land of Israel and handing it over to foreigners is the gravest of sins and uprooting a Jewish settlement is a horrible edict which cannot be accepted. Retreat from the Yamit region and the destruction of its flowering towns are liable to hasten the bloody war for which our enemies are preparing, even proclaiming—and endanger the IDF's soldiers. The command to remove the Yamit area from the State of Israel and to uproot the region's settlements is, therefore, illegal and immoral. The Jewish community living in Yamit will struggle with all might and main to hold onto this holy soil, the soil of the Land of Israel and, under no circumstances will they budge from this place . . . In our steadfast and resolute stand we empower the State of Israel and protect the welfare of the IDF. May the salvation of God lift us up and strengthen us. (Bedichi, 2005: 377–78)

A careful analysis of this rabbinical directive reveals a compound of justifications: religious justifications ("the gravest of sins," "holy soil"), security justifications ("liable to hasten the bloody war . . . endanger the IDF's soldiers"), and moral justifications ("the destruction of its flowering towns," "illegal and immoral"). Among these justifications, the main thrust, the dominant tone, is religious in character. Note as well the conclusion of their statement: despite their fierce opposition to the evacuation, they speak the language of Mamlachtiut; "we empower the State of Israel and protect the welfare of the IDF." Much of the same kind of rhetoric was heard during the second and much more painful evacuation that took place twenty-three years later—from Gush Katif in the Gaza Strip. Not surprisingly, the discourse related to the Gaza withdrawal remained religious but its character had become far more aggressive and threatening.

Among those who advocated disobedience there were also voices that called upon soldiers to disobey orders and refuse to evacuate Yamit. In a demonstration (February 1982) against the military barrier set up by the army to prevent infiltration into Yamit, the protesters, some of whom wore yellow stars, were addressed by Yamit's rabbi, Yisrael Ariel. He proclaimed:

Disobey orders! No mortal has the moral right to command Jewish soldiers to evacuate Jewish settlers from the holy land . . . We will not raise a hand against you, forbid it, in no case, in no way, in no place. And therefore I say to you: Disobey the orders. Tell your commanders that you cannot take part in this work, because it is not in your soul. (Weissman, 1990: 263)

Because of these words, Rabbi Ariel was arrested and charged with sedition. And indeed, some soldiers asked to be transferred and the army acceded to their request (Weissman, 5759: 263). For its part, the IDF treated soldiers who were distressed over the evacuation with considerable tolerance. This resulted in few incidences of disobedience as well as in the mitigation of the long-term effects of a potentially serious confrontation (Minka-Brand and others, 2006; Amitai and Minka-Brand, 2010).

A month and a half before the evacuation, Rabbi Issar Klonski (a Gush Emunim activist, rabbi of *Chatzer Hadar* in the vicinity of Yamit and editor of Rabbi Tzvi Yehuda's writings) declared that it is the "Halachic judgment that one must refuse to carry out orders . . . It is forbidden to give an order that opposes the State of Israel's Declaration of Independence. One must refuse to obey such orders" (Segal, 1999: 249). Yoel Bin-Nun, one of Gush Emunim's more moderate leaders, posted the following letter on the door of his house:

> The second day of the Sabbath [Monday], the 5th day of Nisan 5742 [29 March 1982], Talmey Yosef, the Yamit region. Officer/ soldier . . . peace to you. If you have come to implement a com- mand to expel Jews from the Yamit region you are hereby warned that your act constitutes a crime against the people of Israel in its land and is opposed to natural justice that is expressed in Jewish history and also to Divine justice as it is presented in the Torah of Israel. (Segal, 1999: 122)

More than fifteen years later, looking back at the Yamit withdrawal, Yoel Bin-Nun claimed that:

> In the Yamit period I opposed any physical confrontation with IDF soldiers after they had received the order to expel Jews from their homes. The letter cited above [previous citation] was a kind of substitute for violent confrontation on the roofs of Yamit. I went down to the Yamit region only after I was convinced that there was no way of preventing the retreat with force, and the struggle was directed to the future, to the next phases of the 'peace process.' In my view, even if it were possible to forcefully prevent the implementation of the government's decisions, it would [still] be absolutely forbidden to do so because this would mean the abolition of the state and the abolition of its ability to make critical decisions in matters of war and peace. This was my

view then as well, as my students in the *Tanach Kollel* in *Ofra* will attest—in a discussion held before deciding to go down to the besieged Yamit region. (Segal, 1999: 344–45)

In contrast to the approach of Rabbi Yisrael Ariel, Rabbi Yaacov Ariel (the former's brother) who was the head of the yeshiva in Yamit and who later became one of the central rabbis of religious Zionism, was committed to a Mamlachti approach according to which no benefit would come from actively confronting the State of Israel. He instructed his students to continue studying until the bulldozers came to raze the yeshiva building. Not that he rejected the possibility of confrontation in principle; rather—and this is something quite different—he claimed it was futile.

> Were there a chance that through violent resistance the retreat could be prevented it might be permitted, but there is no such chance and therefore violent resistance is forbidden. Only the blind believe in the possibility of resistance of a few thousand people against the entire state and a powerful army. We have no choice but to rely on our Father in Heaven, to accept His edict and justify His ways. Let us hope that blood will not be spilt here. Not of a soldier, not of a policeman and not of a settler. (Segal, 1999: 196)

Rabbi Yaacov Ariel's pragmatic Mamlachti argument that rejected disobedience to law and to military orders shifted toward a more principled one some five years later. Here it is not merely a matter of resistance being futile. In a retrospective glance, Rabbi Ariel claimed that left-wing disobedience during the Lebanese War—that broke out shortly after the evacuation of Yamit—was influenced by the right-wing struggle in Yamit. In an interview with Chagai Segel, Rabbi Ariel presented a resolute Mamlachti position:

> If we are permitted to fight against the soldiers, the leftist are permitted to do so as well. We must explain the subject of accepting authority (*marut*) to the students so that they know where the border lies . . . There are subjects where Halacha does not permit flexibility, but the moment of 'no choice' must be minimized as far as possible. Denying authority is a national and spiritual danger. The State of Israel is the vehicle chosen by Divine Providence to settle the land, and the disintegration of this vehicle is a national and spiritual danger. (Segal, 1999: 197–98)

A year after the evacuation of Yamit and in the wake of the Lebanese war, Rabbi Yaacov Ariel published an important essay entitled "Disobeying orders for the sake of a Mitzvah or because of moral considerations." In it he asserts:

> In the same way that disobeying orders endangers public peace, so an order that opposes the law of the Torah endangers the public peace. However, it is apparent that it is not enough for the recipient of the order to believe, according to his *subjective* view, that the order is opposed to Torah law, rather he needs to consider the matter from an *objective* view—insofar as he can. And if he cannot do so on his own, he needs to consult with an objective Torah personality who will judge whether the order does in fact oppose Torah law *absolutely* or whether it opposes Torah law only according to the view of the order's recipient. And in a controversial issue, the danger that lies in disobeying an order is greater than the prospect of cancelling the law. (Ariel, 1983: 177) [Emphasis in the original]

From these premises, Rabbi Ariel derives the following conclusions:

> Soldiers who have not reconciled themselves to the government's decision to destroy the Yamit region and to expel its Jewish residents were obliged to obey the order. Because they too would agree that the government, at very worst, erred in its judgment but did not deliberately intend to sin; rather it believed that in so doing it was benefiting the people of Israel and the Land of Israel. . . . Even so, it was known that a soldier who requested being freed from participation in the uprooting of settlements in Sinai for reasons of conscience was usually responded to positively. (Ariel, 1983: 178)

The evacuation of Yamit was executed in three stages: During the first stage (31st of March 1982) the permanent residents were evacuated. In the second stage (22nd of April 1982), the opponents of retreat were expelled, most of them being non-permanent residents. The third stage (25th of April 1982) saw the withdrawal of the remaining IDF soldiers from Gaza's Rafah Salient (Weissman, 1990: 298). In home study circles the members of the Stop the Retreat Movement made it clear that they opposed violence, and that resistance to the evacuation would be passive at most. Still, they knew that there were others who were not members of the movement who might respond violently (Weissman, 1990: 174). Moreover, the rabbis of Atzmona in the Yamit region cautioned their students against the use of violence. The rabbis warned that when violence was used against IDF soldiers it would only intensify the violent reactions of the soldiers and distract them from what they were actually doing: expelling Jews from their homes. They concluded that the preferred form of resistance is passive (Segal, 1999: 245).

In the course of the second stage of the evacuation, 3,000 demonstrators organized to resist the IDF forces. They fought the army from Yamit's roofs. The struggle focused on two roofs in the town's center: "Kiryat Arba Roof" and "Ramat Hagolan Roof." Crowded onto each roof were a few hundred resisters. A group of students under the leadership of Tzachi Hanegbi (who later served as a Minister in a number of governments) barricaded themselves at the top of the Steel Brigade Monument. The protesters had collected tires, sandbags, and metal rods; confronting them were thousands of soldiers under the leadership of Regional Commander Chaim Erez (Weissman, 1990: 333). When the moment of evacuation came and soldiers attempted to climb ladders to the occupied roofs, violent acts did take place. The violence that did occur included throwing of objects—even metal objects—at the soldiers. At times there was hand-to-hand fighting. But real danger to life and limb, danger of violent bloodshed, was minimal (Segal, 1999: 209). Atop the monument, Hanegbi and his fellow protesters manacled themselves with heavy chains to make evacuation more difficult but they did not resist the commando unit that came to evacuate them.

It needs to be emphasized that the level of violence was far from what the media and public commentators anticipated. Given the prophecies of doom, the actual evacuation—with a few exceptions—was rather subdued. Neither did the IDF face mass disobedience in its ranks. Although tens of thousands of soldiers took part in the evacuation, only a handful asked to be excused from participating (Segal, 1987: 133).

Although it is impossible to know for certain, the process of evacuation does not seem to have created deep residual anger between the evacuees and those that evacuated them. Notably, even among those who supported the evacuation, feelings were sometimes mixed. Arik Nechamkin, a Knesset member from the Ma'arach (A Labor Party-centered coalition of parties) probably spoke for many when he declared that the resolute struggle of the resisters was extremely important. In a Knesset meeting held seven weeks before the evacuation he said:

> In contrast to some of the party members, I believe that had
> there been no Movement to Stop the Retreat, a real movement,

it would have been necessary to invent it. Do you think it is possible to leave such an area without a loud protest? Did someone
in this movement do things that go beyond what is acceptable
in normal protests? Are there protests that are more moral
than these? Which and what for? Improving salaries, improving
housing conditions? . . . It is unacceptable for the Egyptians to
entertain the thought that we do this easily. (Segal, 1999: 193)

Even the commanding officer of the evacuation, the Southern Regional
Commander, Lieutenant General Chaim Erez, expressed equivocal feelings.
He said in an interview a number of years later:

I believe that it would have been very very grave if such a
move were carried out in silence, in serenity, without resistance,
without argument. Therefore, broadly speaking, it is possible to
say that both sides did important work. The army fulfilled the
government's decision while the opponents of retreat expressed
their pain and loss. They carried out a natural and clear function. (Segal, 1999: 229)

The single most serious case of resistance took place in one of the
town's shelters, named by its occupants "the sanctification of [God's] name
bunker" (i.e., those who were willing to die the death of a martyr) in
which eleven young people from the extreme right-wing *Kach* movement
barricaded themselves against the soldiers. Twenty-year-old Yehuda Richter
was the group's leader and he presented himself as the agent of Rabbi Meir
Kahane, the leader of the Kach movement. Richter threatened that he and
his fellow protesters would commit suicide if the army broke into their
fortified chamber. They had, Richter warned, six canisters of cyanide for
that purpose. A day after the Passover holiday, less than a week before the
evacuation, a Molotov cocktail was thrown from the vicinity of the bunker
at the jeep of operation's commander, Brigadier General Oded Tirah. The
Chief Rabbis, Rabbi Shlomo Goren and Rabbi Ovadia Yossef were brought
to the bunker in order to convince the blockaded young people not to
commit suicide, but without success (Segal, 1999: 111–15). The barricaded
group passed a note out to Rabbi Israel Ariel, the rabbi of Yamit, in which
they wrote: "Exactly when the evacuation begins we will start putting an
end to our lives, one by one, 120 minutes apart from each other until we
are all dead . . . We hope that the shock that comes from our deaths will
drive the people to understand how important the Land of Israel is to the
people of Israel" (Segal, 1999: 113).

Yet despite Yehuda Richter's pronouncements that he and his fellows "meant it in all seriousness," from the testimony of the barricaded group (taken at a later date) it appears that their intention was more to deter the army and the government leadership than to actually commit suicide (Segal, 1999: 113–14). Rabbi Meir Kahane was urgently summoned from the United States and was allowed to enter the bunker on condition that he made sure there would be no suicides among the barricaded youth and that they would not use excessive violence when they were evacuated by the army. And, in fact, in the course of the evacuation four days later, there were struggles between the barricaded band and the military police who removed them but at no point was there a real risk of serious bloodshed on either side (Segal, 1999: 114–15). More than two decades later, during the disengagement from the Gaza Strip, the same Yehuda Richter called for "spreading as many bunkers as possible all over Gush Katif." His advice was not heeded.

Despite their inability to deter the government from going through with the evacuation, many of the settlers did not see the struggle as a failure. It was meant to traumatize the country and prevent future evacuations, and in this regard they judged it a success. In a number of interviews given over the years, the then-Regional Commander, General Chaim Erez said repeatedly that having experienced one evacuation he hoped that there would be no further repetitions of such a wrenching act. Indeed, some scholars believe that Yitzhak Rabin avoided evacuating territory during the Oslo process because of the trauma of Yamit (Zertal and Eldar, 2007).

The impact of the evacuation deeply affected the settler movement. The Yamit trauma was linked in their minds to the death of Rabbi Tzvi Yehudah Kook in February 1982—a short time before the evacuation. The settler camp remained without its charismatic spiritual leader who might have consoled them in the wake of the painful evacuation. Although already visible in the reactions to the retreat from Sinai, from this point onward two opposing positions regarding disobedience developed and diverged. The first approach—the Mamlachti one—was led by one of the heads of the Mercaz HaRav yeshiva, Rabbi Tzvi Tau, a devoted student of Rabbi Tzvi Yehuda. In a eulogy for Rabbi Kook delivered shortly before the withdrawal (in the later-evacuated settlement of Atzmona) Rabbi Tau stated:

Sometimes it is necessary to teach . . . what not to do. Rabbi Tzvi Yehuda, of blessed memory, always asked, are the people with us? And if Gush Emunim nevertheless executed bold actions, this was because we knew that the actions were being done in the light of a careful judgment that the people would follow

> us . . . We will struggle for the Land of Israel with the will to
> create proud independence out of faith . . . For even all the
> retreats are positive and constructive. (Don Yehiya, 2003: 206)

In this eulogy, the religiopolitical position of Rabbi Tau and his followers is already apparent: it is wrong to act against the will of the people.
Weakness and retreats reflect the weakness of the people; changing this
condition cannot be done by radical, coercive political actions. To effect
change, intensive educational and spiritual work is necessary, first of all
within the religious Zionist camp itself and only then, by spreading out
from this energized core, will it be possible to influence the entire public.
At the heart of Rabbi Tau's teaching lies a charged conception of "the
spirit of the people." In the tradition of Mercaz HaRav he believes that
enormous spiritual powers reside within the Jewish nation, even if they
are not immediately apparent. It is imperative to transform these potential
energies into actual dynamism. The manner in which many of the Yamit
settlers bargained over the amount of government compensation they were
to receive was proof of the weakness of the nation that could be corrected
only by intense didactic and religious outreach (Don Yehiya, 2003: 207).

A considerably more radical approach was that of Rabbi Israel Ariel.
He argued that uncompromising activism was imperative because the truth
upon which it was based was uncompromising as well. To be truly committed
meant to act unconditionally. The public, he declared, would be brought
to true understanding by the resolute spirit of a vanguard (Don Yehiya,
2003: 208). The ties between this position and that of Rabbi Tzvi Yehuda
are dubious. Rabbi Kook was inclined to reject the idea that a select elite
would lead the nation despite its refusal to be led.

Both the radical and the more moderate positions, as we have noted,
emerged from Rabbi Kook's teachings. They shared the belief that the State
of Israel ("the throne of God in the world") is historically "determined"
to express the true "general will" of the nation and nothing expresses this
will more genuinely than settling the land. Although this project involved
clashes with the legal authorities, those students of Rabbi Kook who tended
toward the more moderate Mamlachti position considered this a technical
problem because, in the end, the "people" really supported the settlers. In
Yamit many were disabused of this belief; they realized that this determined
process involved serious difficulties, that the vast majority of Israelis supported the withdrawal from Sinai, and that the people's support could not
be counted on. They therefore turned to educational work to raise public
consciousness in regard to Judaism generally and to the Land of Israel in
particular. By contrast, the radicals believed that the people needed to be

aggressively "helped" to understand their true role. Through radical activism—that the moderate Mamlachti'im saw as heretical mutiny against God's will—they would bring about the desired messianic consciousness (Fischer, 2007: chapter 6).

In this way, the retreat from Yamit acted as a catalyst for a major educational campaign to deepen and spread the religiopolitical message of Gush Emunim. Leaders like Rabbi Tzvi Tau, convinced that the intensification of religious education was the answer to their inability to win over the people's hearts, helped create a dynamic, inspired Torah-elite that would accomplish what the militants could not—prevent further retreats from the Land of Israel. A network of yeshivot and seminars was established: the yeshiva high-school system was expanded, institutions of higher religious learning proliferated, *Hesder* yeshivot (that combined Torah study with military service) multiplied and pre-army religious preparatory programs (*Mechinot*) were established and spread. These institutions were anything but lax in their demands; they promoted uncompromising piety and the scrupulous observance of religious commandments. A new religious category was born: *Hardelim*—a synthesis between Haredim and national religious. They studied Torah and observed the Mitzvot like Haredim, while being religious Zionists whose faith was centered on the holiness of the State and the Land of Israel.

This religious revolution had dramatic consequences for the military. Moved by national and religious duty, young men from the yeshivot enlisted for front-line combat duty in far greater numbers than ever before. The pre-army Mechinot prepared a cadre of religious Zionists whose messianic, Mercaz HaRav views led them to seek out command positions as an expression of both piety and national commitment. Combat duty became a form of religious duty. The result: at the lower- and mid-level officer ranks, these young men are substantially overrepresented, changing the religious complexion and ideological character of Israel's army. One knowledgeable expert speaks of the "theocratization" of the IDF. Indeed, he argues, that if a retreat from Judea and Samaria were ordered by the government, it would face an unprecedented problem: a recalcitrant army (Levy, 2015). Although others feel that this argument is overstated, it is impossible to deny the increasingly religious character of the IDF (Gal and Liebel, 2012).

Whatever the future may hold, in Yamit the army stood firm and Gush Emunim—in spite of its radical rhetoric—did not resort to life-threatening violence. And when resistance did take place, it was limited and local. Despite prophesies of large-scale bloodshed and despite the militant's "do or die" proclamations, the withdrawal passed with theatrical, media-savvy turmoil but without egregious violence. We contend that what prevented mass defiance was the "theological-normative balance" argued for in the first chapter. Convinced of the state's sanctity, the leaders of Gush Emunim acted with marked restraint when dealing with the government, its institutions and the IDF. To be sure, there were confrontations with much screaming and shoving between religious militants and security forces but the conflict did not deteriorate into the kind of violence that would have threatened the bridge linking religious Zionists and Israel's secular majority. The center held.

Nevertheless, radicalization was in the air. Frustrated by their powerlessness, die-hard zealots in the settler camp turned to terrorism.

The Jewish Underground (1980–1984)

Violence against Palestinians by militant settlers did not begin with the Jewish Underground. Notably, these early attacks were not unequivocally condemned by the settler community and its leadership. Neither did Israel's judiciary rise to the occasion. In 1982, a report authored by the deputy to the government's legal advisor, Yehudit Karp, denounced "the connection between the many filed complaints [against the settlers] that were closed, and flawed investigations—whether because the investigations were not carried out with the necessary speed directly after the event or because they failed to locate the perpetrators in time." According to the report "the situation in which [a settler's] need to protect himself stands in the way of police's ability to clarify whether it was indeed self-defense or rather taking the law into his own hands—this is an unbearable situation that encourages flouting authority" (cited in Negbi, 2004: 225–26). Karp's report was condemned by many on the Right who saw it as a left-wing tract. It was especially argued that Karp ignored the extenuating contexts in which the settlers acted.

The most challenging research on the subject of "vigilantism"—understood as taking the law into one's own hands often including the use of violence—was conducted by David Weissburd (Weissburd, 1989). He conducted field research trying to determine the degree and character of settler support for these illegal activities. Settler vigilantism, he contends, had a calculated, instrumental side to it. They employed violent actions as a means of preventing retreat from the territories and as a strategy aimed at enforcing the policies they supported (Weissburd, 1989: chapter 2). Vigilante behavior—blocking roads, uprooting olive trees, torching mosques, damaging cars, and threatening, injuring, even killing Palestinians—grew out of an identifiable motive: the need to correct what they believed to be "deviant" government behavior, that is to say, the government's lax attitude toward violent Palestinian actions. Palestinians threw stones and Molotov cocktails, launched guerrilla attacks against settlements, and killed settlers, but the government failed to employ the forceful—even drastic—measures necessary to deter these attacks. In their view, the Israeli military that administered Judea and Samaria/the West Bank failed in its job to protect them. Vigilante activity was seen as making up for this failure and, hence, was supported by a sizeable part of the settlement community. Without the deterring power of vigilante attacks, many settlers were certain that Palestinian attacks would be even more damaging than they were (Weissburd, 1989: chapter 4). As Weissburd writes: "The vigilante settlers operated as 'agents' of the Gush Emunim community. They executed a strategy of social control, which they often explicitly discussed, and which won broad support in the settler community" (Weissburd, 1989: 94). It should be added, that there were some who believed that segments within the IDF did not see all these attacks on Palestinians in a wholly negative light. In an important way, it made their objective of controlling the Palestinian community that much easier.

The behavior of the Jewish Underground belonged to a different category of settler vigilantism—so extreme in fact that it did not win support among the settlers. As opposed to other less violent vigilante actions, which were often not frowned upon, the egregiousness of the Underground's assault on Palestinians and the wild improbability of their plans led to a clear rejection of their deeds and their strategy. Arguably, the actions of the Underground were the radical, perhaps even the logical, denouement of the more moderate forms of vigilantism. Nevertheless, there are important differences between them. What stands out in the Underground's motives and actions, what separates them from the less errant vigilantes was the desire to transform the character of the State of Israel through spectacular actions. They believed that individuals, even if they are few in number, could trigger cataclysmic change if they are bold enough. Nowhere was this more apparent than in the Underground's plan to bomb the mosques on the Temple Mount (Fischer, 2007: 327).

In April 1984, it became known that twenty-five members of a Jewish Underground had been arrested. Although most of them had links to Gush Emunim, they were not central figures in the movement. They were caught "in the act" of planning to bomb five civilian, Arab buses in east Jerusalem and were suspected of having been active in attacking Arabs for a number of years The hard core of the Underground centered on settlers from Hebron and Kiryat Arba and its most prominent operational leader was Menachem Livni. The group's major ideologue was Yehuda Etzion who made the case for sensational actions that would catalyze the onset of the messianic era. Other prominent members were Sha'ul Nir, Yeshua ben Shoshan, and Chagai Segal.

The Underground reacted murderously to the many terror attacks perpetrated by Palestinian terrorists and militants against Jews that led to feelings of frustration, vulnerability and insecurity. Moreover, as noted, some in the IDF were not unhappy with the deterring impact of settler violence on hostile Palestinians. Also influential was the uncertainty caused by the resignation of the Defense Minister Ezer Weizman and the assumption by Prime Minister Menachem Begin of the defense portfolio. This abrupt change in responsibility for administering the territories—Begin had little if any experience with security matters—caused an interim security vacuum into which stepped the army's Chief of Staff, Raphael Eitan known for his very hawkish views. It is not impossible that this led the Underground to believe that they had friends in high places. Taken together, these factors provide some explanation for why the Underground succeeded, in its early years, in avoiding the attention of the security services (Gal Or, 1990: 66–67).

The event that directly triggered the rise of the Underground was an attack (Sabbath, May 2, 1980) carried out by Palestinian terrorists against a group of yeshiva students on their way from Kiryat Arba to Hebron. In a hail of gunfire and hand grenades, six students were killed and sixteen wounded. After initial hesitation, the government responded by expelling to Jordan three Palestinian leaders from the outlawed "National Guidance Committee" that were charged with justifying the murders. They were the mayor of Hebron, Fahed Qawasmi, the Kadi of Hebron, El Tamimi and the mayor of Halhul, Mohamed Milchim. But this punishment was seen as too little and too late by the settlers. A group of Kiryat Arba and Ofrah residents led by Menahem Livni and Yehuda Etzion prepared a counterattack. Members of this group booby-trapped the cars of three West Bank mayors (June 2, 1980) who were members of the PLO. The mayor of Nablus Bassam Shakah and the mayor of Ramallah Karim Chalaf were severely wounded and needed to have their legs amputated. The third intended victim was the mayor of El Bireh, Ibrahim Tawil, who alerted the military administration; soldiers were sent among whom was the Border Guard's demolitions expert Siman Herbawi. He was blinded when he opened the door of the booby-trapped garage. This action won the silent support of many in the Israeli military administration and was greeted with substantial approval among the settlers (Segal, 1987: chapters 8–10).

In his book on the Jewish Underground, Chagai Segal, himself a member of the group, attempts to minimize the disobedience to law involved in the attack on the mayors. It was a "technical problem" he indicates, to be understood in the context of *Pikuah nefesh* or self-preservation. He writes:

The answer to the question: what caused people with families to risk extended jail terms is the growing power of the Committee [the Palestinian National Guidance Committee] that by its very existence threatened the safety of every Jew in Yesha. It explains why the perpetration of such a serious crime [the attack on the mayors] was more a technical than an ethical problem, a matter of self-preservation that momentarily set aside the laws of the state and the principle of exclusivity given to the legal authorities for establishing the law and punishing criminals. Indeed, we related to the deed as a onetime act that had no intention of replacing the authorities, or to serve as a model for transgressing the law. (Segal 1987: 83)

In the eyes of many, however, Segal's protestations are dubious because leading figures in the Underground organization continued their terrorist actions even after the attack on the mayors. In truth, radical Underground vigilantism expressed nothing so much as an extreme doctrine of disobedience to law. Indeed, for a small minority this constituted a genuine rebellion against the sovereignty of the Israeli regime, a rejection the "theological-normative balance."

The failed attempt to prevent the Sinai withdrawal and the government's disregard for their deeply held principles also contributed to radicalization in some settler circles and to the growing ambition of their grandiose vigilante plans. Most notably, in an attempt to thwart retreat from Yamit some members of the Underground like Yehuda Etzion, Menahem Livni, Yeshua ben Shoshan, and Dan Be'eiri accumulated explosives in order to demolish the mosques on the Temple Mount. Yehuda Etzion, the inspirational mastermind behind these Underground plans, was convinced that destroying the mosques would not endanger Israel; he believed that the mass of Moslems would not take action against the State of Israel. In his messianic vision, the people of Israel would stand behind the destruction of the mosques. With the mosques gone, it would be possible to construct the Third Holy Temple and to revive the ancient monarchy of Israel. In the end, the plan was never executed because of the second thoughts of some Underground activists and particularly since the Yamit evacuation had already become a fait accompli (Segal, 1987: chapter 12; Inbari, 2007).

In the wake of the murder of the yeshiva student Aharon Gross (7 July 1983) which took place in the market plaza of Hebron witnessed by hundreds of Arabs who did nothing to prevent the slaying, two members of the Underground—Menachem Livni and Sha'ul Nir—decided to take revenge so radical that it would deter further Arab violence. A few days later a defining act of Underground bloodshed took place: an attack with rifles and grenades on the Moslem College in Hebron which took the lives of three students and injured thirty. In order to make the attitudes of radical settler circles clear, it must be added that in the deliberations of the municipal council of Kiryat Arba after the event, opinions were divided about whether to support or condemn the attack. This murderous attack led Prime Minister Menachem Begin to direct the head of the *Shabak* (General Security Services) to make every effort to reveal the identity of the attackers (Segal, 1987: chapters 14–15).

The continuation of terror against Jews as well as the release of thousands of Palestinian militants in the context of prisoner exchanges—including those involved in the 1980 Hebron murders—only exacerbated the rage of the Underground. Menachem Livni and Sha'ul Nir began planning further attacks against Arab civilians. After his period of imprisonment, Sha'ul Nir explained—without apology or expressions of regret—that there is indeed a problem with harming the innocent as well as in taking the law into one's own hands, but the action was mandatory

> in order to sear into the Arab consciousness that continuing terrorist activity or the sympathy for it would bring unpleasant consequences. But more than anything else, they intended to signal the Israeli authorities that they needed to enforce law and order and to stop standing by idly when Jewish blood was being spilt. (Segal, 1987: 159)

As opposed to Livni and Nir, Yehuda Etzion (who had supported the demolition of the Temple Mount mosques without harming innocent civilians) demurred: he believed that only

> war could include within its conduct indiscriminate killing of the enemy. But only a government is entitled to declare war and to decide who among the enemies should be killed. Moreover, even a government that acts properly in accordance with the Torah of Israel—will not see every Arab in Judea and Samaria as an enemy who should be killed. (Segal, 1987: 159–60)

Therefore, Etzion was excluded from the secret deliberations about the attack on the Islamic college or the proposed attack on Bir Zeit University. (The latter plan was never implemented because the Minister of Defense Moshe Arens closed the university after riots took place on its campus). Etzion's reluctance to harm civilians, like the attempt of Nir to justify the murder of innocents, indicates that despite their egregious disobedience to law, what the Underground's members longed for was draconic, iron-fisted Israeli sovereignty that would obviate the need for the violent actions they employed. As violent as their plans/actions may have been, it is clear that we are not dealing with an impulsive anarchist group.

The final plan of the Underground came after the attack on the number 300 bus that was waylaid en route from Tel Aviv to Ashkelon. This attack prompted Nir and Livni to prepare a retaliatory attack against Arab public transportation. It was proposed that they attach explosives to five Arab buses in east Jerusalem. But before the plan could be executed, the *Shabak* exposed the plot and arrested the Underground members (Segal, 1987: chapters 15–16).

The Jews of the Underground movement were not the only ones who indulged in or planned terrorist activities during the 1980s. Yoel Lerner attempted to blow up the Dome of the Rock in 1982. He was the coordinator of the Hashmonean Youth and a teacher in a yeshiva high school. Similarly, members of Kach (followers of Rabbi Meir Kahane) torched cars and busses in 1984. Also in 1984, David ben Shimmol fired a (Lau) missile at an Arab bus killing one and wounding ten. Prior to that attack, he lobbed a grenade into an Arab café in east Jerusalem wounding eight. The Lifta Gang also sought to blow up the Dome of the Rock in 1984, believing that it would hasten the coming of the Messiah (Gal-Or, 1990: 31–34). Gal-Or distinguishes between these one-time actions and those of the Jewish Underground, which was an organized group that carried out a series of violent attacks against Arabs from 1980 to 1984. In her view, the Underground cannot be defined as anything but a genuine terrorist cell. They were, she claims, very similar in organization and modus operandi to the terrorist movements in the pre-state era. On the other hand, Chagai Segal, an active member, argues that the Underground was not a disciplined terrorist organization but a weakly associated group based on personal ties (Segal, 1987).

An important difference between the Underground and other terrorists (and would-be terrorists) in the 1980s was that the Underground received some tacit support from members of right-wing parties like the Likud, Hatchiya, and the National Religious Party. Moreover, the Underground's close ties with Gush Emunim provided them with a not insubstantial number of fellow travelers. Interestingly, the bonds between the Underground and the Gush were not only ideological; they were united by significant family ties as well (Gal Or, 1990, chapter 3). Some even claimed that the Underground received the blessing of important rabbis like Eliezer Waldman, Dov Lior, and Moshe Levinger (Bin-Nun, 2001: 84) By contrast,

Menachem Livni claimed that religious Zionist rabbis including Rabbis Waldman, Lior, and Levinger were opposed to blowing up the Dome of the Rock (Shragai, 2007).

Although mostly rejected in yeshiva Torah circles, some of the members of the Underground stressed the sharp (and by now quite familiar) opposition between the laws of the Torah and the laws of the Knesset. Clearly, the state's legitimacy was conditional. For example, Yehuda Etzion asserts:

> It is not the laws of the state that will decide for us what is permissible and what is prohibited in our revolutionary striving against it; only the Torah of Israel and the sense of national responsibility that is imposed upon us will decide to what extent we recognize the state's laws or reconcile ourselves to them in our practical struggle. (Segal, 1987: 45)

Another member of the Underground, Sha'ul Nir, in an article written after his arrest (*Haaretz*, 16 November 1984: 15), declares:

> The nation strives toward the founding of the Kingdom of Israel that is based upon the principles of faith and divine morality as a dominant and powerful instrument for the embodiment of the Good that is able to rule the world. From the early stirrings of our nationhood, we knew that the spiritual fabric that would fill us with substance and set us on a good path is present in the infinite system of the Torah that was given to us; it is in our power to apply it to the varying worldly circumstances we face. (Cited in Gal-Or, 1990: 91.)

Nir's theological ruminations look forward to the establishing of a modern Kingdom of Israel. Ideas such as these were present (in secular form) in groups like the *Brit Habiryonim* and *Lechi* (two pre-state extreme right-wing groups) and in the messianic teachings of Shabtai ben Dov (an extreme right-wing thinker of the 1950s) whose views deeply influenced some members of the Underground (Segal, 1987: chapter 5).

Gideon Aran maintains that the struggle against the withdrawal from Yamit and the actions of the Jewish Underground were closely related. While the struggle for Yamit remained, for the most part, within the basic framework of nonviolent civil disobedience that did not deny the legitimate sovereignty of the state, the Underground's activities clearly crossed the line of normative civil disobedience and turned to outright terrorism. And yet Aran believes that a common denominator unites them: they both reflect security distress fused with a desire for radical messianic revival (Aran, 1985: 4). In the same vein, Ehud Sprinzak, consistent with his view that Gush Emunim was a movement characterized by what he famously calls "illegalism," argues in regard to the Underground:

> One of the dangers hovering over every radical movement that adopts a practice of illegalism together with a rationalization of this practice is the deterioration of the movement or parts of it into deliberate violence. Cutting edge research on this subject today clearly distinguishes between the 'stages' of radicalization that mark the unintentional deterioration into violence of even the greatest idealists . . . When the shocked residents of Israel were notified on Friday, the 27th of April 1984 that 25 members of Gush Emunim were arrested because they attempted to blow up six [sic] busses filled with Arab passengers, it became clear to them that the law of radicalization operating in many radical idealist movements was operating here as well and with great intensity . . . We can certainly say that behind these actions stands an entire philosophy of extremist illegalism . . . since the issue is no longer passive disobedience to the representatives of the authorities or bypassing the law for the sake of 'construc-tive' actions like the establishment of settlements. What is at stake, and this matter needs to be sharpened, is illegalism whose consequence is murder. (Sprinzak, 1986: 135–36)

According to Sprinzak, the radical messianism that erupted after the Six Day War lies at the heart of the Underground's terrorism. Even if they did not win backing in their attempt to blow up the mosques on the Temple Mount, they nevertheless enjoyed broad support in their turn to violence. Indeed, the deterioration into violence came in large measure because the illegal actions of Gush Emunim were sympathized with, even legitimized, by many (Sprinzak, 1986: 142). The more virulent critics of the settler camp draw a direct line between the radical, fantasist plans of the Underground and the entire messianic settlement project (Zertal and Eldar, 2007).

In opposition to Sprinzak and Aran, Yoni Garb attributes the Under-ground and its violent activities first and foremost to the distress settlers felt in the face of Palestinian terrorism. Messianic dreams were surely present, but they were secondary to the genuine fear of their Palestinian neighbors' hostile intentions. In Garb's view, there is no linear continuation between Gush Emunim's struggle again the withdrawal from Sinai and the Underground's terrorist violence. He reminds us that while virtually the entire leadership of

Gush Emunim threw its weight behind the struggle for Yamit, the Underground fielded at best only a small minority for their terrorist attacks. And of course, to repeat the obvious, the Yamit struggle was only peripherally violent while the Underground's actions were violent in the extreme (Garb, 2004b: 354). Garb also accepts Segal's view that the Underground was only a loose name for a few subgroups who perpetrated various actions from different motives. Notably, actions such as the attack on the Arab mayors took place before the withdrawal from Yamit (Garb, 2004b: 355). One of most striking proofs that Garb brings to bear is that the central figure in the Underground, Yehuda Etzion, did not participate in the Yamit demonstrations. On the other side, there were central figures in Gush Emunim like Chanan Porat who censured the Underground (Garb: 2004b: 357).

Yet, it is not unreasonable to claim that the linkage between the kinds of justifications offered by the activist branch of the Yamit resisters and those expressed by the Underground bears comparison. This affinity is revealed implicitly in the arguments of Rabbi Tzvi Tau, perhaps the most widely respected among Rabbi Tzvi Yehuda Kook's protégées. After the arrest of the Jewish Underground's members and even more so after the letters written by Underground militants while in prison were publicized, a deep controversy shook the religious Zionist movement: how to relate to the Underground, its plans and its violent actions? The rabbis who supported the Mamlachti approach, like rabbis Yaacov Ariel and Shlomo Aviner, expressed vigorous objections to the Underground. Especially noteworthy for our purposes is the telling lecture that Rabbi Tzvi Tau delivered to his students in the Mercaz HaRav yeshiva. He declared that the Underground represented false messianism and, as such, it was very dangerous. But Rabbi Tau, entirely cognizant of the connection—pointed out by both the supporters of the Underground and their left-wing opponents—between the support of Rabbi Tzvi Yehuda Kook for Gush Emunim's disobedience in the case of Yamit and the brutal violence of the Underground. Despite conceding this affinity, he makes an important distinction between the two. Two months before the evacuation of Yamit Rabbi Kook had asserted that it is permissible to act even in illegal ways only if the people as a whole support such action; it is prohibited to resort to illegality when they do not:

> When he [Rabbi Tzvi Yehuda] founded Gush Emunim he did so knowing the pulse of the people. He understood that the spirit of the people did not correspond to that of the government that ruled them: The spirit of the people was high while the government was made up of private wheeler-dealers who suffered from weakness. He understood that the people were prepared for self-

sacrifice at a much higher level than the government . . . that is, the government exercised coercion against the people. It did not express the popular will . . . But when Begin returned from Egypt and one hundred and forty thousand people gathered in Kikar Malchei Yisrael and danced because peace had come, Rabbi Tzvi Yehuda declared that 'the people are not with us' and, therefore, we need to stop. The activists of Gush Emunim were unwilling to accept this and, as a result, our paths diverged. There is no mandate for five thousand people to force its will on the people of Israel, to rebel against the spirit of the people, to dismiss things that were done in a public way—this is rebellion against the Kingdom of God . . . We must understand that Tel Aviv is in our hands because all of the Jews . . . see it as part of their homeland and in their national spirit are committed to this territory. In regard to Yamit, by contrast, we did not succeed in arousing recognition and national consciousness and what happened happened. (Segal, 1987: 216–17)

Rabbi Tau believed that the legitimate struggle for Yamit was profoundly corrupted by the Underground. Their antinomian ideas and strategies arouse from the frustrations that marked the last stages of the struggle against the withdrawal from Sinai. And these ideas badly fractured the religious Zionist camp's unity:

The development [of the Underground] which has recently burst into view is constructed on the same mental bases as [those who say] 'we are really a vanguard, we must ourselves be responsible for redemption because the entire people is defective,' and little by little this turns into the disintegration of the Mamlachti belief and of the principle that each one of us is included in the whole of Israel. The bases of the 'revealed end' (Ha'ketz hameguleh) have collapsed, as has the 'a little at a time' paradigm in which we believed; from the same place which should bring us to the principle of the state, to the veneration of its holiness, from this place comes today shameful ridicule and an attempt to uproot the entire Mamlachti establishment. We are dealing with a messianic cult that wants to bring redemption to the people of Israel with weapons in hand; they conceive of truly idolatrous ideas on how we are to leverage the Master of the Universe to redeem Israel by blowing up the mosques on the Temple Mount. (Segal, 1987: 215–16)

At first blush it appears that Rabbi Tau is appealing to Western democratic ideas in which sovereign institutions and popularly elected leg- islatures are the only legitimate sources of authority. But placing Rabbi Tau in the tradition of liberal democracy is problematic. As Eliezer Don Yehiya points out, the sources of Rabbi Tau's ideas are romantic-national and not individualist-liberal. His central emphasis is on the "national spirit" rather than on liberalism or even civic republicanism (Don Yehiya, 2003: 207). We see here once again the idea of a "Jewish democracy" in the spirit of Rabbi Tzvi Yehuda Kook, with which we dealt above. It is not elections or representation in the Knesset that bestow legitimacy on actions but rather the collective spirit of the Jewish people living in Zion (and in distant lands). In Rabbi Tau's view, disobedience to the state can be defended only if official actions contradict the national spirit (Hellinger, 2002: chapter 3).

Another related argument presented by Rabbi Tau focuses on Gush Emunim's self-image as the authentic even mainstream voice of the people of Israel. (Ironically, this argument is also used by severe critics of govern- ment policies (Zartal and Eldar, 2007)). Rabbi Tau contends that Gush Emunim was doing what the government really wanted it to do.

> The government in its heart of hearts did not resist being seduced by the settlers . . . In the period of settlements, government opposition was not really serious. It is true that the soldiers did set up check posts on the roads but they did not arrest you if you detoured off the road and bypassed the check post. All this setting up of check posts was really intended to test whether the people really want this [the settlements]. (Segal, 1987: 216)

The sharp differences between Gush Emunim and the Underground were dramatically evident in a fraught meeting between some of Gush Emunim's leadership and members of the Underground that took place in the prison in which the latter were serving their sentences. In this meeting Chanan Porat and Rabbi Yehoshua Zuckerman claimed that even if Gush Emunim had broken the law, they had not acted in opposition to the will of the people. Rabbi Zuckerman presented the broadly supported criterion by which one could distinguish between different forms of disobedience: disobedience that unambiguously and absolutely tries to impose its will on the people on the one hand and, on the other, disobedience that attempts to motivate the government to discard its unacceptable policies but will, in the end, respect sovereign decisions that are popularly supported. As he writes: "Presenting our views in the form a protest demonstration and even in the form of actions that create a fait accompli—is healthy and justified just so long as we do not coerce those who oppose us and do not tie their hands by actions that are irreversible . . . (Segal, 1987, 236–37). Similarly, Chanan Porat reacted heatedly to the comparison made by the Underground members according to which "the settlement in Sebastia was also an act of coercion" by arguing "that the settlement in Sebastia was not a coercive action against the people. The government gave in because it came to understand that it could not go against the spirit of the nation" (Segal, 1987: 237).

Starting with Gush Emunim's justifications of "simple" disobedience to the law—arguing that these actions were not really disobedience—the development of terrorist violence cannot be dismissed as entirely unforeseen. Gush Emunim believed that the people and the government would soon recognize the legitimacy of their initiatives, follow their lead and do the "right" thing. The Underground members, as different as they were from Gush Emunim, appealed to this genre of arguments as well. Fantastic though their ideas may have been, a certain family resemblance in their manner of thinking cannot be rejected out of hand. This should come as no surprise given the undeniable fact that the Underground came into being as an offshoot of Gush Emunim. Underground members were numerically marginal of course but it is impossible to understand their behavior unless it is seen in the context of Gush Emunim's self-justifications.

The Underground sparked a profound controversy within the ranks of Gush Emunim, a controversy that over time has not entirely abated. The question: "How to relate to their terrorist actions?" divided Gush Emunim's leadership, both lay and rabbinical (Sprinzak, 1995: 45). On the one side stood Underground-valorizing rabbis such as Moshe Levinger (who was arrested under suspicion of being involved with the Underground; he was subsequently released) and rabbis such as Dov Lior and Eliezer Waldman from Kiryat Arba with whom the Underground circle felt ideological affinity. Also sympathetic to the Underground's cause was Rabbi Yisrael Ariel who, after the eviction from Yamit, supported the radical wing of Gush Emunim and devoted himself to the Temple Institute whose purpose is to prepare for the building of the Holy Temple. Like others who followed Rabbi Tzvi Yehuda Kook, Rabbi Ariel also insisted that there is a critical distinction to be made between the State of Israel and its government. The State of Israel is holy; its government is not. Only if the government acts according to Halacha and is appointed with the blessing of Torah sages (*Da'at Torah*) does Rabbi Ariel consider disobedience to the law as "rebellion against the Kingdom" (*Merida be'malchut*). In his view, the plans to blow up the mosques on the Temple Mount were, in themselves, not problematic (Don Yehiya, 2004: 211–12).

On the other side, most of the rabbis and leaders of Gush Emunim were strenuously opposed to the Underground. The great majority of Rabbi Tzvi Yehuda's followers remained loyal to the idea of Mamlachtiyut. Still, for the sake of fairness it must be added that it was not the attack on the Arab mayors per se to which they objected—they were, after all, sworn enemies of Israel. The problem was the assault on the "Kingdom of Israel." For example, Rabbi Shlomo Aviner, who was one of the foremost leaders of the Mamlachti position, authored an article entitled: "Let us renew the Kingdom: More on the matter of the Underground." Note the equivocal language:

> We are dealing with the establishment of the Kingdom of Israel. It is not the ideal Kingdom but it is the Kingdom in process (*She'baderech*). We are therefore loyal to the State and our loyalty is greater than that of the secular nationalists . . . We are obliged to accept the government's discipline. It is permitted to argue aggressively but with honor and humility . . . It is self-understood that if they [the Palestinians] abuse the trust and the respectful relations [they enjoy] and involve themselves in murder and incitement to murder—we ought to act against them with all power . . . Every act of vengeance whose purpose it is to ensure the existence of the nation does not derive from a corrupt soul but rather from a healthy soul. (Cited in Gal-Or, 1990: 92.)

The most outspoken critic of the Underground and its terrorist actions was Rabbi Yoel Bin-Nun. In an article that appeared in the weekly magazine *Koteret Rashit* (9 June 1984) he says of the Underground members, some of whom were personal friends, some like Yehuda Etzion, his one-time student:

> We are talking about people who were educated not only about the holiness of the Land of Israel, but also that the State of Israel is a stage in the process of Redemption. They were educated about the holiness of Independence Day . . . And now, people like this arise to uproot the concept of the State, to take from it the authority to deal with military and security issues. (Cited in Gal Or, 1990: 93.)

And yet, despite the widespread opposition to the Underground it must be conceded that virtually all the authorities acted toward the terrorists with a measure of ambivalence. Although their terrorist activity posed a clear and present danger to public authority, a certain grudging understanding for the rage that precipitated their violence was not uncommon. After all, the Underground was composed of recognized individuals who were close to the settler establishment. They were not moonstruck, marginal figures like Yonah Avrushmi, David ben Shimmol, Ami Popper, Alan Goldman, and their like. Consequently, they received very different treatment than other violent political activists. This is apparent in a great number of ways: the Shabak's turning a blind eye toward their activities, expressions of joy in the military headquarters of Judea and Samaria when their acts became known, the statement made by the commander of Judea and Samaria division Brigadier General Binyamin Ben-Eliezer (later a high-placed Minister) to the apprehended Underground members that he had not educated them to fire only at the legs, and so on. So indulgent were the authorities that it took the Shabak a number of years to apprehend the members of the Underground by contrast to the great efficiency they demonstrated in catching Palestinian terrorists. Only after the massacre in the Islamic College in 1983 did the security forces begin a serious search for the Jewish terrorist cell. The special treatment received by the Underground members in prison also points in the same direction. Notably, they were also granted an unusual measure of freedom during the period of their trial.

In short, much of the political establishment acted toward the members of the Underground as if they were wayward patriots but not terrorists in the full sense of the term. This atmosphere of exoneration reached its peak in the campaign conducted by religious Zionists to grant pardons to the Underground militants—a struggle for which Yitzchak Shamir, the then-Prime Minister, displayed sympathy. Indeed, many of them did receive pardons from President Chaim Herzog. In the end, not one of the Underground members served his full term (Gal Or, 1990: chapter 7). Many of the prisoners (such as Chagai Segal, Uzi Sharbaf, Moshe Zar, and even Menachem Livni himself) were received, upon their release, as "normative" figures in their communities.

From the Beginning of the Oslo Process until Rabin's Assassination (1993–1995)

The Struggle against the Oslo Process

The period between 1984 and 1992 was mostly quiet on the settlement front: no major confrontations related to the Greater Land of Israel upset the good working relationship between the religious Right and Israel's governments. Gush Emunim grew increasingly institutionalized, merging into the more moderate Judea and Samaria Council while its operational settling programs were taken over by the Amana movement. Moreover, much of Gush's leadership underwent a process of *embourgeoisment* that blunted the militancy of the seventies. Politically, many of its members joined right-wing parties like *Moledet* (Homeland) the Mafdal and Tehiya. The death of Rabbi Tzvi Yehuda Kook in 1982 also created an ideological vacuum into which the more pragmatic members of the settlement movement entered.

But this period of relative calm was followed by one of great passion and tragedy. During the more peaceful period, two national unity governments under Yitzchak Shamir and Shimon Peres—with Yitzhak Rabin acting as Minister of Defense—served from 1984 to 1990. The settlement issue remained relatively muted. In addition, religious Zionism's trauma brought on by the revelation of the Underground and its activities kept extremist settler voices in check. A period of relative de-radicalization followed (Sprinzak, 1995: 95–97). During the first part of this period, the issues that were uppermost on the public agenda were the hyper-inflation crisis (it reached 445 percent in 1984) and the attempts to reduce Israel's military presence in Lebanon during the First Lebanese War.

In the latter half of the period, however, public attention was redirected: it was now focused on the Palestinian Intifada that broke out in 1987 and continued into the early 1990s. The Iraq War (1991), in the course of which Israel was attacked by missiles, also diverted attention from the settlement issue. Nevertheless, Prime Minister Shamir, true to his right-wing agenda, devoted very substantial resources to strengthening the settlements in Judea and Samaria. Tens of thousands of new settlers streamed into the territories: there was little for religious Zionists to complain about. Nonetheless, Palestinian attacks against the settlers continued and demands for more forceful government responses created substantial tensions, although they were mostly low-level and did not trigger serious confrontations between the settlers and the government.

This reality changed abruptly in 1992 with the election victory of the Labor Party under the leadership of Yitzhak Rabin. He formed a mostly dovish minority government (Labor, *Meretz* and *Shas*—the Mizrachi Haredi party) that rested on the external tacit support of the Arab parties. Rabin was now the driving force in the government and he made no secret of his desire to effect a decisive change in the country's political direction. Pride of place should be given to promoting a peace process with the Palestinians. He spoke of transferring resources away from "political" settlements to civilian needs inside pre-1967 Israel. (It should be added parenthetically that Rabin was also prepared to return most of the Golan Heights in return for a peace treaty with Syria. Only Hafez Assad's hesitations and prevarication prevented these negotiations from advancing).

From the time of the Madrid Conference in 1991, private discussions between Israeli and Palestinian representatives took place in Washington but the Palestinian delegation was not authorized to make any decision without Arafat's express approval, which made negotiation next to impossible. However, a secret channel, led by two Israeli academics (Yair Hirshfeld and Ron Pundak) under the auspices of the Deputy Foreign Minister Yossi Beilin, opened up in 1993. Abu Alaa (later a Prime Minister of the Palestinian Authority) represented the Palestinian side and the Norwegian government acted as mediator. These talks eventually received the go-ahead by Foreign Minister Shimon Peres and eventually also of Yitzhak Rabin—although the government's ministers were kept in the dark. Led on the Israeli side by the general manager of Israel's Foreign Office, Uri Savir, an agreement was finally reached (Savir, 1998; Hirshfeld, 2000).

Rabin and PLO chairman Yasser Arafat exchanged letters that included the PLO's acceptance of decisions 242 and 338 of the United Nations and a commitment on its part to end terrorist attacks. More critically it included the assurance that the Palestinian National Council would cancel some of the clauses of the Palestinian Charter that rejected the existence of the State of Israel. For its part, Israel recognized the PLO as the single legitimate representative of the Palestinian people and committed itself to canceling the law that prohibited meeting with members of the PLO. On the 13th of September 1993, the Oslo Accords were signed with great fanfare on the White House lawn, with Rabin and Peres representing Israel, Yasser Arafat representing the Palestinians, and President Bill Clinton serving as the master of ceremonies. Especially memorable was the demonstrative displeasure expressed by Rabin's body language when he was prodded into shaking hands with Arafat (Savir, 1998; Hirshfeld, 2000).

With the aid of the Shas party that abstained from voting and with support of two right-wing members who crossed party lines, Rabin was able to ratify the agreement with what became a lightning rod issue in Israeli politics: a "Jewish majority." Even for Rabin, securing a Jewish majority was critical in order to bestow public legitimacy on the vote. Sixty-one MKs voted in favor of the agreement (all the fifty-six members of the Labor Party and Meretz and five members from the Arab parties. Fifty cast negative votes, eight abstained and one Knesset member absented himself from the plenum. Those who insisted on a "Jewish majority" received their wish: a majority of Jewish MKs had indeed supported the accords.

In June 1994, Rabin and Arafat signed the Cairo Agreement—also known as the Gaza and Jericho Agreement—after which the IDF began retreating from the cities of Gaza and from Jericho. In place of the Israeli military administration, a self-ruling Palestinian government was to be set up in these areas. The agreement was ratified by the Knesset in July 1994 and soon afterwards Arafat returned to Gaza from Tunis. A 9,000 man police force was set up (most of them from the PLO's Tunis exile) and 5,000 Palestinian security prisoners were freed from Israeli prisons. Nevertheless, Rabin insisted that the responsibility for security matters in all these areas remain in Israeli hands and that no settlements would be evacuated. In his Cairo speech Rabin expressed the belief that this was a new path, full of hope, and that it would permit the two nations to live together on one piece of land—in the words of the Bible—each man under his grapevine and his fig tree (Goldstein, 2006: 418–19).

These agreements were intended to set into motion an interim process which would lead to the establishment of a Palestinian authority in five years. The Palestinian Authority was to begin operating in Gaza and in Jericho and, over time, to take upon itself more and more responsibilities leading to a final status agreement. In September 1995, the interim agreement (Oslo B) was signed; it granted the Palestinians self-rule in six cities and in many villages. The territory of the West Bank/Judea and Samaria was divided into three regions, each with its own civil-military status. Area A would be under both the civilian and the military control of the Palestinians. In area B, while civilian authority would be in Palestinian hands, military control would continue to be held by Israel. Area C would be Israeli-ruled, both in regard to military and civilian matters.

But the Shas party, which was critical for the coalitional majority, was rocked by corruption scandals. Two of its leaders were charged with illegal economic dealings and, in the end, this led to the exit of Shas from the government. The Rabin government found itself in a serious bind: two members left the Labor party and the government "had no choice" but to "draft" two Knesset members who were elected on right-wing tickets. It was only with their support that the agreement passed by the slimmest of majorities: 61 to 59. Condemnations from the right wing were savage. The Rabin government, they charged, had "bought" these Knesset members and hence, the parliamentary ratification lacked legitimacy (Savir, 1998; Goldstein, 2006: chapter 8). For their parts in the peace process, Rabin, Peres, and Arafat were awarded the Noble Peace Prize (December 1994).

Although the polls showed that a majority supported the Oslo Accords (53 percent for, 45 percent against) according to a *Yediot Achronot* newspaper poll (cited in Goldstein 2006: 414; 538) the opposition became more aggressive and more uncompromising. In public demonstrations of the Right, Rabin was branded a "traitor." The continuation of Palestinian terrorist attacks as the peace process unfolded only strengthened the Right's commitment to prevent and undo the Oslo Accords. It was a two-pronged attack: parliamentary and extra-parliamentary. The parliamentary struggle was led by Benyamin Netanyahu; the extra-parliamentary struggle by the settler's Yesha Council. Mass demonstrations followed one another; Yesha's struggle was blunt and verbally violent. Already in 1986, it had made its "red lines" quite clear. Returning land from Judea and Samaria was labeled a crime. They would relate "to any government in Israel that perpetrates this crime as an illegitimate government just as de Gaulle acted toward the Vichy regime of Marshal Pétain when he betrayed the French people by signing away most of France's historical territory" (Goldstein, 2006: 419).

The Yesha Council devoted much time and energy toward developing strategies that would topple Rabin's government. They set up a joint Likud-Yesha team called "*Ma'amatz*" (Effort) to oversee the demonstrations and to provide funding for them. At the Yesha Council's deliberations, there was no talk of violence but when the substance of their meetings trickled down to the more radical Ma'amatz group, incitement became more pronounced. The Yesha Council under Uri Ariel refrained from confronting Ma'amatz and so, even in cases when they disapproved—as when the "Rabin is a traitor" slogan was being chanted—Yesha leaders held their peace. Some of the activists in Ma'amatz were Kahane supporters (like Baruch Marzel and Noam Federman) but this did not stop them from deliberating with the Likud in the Knesset building (Karpin and Friedman, 1998: ch. 3).

The demonstrations against Rabin gave rise, at the margins, to various forms of illegal actions. New unauthorized settlements were set up, Palestinian property was vandalized and severe rioting marked Rabin's public appearances. As time passed, the harsh voices accusing Rabin of being a traitor increased in volume and in truculence. Rabin denounced these attacks vehemently (Goldstein, 2006: 419–22). Many on the religious Right argued that even if Rabin believed wholeheartedly in the political direction he was taking, he should have at least expressed sympathy for the authentic pain felt by the settlers and their allies. His callousness toward his opponents, they claimed, was selfish and deeply offensive. Feeling themselves powerless and frustrated, the Right's demonstrations became all the more vociferous and aggressive. In one such demonstration in Jerusalem's Zion Square in July of 1994 posters of Rabin in a kafiya were held aloft as the chanting of "Rabin is a traitor" was heard in the background. After the Oslo Accords, on the 5th of October 1995, again in Zion Square, a demonstration—at which the leadership of the Likud was present—was held amidst cries of "Rabin is a murderer," "Rabin is a traitor," "With blood and fire we will drive Rabin out," they chanted. A poster of Rabin in an SS uniform was displayed by Avishai Raviv, who was later discovered to be a rogue Shabak agent. TV crews filmed the poster and it was televised, potentially to every home in Israel. Incitement had reached its peak.

The leaders of the Likud were split in the way they reacted to these acts of incitement. Binyamin Netanyahu, Ariel Sharon, and Moshe Katzav remained on the speaker's dias without attempting to rein in the goings on. Benny Begin, Dan Meridor, Ehud Olmert, David Levi, and Michael Eitan left the demonstration in protest. In what followed, a few hundred protesters marched carrying torches from Zion Square to the Knesset where they "discussed" the Oslo Accords, rioted violently, attempted to break into the Knesset Plaza, damaged Rabin's car and the cars of other government's ministers. In all of these events, the part of religious demonstrators, some of them Kahanists, was very great.

The car of Binyamin Ben Eliezer, the Minister of Housing, was attacked as he drove to the Knesset. The rioters shook the car, rocked it from side to side, and struck it with clubs. Ben Eliezer, a former battle-hardened Brigadier General, walked into Knesset pale and alarmed and said that he had never been closer to death. He approached Binyamin Netanyahu and warned: "I suggest that you restrain your people, otherwise it will end in murder. They attempted to kill me just now." When Netanyahu replied with a smile, Ben Eliezer said: "I suggest that you wipe that smile off your face. Your people are crazy. If someone is murdered, his blood will be on your head" (Karpin and Friedman, 1998; 97).

Many of those in the security and judicial elites felt there was a real risk of a political assassination (Kapliouk, 1996). An angry assault on Rabin himself at a conference of mostly religious Olim from English-speaking countries was a harbinger of tragedies to come (Peri, 2005: 39–45). Benny Elon, one of the leaders of the radical right "This is Our Land" movement warned that "Rabin is leading the state to a civil war. If he's not careful he is liable to be killed." According to a biographer of Rabin:

> In the end we can see that Prime Minister Rabin himself con-tributed indirectly to the intensification of the incitement against him. In his pronouncements he did not express an understanding of the deep pain and shock that the accords caused among the settlers. He did not express empathy for the day to day anxiety that Palestinian terrorism produced in the residents of the ter-ritories. Moreover, he did not feel the hurt and rage that the Oslo agreements ignited among those who would bear their consequences on their backs. Nevertheless, there was truth in Rabin's accusation that the 'leaders of the Likud were being hypocritical . . . They resort to intolerable verbal violence against this government and provide legitimacy for hotheaded Kahanists to attack me and the ministers.' As noted, Rabin excoriated the Likud and did not show a measure of empathy for the sufferings of the settlers, but there is nothing that can lessen the guilt of the right wing circles and especially the members of the Yesha Council in regard to the aggressive incitement against him and in the violence that derived from it. The writing was on the wall. The incitement to murder became in October 1995 an unremarkable matter of habit. Rabin comprehended it, the Sha-bak intensified its efforts to prevent the assassination of a state leader, and Ben Eliezer claimed in the Knesset in a loud and clear voice: 'Here there will be a murder, murder, murder.' Now, it was only left to wait for the villain who would take the law into his hand—and he was already there. (Goldstein, 2006: 456)

Rabin's assassination (4 November 1995) was carried out by Yigal Amir. Amir was not a typical representative of the religious Zionist camp. He grew up in a home with Haredi characteristics and was educated for many years in Haredi institutions. Nevertheless, at different stages of his life he studied in institutions associated with religious Zionism like the Hesder yeshiva *Kerem Be'Yavne* and Bar-Ilan University. Amir took an active role in many of the demonstrations against the government; he even organized a number of demonstrations himself. There were those who claimed that he was deeply influenced by the systematic de-legitimization of Rabin in the various demonstrations that were usually led by religious Zionists. However, it must be noted that this de-legitimization campaign did not—certainly not at the leadership level—include explicit encouragement for a physical assault on Rabin.

Some attributed this de-legitimization specifically to religious Zionist circles in which Rabin was said to fall into the category of a *Rodef*, that is, one whose actions make it clear that he is about to commit a murder. (In such cases, the Rodef may be killed to prevent him from realizing his intent.) On the other hand, there were those who believed that it was the incessant prodding of Avishai Raviv, the aforementioned Shabak agent, which was a cause contributing to Amir's actions. After Rabin's assassination, it was often rumored conspiratorially in right-wing circles that not only did the Shabak know of Amir's intentions prior to the murder, they were also involved in its planning. As fantastic as it may seem, the Shabak, it was alleged, wanted to catch the perpetrator "red-handed" and thereby incriminate the entire right wing. The prevalent argument on the Left is that the Right's conspiratorial theories are only an attempt to exonerate themselves from responsibility for Amir's actions.

Today the conspiratorial narrative has largely vanished. It is clear that the murder committed by Amir was the work of a lone terrorist. It is true that the murder was perpetrated only after a lengthy period of de-legitimizing Rabin and his government especially by the religious Right but also by parts of the Likud. On the other hand, it is also clear that demonstrations, shrill and verbally strident though they may be, are an inevitable part of the democratic process. In this case, when the demonstrators believed that Rabin was leading the country in a calamitous direction, the right to demonstrate forcefully is clearly justified. Such protests are the life's breath of democracy. Where justification ends, however, is when criticism becomes de-legitimation, especially violent de-legitimation, when it claims that the elected government has lost its right to rule. This was more than just robust critique; it was demonization and incitement to violence. If not a "clear and present danger," at times it approached that condition. Although the role of religious Zionists in this process of de-legitimation was uncontrovertibly substantial, assigning direct or unique blame for the murder to them is unjustified. On the other hand, although Amir's actions cannot be directly ascribed to the demonstrators and their leaders, it seems clear that without the prevalent atmosphere of de-legitimation it is unlikely that the murder would have been committed.

De-legitimization was especially vitriolic in the various religious Zionist media platforms, such as the journal *Nekuda* and the Channel 7 radio station.

In the December 1993 edition of the Nekuda journal, the government is presented as the "government of evil" whose behavior is like that of Titus and Nebuchadnezzar (Nekuda, 173: 26, cited in Peleg, 2003: 128–29). In the same number, an essay by Menachem Felix (one of the settlers more prominent leaders) appeared with the lurid title: "It doesn't bother them to upholster their way to 'peace' with our corpses." He writes:

> The present government of the State of Israel has no authority to continue and rule over the state of the Jews. A government that deceived its voters, that is based upon an Arab, PLO-following bloc that preserves it in power, that severs the State of Israel from the history of the people of Israel and from its mission—this is an illegitimate government. (Felix, 1993: 27)

These statements only grew harsher and more bellicose as time went on. An unmistakable escalation in religious Zionist vilification took place from July 1995 onward. First, on July 16, 1995, right-wing rabbis issued a ruling justifying disobedience to government directives to evacuate settlements. The second stage of the Oslo Accords (signed in Taba, Egypt) prompted fresh outbursts of furious rhetoric based upon prophecies of impending doom. "The most extreme thing is what this insane sect is doing to us. What is more extreme than taking Jews and delivering them for slaughter?" (Nekuda, 188: 40, cited by Peleg 2003: 180). In the same number of the journal the following appeared: "At this stage, the rebellion is no more than a flowering bud. When it matures, it will develop into a comprehensive position that absolutely negates the legitimacy of the present government, since this government rebels against the God of Israel and his Torah" (Nekuda 188: 40, cited in Peleg, 2003: 180).

An important actor in the campaign of de-legitimation was radio station Channel 7. According to an opinion poll in February 1993, the station enjoyed a 7.2 percent slice of the entire listening audience—most of them from the religious Zionist and Haredi communities (Karpin and Friedman, 1998: 81–83). One popular broadcaster, Adir Zik, devoted parts of his weekly programs to denunciations that blatantly incited against Rabin and his government. He repeatedly called Rabin a "traitor," and claimed that rabbis had ruled he was a Rodef. Reaching for superlatives, he argued that "this is a government out to destroy Judaism . . . they are eradicating everything Jewish . . . This government lacks legitimacy. It is a government that has betrayed me, my ideas and my principles with its [one vote] majority and a few traitors" (Karpin and Friedman, 1998; 82).

Rabbi Zalman Melamed from the Beit El settlement added a particularly hostile voice to the chorus of condemnation and de-legitimation. In one of his monologues entitled "The left has crossed all the red lines," he asserts:

> The extreme left has crossed the last of the red lines; the rule that 'all Israel are responsible for one another' no longer exists for them. They expose the blood of the Yesha settlers to attack. They abandon part of the nation for allegedly lofty ends. Allegedly for the sake of justice, integrity and peace they join the Arabs against their brother Jews and expose their blood to attack . . . [Our] healthy Jewish nature awakens and understands the danger latent in their poisonous language, that of abandoning the blood of their brothers. (Melamed, 1998: 167)

In different articles appearing in the weekly Haredi newspaper *Hashavua* (The Week), Rabin was deemed mentally ill, crazy, and a murderer. He was referred to as "Judenrat," "Kapo," "drunkard," a "destroyer of Israel," and the like. Rabin and Peres, an editorial opined "must be placed before a firing squad" (Karpin and Friedman, 1998: 84).

The peak of incitement came in the deliberations of different rabbis on the subject of *Rodef* and *Moser*. To repeat: The Halachic category Rodef comes into play when an individual pursues another with the clear intent of murder. In this case, the pursued and even others are permitted to attack him, and, if there is no other way to stop him, kill him (Maimonides, *Mishneh Torah*, "Laws of Murder and Preserving Life," Chapter 1). A *Moser* is one who "delivers" Jews into the hands of Gentile enemies, and, in so doing, causes harm to befall them. The punishment of a Moser is "destruction and descent into the pit of hell" (Maimonides, *Mishneh Torah*, "Laws of Idolatry," chapter 10, Halacha 1). Nevertheless, it is important to caution that this kind of inflammatory rhetoric worried some of the more sober members of the religious Zionist establishment. For example, Rabbi Ya'acov Ariel, the rabbi of the city Ramat Gan, published an essay in the religious Zionist newspaper *Hazofeh* as early as December 1993 in which he attacks those who speak of Prime Minister Rabin as a Rodef; this, he argues, is absolutely forbidden. Similarly, Rabbi Shlomo Aviner called upon the rabbis of Yesha to cease speaking about Rodef lest it lead to severe consequences (Sprinzak, 1999: 255–56).

In January 1995 a letter was sent to forty Orthodox rabbis in Israel and the United States in which they were called upon to express their views on the question: Were Prime Minister Rabin and his government

Mosrim (plural of Moser) according to Halacha? The letter was sent from the *Bracha* settlement in Samaria at the initiative of three rabbis: Rabbi Eliezer Melamed coordinator of the Yesha rabbis, Rabbi Dov Lior of Kiryat Arba, and Rabbi Daniel Shilo of Kedumim.

The letter, (*which because of its importance is cited in full in the book's Appendix 1*), asserts that since the Oslo agreement, the number of Jewish casualties has risen dramatically and will only grow in the future. The government gave the Palestinian police guns and they are using them against Jews. If Gaza and Jerico are "test cases," for the peace plan, the agreement has failed. Nevertheless, this "evil government" wishes to apply it to Judea and Samaria. We have been asked: "What is the law in regard to this evil government and to he who stands at its head?" Are they "accomplices to acts of murder?" Does Halacha mandate that they be put on trial and punished? Without a "Jewish Majority" is the government halachically legitimate? If members of the government continue with their dangerous policy can they be seen as Mosrim, even if they act unintentionally? Although anarchic murder of government member by individuals—even if they are Mosrim—is unacceptable, should the sages of Israel warn the political leaders that according to Halacha they will be put on trial as Mosrim? Are the heads of the army accomplices as well? Is "every man in Israel" obligated to bring them to justice? "The voice of our brother's blood calls out to us from the ground" and therefore it is incumbent [upon the rabbis to whom the letter was sent] to consider the issue with great seriousness. We turn to you "the chief sages of the generation" to make your voices heard (E. Melamed, 1995, in Forum Eretz Moledet [2008].

The very posing of these questions reveals the degree to which de-legitimization of the Rabin government had progressed among parts of the religious Zionist rabbinate. There can be no doubt whatever that in the mind of the letter's authors, Halacha overrides representative institutions and popular government. The justification for political sovereignty is to avert chaos but the legitimacy of a democratically elected government is not, in their eyes, a serious consideration. There is here an audible subtext. It certainly cannot be ruled out that the questioning rabbis entertained the possibility that Rabin and his government did indeed fall into the category of Mosrim, even if they did not directly encourage political murder. Whatever may be its subtexts and possible intimations, nowhere in this document do they advocate assassination. Suggestions to the contrary are based on selective and distorted reading of the text.

The rabbis responsible for formulating this letter sent it privately fearing that if their query were to become public, it might trigger a hothead to respond violently. Hence their equivocal, to-and-fro language. There is no reason to doubt the rabbis's heartfelt sympathy for the victims of the terrorist attacks ("the victims of peace," as they were sardonically called) or with their attempt to provide these unfortunates with an answer to their charged question. Nor should the context be forgotten. Whatever one's ideological predilections, it cannot be denied that terrorist attacks peaked in the wake of the Oslo Accords and in the eyes of many they were its direct consequence. The Intifada had declined before the Oslo Process began and, in the eyes of many of its opponents, the Rabin government's actions had served to revive PLO violence. It was also charged that the government deliberately ignored Arafat's devious involvement in the terror. Clearly, it was unfortunate that the letter was ever written—it crossed red lines never crossed before—but however damning it may appear after the tragic events of the evening of November 4, 1995, this may well be the wisdom of hindsight.

Only eleven of the petitioned rabbis answered Rabbi Melamed's query. Two of them replied that Rabin did indeed fall into the category of a Moser. Others offered, in varying degrees, hazy, ambiguous answers. On the other hand, one of them answered bluntly "you are playing with fire." In the wake of Rabin's assassination an investigation was conducted by Attorney General Michael Ben Yair into the various declarations we have described. It concluded that there was no incitement to murder present (Karpin and Friedman, 1998: 115). The Left criticized this decision bitterly. The question of whether Yigal Amir was directly influenced by the rabbis or acted without any rabbinical prompting must, in the end, remain moot. Notably, at his trial Amir asserted forcefully that he acted alone and without directives or support from any religious authorities.

Other personalities accused of being complicit in describing Rabin as a Rodef and Moser were Rabbi Shmuel Dvir, who taught in the relatively moderate yeshiva *Har Etzion*; Rabbi Nachum Eliezer Rabinovitch, the head of the *Birkat Moshe* yeshiva in *Ma'aleh Adumim*; and Rabbi Dov Lior, head of the *Nir* yeshiva in Kiryat Arba (one of the initiators of the aforementioned letter). In the course of his interrogation after Rabin's murder, Rabbi Rabinovitch denied having said the things attributed to him. Nevertheless, for the record, in an article published in the *Jerusalem Post* in December 1993 he asserted clearly that the government's attempt to impose cooperation with the Palestinians onto the Israeli people can be seen as falling into the category of Moser.

Yizchak Frankental, among the leaders of the religious Left, reported that in a conversation (spring 1995) with him Rabbi Rabinovitch likened Rabin's government to Nazis. Frankental recounts that Rabbi Rabinowitz repeated what he had previously said to a number of rabbis: the settlers would spread explosives on the paths leading to their villages in order to deter soldiers who might come to evacuate them. In the same vein, according to Frankental, Rabbi Rabinowitz declared that IDF soldiers should know that they are forbidden to enter Jewish settlements (Karpin and Friedman, 1998: 118). In an interview on the Kol Yisrael radio station in August 1995, Rabbi Rabinowitz declared that Rabin was a Moser who, according to Maimonides, was deserving of death (Mitcha'yev be'nafsho) although he added that "I didn't say that it's permissible to harm him" (Karpin and Friedman, 1998: 119).

A prominent voice in the chorus of de-legitimation both of Rabin personally and of his government in general was that of Elyakim Ha'etzni, a former Knesset member from the Tehiyah party, a settler from the town of Kiryat Arbah, a leader of the Yesha Council but, notably, not a religious figure. In March 1995, he told the Central Military Command "in Hitler's Germany there were officers who understood that their government was leading the German people to oblivion, and they stood up and threw down their insignia and paid for it with their lives. Here too the government is leading the people to oblivion" (Karpin and Friedman, 1998: 69). He published a pamphlet of caricatures entitled "Peace Criminals" containing cartoons in the style of Der Stürmer: for example, Rabin is seen washing his hands in a sink full of Jewish blood. In Yesha Council deliberations, he repeatedly said that the government was like the traitorous government of Vichy France. Indeed, he said to the press that the Oslo Accords should be related to just as the French regarded occupied France as having cooperated with the Nazis and it is not unlikely that the day will come when Rabin will be put on trial just as Pétain was put on trial (Karpin and Friedman, 1998: 69). Nevertheless, it is important to note that the Yesha Council did not endorse Ha'etzni's comments.

Significantly, a number of Rabin's close army friends denounced him in the strongest terms—terms that border on true incitement and de-legitimation of the democratic process. Member of Knesset Rehavam Ze'evi ("Gandhi") in September of 1995 defined Rabin's government as "the Jewish Munich government." Ariel Sharon, who had a long history of close relations with Rabin wrote in the Hayarden newspaper (5 July 1995) that the government is delivering settlers into the hands of Palestinian gangs. Being a Moser, he continued, is in the very nature of the Left. In September of 1995, less than two months before Rabin's murder, he said in an interview with a Chabad newspaper that "what is involved is the cooperation [with the Palestinians] of two personalities, Rabin and Peres; in any other country they would be put on trial."

To summarize a complex and delicate subject: It seems clear that despite the incitement and de-legitimation, it is unfair to saddle the right wing religious Zionists with direct (and certainly not with unique) responsibility for the murder. As to indirect responsibility, the issue is harder to resolve. Perhaps Amir did what he did in an atmosphere of verbal violence, but passing from talk to deed, from threats to assassination seems to have been the project of one person: Amir. Nevertheless, it cannot be doubted that many in the radical camp, were pleased that Rabin had been removed from the political horizon. It is arguable that without the fierce atmosphere on the religious Right, without the talk of Rodef and Moser, Amir would not have been prone to kill, but his homicidal proclivities were, in the end, his own. Moreover, even if a tie between the talk and the deed can be established, it implicates only a relatively small part of the right wing and the religious Zionists. What can be said unequivocally is that the words and deeds of the extreme right wing and of a sizeable portion of the religious Zionists community constituted a profound de-legitimation of the democratic process. No apologetics can change this.

The Radical Religious Right:
Violence against Arabs and the Goldstein Massacre

Investigating the massacre in Hebron's Cave of the Patriarchs (February 1994), the Shamgar Committee broadly surveyed violent acts that settlers in Judea and Samaria had committed over the years. The committee cited a report of *Be'tselem* (The Israeli Information Center for Human Rights in the Occupied Territories) according to which many attacks on Palestinians and their property had taken place without the authorities attempting to prevent them or, afterwards, punishing the guilty. Some of these acts of settler violence, the Shamgar Committee claimed, were, in fact, "deliberate punishment actions, well-organized and backed by the established leadership." At the other ideological pole, the committee cited the testimony of Tzvi Katzover, head of the Kiryat Arba municipal council, according to which the police and the army were derelict in preventing Palestinian violence (*Din ve'cheshbon*, 1994: 157–58).

The main perpetrators of violence against Palestinians were members of the Kach organization—followers of Rabbi Meir Kahane among whom the militant Baruch Marzel stands out. Marzel attacked Palestinians and assaulted IDF soldiers. He was convicted of attacking soldiers in 1996 as they tried to arrest a settler who had damaged a Palestinian's car. The judge noted that Marzel had

> chosen a way of life that expressed his political outlook by violent means and by callously scorning the rule of law . . . He does not

recognize the obligation to respect the law, and advancing his
ideological objectives, so far as he is concerned, can be carried
out while trampling on the principles of the rule of law, even
though violent actions against those appointed to preserve it.
(Negbi, 2004: 230–31)

Nonetheless, Marzel received only a suspended sentence.

Kahanists do not belong to the normative religious Zionist camp
even though they broadly espouse religious Zionist views. Their unique
brand of religious Zionism is synthesized with Haredi religious stringency
and a strong tendency toward cultural isolation and xenophobia; it is also
seasoned by radical Jewish "self-defense" ideas whose source lies in the
United States. Racist anti-Arab rhetoric—Jewish women are threatened by
Arab seducers—bring to mind other times and places. Violence is central
to their belief system. They do not feel at home in the *Hesder* yeshiva
atmosphere (that combines Torah study with service in the IDF); neither
do they gravitate to the teachings of the Rabbis Kook. Kahanists often live
in religious Zionist settlements and are usually accepted by their neighbors
who regard them as potentially useful allies. With the growing radicalization
of religious Zionism in the past decades, there has been a blurring of lines
between its extreme right-wing faction and Kahanist militants—particularly
among the youth. Nevertheless, Hebron and Kiryat Arba have witnessed
deep ideological rifts between the two—between the religious Zionists who
follow Rabbi Tzvi Yehuda's teachings and the Kach adherents for whom
Kahane is political mentor and spiritual guide. This split was most evident
in their reactions to the most grievous case of Jewish terrorist violence in
Israel's history; the massacre of Arab worshipers by Baruch Goldstein in
the Cave of the Patriarchs.

On a Friday morning, 25th of February 1994 (Purim day), Dr. Baruch
Goldstein wearing his army reserve fatigues as a Captain in the IDF and
carrying his Galil automatic rifle, burst into the Isaac hall, the largest of
the halls in the Cave of the Patriarchs and opened fire on the Arab worshipers as they prayed. That morning there were about 500 worshipers in
the hall; he killed 29 and wounded 111. The slaughter continued until his
rifle jammed and he was attacked by the outraged congregants and beaten
to death. Subsequent to the attack, in the course of violent confrontations
between Arabs and the army, another nine Palestinians were killed and
200 wounded.

Goldstein was already a Kach activist in the United States before
he immigrated to Israel in 1983. He continued his Kahanist activities in
Kiryat Arba. Incongruously, he was a prominent and devoted doctor in the

Hebron area and earned the admiration of the settlers and even of the IDF. There are conflicting reports about his willingness or refusal to treat Arab patients. Not surprisingly, both Prime Minister Rabin and the settler leadership claimed that he was insane when he committed his mass murders. Nonetheless, the Shamgar Committee set up to investigate the massacre found that Goldstein had planned the slaughter coldly and methodically. The murders derived from his Kahanist ideology which was exacerbated by frustration over the concessions the government had made to the PLO and by the many attacks against settlers in Judea and Samaria. He treated many of the victims of these attacks himself. The Shamgar Committee determined that his act was that of a sole perpetrator. Despite the severity of his crime, after the murder some saw Goldstein as a "saintly person" (*Tzadik*) who had died the death of a martyr—for the "sanctification of God's name" (*Kidush Hashem*) (Sprinzak, 1995: 101–03).

Rabin considered evacuating the Jewish settlement in Hebron as a response to the Goldstein murders but, in the end, he relented because of right-wing threats of mass violence should he do so. Some claimed that Rabin was disinclined to undertake such a fraught step because of a ruling by religious Zionist rabbis (see below) that soldiers should disobey orders in the event of an eviction. In the end, Hamas responded to the Goldstein murders with an unprecedented series of suicide attacks in Jerusalem and Ashkelon. These attacks seriously weakened the legitimacy of the Oslo Process in the public mind. Moreover, they were effectively exploited by Rabin's opponents to justify an even more strident level of incitement.

The right wing's response to the Goldstein massacre was diverse and uneven. To be sure, the vast majority of the religious Zionist camp denounced the murder but there were variations in tone and in the apportioning of blame. Some argued that the main guilt lies with the government that had led the country into a dangerous corner which threatened Israel with unprecedented catastrophe. It was, they claimed, fear of this disaster that prompted Goldstein to murder the innocent. A more moderate position claimed that the murder of defenseless worshipping civilians was inexcusable but, in the same breath, they attacked the government for its heavy-handed actions against the settlers, such as administrative detention. The third group—arguably a minority—directed the blame inward and called for introspection and soul searching. They lamented the breakdown of dialogue between the settlers and the majority of the Israeli people (Peleg, 2003: 141–43).

It must be said, however, that there was a small minority of the radical religious right that justified, even glorified the murder. Yigal Amir, Rabin's assassin, confessed that he was deeply impressed by Goldstein's fearless selflessness. In his mind, the murders prevented a planned slaughter of Jews in Hebron. In his interrogation, he stated that he had travelled to Kiryat Arba for Goldstein's funeral. Amir claims that he found great love for Goldstein among many residents and associates. He declared that it was then, "when I had the idea that it was necessary to take Rabin down" (Karpin and Friedman, 1998: 16).

Surely, the most fervent support for Goldstein came in the form of a hagiographical book entitled *Baruch Hagever: Sefer Zikaron Lakadosh Dr. Baruch Goldstein—Hashem Yikom Damo* [Baruch = Blessed, Hagever = is the man, i.e., a real man: A Memorial Volume for the Martyr Dr. Baruch Goldstein, May God Avenge his Blood]. (Ben Horin, 1995). (The name of the book disfigures Jeremiah's declaration: "Blessed be the man who puts his faith in God," 7:17). The book is an anthology of articles dealing with "sanctifying God's name," i.e., dying a martyr's death, the laws regarding killing a Gentile, revenge against Gentiles, and general essays on religious and social issues that confront Israel. A large section of the book is devoted to many stories about Goldstein's exemplary life, of Goldstein as a doctor dedicated to healing the sick. The book's central contention is that Goldstein's actions cannot be separated from his devoting his life to helping the sick and wounded. On the contrary, the massacre is the expression of his greatness and his dedication. Knowing that the IDF had warned against an outburst of deadly Palestinian violence against the Hebron settlement, he preempted the attack and selflessly gave his life for the sake of others. This self-sacrificing behavior was of a piece with his altruism in diligently treating the sick and the wounded in the entire Hebron area. Indeed, the book concludes with the factually unimpeachable statement that Goldstein had received an award from the IDF for his selfless work.

Justifying the act of mass murder and calling Goldstein a martyr represents a position that is at least as radical as that of Meir Kahane—Goldstein's spiritual mentor. Implicit in Goldstein's behavior is the defense of killing Palestinians for the sake of revenge, killing them as a means of allegedly protecting Jewish security, and killing them as part of a "pre-emptive attack" (Sprinzak, 1999: 258–66). In the book's showcase article, Rabbi Yitzhak Ginsburgh (surely the most radical religious right-wing ideologue since Kahane), focuses on Goldstein's many altruistic deeds as a person and as a doctor. Ginzburghh, head of the Joseph's Tomb yeshiva in Shechem (Nablus) and later the *Od Yosef Chai* yeshiva (Joseph Still Lives) in the radical settlement *Yitzhar*, takes up cases in which there is justification for killing Gentiles in revenge for their actions, killing them in the context of war, and killing them for the sake of "eradicating evil."

Ginzburghh believes that Goldstein's mass murder should be understood as incarnating five distinct virtues: the sanctification of God's name, the saving of lives, revenge, the eradication of evil, and the struggle for the Land of Israel (Ginzburgh cited in Ben-Horin, 1995: 20).

A. The sanctification of God's name: The crowning glory of Goldstein's act is the sanctification of God's name. He sacrificed his life and annulled his ego for the sake of his comrades. He acted against the profanation of God's name that is inherent in the Arab threat to Israel. In his act, Goldstein sanctified God's name by sowing fear in Arab hearts. He acted like Jacob's sons Simon and Levi who took revenge for Shechem's rape of their sister Dina by killing all the men of the town (Genesis: 34) (Ginzburgh in Ben Horin, 1995: 21–25).

B. Saving lives: Goldstein saved the lives of Jews threatened by Arabs who planned to attack them. He preferred that non-Jews die rather than Jews. As Rabbi Shimon Bar Yochai taught: "Kill even the best among the Gentiles." This statement is relevant for any Jewish national conflict and not only for the battlefield (Ginzburgh in Ben Horin, 1995: 25–29).

C. Revenge: The heart of Goldstein's deed is revenge without any consideration of personal gain. It was done out of identification with the good of all. Revenge goes beyond any rational concern. Revenge arises from a bond with nature and its rightful place in relation to God. Revenge vindicates the revelation of the world's judge in that the hand of Israel prevails (Ginzburgh in Ben Horin, 1995: 29–32). Ginzburgh writes:

> All who knew him felt that Baruch [Goldstein] acted out of his Jewish character. His deed was not 'another aspect' of his character but was totally integrated with his 'Yiddishkeit.' Therefore, beyond what was revealed about revenge as a natural reaction found in all of nature, this revenge was experienced as pure Jewish revenge and not as an outburst of coarse brutishness (as legitimate as that may be). This was not the reaction of an ignorant Jew—although even this kind of reaction should be blessed—but of a

learned man and a model individual. (Ginzburgh in
Ben Horin, 1995: 33)

D. The eradication of evil: The Palestinians who attack Jews
today are the continuation of Amalek and they must be wiped
out. "The Palestinian Nation" is a fabrication the purpose
of which is to undermine the existence of Israel. Palestinian
hostility derives from hatred of the "Jew" and not only from
a conflict over land. Therefore, Goldstein acted to eradicate
evil.

E. The struggle for the Land of Israel: Jews are commanded to
take over the land from the nations that occupy it. As was
the case with the seven Canaanite peoples in the time of
Joshua, so it is with the Palestinians today. Goldstein's action
furthered the cause of ridding the land of Palestinians and
in so doing he took a step toward the establishment of the
Kingdom of Israel.

At the end of his essay Ginzburgh concedes that there may be other ways
of looking at the Goldstein's massacre. It could well cause a profanation
of the name of God in the world's eyes and trigger Palestinian retaliation in which Jews will be killed (as actually happened). He realizes that
sometimes revenge can be problematic, that the Palestinians may not be
comparable to Amalek and that there may not be a command to rid the
land of its inhabitants as was the case in the time of Joshua. These doubts
do not deter him. He concludes with a bravura flourish: When there are
arguments that can be made for both sides there is often the need for an
"emergency decision" (Hora'at sha'ah), for a moment of resolution when
there occurs an internal revelation, when a person reaches down to the
roots of his soul—but this can happen only when there is a nullification of
the self and no regard for personal needs. It is in moments like these that
authentic human power arises (Ginzburgh in Ben Horin, 1995: 45–47). He
clearly believes that Baruch Goldstein had such a moment of epiphany and
that his massacre came from the deepest and purest recesses of his soul.

Tomer Persico contends that what lies at the heart of Ginzburgh's
Baruch Hagever essay is a belief in the goodness, indeed the holiness of
Goldstein's soul. Attempting to recreate the moment of Goldstein's mas-
sacre, Perisco writes:

In that early hour of morning when Baruch Goldstein's middle
finger rested on the trigger of his 'Galil' rifle his soul sloughed
off the shell of rational falsehood, nullified itself and became

one with the Divine spark that is hidden in very depths of its being. Out of this pure and holy place the voice arose to take blind and murderous revenge, revenge so natural and nevertheless holier than all holiness. A moment thereafter Dr. Goldstein freed the natural Divine vitality within him and transformed the Tomb of the Patriarchs into a blood bath. (Persico, 2014)

Ginzburgh never retracted—even years afterwards—his justification for Goldstein's massacre. In a book written a decade later he once again declared that the killing of Moslem men at prayer can be compared to the killing of the seven idolatrous Canaanite nations:

Because this is so, it is possible to relate to a Gentile who holds onto a religious faith—even when he turns to the Creator of the Universe—as absolute evil that must be completely destroyed—if he sets himself and his faith against Israel and its faith. We can come in the name of God to attack those who devote themselves fervently to their religion, even during the liturgy itself (and maybe precisely then) as in the commandment to destroy the seven nations who are immersed in their coarse idol worshiping. We should not be impressed by bogus compassion: 'how terrible it is to attack those at prayer at the moment they bow down to their god'—this is a claim heard from those who do not have God in their hearts. He who has God in his heart and toils endlessly to cleanse and purify his relationship with Him, he experiences and knows how such crude and coarse attitudes toward Godliness can attach to his efforts, how likely they are to strengthen all that is inferior and evil in his heart. (Ginsburgh, 2005: 101)

According to Sprinzak (1999: 265–66), the publication of *Baruch Hagever* enhanced the standing of Rabbi Kahane's followers—both Kach and its rival "Kahane lives" organization, led by Kahane's son Binyamin Ze'ev—among the settler community. Kahane's followers were viewed as the militant spearhead of opposition to the Oslo Accords. Most visible in attacking Arabs was "The Committee for Security on the Roads" that was established by Rabbi Kahane in the 1980s. In an interview with Tiran Pollack, one of the leaders of the committee, whose two sisters had been murdered in 1983 by Palestinian terrorists, he claimed that between 1992 and 1993 his people were involved in more than 500 violent confrontations with Arabs (Sprinzak, 1999: 124–30). It is impossible to verify the numbers that Pollack alleges. And yet it is clear that Shmuel Ben-Yishai (head of the Kach faction in the radical Kiryat Arba settlement), Tiran Pollack, and especially Baruch Marzel were part of the tens of armed Kach and Kahane Chai activists that patrolled the roads of Judea and Samaria and the "borderline" neighborhoods (between Jewish and Arab residents) in Jerusalem. Not infrequently, they attacked Arabs and vandalized their property—at times, allegedly while the official security forces turned a blind eye. It is difficult to determine definitively what part radical religious Zionists took in these actions (Pedazur, 2012; Sprinzak, 1999). Notably, Kahane's son Binyamin Ze'ev, his grandson Meir Ettinger, and of course Baruch Marzel have rich criminal records related to violence against Arabs; they have been arrested many times for vigilante activities although usually freed without serious punishment.

Rabbinical Calls for Soldiers to Disobey Orders and for Civilians to Resist Evictions

Among the most divisive reactions to the government's Oslo policy was the appeal to IDF soldiers to disobey orders if they were commanded to vacate settlements or army bases in Yesha/the West Bank. This call was sounded by right-wing and religious journalists, intellectuals, publicists, politicians. But perhaps the most dominant and influential voice was that of leading rabbis in the religious Zionist community who publicly appealed for personal and collective disobedience. This call echoes similar rabbinical appeals from the past: during the attempt in the 1970s to evacuate the earliest Gush Emunim settlements and, once again in the early 1980s with the retreat from Sinai. However, as opposed to the earlier cases where equivocations were frequent and many important rabbinical authorities desisted from making such appeals, the calls for insubordination during the Oslo period came from the front line of religious Zionist rabbis.

    This confrontation marks a watershed in the relationship between religious Zionism and the State of Israel. From the Mizrahi's origins in 1902 up until the 1990s, religious Zionists never engaged in an out-and-out battle with the official representatives of the Zionist movement. Even Gush Emunim's disobedience did not question the principle of Mamlachtiut as understood by religious Zionism. Now however, when the struggle focused on the Oslo Accords, all the stops were pulled and the leading religious Zionist adjudicators (*Poskim*) explicitly called for soldiers to disobey orders.

    These Poskim included, among many others, Rabbi Avraham Shapira, head of the Mercaz HaRav yeshiva in Jerusalem and former Chief Rabbi of Israel; Rabbi Shlomo Goren, former Chief Rabbi of the IDF and later of the State of Israel; Rabbi Shaul Yisraeli of the Mercaz HaRav yeshiva; and Rabbi Moshe Tzvi Neria, founder of the Bnei Akiva yeshivot. In a single voice, they unambiguously called upon Israeli soldiers to disobey orders to evacuate territories in Yesha—even if it involved only the evacuation of an army base without retreating from settlements, even if it did not mean giving up any territory to the Palestinians.

Nonetheless, these calls for disobedience did not lead to significant acts of noncompliance on the part of religious soldiers. This may be due to Rabin's decision not to vacate Jewish settlements before signing the final Oslo agreement. Given the absence of actual insubordination, there are those who argue that the rabbis's pronouncements were of no great consequence. We believe this to be false; the precedent was, in fact, crucial. It is hasty and short-sighted to ignore such prominent voices from within the religious Zionist camp. These rulings constituted a clear and present signal that rabbis who were at the very center of religious Zionist thought and practice endorsed disobeying the directives of a democratically elected government.

The immediate issue at stake was disobeying orders for the sake of the Greater Land of Israel but it established a precedent and, as we shall see, eventually went beyond its original objective. As soon as the rule of law is breached in principle, the practice—sometimes unforeseeable—is not far behind. It often does not take long until the very legitimacy of the democratic process is placed into question. Although even the most painful of all the withdrawals—the disengagement from Gush Katif/the Gaza Strip in 2005—did not precipitate life-endangering violence, after rabbinical calls for flouting the rule of law are voiced, the door is open. Other issues—the early 2013 much-publicized conflict over the integration of women into the army comes to mind—may well trigger the same dismissive attitude toward decisions not congenial to religious leaders. It can only be conjectured what might occur if the government of Israel decided to vacate substantial parts of the occupied territories. As we shall see in the following chapter, more recent events—notably the "Price Tag" (*Tag Mechir*) violence of certain settlers—bear out the fear that rejecting the rule of law is a very slippery slope.

One might be led to draw the conclusion that the split in the religious Zionist camp between those who support disobedience and those who reject it is deep and abiding. This is not the case. There is more that unites than divides them. Most of the religious Zionist camp and virtually all of it radical right-wing faction accept the political theology of Rabbi Tzvi Yehuda Kook according to which settling the Land of Israel is *the* cardinal Mitzvah for our generation and that it is forbidden to transfer land to the Palestinians once it has come under Jewish control. For a vast majority of religious Zionists, settling in Judea and Samaria—even if they do not do so themselves—is a central expression of their religious-Jewish-Zionist identity. Indeed, during the Oslo period, opposition to the Accords was perhaps the defining element in the religious Zionist camp, its rabbis, and its lay leaders. (Some important religious intellectuals protested but they were numerically insignificant and religiously without authority). This opposition to the Oslo Accords embraced both those who supported disobedience and those who were against it.

A clear example of this broad unity of outlook can be seen in the writings of Rabbi Shlomo Aviner, one of the most vigorous opponents of disobedience. According to Rabbi Aviner, settling in the Greater Land of Israel is morally commendable and transferring territories to the Palestinians is prohibited (Aviner, 1990b: 57). It threatens Israel's security and violates the biblical injunction that prohibits Jews from selling land in Israel to Gentiles (*Lo Techonem*, Deuteronomy 7:2). Moreover, most of the land was desolate and uninhabited and Jewish settling did not injure any moral right of a sovereign Arab government (Aviner, 1983: 129–35).

In his article "Let us renew the Kingdom" that was published after the Jewish Underground was exposed in the 1980s, Rabbi Aviner writes that not every Knesset law is beyond reproach. A law that violates the "internal essence" of the people of Israel is invalid. And citing Rabbi Tzvi Yehuda he declares: "Torah takes precedence over government." The government has no legal authority to evacuate settlements, and clashing with such a government is entirely legitimate (Aviner, 1990a: 240–41). In this regard, Rabbi Aviner was in full agreement with the Yesha Rabbis who wrote on the front page of their *Va'ad Rabanei Yesha* Journal (September 1992):

> Certainly we are obliged to settle all of our land; a government that decides as a matter of principle that the land should not be settled subverts the mission it has and its words are null and void. And it does not matter if the government decides to stop settlements partially or entirely, like the heretic who denies a single letter of the Torah denies the whole Torah, such is the case in regard to the land of our lives (Signed by: Rabbis Shlomo Aviner, Elyakim Levanon, Zalman Melamed, Gideon Perl, Yigal Kaminatzky and Daniel Shiloh.) (The Association of Yesh'a Rabbis, 1992)

What stands out in Rabbi Aviner's position is his prohibition of disobedience. He contends that it is forbidden to wage violent or even passive struggles against soldiers who come to vacate settlements (Aviner, 1990a:

208). Resisting the army, Rabbi Aviner claims, causes it to be weakened. Thus, even if the army carries out an invalid government decision to vacate parts of the Land of Israel, we are forbidden to weaken it by disobeying orders. Such noncompliance endangers the existence of the people because it harms the IDF's ability to function. Therefore, insubordination is counted as a "revolt against the Kingdom" (*Mored be'malchut*) that is explicitly prohibited by Halacha (Aviner, 1990b: 57).

Rabbi Aviner's paradoxical position heatedly contests the authority of democratically elected governments while, simultaneously, and with no less passion, rejects civil disobedience against the government. As he writes:

> [I]t is simply forbidden to give parts of the Land of Israel to the enemy; on the contrary, we are commanded that all of the Land of Israel belongs under our national sovereignty . . . Abandoning parts of the Land of Israel is a sick and traitorous policy and those responsible will need to give an account of themselves before the nation, before all of human history and before the Master of the Universe . . . Against this national treason we should act with all might and main and with all the means at our disposal. And even if it turns out that a majority of the people supports such a disgraceful and dangerous move—this does not constitute a moral justification. It is not enough that a decision be taken by a state organization for it to be moral. 'You shall not be led into wrongdoing by a majority' (Exodus, 23:2). When I say 'all the means at our disposal' it clearly is not referring to technical means but rather to moral and halachic possibilities. Every sentient person understands that we should not build something on the wreckage of something else. Just as giving over parts of the Land of Israel is a sin and a crime, so also is injuring the government a sin and a crime . . . We will not crush Israel into fragments. Even talk of it is forbidden in times of war and danger, because it causes weakness. We will not contest the government that we have been blessed to have by the grace of God. Our loyalty to the state is greater than that of empty people because it derives from the Torah. (Aviner, 2002: 259–60)

Rabbi Aviner derives the prohibition of "rebelling against the Kingdom" from the words of the people of Israel to Joshua: "If anyone rebels against your orders or will not listen to your commands, let him be put to death. Only be strong and stand firm" (Joshua, 1:17). This uncompromising language reflects the recognition that rebellion endangers the Jewish collective (Aviner, 2002: 261). Rabbi Aviner is well aware of Maimonides's ruling that a king who abrogates a Mitzvah is not to be obeyed (*Mishneh Torah*, "The Laws of Kings," chapter 3, Halacha 9), a text which was central to rabbis who supported disobedience. But he introduces a principled distinction between, on the one hand, a Jewish government that coerces an individual Jew to disobey a law of the Torah and, on the other, a transgression committed by the government itself, even it involves the participation of the individual. In such cases, the individual does not sin if he obeys:

> Maimonides speaks of a king who coerces an individual to commit a personal sin, such as to violate the Sabbath, and not about a sin that the king commits. Therefore an individual Jew who is forced to move his residence from one part of the Land of Israel to another because of government machinations—does not commit a sin. There is no Mitzvah to live specifically in a certain place in the land; the important thing is live in the Land of Israel. Therefore, the transfer of the Land of Israel [to Gentiles] because of mistaken political considerations is a terrible and appalling sin of all Israel but it is not a personal sin of which Maimonides spoke. Of course, one should fight against this calamity with all might and main, but not by inciting people to revolt against the government but rather by inciting all the people of Israel to 'rebel,' that is to change the direction of the government. It is clear that this work needs to be done in a democratic fashion . . . We will renounce nothing, not our land, not our government and not our unity. 'The Laws of God are true and righteous altogether' (Psalms 19:9). (Aviner, 2002: 262)

Rabbi Aviner's fierce opposition to the Oslo Process did not alter his consistent rejection of de-legitimizing government decisions and the demonization of Rabin as a traitor. Although this government, he writes, sadly lacks a consciousness of the Land of Israel as our irreplaceable motherland, it surely is not interested in "selling off the state" (Aviner, 1996: 9). Nevertheless, his ideas should not be mistaken for liberal democratic ones. For example, he argues that

> there is room for democracy and for the joining of Jews from different factions; more or less Zionist, more or less religious that together create a majority that is healthy and normal. But a majority that is composed of a minority of Jews together with Gentiles is a sick and rotten majority, haughty and insolent.

It is a terrible tragic-comedy of a state without a government. (Aviner, 1996: 23)

All the same, despite its egregious misdeeds and although the government relies on Arab coalitional support, the state remains holy (Aviner, 1996: 11–12). In his view, under no circumstances is it permissible to direct violence against the government because it is precisely internal violence that destroyed Israel in the past (Aviner, 1996: 25). In particular it is strictly forbidden to call the Prime Minister a traitor: "The Prime Minister is making a crucial, frightening mistake and his name will live in eternal disgrace, but he is no traitor. His intention is to advance the good of the state" (Aviner 1996: 31–32). It is prohibited to even think of him in the category of Rodef; indeed "we must think of the one who says the Prime Minister is a Rodef as a Rodef himself for there is no greater Rodef than he, and this is what will destroy Israel" (Aviner, 1996: 48).

It is fascinating that Rabbi Aviner looks far afield to bolster his position against violent disobedience—to the teachings and practices of Mahatma Gandhi and Martin Luther King. Both conducted a nonviolent struggle and their tactic of passive resistance succeeded brilliantly. Nevertheless, Rabbi Aviner makes a sharp distinction between Gandhi and King on the one hand, and the Jewish/Israeli case on the other. Opposing the Oslo process does not fall into the same category as the struggle against imperialism and racial prejudice. The struggle against the Rabin government takes place uniquely against the background of a deep common loyalty of a people to its collective good. Both the government and its fiercest critics belong to one people and only then branch off into rival movements. We must therefore continue to pray for the well-being of the government and obey its decisions (Aviner, 1996: 101–06).

In all likelihood, Rabbi Aviner's defense of obedience to orders was a minority position. Perhaps more representative of the right-wing rabbis's opposition to the Oslo process was the position of Rabbi Ya'acov Meidan one of the main figures in the *Har Etzion* yeshiva located in *Alon Shvut*. Although he parts company from Rabbi Aviner and his insistence on virtually unconditional obedience, he stops short of advocating outright disobedience. In his essay, "Between disobedience and tears" that appeared in the settler's journal *Nekuda* (April 1994), Rabbi Meidan expresses the doubts, confusion, and anguish caused by the right-wing rabbis' ruling (with which we will deal shortly) that soldiers should disobey orders if asked to dismantle settlements. According to Rabbi Meidan, a complex, even tormented road between loyalty and disobedience must be sought. On the one hand, there should not be outright disobedience by soldiers to the orders they receive from their officers but, on the other, it is important that the soldiers approach the implementation of their orders with tears and distress. They ought not to contribute enthusiastically to the command's execution. Not passive resistance but the passive following of orders; a squaring of the moral circle. During the 2005 evacuation of the Gaza/Gush Katif settlements Rabbi Meidan's prescription became the dominant *modus vivendi* of the religious Zionist camp.

But what of those rabbinical authorities who explicitly called upon soldiers to disobey orders when commanded to vacate settlements? In July of 1995, prominent rabbis belonging to the religious Zionist elite published a ruling *requiring* soldiers to disobey orders for the sake of the Land of Israel. This was not the first such ruling but it was doubtless the most detailed and specific; it was also the one with the greatest public resonance. Rabbi Eliezer Melamed, the secretary of the Yesha Rabbinical Council and one of its pivotal personalities cites the content of the ruling. (*Because of its length, it is here paraphrased and cited in its entirety in Appendix 2*).

The rabbis issued the following halachic ruling: (1) The Torah prohibits vacating army bases which are part of the Land of Israel and transferring them to Gentiles, and (2) Nachmanides insists that the land be conquered and not relinquished. Moreover, giving up land endangers both the lives of Israelis and of the well-being of the state. It is therefore "clear and simple" that every Jew is prohibited from taking part in the evacuation of land held by Jews. An evacuation order puts soldiers in the position of having to act against their religious, moral, and national conscience. The rabbis call upon the government to rescind the order that fractures national unity. Although the IDF is holy, it may not endanger the lives of Jews. Moreover, half the nation opposes the government policy and hence it is immoral to impose evacuation on soldiers who oppose it on religious, etc., grounds. This would be a "moral crime" (E. Melamed, 1994).

Summarizing our discussion to this point.

1. There is much in common between those supporting and opposing disobedience. They both believe that settling of the Land of Israel is a cardinal Mitzvah. Basing themselves on Nachmanides, they reject giving up any part of the Land of Israel. A governmental evacuation order both abuses its rightful authority and endangers Israelis, the army and the state. Basing themselves on Maimonides, both argue that a king (or government) that orders individuals to violate Torah laws should not be obeyed.

2. Rabbi Aviner presents a distinctly minority opinion. Soldiers, when so ordered, may evacuate a settlement or a military base. He draws the distinction between individual infractions and government sinfulness. When a rogue government pursues an illegitimate policy, individuals may not disobey it because public order and security trump other concerns.

3. The rabbis appeal to the government—beyond the more important issues of Halacha and security—not to place religious soldiers in a moral bind, that is, not to demand that they violate their conscience.

4. Inevitably, questions arise regarding the right of a sovereign, democratically elected government to impose a single policy on its citizens. Democracies rest on their armies to execute policy decisions they make. Besides, many on the Left contend that substantial numbers of soldiers sent to defend the settlers are no less opposed to the settlement project than the religious Zionist soldiers are devoted to it. Why should they not be released from their military duties as well?

A largely identical "Torah judgement" was promulgated a few years earlier by three of the most prominent of religious Zionist rabbis: Avraham Shapira, Shaul Yisraeli, and Moshe Tzvi Neria. (See *Appendix 3*. For another statement made by the Union of World Rabbis for the Land of Israel in 1996 see *Appendix 4*).

Rabbi Avraham Shapira, seen by many in the religious Zionist community as their most important Torah authority during the Oslo period played a central role in calling for disobedience. In his comments on Professor Eliav Shochetman's book *And He Legislated it to the Ancestors of Jacob* (Shochetman, 1995) that contains the most thoroughgoing discussion of issues surrounding withdrawal from the Land of Israel (see below), Rabbi Shapira is particularly incisive on the obligation to disobey orders when the Land of Israel is at stake. It may be seen as the "document of record" in the debate over disobedience and as such it bears reiteration. We compress what is a lengthy argument.

1. The halachic grounds: The superiority of Torah law over state law.

> . . . Is it possible that a person who obeys the Torah and the Mitzvot might think that it is permissible

to transgress the Torah because there is a military directive against it and think that he is still to be considered a religious man? This is a contradiction in terms. This was among the simplest matters for all Jews from their childhood onwards—that the supreme thing is observing God's commands, as they are determined in Halacha . . . The Mitzvah of settling the Land of Israel is accepted among the Poskim as a performative Mitzvah (*Mitzvaht a'seh*) demanded by the Torah . . . and if a Jew is coerced to evacuate a settlement and to give it over to Gentiles, it is a coercion to transgress a Mitzvah and it is forbidden to do so. And therefore the rabbis ruled as they did. In addition there is also a prohibition from the Torah of *Lo Techonem*—not to give the Gentiles a foothold in the land (Deuteronomy 7:2). Now the time has come to protest . . . against 'rebalech' [inconsequential rabbis] who come to flatter the government and rely on selected flowery phrases to rule in favor of obeying the government and to approve a prohibition that is against Halacha. (Shapira in Shochetman, 1995: 67–68)

Rabbi Shapira uses the mocking term "rebalech" a number of times against religious Zionist rabbis who do not seem to him to be Poskim of the first order. In our case, the denigration is aimed at the distinction made by Rabbi Aviner between a personal sin and participation in the evacuation of a settlement which is a government sin and not one of a soldier who executes its directive. Rabbi Shapira believes that this distinction is hollow casuistry and excoriates it. A sin is a sin is a sin and no excuses can change that.

2. The current government is a religion-transgressing government.

A number of laws have been passed by the Knesset with which the Rabbis (*Chachamim*) are unhappy but they did not coerce a Jew to transgress his religion and his will . . . But this time they have upset the balance and the government is comprised of people some of whom have no faith in the Torah in Scripture and in the Land of Israel as their heritage for generations; they write that Yehoshua Bin Nun [the

biblical Joshua] was a fascist and that his story should
be excised from Scripture; they deeply injure the unity
of the nation. (Shapira in Shochetman, 1995: 69)

3. The government and Knesset have no authority to renounce
parts of the Land of Israel.

> According to Halacha there is no one who is autho-
> rized to relinquish the holy assets of Israel, not parts
> of the Torah and not parts of the Land of Israel,
> following the well-known words of the Rabbi, the
> genius, Menachem Zamba, may God avenge his blood.
> [He perished in the Holocaust. Rabbi Shapira is refer-
> ring to the decision of the Haredi Council of Torah
> Sages of Agudat Yisrael in 1937 that prohibits ceding
> parts of the Land of Israel.] Even the entire Knesset
> cannot so relinquish—all the more so a temporary
> government that lasts four years that relies on Arab
> representatives cannot cede something that belongs
> to all of Israel for generations. Such a renunciation
> is not valid and what is done by the illegal use of
> force, pressure and extortion, any time that it can
> be cancelled, it is a Mitzvah to cancel it. (Shapira
> in Shochetman, 1995: 69–70)

Part of Rabbi Shapira's judgments derives from his patent distrust of the
Palestinians, specifically Yasser Arafat. *Prime facie* one might suppose that
were this suspicion allayed, disobedience would not be mandatory and
making concessions for the sake of peace would be halachically permitted.
This, of course, is not the case. One must distinguish between the heart of
Rabbi Shapira's argument that rests upon the absolute obligation to retain
the Land of Israel and the ancillary rhetoric that provides it with added
cogency. Much the same can be said for the next paragraph.

4. Saving lives and ceding territories: Only military experts can
decide.

> The only justification for ceding territory in the Land
> of Israel is when military experts clearly determine
> that it is strategically impossible to defend the place
> and the lives of the Jews that reside there. And if we
> do not retreat from there soldiers' blood be spilled in

vain. In such a case, it is forbidden to spill blood in vain and it is necessary to retreat . . . Considerations such as these in the matter of saving lives are given only to the judgment of military people and experts in strategic matters in the same way that in the matter of the dangerously ill, the judgment is only according to the consideration of doctors expert in medicine which is a scientific, objective profession. On the other hand, diplomatic considerations that are not, as is well known, objective and scientific, are all based on personal speculations that are always bound up with previous assumptions, with personal temperament, with biased concerns . . . In our case, the statesmen are aware of the fact that this [retreat] constitutes a military danger, but in their view it is worth taking the risk; their hearts tell them it will be good, and they truly want it to be good. But the rationale 'it is worth taking the risk' is in no way a reason to permit the forbidden and to endanger souls. (Shapira in Shochetman, 1995: 70)

5.   There is a real security danger in retreat from Judea, Samaria, Gaza, and the Golan Heights.

If, forbid it, it [Israeli retreat] should take place . . . then all [Israel's] neighbors . . . will join the haters of Israel because they too are haters of Israel . . . This is so in the case of the Golan where everyone sees the terrible danger involved in the removal of settlements and tanks. And the same is relevant for the evacuation of Judea and Samaria and the retreat of the IDF and transferring the territory to the armed military of the PLO. This is no saving of lives but the reverse—the endangering of life. For it is clear that after a few years when they become strong, they will become a terrible danger to the area near them and especially since we have heard in a recording the view of the head of the PLO to fight Israel as Mohamed did his opponents a year after he made peace with them. This peace is a false peace and not a true peace. (Shapira in Shochetman, 1995: 70–71)

True peace is of great value but it must be genuine and durable. At least a generation must pass in which the hatred for the Jews ceases and the state's security is preserved, which can only happen when a Jewish army controls all of the Land of Israel, even if local autonomy can be accepted. This, Rabbi Shapira contends, is surely not what has happened since the Oslo Accords were signed—on the contrary, bloodshed has only intensified (Shapira in Shochetman, 1995: 72–73).

Rabbi Shlomo Goren, the IDF's Chief Rabbi and, subsequently, the Chief Rabbi of Israel is another central figure who pressed for disobedience when withdrawal from the Land of Israel was proposed. Few are the religious Zionist Poskim who compare with him either in learning and stature or in his willingness to make bold and controversial rulings. For religious Zionism, he was the most important figure located at the interface between the army, religious practice and the public sphere. (His book *Mayshiv Milchama* (Fighting Back but also translatable as Answering Questions about War) is the foundational religious text on civil-military relations in Israel). Although in his teaching and actions he was the most outstanding symbol of Mamlachtiut, when it came to evacuations from the Land of Israel he became a leading voice in the anti-Mamlachti camp. His demand that religious soldiers disobey orders when evacuation was at stake was repeated regularly and tenaciously. In his essay "Disobeying orders" he writes:

> It is clear that a soldier who receives an order that is in opposition to the laws of the Torah must observe the Halacha of the Torah and not the secular command . . . One must not obey a military command that violates the Torah; it is clear that the Mitzvah to settle the land is a weighty one—equal in importance to all the other Mitzvot combined . . . [Moreover] the prohibition of *Lo Techanem* (Deuteronomy 7:1–2) forbids giving [Gentiles] a foothold in the land . . . And in our case, evacuating settlements from Judea and Samaria means giving the soil over to Arab settlements, which is a compounded sin; it is certain that a soldier should not be forced to transgress a number of severe sins whose origin is in the Torah itself.
>
> An additional answer in this regard [disobeying evacuation orders] is that this government is not based on a Jewish majority, but rather on Arab voices that according to Halacha do not possess the legitimacy of a majority; therefore the government's directive to evacuate Jewish settlements does not have the validity and authority of a majority of the people. In this light it is clear that soldiers must disobey orders to evacuate settlements from

the Land of Israel that contradict the Mitzvot of the Torah about which the Sages said 'The words of the rabbi and the words of the student, heed the words of the rabbi.' (Goren, 1994: 1–2)

Rabbi Goren's reasoning is identical with that of the rabbis mentioned above: Halacha overrules state law. Still, it is important to caution that as opposed to the ruling of Rabbi Shapira, Rabbi Goren does not base his argument on security concerns. (Perhaps after a life in the army he was aware of how complex security considerations could be). Moreover, he does not appeal to the leaders of the army to show sensitivity to the soldier's Jewish/moral conscience or to respect the freedom of religion in the spirit of liberal democracy. In the end, Rabbi Goren bases his position on the simple proposition that Halacha is superior to state law.

A number of other rabbis took part in the "discourse of disobedience" as well; lesser lights perhaps than Rabbis Shapira and Goren but their influence on the ground was arguably greater than the more prominent figures and as such deserve our attention. One such figure was Rabbi Zalman Melamed. Before dealing directly with his views on disobedience, it is enlightening to examine an earlier essay of his entitled "Torah judgments in political matters" (October 1992). In this essay, Rabbi Melamed, basing himself on the arguments of Rabbi Tzvi Yehuda Kook, contends that Rabbis not only can but are required to intervene in political issues; if they do not, they abuse their religious authority.

The Torah encompasses and illuminates all of reality and instructs us in all areas of life. There is nothing in reality that is outside the instructive power of the Torah . . . And if in private individual matters there is comprehensive instruction, *a fortiori* in affairs that involve the whole Jewish people, the entire nation. It is therefore the responsibility of every learned student of Torah and every rabbi in Israel, to express the judgment of Torah and to instruct the public according to the Torah, and it is forbidden for him to shrink back from making his voice heard even if it arouses opposition. On this subject the Torah said: 'You shall not fear anyone.' Matters relating to settlements in the Land of Israel and the rule of the people of Israel over all of the Land of Israel are absolutely Torah matters and every rabbi ought to act in order to exert influence so that the Torah commandment 'You shall possess it and live in it' (Deuteronomy 11: 31) will be fulfilled. (Z. Melamed, 1998: 1–2)

Like his mentor. Rabbi Tzvi Yehuda, Rabbi Melamed is an ardent Jewish "particularist," that is, very different from universalistic Western conceptions of liberal democracy. If liberal themes do enter his worldview at all, it is only by the back door and in a very conditional way. In an essay entitled "The limits of democracy" (June 1993), he asserts that he is no democrat if it involves "blurring the borders between Israel and the world" or if it entails a "Jewish-Arab coalition" that "overwhelms a Jewish majority." Indeed, liberal democracy constitutes the most serious danger to the existence of the people of Israel." It is "viper-poison that percolates and destroys the very core of the nation."

> If pluralism means giving full legitimacy to mentally and spiritually diseased perversions and to the complete freedom of ideas and opinions for everyone, without striving to preserve and build what is unique to us as the people of Israel, the barrier not only to assimilation is breached but also to religious conversion . . . There is definitely a place for the striving to liberty, personal freedom, democracy, but not for democracy that cancels Jewish national existence. There is definitely a place for respecting each person whoever he may be and every creature that God created in the world but we must not blur the distinctions between the ranks. 'Man is beloved because he was created in the Image.' But above this there is another rank, a second story: 'Beloved are Israel, for they are called children of God; even greater love is bestowed upon them that they are called children of God' (Ethics of the Fathers 4: 14). (Z. Melamed, 1998: 29–30)

On the subject of disobedience, Rabbi Melamed could not be clearer. Like Rabbis Shapira and Goren he insists that a democratic state is entirely subject to the Torah. Therefore, fighting against fragmenting the Land of Israel—a profound religious transgression—is no different than struggling against a government that would prohibit Sabbath observance or circumcision. "The struggle for the Land of Israel is a Torah-based struggle and it is remarkable that there are religious people, students of Torah who do not join the struggle" (Z. Melamed, 1998: 35–36). For the religious community "loyalty to the Torah and Mitzvot is absolute" overriding "every other national-Mamlachti responsibility." He reports "that I teach [students to] disobey orders to evacuate Jewish settlements in the land according to the religion and Torah of Israel that obligates us to disobey. But, do not worry; I believe that there will never be an army order that is opposed to the Torah (Z. Melamed, 1998: 88–89). Rabbi Melamed concludes in a way that reflects the deep dilemma of religious Zionism drawn taut between the sanctity of the state and Torah law:

> The instruction of the major rabbis to disobey an order to evacuate Jewish settlements derives precisely from recognizing the value of a Jewish State, the State of Israel . . . They see the State of Israel as a spiritual and religious value. Its reality is sanctifying God as opposed to the Diaspora which is in the state of profanation of God. Precisely because of the view that values and loves the land and its army, precisely for that reason, the rabbis instructed disobeying the order to evacuate Jews from their homes, if, forbid it, an illegal order of this kind is given. After all, the power behind the existence of the Jewish State in the Land of Israel derives from the exclusive right of the people of Israel over the Land of Israel. The right was given to us by the Lord our God, creator of the world and its ruler and every action that harms this right weakens the very basis upon which the state rests. Evacuation of Jewish settlements entails the recognition that our living in this place is allegedly unjust, and such recognition undermines the basis of our claim to have a right to our land. Therefore, anyone who opposes such an order, anyone who refuses it, it is he who is loyal to the state and to the people, he is the person of law and justice, and anyone who, forbid it, allows it to cross his mind to evacuate Jewish settlements in the Land of Israel, he inflicts a mortal wound on the existence of the state. (Z. Melamed, 1998: 107–08)

These arguments with their unconditional, unqualified rhetoric provide a genuine sense of how the struggle over the Land of Israel became, for its advocates, a non-negotiable issue. If the right to the Land is absolute and exclusive, any retreat whatever involves the admission that the Jewish right to Israel exists in a world of competing rights, that there is justice to other claims as well. And if the principle of exclusivity is breached, the very belief in the Divine provenance of Israel's territorial rights is in jeopardy.

Rabbi Melamed's adversaries—some of them part of the religious Zionist camp—reject the parallel he draws between the outlawing of circumcision and the retreat from territories. While criminalizing circumcision is absolutely clear and unmistakable—there are no gray areas—evacuating land is not an all or nothing affair; it is obviously a far more complex issue. There are important differences between Poskim on the subject: what counts as the Land of Israel is contentious; considerations of geopolitical realities inevitably intrude and *Pikuach nefesh* (saving lives) must be factored into the equation. The argument in favor of an historical compromise as a prudential solution to a potentially deadly all-out war cannot be categorically rejected even by those who remain loyal to the holiness of the land.

Although he has little sympathy for liberal democracy, Rabbi Zalman Melamed, nevertheless, appeals to democratic arguments to undergird his position and, with the passage of time, this line of argument became increasingly dominant in his discourse. For example, in January 1995 he said:

> An order to evict a Jewish settlement in the Land of Israel is illegal, inhuman, against the Torah and lacking validity. The people will not accept it and a democratic government cannot coerce it on the people in opposition to its conscience and its basic principles. In a healthy democratic regime, there is a freedom to criticize; this is good, desirable and necessary in today's reality and does not oppose the laws of the Kingdom of Israel. (Z. Melamed, 1998: 163)

Another prominent rabbinic figure who lent his voice to the chorus advocating disobedience was Rabbi Nachum Eliezer Rabinovitch whom we came across in our discussion of the Rodef issue above. Following the rabbinic ruling that forbad the evacuation of military bases in Yesha, he presented his reasoned position in the journal of the Yesha rabbis in September 1995. In his view, the decision as to whether or not to return territories is not one for military experts to decide. The reality is clear and unambiguous—every retreat from territory will create dangers for the State of Israel.

> When the issue is the IDF's leaving and abandoning territory, it is clear as the sun at noon that there is a clear and present danger for thousands of Jews and there is no reason to assign such a decision to experts. And even were the opinions of all the experts unanimous that this political step would lead to saving lives in the long run—even in such a case it is only an opinion of uncertain status; how much more true is this when the military experts are divided in their views. Uncertain long-term doubt is trumped by certain immediate danger. (Rabinowitz, 1995: 1–2)

Not surprisingly, the most methodical and inclusive essay about the obligation to settle the Land of Israel and the prohibition of evacuating or participating in dismantling settlements was written during the deeply conflicted period of the Oslo process. It was entitled *Confirmed for Jacob as a Law* (*Va'yamedah leYaacov lechok*) (Psalms 105:10) and was written not by a rabbi but by an academic, Professor Eliav Shochetman, later an Israel Prize laureate in Jewish Law. This study was deeply influenced by the teachings of Rabbi Avraham Shapira who affixed his seal of approval to the book and added his own supporting comments. Shochetman's arguments are perhaps the most comprehensive formulation of the religious case against evacuation that exists. Careful perusal of his wide-ranging, systematic and learned treatise will reward the reader who wishes to comprehend religious anti-evacuation sentiments in all their breadth and depth. Nevertheless, many of these contentions have already been presented in our dealings with Rabbis Shapira, Goren, Z. Melamed, E. Melamed, Rabinovitz, Aviner, and the Yesha Rabbinical Council (not to speak of all the others mentioned in earlier chapters) and it would be tedious to repeat them once again. Nevertheless, some of the arguments raised by Shochetman, especially those related to the democratic aspect of disobedience and settlements, were to be of great consequence in the years to come. Notably, they attempt to address the secular world's democratic concerns as no other text does. In essence, Shochetman rejects Christian duality between religion and state insisting that halachic authorities and Jewish law ought to be central in shaping Israel's public life (Shochetman, 1995: 76–83). Even at the risk of some repetition, a condensed analysis and critique of the most important elements in this multifaceted work is mandatory.

1. Unless the people of Israel are substantially threatened by an overwhelming loss of life, retreat from the Land of Israel is impermissible (Shochetman, 1995: 15–46).

2. All the halachic justifications for obedience to the state do not hold when the evacuation of settlements is at stake (Shochetman, 1990–1991; Shochetman, 1995: 47–54). Three such justifications exist in halachic literature: a king's decree; the law of the land and the validity of community ordinances.

   Even if the Knesset is regarded as a latter-day king (as argued by Rabbi Kook the father) the dominant halachic authorities (Maimonides and Rabbi Nissim Ben Reuven Girondi (known as the "Ran") 1320–80) disallow obeying a king's law that contravenes Halacha. Arguments based on the putative "public good" do not prevail against halachic imperatives. Halachists ought to decide on the basis of Halacha, not ancillary considerations.

But Shochetman's adversaries argue that an exclusively Halacha-centered focus ignores other critical considerations. Even if evacuation has religious repercussions, deciding on borders and on where to settle are inalienable elements of state sovereignty. Public order could not be maintained without them. Lacking these powers the state would collapse into anarchy. Moreover, granting a veto power to the rabbis raises the inevitable question of "which rabbis"? Rabbis differ on the subject of retreat and Shochetman chooses to empower those rabbis who support the settler's position.

If "the law of the land is the law" (*Dinah de'malchuta dinah*) then, prime facie, Knesset laws ought to be obeyed. This dictum, Shochetman claims, is inapplicable in our case. It applies to laws of a non-Jewish regime whose civil statutes, although not based on Halacha, do not coerce Jews to violate Torah law. In such cases obedience is the rule. However, when coerced by a non-Jewish regime to violate Halacha, Jews must refuse to obey. All the more so when a Jewish regime that is obligated by Jewish law demands sinful behavior.

Shochetman's critics are not convinced. Maimonides does indeed prohibit obeying a halachically errant government. But his position is more complex. To wit: in close proximity to this oft-cited prohibition, Maimonides declares that a king of Israel may, in clear violation of Torah law, execute a murderer on the basis of one witness's testimony (Halacha insists on two) and to publically display his body for many days (another violation of Torah law) in order to create deterrence. This is justified on the grounds of the state's needs. Clearly, if public welfare is involved, broad autonomy is granted to the sovereign Jewish state, even if it entails acting against halachic norms. And once again the question may be asked: is retreat a state need; does it serve the public welfare? Who decides?

Major halachic decisors attributed great weight to the authority of medieval communal ordinances in the public sphere (e.g., Rabbi Shlomo ben Aderet, known as the Rashba, 1235–1310) even when they were at variance with accepted halachic norms. It could be argued that Knesset legislation enjoys similar latitude. Shochetman rejects this claim. Public ordinances apply only to certain civil issues (e.g., finances); they cannot set aside halachic imperatives such as settling the land. Halacha must be determined by halachists.

But here again, critics argue, the issue is more complex. The greatest halachic adjudicator in thirteenth-century Spain, the Rashba, ruled that in questions of the public welfare, even those involving religious law, elected communal authorities or a communal assembly may pass ordinances that do not accord with halachic norms (Elon, 1994: chapter 19).

3. Although the imperative to lay down one's life rather than sin applies only to idolatry, incest and murder, in times of forced conversions and religious persecution it applies to all Mitzvot (Maimonides, Mishneh Torah, Laws on the Fundamentals of Torah, chapter 5, Halacha 3). Shochetman contends that persecutory edicts include those originating from Jewish authorities, such as in the case of forced evacuation (Shochetman, 1995: 54–56).

4. Since the state's sovereignty over the Land of Israel is halachically mandated, retreating from it is violates a religious prohibition and, therefore, it is rightfully resisted. This principle, he declares is the "life's blood of our democratic regime." Resisting evacuation is therefore tantamount to resisting religious coercion (Shochetman, 1995: 58–59).

The counter-argument raised against Shocheman is that he ignores the distinction between an order given to an individual soldier to violate the Sabbath and a government decision to evacuate settlements, which is not a personal issue but a right that inheres in a sovereign state. If the state cannot command religious soldiers in matters of geo-politics, it forfeits its sovereignty. Religious freedom, in such cases, is not a relevant consideration.

5. As a Jewish and democratic state, evacuation of settlements is unacceptable. This is so because:

A. The settlers acted lawfully in setting up settlements; they were even encouraged to do so by the government. They fulfilled the Zionist imperatives of settling the land and defending the country's security. Expelling them from their homes is a grievous blow against the values of the state and their basic rights.

B. Evacuation violates the Basic Law: Human Dignity and Freedom according to which "the life, body and honor of a person, qua person, are not to be harmed" and "the property of a person is not to be harmed." Forcibly evicting settlers who fulfilled a national mission and acted lawfully is "a gross violation of the right of a person not to be harmed in his body, his honor and his property."

C. "Transfer" of Arabs is broadly rejected as anti-democratic and as violating basic human rights. "Is it possible that an act that is thought to be improper will be considered valid when Jews are involved?" (Shocheteman, 1995: 11013). (In the heat of argument Shochetman employs the heavily laden term "Judenrein" to describe a territory from which Jews have been expelled (Shochetman, 1995: 124). He concludes that "if the act of expelling Jews from their homes is, in fact, against the laws of the State of Israel, there is no obligation on the part of soldiers to obey such an order" (Shochetman, 1995: 113).

Shochetman's arguments were quite influential, especially those that were grounded in democratic principles (numbers 4 and 5 above). As we shall see in the next chapter, these claims became central to religious Zionist discourse during the "disengagement" from Gush Katif/the Gaza Strip in 2005 and continue to be heard a decade later.

Shochetman's opponents reject his reliance on democratic principles. First, if Western democracy is his standard, it is odd that he should ignore the unanimous Western democratic objections to the settlement project as a whole. The democratic world insists that settlements violate universal conceptions of justice and are prohibited by international law. Indeed, their removal is thought to be a democratic necessity, a condition for Israel's remaining a liberal democratic state.

Moreover, they maintain that there is a profound difference between civil disobedience against discrimination based upon universal democratic norms—as was the case with Martin Luther King's struggle against racial segregation—and the narrowly partisan disobedience of a minority who support settler ideology and demand a privileged status for their views and program.

Besides, the argument that the government encouraged the settlers to settle and hence is prohibited from evacuating them is seen by his critics as containing an inherent contradiction. If the sovereign state has the right to establish settlements then, by the same token, it has the right to evacuate them—traumatic though it may be. If the government sees evacuation as necessary for the public good or for geo-political and strategic reasons, it is entirely within its rights to implement such a policy. Compensating the settlers for their loss may be necessary, but the right of a democratically elected government to revise its policy in the light of new political realities is utterly basic. It is the heart of prescient diplomacy. To reject this state prerogative is to subvert its sovereign democratic character.

Moreover, they continue, the claim that evacuation is a form of "transfer" or "ethnic cleansing" is an unsustainable argument. Expelling Arabs from the State of Israel and depriving them of their citizenship is properly dubbed "transfer." By contrast, deciding on the country's borders and returning the settlers, as full citizens, to within these borders is the prerogative of a sovereign state.

Similarly, the contention that evacuation violates personal freedoms and property rights has no relevance when vital strategic and national interests are involved. If a democratic state can forcibly draft individuals to fight in a war of which they may not approve and in which they may be killed, then it certainly has the right to evacuate citizens if it believes that its critical interests and security needs are at stake. If the elected leaders of the state make such a judgment, its legitimacy—even if settler rights are compromised—cannot be gainsaid.

Finally, opponents point out that evacuations do not leave the settlers behind rendering them vulnerable to the depredations of a hostile population. When it withdraws from territories, Israel withdraws its settlers as well. Were setters abandoned defenseless in a hostile environment, this would indeed constitute a violation of Jewish tradition, Jewish solidarity, and Jewish law.

The Varieties of Nonviolent Civil Disobedience

The call for bolder but still nonviolent disobedience was led by Elyakim Ha'etzni, a resident of Kiryat Arba and one of the founders of the settlement project. He was among the earliest right-wing intellectuals to justify soldiers disobeying orders. Although closely allied with the radical religious Right, Ha'etzni himself is not an observant Jew. In his essay "From a defending army to an abandoning army" published (February 1994) in the settler journal Nekuda, Ha'etzni writes:

Refusing to obey an order to uproot a Jewish settlement and to expel its residents is not illegal. On the contrary, it is executing an order such as this that is clearly illegal—here is the true trans-gression and a soldier who obeys is liable to stand trial . . . It is prohibited to blow up the home of a terrorist-murderer without a special law, and a Jewish house, yes? We do not yet have a 'law for the uprooting of Jewish settlements, the destruction of their homes and the expulsion of their inhabitants' and even if it did exist, it is doubtful that even then it would be legal. Therefore, he who 'educates' soldiers to uproot Jewish settlements, to commit the crime of 'transfer' against their own people—it is he who incites to violate the law. (Ha'etzni, 1994a: 24)

Soon thereafter, in another article in Nekuda (September 1994) entitled "Civil disobedience now," Ha'etzni intensifies his argument. He dramatically called for a nationwide movement of civil disobedience. Although it is not a call for armed insurrection, Ha'eztni refuses to be satisfied with the mere refusal to obey orders. One need not read between the lines to grasp that when he compares Rabin to Pétain his objective is to thoroughly delegitimize Israel's democratic process, to declare "open season" on Rabin's leadership and (perhaps) his life and to encourage more than passive resistance. Comparing a democratically elected Prime Minister to a Nazi puppet leaves little to the imagination.

For Ha'etzni, passive resistance is no longer sufficient; he insists that the enemies of Rabin and his government need to up the ante on civil disobedience. A strategy of active confrontation with the authorities is required although he adds that, hopefully, bloodshed will be avoided.

In defeated France of 1940, when Marshall Pétain capitulated to Hitler and, afterwards, concluded a treaty with him—just as General Rabin shook the contaminated hand of Arafat—General de Gaulle did not "protest" or object. He defected from active service and rebelled against the regime that collaborated with the Nazis, even though this regime was born in a democratic process. All the more so in our case: Israel was not defeated, certainly not by Arafat, whom it lifted up from the sewers. Moreover: Hitler did not plot to destroy the French people, while destroying us is the life's blood of the charter of the 'Palestine Liberation Organization,' a charter it refuses to rescind . . . We present the following question to ourselves: what are the legal and moral limits to the policies that a democratic majority may impose upon the minority? Where is the boundary of resistance that a minority is permitted to draw against a democratic major-ity that wishes to bring a holocaust (Shoah) upon its homes, its cities, its towns? . . . For this too is among the main principles of democracy: protection of the minority against the despotism of the majority as well as marking those areas over which even the majority has no authority . . . Let us then sum up: uprooting of settlements and turning their residents into refugees not in the heat of battle or as a consequence of it is an absolute crime. A government that does this to its people commits a national crime . . .

Therefore I say here without reservation: An IDF soldier, also as a Jew, if he drags us, our wives, our children and our grandchildren from our homes in order to destroy them and turn us into refugees—in our eyes this is a pogrom and we will see him as a violent rioter performing a Cossack deed . . . We will speak to the soldiers, our brothers, we will call to them from the depth of our hearts to refuse to obey all commands that will transform them into our enemies. But to those who do not heed our cry we will use reasonable opposing force and we will not allow them to hypocritically bandy about talk of 'civil war' . . . To the best of our ability we will behave toward those who come to hurt us—in the same coin. If they come to drag us with their hands—we will protect ourselves with our hands. If they use other forms of force, we will reply with an active defense but we will not carry arms and we will not spill blood. (Ha'etzni, 1994b: 27–28)

A far more moderate variation on the theme of civil disobedience was voiced by Yisrael Medad, a right-wing journalist and resident of the *Shilo* settlement. Although he too advocated widespread civil disobedience and called upon the settler community to publicly disobey the law *en masse* so that it would be impossible for the government to carry out its policies, Medad's heroes are the democratic, nonviolent, passive resistors and not the delegitimizing active confronters. Nekuda (May 1994) published his political credo:

We should learn from the civil struggles of Martin Luther King and others. The leaders must be prepared to be imprisoned, which only contributes to their leadership . . . This should be done non-violently and not by calling Rabin a murderer and a traitor . . . It should be understood that a non-violent struggle is intended to attack the source of the political strength of the government, not its legal authority. And nevertheless, the struggle must deprive the government of the option of carrying out a policy that opposes the very foundation of the state as a Zionist entity that represents the Jewish people, which incarnates its beliefs, its traditions and the will of thousands of years of history in which the Jewish people sought to renew its political liberty. (Medad, 1994: 50)

Arguably the most publically visible force dedicated to nonviolent civil disobedience was the Zo Artzenu (This is our land) movement. Set up because of what they saw as the disappointingly lukewarm struggle conducted by the Yesha Council against government policy, Zo Artzenu activists blocked many major transportation arteries at critical traffic hours throughout the entire country. Led by Moshe Feiglin from the Likud's extreme right-wing and religious Zionist allies, Zo Artzenu activists publicly declared their willingness to be imprisoned for these actions—in the spirit of Gandhi and Martin Luther King. On August 9, 1995, Zo Artzenu blocked seventy-eight different intersections at the same time, effectively shutting down the country for a few hours. Feiglin claimed that seized by fear, the government panicked and ordered the police to employ extreme violence against the protesters (Feiglin, 1998: 122). More moderate than Ha'etzni but more militant than Medad, Feiglin understood his strategy as lying well within the venerable tradition of civil disobedience as practiced in liberal Western democracies. Here at least, messianic motives are not an overt part of his terminology. He declares:

It is clear to every sane person that there is a boundary to obedience and that the dry law is liable to become a vehicle of evil in the hands of an immoral government. The question is certainly not if 'there is a boundary' (Yesh gvul) to obedience: the question is where the boundary passes, and, if we are forced to break the law, what is the right way to do so without shattering the foundations of society. It was absolutely clear to us that in the State of Israel this boundary was passed long ago . . . How then to violate the law and yet not 'throw out the baby with the bath water'? That is, how will we avoid anarchy?

Three principles guided us in our actions: no use of violence, either physical or verbal; an effort to reduce to a minimum the danger of injury liable to be caused by our actions, and the full willingness to pay the price that the courts impose upon us. This willingness is very important because it means that we respect the law and do not attempt to evade it; on the contrary, we humbly accept the consequences of our actions according to the law that we openly violated. A rebel will be punished for his action if he fails. As opposed to the rebel, one who resorts to civil disobedience will be punished in any event; even if the government is replaced (which was in fact what happened in our case). (Feiglin, 1998: 97)

Although it is questionable if Western liberal democrats would accept Feiglin's claim that he acted as a committed democrat his argument deserves our attention:

Large publics that are no longer able to tolerate extreme governmental injustice and are prepared to passively transgress the law while paying the price involved, point to the radical injustice that an insensitive government is visiting upon its citizens. The widespread outbreak of civil disobedience provides an excellent test for the democratic character of the government . . . An entire community that turns to the streets in a restrained way (as opposed to a mob) prepared to violate the law and pay the price, must set off a red light in every democratic government. A light that cries out in giant letters: you have broken the rules—not the formal rules but more important rules, the foundational grounds upon which the national values are based. A government that ignores such a protest—even if the law is on its side—cannot pride itself with the title 'democratic.' (Feiglin, 1998: 97)

Nevertheless, Feiglin is fully cognizant of the "slippery slope" that his arguments can invite. To this he responds:

The clear line that is drawn between the proper preservation of law and order and, on the other hand, the rare but vital necessity to violate it under certain circumstances, allows the existence and strengthening of two principles simultaneously: the principle of obeying the law and the principle of morality. It is today accepted that in all the Western democratic countries where civil disobedience has broken out, this disobedience has advanced the cause of the rule of law and of democracy . . . and prevented severe moral distortions that had spread in their institutions. What is at stake is a balancing instrument that is of unparalleled importance against the callousness of the authorities, an instrument that has always benefited states that accepted it and has never led to anarchy. (Feiglin, 1998: 99)

Despite the differences between Feiglin's ostensibly liberal democratic discourse and the religious-messianic claims of the radical Zionist rabbis, Zo Artzenu's activities won the support of the Council of Yesha Rabbis. In a special declaration the Yesha Rabbis voiced support for the struggle of the Zo Artzenu movement "that has succeeded in expressing broad public protest against the minority government and calls upon the public to participate in its activities" (The Association of Yesha Rabbis, 1995).

Nonetheless, many in the more moderate camp opposed blocking roads, pointing to the serious damage it can potentially cause. Drivers stuck in traffic for hours, especially if they are in poor health, can lead to calamitous results—not to speak of blocked ambulances, fire trucks, police cars, etc. Moreover, Zo Artzenu's protestations of being a disciplined and responsible group did not always live up the test. In demonstrations that it organized there was frequent incitement against the government and demonization of Prime Minister Rabin as an individual.

Feiglin's use of liberal democratic theory in order to justify civil disobedience renders his position accessible to those for whom religious arguments are remote if not entirely irrelevant. To be sure, this kind of democratic argumentation is tangential to the mainstream of disobedience discourse which was theological, halachic, Zionist, and security-based, but it did win some hearts and minds in the religious Zionist community. Indeed, it became a staple of religious Zionist rhetoric when, a decade later, Sharon's "disengagement" plan triggered another fierce struggle between the government and the religious Zionist camp.

4

The "Disengagement" from Gaza/Gush Katif (2005)

Introduction

For the decade following Rabin's assassination until Ariel Sharon announced his plan to "disengage" from Gaza/Gush Katif and from a number of settlements in northern Samaria (2005), a tense calm prevailed between religious Zionism and the state's institutions. Perhaps nowhere else in Israeli society was the murder of Rabin as traumatic as in the religious Zionist community; first because it was widely charged with having created the atmosphere in which such an unprecedented act could take place, and second because, inevitably, many in its ranks felt that they could not blithely dismiss the charge. The harsh criticism directed against them by large parts of Israel's citizenry—especially from the Center and the Left—led the religious Zionist leadership to rethink the boundaries of political protest as well as their commitment to the rule of law.

Indeed, in the wake of the assassination, a series of initiatives to strengthen dialogue between the religious and secular camps proliferated; not infrequently, these meetings were more heavily attended by religious than by secular participants. These were also the years in which a movement among secular, often left-wing Israeli Jews to return to the "Jewish bookshelf" (the canonical works of the Jewish tradition) thrived. In an attempt to challenge the Orthodox religious monopoly on Jewish sources, secular study groups, seminars, and conferences were organized and institutionalized. This too helped mitigate the gaping chasm that had opened up since that fateful evening in November 1995 (Sheleg, 2000: chapter 4).

In political terms, the Prime Ministers who served after Rabin's murder: Shimon Peres 1995–1996, Binyamin Netanyahu 1996–1999, Ehud Barak (1999–2001) and Ariel Sharon (2001–2005), did not initiate major policy changes—apart from the one-sided retreat from Lebanon presided over by Prime Minister Ehud Barak in 2000. Barak even conducted advanced negotiations with the Syrians on the future of the Golan Heights and with the Palestinians on a peace agreement regarding the future of Yesha/the West Bank and the establishment of a Palestinian state. But in both cases the negotiations ended in failure: in Shepherdstown with the Syrians and in Camp David—actively presided over by President Bill Clinton—with the Palestinians. In the Palestinian case, Barak succeeded in convincing most of the Israeli public that Arafat's lack of political will to enter into a conflict-resolving agreement was the cause of the negotiation's failure. Although less explicit, President Clinton echoed Barak's assessment. The sense that the Palestinian negotiating position was merely tactical rather than authentically strategic precipitated a surge to the political Right in Israeli public opinion.

The Al-Aqsa (second) Intifada that broke out soon after the failure of the Camp David meetings in 2000 led, in short order, to another especially violent struggle between Israel and the Palestinians—including a bloody confrontation with Israeli Arabs—that resisted solution even after Barak expressed willingness to make additional concessions in the context of Clinton's initiatives. This struggle continued, becoming even more violent after Barak's very poor showing in the 2001 elections and the rise of Ariel Sharon to the office of Prime Minister. Between the years of 2001 through 2005, the Intifada resulted in the death of more than 1,000 Israelis in numerous suicide attacks and, on the other side, more than 3,000 Palestinians were killed by IDF fire. At the height of the violence in mid-2002, Ariel Sharon instructed the IDF to recapture the cities of Judea and Samaria/the West Bank under Palestinian control in a campaign dubbed "Defensive Shield." Militarily, the campaign achieved its aims; the cities were retaken and the Intifada-related attacks and fatalities dropped by roughly half, even if the Israeli objective of breaking the back of Palestinian resistance remained elusive. Once again, public opinion gravitated to the Right. Presciently foretelling the tale of many subsequent Israeli-Palestinian clashes, the Chief of Staff Moshe Ya'alon commented: "in their story they won, in our story we won" (Shelach and Drucker, 2005: 403).

The weakening of the terror infrastructure in Judea and Samaria succeeded in substantially reducing violence for some years to come. Moreover, the pragmatic approach of Abu Mazen (Mahmoud Abbas) Arafat's successor and his coterie of colleagues led to security cooperation between the Palestinian Authority and Israel—it was in both of their interests to prevent terror attacks. Many conceived of these developments as proof positive that Sharon's tough military reaction to the Intifada had been vindicated and that Israel had emerged victorious from the second Intifada.

Moreover, the many terrorist attacks against innocent civilians had the effect of strengthening Israel's internal unity, of creating a sense of solidarity between Left and Right, between religious and secular. In the religious Zionist community this relative calm provided confirmation that national steadfastness, both in terms of morale and of military power, was the key to success. Expanding the settlements in Yesha, they believed, would serve both purposes. National unity however, took precedence over provocative settlement activity. Not surprisingly, clashes between the religious Zionist community and the state's authorities abated substantially.

This relative calm ended abruptly when Ariel Sharon announced his "disengagement" initiative in 2004. Sharon's plan was to evacuate all of Gush Katif/Gaza (twenty-one settlements in all with about 8,000 residents) as well as four settlements in northern Samaria. Many theories accounting for the disengagement initiative have been proposed. Some believe that the plan was born of Sharon's fear that the vacuum created in the absence of an Israeli peace plan would lead to the renewal of Palestinian violence. In a similar spirit, it was argued that among Sharon's associates ("the ranch forum"—after Sharon's ranch) the dominant attitude was that there was no political "horizon" apart from a unilateral separation from the Palestinians (Waxman, 2008). Others pointed to the rival "Geneva Initiative" presented by left-wing leaders together with central Palestinian figures. Moreover, it was argued that Gush Katif, surrounded by more than a million hostile Palestinians, was not a viable affair. It required too many military resources to defend and would only come under increasing Palestinian pressure in the future. For the more skeptical, it was alleged that the initiative grew out of ongoing investigations into serious criminal acts of which Sharon was suspected. A major political initiative—in this view—would distract attention from Sharon's legal imbroglio (Shelach and Drucker, 2005: chapter 26).

Sharon was a national hero for the Center, the Right, and the religious Zionists. As a Likud stalwart and Minister of Agriculture in the late 1970s, he was the dominant force in energizing the settlement project and was known as "the father of the settlements." His policy of brooking no opposition to his settlement policies earned him the nickname "the bulldozer," and together with his allies in the former Gush Emunim they changed the demographic and geographic face of the West Bank. His reputation as a bold military powerhouse—especially his part in the commando unit 101 in 1953 and the retaking the Suez Canal in the Yom Kippur war two decades later—lent him an almost mythological status among many Israelis, the settlers among them. (Although his reputation was badly tarnished in the Lebanese Sabra and Shatila affair, among those in his camp he remained the *ne plus ultra* of military valor). Even his support for the evacuation of Yamit was forgiven and forgotten. As Prime Minister, the success of the Defensive Shield campaign in hobbling the Second Intifada fortified his image as a hard-hitting and effective political leader. During the early period of his second term in office (starting in 2003) Sharon was a dominant and experienced Prime Minister who enjoyed great popularity among substantial parts of Israel's Jewish population. Imagine the shock and disbelief of his followers when he announced with his usual *sangfroid* that Gush Katif/Gaza was to be evacuated.

Sharon's initiative reshuffled the deck entirely. His disengagement plan created an unprecedented threat to the settlement project—far more menacing than the evacuation of Yamit in the early 1980s. Notably, the Yamit and the Gush Katif populations were very different from each another. While the Yamit residents (about 2,500) were largely secular and for the most part not driven by ideological motives, the Gush Katif settlers were mostly religious, ideologically committed to the settlement project and often motivated by messianic ideals. Another essential difference was that Yamit settlements were relatively new when they were dismantled, while Gush Katif included many who had lived there for thirty years with the full financing and support of Israeli governments. Predictably, these differences had far-reaching consequences for the kinds of struggle that the two evacuations triggered. One telling example: as opposed to the Yamit residents, the Gush Katif settlers flatly refused to take part in any talk of compensation for their removal.

This chapter deals with the spiritual, political, and practical attitudes of the Gush Katif settlers—especially their intellectual and religious leadership—toward the disengagement. The religious media's role in encouraging resistance and disobedience will be addressed as well. Illegal actions committed in the lead-up to and in the course of the actual evacuation will be given special attention. But, above all, the focus will be on the underlying ideas, the inner mental universe that justified these acts of disobedience in the eyes of their perpetrators.

The evacuation of Gush Katif is remarkable for its lack of bloodshed, for the mostly token level of violence it triggered. To be sure, disobedience at times spilled over into low-intensity clashes with the security forces, but the feared bloody confrontation did not materialize. Despite the warnings that came from many quarters—academia, the media, the politicians—the evacuation drama resulted in much that was theatrical and little that was life threatening. Disobedience came in many forms: entering closed military areas, blocking intersections, and protesting without a permit, but serious, deadly acts of violence were, if they took place at all, extremely rare.

Moreover, it seems probable that those who flaunted their disobedience represented a relatively small minority of Gush Katif's inhabitants. The majority accepted the decree either with pained resignation or, at most, with passive resistance. No arms were brandished, there was no deliberate strategy to injure the evicting soldiers and, above all, the fabric of national unity was not decisively rent.

For its part, the army did all it could to show sympathy for the evicted and to make the expulsion as non-traumatic as possible. Part of what remains in memory are the incongruous moments in which soldiers comforted the residents in their difficult moments. Although they were at times sorely provoked by the resistors, soldiers kept their cool throughout. The predicted mass refusal of soldiers to carry out orders also proved to be a false alarm. In sum, the Gaza evacuation, although traumatic for some, was not the Armageddon-like confrontation that had been predicted.

Our fundamental thesis is that the relative lack of violence can be attributed to what we have called a "theological-normative balance." But even a cursory and preliminary mention of this "balance" requires important reservations. It has not continued to hold sway as it did in Yamit and Gush Katif. In the years following the relatively mild character of the disengagement, a sharp rise in the level of disobedience and violence occurred. The evacuation of a number of outposts (most notably *Amona*) deteriorated into pitched battles between the settlers and the police. The rise (2008) of the "Price Tag" (*Tag Mechir*) gangs—peripheral perhaps, but violent, vigilante, and at times terrorist nevertheless—has shaken the balance and casts a dark shadow on the future. But we are getting ahead of ourselves.

We have already encountered some of the public personalities who were central to the discourse of disobedience. Here they appear a decade or so later with their thought evolved, and in many cases, radicalized. Rabbis Dov Lior, Zalman Melamed, and Nachum Eliezer Rabinovitch, who are all prominent Poskim (halachic adjudicators) in the religious Zionist camp, will figure significantly in our analysis. Other voices in the disobedience debate whose influence upon the young was particularly great will be taken up as well. They include Rabbis Eliezer Melamed, Shlomo Aviner, Yuval Sherlow, Elyakim Levanon, and others. Despite the important differences between them, what unites all these figures is their wholehearted identification with the religious Zionist camp and their belief that the State of Israel, as the national and religious focus of world Jewry, possesses a lofty messianic standing.

The opposition to the disengagement, like the opposition to the evacuation of Yamit and the Oslo Agreements, was not born *ex nehilo*; they were the products of a century-long educational and philosophical project which climaxed in the Six Day War and its aftermath. To repeat what has been made clear above: the war and the settlement project that followed were seen as portents of Divine redemption and the State of Israel was conceived as its vehicle.

The past forty years have witnessed an explosion of settlement activity as well as wrenching territorial retreats and political defeats. Starting from a few score in the early-mid 1970s, today more than 400,000 settlers live in Judea and Samaria/the West Bank (excluding about 200,000 in annexed Jerusalem). Nevertheless, Yamit was evacuated and the Oslo Accords were signed. This mix of success and failure has created a complex intellectual and emotional mindset among the settler community and its supporters. On the one hand, they have no doubts about the world-historical, apocalyptic significance of the settlement project and its ultimate triumph, but on the other, they cannot ignore the fact that the state is controlled by many who do not share these sentiments. Nevertheless, whatever its policies and whomever its leaders may be, in their eyes the state remains holy—even if the government's policies need to be resisted. Settler political theology rests therefore on dissonant foundations. Although everything that occurs in the Land and in the State of Israel is meticulously directed by God Himself, the logic of His ways is not always obvious. Despite defeats and failures, the sacredness of the state endures and the religious imperative to settle the land remains as obligatory as ever. To understand the Divine mystery of the State of Israel and the Jewish people who populate it, one must, religious Zionist rabbis tell us, rise above mundane logic. One must acquire, what Rabbi Kook the father spoke of as a "Divine eye"—"for with their own eyes they have seen God returning to Zion" (Isaiah, 52:8) (Kook, 1962, vol. 2, letter 409; Kook, 1984: 14). The father's views were repeated and elaborated upon by the son (Kook, 1998: 89). Diverse developments and extensions of this line of thought continue among contemporary religious Zionist rabbis who view it as a paradigm for understanding the inner reality hidden by the external shell of the rebirth of Jewish sovereignty in the Land of Israel.

Confronting tribulations along the way to redemption should not, they insist, undermine the messianic vision. Indeed, these trials shape and consolidate it. They present challenges that preserve the vision's vitality and continually refresh and update the religious Zionist outlook. Yet this resilient perspective is workable only so long as the retreats from the path of redemption are minor and do not mortally wound the vision as a whole. Hence, when major retreats from the Land of Israel take place—as was the case most especially in Gush Katif—this worldview is severely challenged.

It becomes more difficult to justify and sustain when vibrant Jewish communities representing the driving force of the messianic process are removed from the Land of Israel upon which they lived and thrived.

Their failure to prevent stinging defeats (Yamit, Oslo, and Gush Katif) triggered internal developments within the religious Zionist community leading to far-reaching conceptual adaptations. To be sure, the messianic vision did not dim, but a new, more realistic awareness developed, one that dampened the initial burst of messianic euphoria. The most challenging difficulty with which the right-wing religious Zionist community needed to contend was that their vision had failed to win broad public sympathy, that it had not become a uniting national ideal.

Despite its demographic successes, the settlement mission remained, in essence, the project of only a single sector of Israeli society. Hence, it became clear that preserving the already established settlements and not permitting a replay of the Yamit and Oslo failures was a goal no less vital than the triumph of their theology of redemption. Although they continued to be convinced that the inspirational settlement project would ultimately win over public sympathy, a certain alienation—one might almost speak of a mild form of siege mentality—developed. They were indeed responsible for destiny of the Jewish people, but they could not ignore their status as an ideological minority. The recognition that the broad secular and non-committal majority did not share their ideals made its way into religious Zionist circles with important consequences for their religious credo and their political strategies. Neither could they dismiss the influential campaign of de-legitimization against the settlement project led by academic, economic, cultural, and media elites who, more often than not, espoused liberal and left-wing positions (Newman, 2010; Feige, 2009: 247).

While the religious Zionist camp needed to continue shouldering the mission to bring salvation to Jewish people, it could not forget that large parts of the Israeli public were estranged from the settlement project—and draw the necessary strategic conclusions. One such conclusion was the willingness to support increasingly vigorous civil disobedience and to call upon soldiers to disobey orders. As we have already seen, settlers and their religious Zionist sympathizers were drawn to disobedience, first by their unshakable credo that uprooting settlements was a moral, strategic, ideological and religious blunder, and second by their deep emotional and mystical attachment to the soil of the Land of Israel and its Jewish settlers. In this light, it has often been charged that their loyalty to the land and to its settlers overwhelmed their commitment to Israel as a genuinely united nation.

Disobedience in the face of hostile majority decisions necessitates the development of complex, nuanced justifications. From the moment that the majority is defied, all the more so when the majority acts to uproot settlements, radical religious Zionists are driven to adopt the position that whatever the merely numerical majority decides, it is they who remain the moral, essential majority. But disobedience to the state's decisions inevitably involves a certain retreat from the attribution of holiness to the state and its institutions. Elaborate and sophisticated ideological strategies are needed in order to square the circle. One such common strategy involved distinguishing between the state's sacredness and the government's profane character: the former to be honored, the latter resisted (Shochetman, 1995; Bick, 2007).

This dissonance between sacredness and resistance created wrenching tensions, especially when it appeared that the messianic project was being derailed by government-mandated evacuations. Popular hostility to the settlement project did not make it any easier. And yet, as hard-pressed as Yesha rabbis and political leaders became when retreat was imminent, their commitment to the holiness of the state persisted—at least for the most part. Despite the patent challenge involved, advocating disobedience could not be dissociated from Mamlachtiut. Locked into a permanent dilemma, settler political theology took some quite creative turns (Ravitsky, 1998; Schwartz, 2002; Schwartz, 2008; Inbari, 2009; Inbari, 2010: 194–206).

Settler media channels took up this challenge repeatedly. First, there was *Nekuda* (Period), probably the most respected mouthpiece of the Right's (especially the religious Right's) worldview. It carried thoughtful—if at times very radical—essays on Jewish ideas, messianism, the settlement project, faith-based ideology, and political strategy. Almost everyone who was anyone on the religious settler Right published, at one time or another, in this bi-monthly journal. (In 2010 it was sold to the mass-circulation *Mekor Rishon* (Primary Source) weekly newspaper and in 2014 it was purchased by the *Yisrael Ha'yom* (Israel Today) owned by the right-wing American casino mogul, Sheldon Edelson).

The veteran religious Zionist newspaper *Ha'tzofeh* (The Observer), which began publishing in 1937, changed its moderate ideological line as the religious Zionist community moved sharply rightward. *Ha'tzofeh* had a relatively varied readership in the religious Zionist community but its clear ideological tendency—under the editorship of Gonen Ginat—was to support disobeying orders. Ginat called the disengagement "a crime against humanity," defended soldiers who refused to obey orders and condemned those who did. He spoke of the Supreme Court as "an unprecedented dictatorship in the Western world."

The weekly newspaper *BeSheva* (At Seven) consistently and explicitly preached resistance and refusing orders during the disengagement period.

Its editorial policy, its publicists and columnists were associated with the religious Right, if not the radical religious Right. (Notable contributors were its editor Emanuel Shiloh, Chagit Rotenberg, and its "spiritual mentor" Rabbi Eliezer Melamed—about whom more below). Associated with the *BeSheva* newspaper is the Radio channel *Arutz Sheva* (Channel 7) which also catered to radical right-wing tastes.

Settler Leadership and the Sharon's Government Prior to the Disengagement Initiative

Tensions between Sharon and the religious Zionist camp did not begin abruptly with the disengagement plan. In July 2004, Sharon personally and controversially appointed, without a public tender, Talya Sasson (the previous director of the Department for Special Tasks in the State Attorney General's office) to report on the legal status of the various "outposts" (settlements without government or bureaucratic approval) in Yesha. The Sasson Report asserted that most of the outposts were illegal and that it was incumbent upon the government of Israel to remove them. The report presented a scathing critique of collusion between the government, the law enforcement agencies in Yesha, and the outpost's founders. The outposts, so the report alleged, were extremely problematic legally (Sasson, 2004; Sasson, 2015).

Critiques of the Sasson Report concentrated on its author's left-wing politics. Indeed, she would later join left-wing organizations such as *Yesh Din* (Volunteers for Human Rights) and run for Knesset as a candidate of the *Meretz* party. The report, Yesha leaders alleged, was ideologically motivated. Similar critiques were leveled against another report submitted by Yehudit Karp and against the Legal Advisor to the Government, Michael Ben Yair, both of whom, after their period of government service, expressed hostility toward the settlement project. Settlement leaders argued that Sharon himself had initiated the building of tens of settlements, right at the start of his incumbency as Prime Minister. He later appointed Talya Sasson, they charged, in order to clear his name and to prepare the land for evacuation (Shragai, 2004; Elizur, 2005). Adi Mintz, formerly the CEO of the Yesha Council, described the establishment of the outposts in the early years of the twenty-first century as follows:

> The outposts are not related to the 'hilltop youth.' Strict planning takes place here. They are set up in order to occupy strategic locations. The outposts were coordinated with the Prime Minister. One of our people sat with Sharon and told him:

this spot is strategic and important. The Prime Minister would get back to him within a few days and say: 'you are right, that is an important spot. It should be occupied.' All the outposts were established in coordination of the political authorities. The political authorities knew about them. This was the process. Even [Binyamin] Ben Eliezer [of the Labor party], serving as the Defense Minister under Sharon, internalized the 'spirit of the commander,' followed his lead, approved, and instructed the system to cooperate. Therefore, the approval and licensing of most of the outposts were successfully accomplished. At a certain point, Sharon switched his views and made a 180 degree turn in his approach. Then the system ceased cooperating but there were already hundreds of outposts on the ground, some approved, and others in the process of being approved. Everything was coordinated. We are not criminals; we were not the bad guys in this story. (Shragai, 2004)

Similar arguments are episodically heard from the Right whenever the issue of the outposts arises (Iserovitch, 2005; Piekrash, 2004). However, before the Sasson Report, the IDF evacuated a number of outposts even before they were officially classified as illegal. As early as 2002–2003 a number of outposts were dismantled such as *Chavat Gilad*, *Nofei Nechemia*, and *Mitzpeh Eshtamoa*. Just before the evacuation of *Chavat Gilad*, the Association of Yesha Rabbis convened and published a statement directed to IDF soldiers: request being excused from executing the evacuation order. Notably, there was here no call for disobedience because the evacuation of these outposts did not involve the transfer of land to Gentile hands and hence, the prohibition *Lo Techanem* (not giving Gentiles a foothold in the Land of Israel) did not apply. To be sure, there was a challenge here to the Mitzvah of settling the land, but the rabbis felt it was appropriately met if the soldiers requested to be excused from the duty. Nevertheless, these evacuations set a precedent of sorts; they were obviously different from, for example, dismantling an illegally built porch in Tel Aviv. The very fact of evacuating outposts had symbolic, perhaps even practical consequences in that it cast something of a shadow on the legitimacy of the settlement project.

This public statement of the Association of Yesha Rabbis can be seen as an initial salvo in the renewed discourse on disobedience. Much that was later to come in the disengagement crisis is already adumbrated in the discussions of the rabbis preceding its announcement. For example, Rabbi Zalman Melamed described his part in these deliberations as follows: "For my part I suggested that we explicitly prohibit taking part in the evacuation of outposts but I accepted the view of my colleagues that it is preferable to express ourselves more delicately. Clearly, the meaning was no different" (Z. Melamed, 2003a: 1). Clearly, the relatively moderate tone of the statement resulted from the unwillingness of the rabbis to precipitate a full-blown collision with the IDF and its soldiers. The context here is critical. Part of the moderation evident in the rabbi's statement resulted from their sense that the army evacuations were, in practical terms, futile. Although the IDF had begun to carry out evacuations regularly, they were largely ineffective; a few hours after the IDF dismantled an outpost, it would be rebuilt by the settlers.

Nevertheless, Rabbi Melamed's activist views expressed much of what was to come. As time passed, the aim of obstructing IDF plans to put limits on the settlement project became increasingly mainstream in the religious Zionist camp. Yet even at this early stage, Rabbi Melamed declares, there was already a frontal clash between state law and Torah law. The only solution is that the state and army leadership find a way to be flexible and avoid violating Torah law, for in such a conflict there is no doubt that Torah law must emerge triumphant. He repeats what had already become the heart of settler orthodoxy:

> The religious community cannot accept a state law that compels violation of the Torah's Mitzvot. A religious soldier cannot obey a military order that forces him to violate God's laws such as honoring the Sabbath or Kashrut. The Mitzvah of settling the land is no less important than other laws, indeed it is more important since it is equal in weight to all the other Mitzvot combined. (Z. Melamed, 2003a: 1)

It is easy to understand Rabbi Melamed's deferral to the more moderate views of his colleagues. First, because following the evacuations, the outposts were quickly rebuilt. Second, and more essentially, because he knew that the halachic case for disobedience in this case was perhaps too weak to justify outright disobeying of orders: the land, after all, was not to be transferred to Palestinians. His argument was therefore couched in more provisional terms. Although the action of evacuating the outposts is, in itself, not forbidden, it should nevertheless be prohibited because it is part of a "tendency toward prohibition." His moderation did not survive the disengagement plan.

The dilemma provoked by the evacuation of *Chavat Gilad* was complicated by the fact that the soldiers were brought to the site on the Sabbath, in clear violation not only of basic Torah law, but also of the army's own regulations. (Infringing upon Sabbath laws may take place only in truly exigent circumstances.) Deploying soldiers on the Sabbath drew stern words from the then-Chief Rabbi of the IDF, Brigadier General Yisrael Weiss. First of all he declared that *"Disobeying orders is not an option for a soldier."* Unless *"saving lives"* is involved, the orders must be fulfilled without fail [his emphasis]. He continues:

> In regard to the operation of the army to evacuate the Chavat Gilad outpost, a grievous and painful mishap took place involving the transport and deployment of the troops on the Sabbath. The 'ruling' of the officers who wrapped themselves in the mantle of the rabbinate and mixed in my name as the one who had ostensibly validated the activation of the soldiers on the Sabbath is grave. I call upon the soldiers of the IDF to obey orders in the future as in the past, to place their confidence in the judgments of their officers, and to restore full trust in the IDF and its Chief of Staff—who perform holy work, night and day, to raise the state's wall of security. (Weiss, 2010: 195–96)

Notably, Rabbi Weiss's critique is directed against the violation of the Sabbath but not against the evacuation of the outposts themselves. He is severe in regard to the Sabbath issue but remains silent about the question of evacuation. As we have noted, the halachic basis of disobedience in the Chavat Gilad case fell into a gray area. During the disengagement, despite threats, banishments, and even physical attacks, Rabbi Weiss remained (mostly) consistent in his opposition to disobedience. After leaving the IDF, he reported a conversation with the previous IDF Chief Rabbi, General Gad Navon, who believed that a soldier who refused an order "even deserved a death sentence." Far more important, however, was the support he received from the previous Sephardic Chief Rabbi, Mordechai Eliyahu, one of the most outstanding spiritual leaders of the religious Zionist community at the beginning of the twenty-first century (Weiss, 2010: 286–87).

But these were the halcyon days before the bulldozers flattened the Gush Katif settlements. When the crisis exploded, the tone of religious Zionist rabbis and intellectuals took a dramatic turn.

Initial Responses to the Disengagement Plan

Prime Minister Sharon presented his disengagement plan for the first time at the fourth Herzliya Conference in December of 2003. The initial version, it must be said, was drawn in general terms and did not explicitly mention the evacuation of Gush Katif; it contained only a broad announcement that there would be a "change in the deployment of the settlements, so as to bring about a decrease, so far as possible, of the number of Israelis living in the heart of Palestinian population" (Sharon, 2003). Still, it was not difficult to guess that Sharon had major changes in mind. He asserted:

> Diminishing the friction will necessitate an action of unparalleled gravity in which there will be a relocation of part of the settlements. I want to repeat things I've said in the past: in a future agreement, Israel will not remain in all the places in which it finds itself today. The relocation of settlements will be done, first and foremost, in order to draw a security line that will be as effective as possible and effect disengagement between Israel and the Palestinians. This security line will not be the permanent border of the State of Israel but until the renewed implementation of the 'roadmap,' the IDF will be deployed along this line. Settlements that will be relocated are those that in a future and final agreement will not be included in the State of Israel. (Sharon, 2003)

This dramatic declaration constituted a total about-face from the positions that Sharon had presented less than a year earlier in the course of the election campaign for the 16th Knesset. As opposed to Amram Mitznah, then head of the Labor Party who advocated evacuating *Netzarim* [an isolated settlement in the Gaza Strip], Sharon touted the bold slogan: "The status of Netzarim is like the status of Tel Aviv."

The disengagement plan was first publicized in detail by the journalist Yoel Marcus in the Ha'aretz newspaper on February 2, 2004. In an interview given to Marcus, Sharon described his plan as follows: "This condition of vacuum [in the peace process] for which the Palestinians are at fault, cannot continue. I have therefore instructed, in the framework of disengagement, to execute an evacuation, pardon, a relocation of 17 settlements with their 7,500 residents from the Gaza Strip to the territory of Israel" (Marcus, 2004).

Still, the disengagement plan did not immediately provoke the religious Right to advocate disobedience because many believed that the likelihood of Sharon actually putting his plan into effect were slim. At the time of the interview, the subject commanding public attention was the Talya Sasson report and its implications for the fate of the outposts rather than the future of the settlements in Gaza and northern Samaria. Many religious Zionist youth took the more moderate step of campaigning among the Likud's members who were slated to cast their ballots in a referendum on the plan. They hoped that a negative vote would cause the plan to be shelved. The assumption was that a "no" vote democratically arrived at by the Likud's ruling body would tie the Prime Minister's hands.

They were bitterly disappointed. Despite the sweeping failure of the Prime Minister in the Likud referendum on 2nd of May 2004 (60 percent voted "no"), he was not deterred. The disillusioned youth sought alternate avenues to express their frustration—without any success. Their frustration was especially intense because many felt deceived by Sharon's erratic policies. He had—so they felt—received an electoral mandate on the basis of his opposition to the evacuation of Gush Katif and yet he now supported just that plan. He pledged to bow to the outcome of the Likud's referendum and yet he did not.

This sense of frustration grew in right-wing circles because Sharon, in their view, was coddled by the media and, even more distressing, by the state's law enforcement authorities. One of Israel's senior media figures, Amnon Abramovitch, spoke of Sharon as an *etrog* [a delicate citron used ritually during the *Succot* festival]: "Sharon was the only one who could execute the disengagement therefore I think that he needs to be protected like an etrog, both in a sealed box and wrapped in cotton wool." Abromovitch explained that he was not referring only to the media; Sharon "needs to be protected not only from the political establishment but also from the legal establishment" (Sach, 2005).

The frustration caused by their lack of influence on the democratic process within the Likud prompted many young people to turn to other avenues of activity. And yet, even after the referendum, as long as the government and the Knesset had not yet ratified the plan, the struggle against disengagement was still largely conducted within the framework of civil disobedience and nonviolence. Martin Luther King's civil rights struggle was called upon to justify their resistance to what they saw as an unjust and anti-democratic decree (Z. Melamed, 2004a; Zik, 2004). Nonetheless, as Roth rightly points out, the great majority of the religious Zionist camp did not turn to outright disobedience, although they were deeply distressed by what they saw as Sharon's duplicity. Notably, Sharon's demarche was broadly supported by the media (Gabél 2011). Roth believes that the mostly restrained approach of the religious Zionist community can be accounted for by the dominance of Mamlachti attitudes among them (Roth, 2014).

In what would become the stronghold of activist, nonviolent disobedience, the *Beit-El* yeshiva, (under the leadership of Rabbi Zalman Melamed), Rabbi Chaim Avihu Schwartz, one of the yeshiva's leaders and a loyal student of Rabbi Tzvi Yehuda Kook, spoke with uncommon harshness against the Prime Minister on Independence Day. In his comments, he laid the foundations for the more extreme forms of disobedience that would develop in the religious Zionist camp. He insisted that they "stand ready to sacrifice their lives against the wicked magician" (a paraphrase on biblical Balaam who is mentioned in the Torah as a magician) reiterating what Rabbi Tzvi Yehuda himself had said about a civil war breaking out over Judea and Samaria (Schwartz, 2004).

An especially fierce remark—that stood out for its radicalism at the time—was made by Uri Elizur, one of the settler's leaders, a journalist and publicist, and former head of Prime Minister Netanyahu's office. On June 17, 2004, in an article authored by Chagit Rotenberg for the radical Right newspaper *BeSheva*, whose title was "How to stop the bulldozer" (Sharon's well-known nickname after his ability to mow down the opposition) Elizur was cited as follows:

> The uprooting of a settlement is illegal and shocking, and therefore justifies refusing to obey an order, violence, and any other way a person can defend his home from which he is being evicted for political reasons. I recommend disobeying orders because what is involved is an illegal order and he who implements it will be put on trial. It is not unreasonable in my eyes that matters reach the spilling of blood. Every population in the world, under similar circumstances, would act the same way although I am not sure this will prevent the evacuation. In my eyes, any use of force, except for firearms, is legitimate in this case. In retrospect, even those who wound those coming to evict him. I will react to his behavior with understanding. (Rotenberg, 2004)

These harsh words ("spilling of blood") are essentially different from the tone prevailing in the rest of Rotenberg's article where she focuses on five major right-wing personalities: Bentzi Lieberman, then the head of the Yesha Council; Sha'ul Goldstein, then head of the local council of Gush Etzion; Michael Puah, head of the Jewish Leadership faction in the Likud; Elyakim Ha'etzni, a former Knesset member and right-wing activist; and Elizur himself. Except for Elizur, the other four—including Ha'etzni and Puah who later advocated more proactive, aggressive disobedience—refrained, at this stage, from calling for violent actions and the use of force in resisting evacuation. Ha'etzni is a borderline case: he called for disobeying orders but argued that these actions should be accompanied by disseminating a

booklet explaining the need for so radical a step. He also calls for resisting evacuation: "In opposition to what is portrayed in the media, the only
force that will be used is the force of muscles. Therefore, if they drag me,
I will drag back, if they hit me with a stick, I will hit back. All in order
to protect my home." This is considerably less than what Elizur advocated
(Rotenberg, 2004). It should be added that there were many right-wing
publicist statements at the time that justified disobeying orders but they were,
once again, considerably less strident than those of Elizur (Segal, 2004).

The government decision of June 6, 2004, ratifying the disengagement from the Gaza Strip was followed by Sharon's dismissal of Ministers
Benny Elon and Avigdor Lieberman—opponents of disengagement—in
order to create a slim majority in favor of the decision. This move was
sharply criticized by Justice Edmond Levy of Israel's Supreme Court. In the
end, a small majority voted for the plan but, beyond some verbal abuse, it
did not bring about a call for violent disobedience. The dramatic change
in the style and content of disengagement struggle took place when the
cabinet ratified (September 14, 2004) granting compensation to those who
would be evacuated from Gush Katif and the establishment of the *Selah*
directorate to reimburse them for their economic losses (Prime Minister's
Office, Notice to the Press, 2004b). From this point onward, the positions
of most of those who called for disobeying orders became radicalized and
unreservedly aggressive.

In the second chapter we presented the Mamlachti approach of Rabbi
Tzvi Yisrael Tau, head of the *Har Hamor* yeshiva and of his colleague and
student Rabbi Shlomo Aviner. Both were central figures in the moderate
religious Zionist camp. We discussed the latter's cautious reading of Rabbi
Tzvi Yehuda's well-known cry: "It will not pass in Judea and Samaria without a war" as a metaphor for a war of ideas and words. By contrast, other
rabbis rejected this metaphorical reading—Rabbi Chaim Schwartz stands
out in this radical group. Indeed, the disengagement plan precipitated a
transformation even in Rabbi Tau's position; he became considerably less
tolerant of the Prime Minister, the government, and the Knesset—a position
he voiced in a closed conference. Even his closest students were surprised:

> Until the conference, all Rabbi Tau's students knew that his
> position was entirely Mamlachti in character. Just as he opposed
> retreating from the Holy Land so did he oppose harming any
> symbol of sovereign Mamlachtiut, most especially the IDF. In
> this spirit, the students of the Bnei David pre-military yeshiva in
> *Eli* [the first and the best-known of the pre-military academies]
> would say "in case of need we will evacuate even our parents."

> But in that meeting, Tau surprised us. He protested against the "mistaken understanding" of his position: explicit refusal is indeed prohibited, but students must clarify to their officers that they are 'unable' to follow such an order. (Sheleg, 2004)

Although we lack documentation definitively charting the changes in Rabbi Tau's position, there is clear evidence that the influence he exerted upon his students, both rabbis and educators, led to their adopting very complex and anguished positions that they transmitted to their students who served in the army.

Whatever may be the intimations of change in Rabbi Tau's position, his Mamlachti position remained firm and unwavering. At a meeting with the organizers of the "Face to Face" program which aimed at disseminating critical attitudes toward the disengagement plan Rabbi Tau expressed himself decisively; he opposed all civil disobedience and other forms of force used against the state authorities.

> If we succeed in stopping the process with belligerence and threats, this 'success' will come with a very steep price that can, forbid it, lead to crises even more serious than the one before us now. There are ways of acting that deal with the branch but fell the main trunk upon which all the settlements in the State of Israel rest. All our actions derive from the love of Israel, from our national mission which includes all of Israel and from our faith in the Divine process of returning to Zion. To create an atmosphere of conflict and hatred in the people, forbid it, to even think that someone will lift his hand against his brother, to speak of part of the nation as 'rabble' and completely despair of the State of Israel, all of these are a blow at the heart of hearts—in the name of saving the Land of Israel. This is liable to cause an incomparably more severe crisis than the one in which we now find ourselves, and who can tell where it will lead. (Tau, 2005: 8)

He argued further that there is no place for civil disobedience unless the government manifestly acts against the will of the people. Since the government does, in fact, faithfully reflect the will of the people, all civil disobedience is nothing but the belligerence of a minority that denies the principle of majority rule, which is unacceptable both in practice and in principle. This position accords with the arguments that Rabbi Tau made more than twenty years earlier at the time of the Yamit evacuation (as noted in chapter 2). Throughout the years, Rabbi Tau consistently rejected active civil disobedience as a challenge to Mamlachtiut and to the doctrine of Rabbi Tzvi Yehuda Kook that the State of Israel is the most complete expression of the Jewish nation in the Land of Israel and that the state should be seen as possessing a clear foundation of holiness (Ravitsky, 1996: chapter 3).

From the time of the Yamit evacuation in 1982, Rabbi Tau repeatedly argued that the crises and retreats experienced in the process of redemption do not alter the inexorable trend toward the creation of a holy Jewish kingdom. Rather than resistance, Rabbi Tau placed emphasis on educational and spiritual outreach to raise the level of Israeli society to a higher plane. In the yeshivot where his influence was strongly felt, two parallel orientations developed concurrently: on the one side there was the strengthening of Hardeli tendencies that sought to institute Torah education from a very early age, that opposed Western individualism and that emphasized strict sexual modesty. But Rabbi Tau himself advocated a more ecumenical approach: reaching out to Israeli society generally by establishing yeshivot in nonreligious areas so as to bring the influence of Torah to the far corners of the country. The imperfect solution he preferred, one that partially fulfilled both parts of his spiritual creed—Israel's holiness and the prohibition against retreating from the Land of Israel—was passive refusal, about which we shall have more to say below. In any event, it is clear that violent struggle against the government and widespread aggressive disobedience are far from Rabbi Tau's Mamlachti program.

Together with Rabbi Tau, his student and colleague Rabbi Shlomo Aviner—the second leading figure in the Mamlachti camp of religious Zionism—publicly and unconditionally decried disobedience. In what would later precipitate intense debate that at times deteriorated into personal abuse, Rabbi Aviner stood front and center against the position of the pro-disobedience school led by Rabbi Avraham Shapira, former Chief Rabbi and head of the Mercaz HaRav yeshiva. "This army is ours," he declared:

> There is therefore no place for disobeying orders. We are not talking about refusing to be drafted . . . but about brave soldiers who are committed both in heart and in soul. But what about evacuation of outposts and uprooting the Land of Israel? If, to our shame and disgrace, we reach such a terrible, insufferable condition, it must be known that an army in which soldiers disobey orders is not an army. This is a matter of life and death and the danger here is worse than the prohibition. *And is not the Torah superior to the army? Certainly. But it is the Torah that says, obey the army . . .* Of course, if the questioner wavers between

the small view of a small man and the great view of a great
rabbi he will surely decide that the view of the small man is
invalidated by the view of great man. But, small I, this is my
view. (Aviner, 2005a) [Emphasis added]

Despite the modesty and caution of Rabbi Aviner, he openly confronts the
leadership of Rabbi Shapira. He asserts:

I should add that even he who is loyal to his rabbi knows that
every rule has its exception . . . Moreover, I am small but I
rest upon the giant of giants, our teacher Rabbi Tzvi Yehuda
Hacohen Kook, who had no trepidation or fear, who did not
yield to anyone, said many harsh things in regard to our struggle
for the Land of Israel and flooded the nation with countless
proclamations, but no one will testify to his saying to a soldier
in practice: disobey an order! . . .
    At the end of his life, when the issue of uprooting many
settlements in Yamit was at hand, he expressed some harsh
positions but he never proclaimed to the many: soldiers disobey
orders! And also there is not a single soldier who reported that
our teacher said to him personally: disobey orders. His great
and loyal students heeded his every word with awe, and yet no
one cited a single decision of his to disobey orders. A call for
struggle—of course. Disobeying orders—no. Our teacher felt
great responsibility about each word he uttered, their content
and their style, and he did not agree that things he did not say
be said in his name. (Aviner, 2005a)

The halachic-intellectual basis of Rabbi Aviner's words rested upon
the same standpoint that he had already formulated concerning the Oslo
Accords: the responsibility for the sin of vacating settlements does not rest
on the shoulders of each and every soldier, as he wrote:

The Mitzvah of conquering the land is a public rather than a
private Mitzvah . . . If the collective does not want to observe
the Mitzvah, the heart bleeds, but this is not the work of the
individual qua individual. All that we do, we do with our people.
If our people are stuck, we will not run forward, rather, we will
always remain in line. Always together. (Aviner, 2005a)

The reaction to these arguments was fast in coming both from Rabbi
Shapira himself and even more publicly in a declaration of the Council of

Yesha Rabbis. Rabbi Shapira (October 15, 2004) granted an interview to his student, Rabbi Aaron Trop which was published in the *BeSheva* journal. Rabbi Shapira expressed himself sharply both on a personal level against Rabbi Aviner and especially about the disengagement and the means necessary to block it. He reacted heatedly to the argument that the sin does not fall on the individual soldier but on the state and hence the individual soldier should not refuse to implement the order to evacuate. He declared: "What?! Every sin is a sin. Heaven does not will it. Rabbi Aviner says that this is a sin of the state and not of the soldier; there is no such distinction. Heaven does not will it. Rabbi Aviner should be told that he is leading the many into wrongdoing. It is a sin" (Trop, 2005).

Rabbi Shapira adds a novel, tactical spirit to his argument. A soldier must disobey not merely in order to avoid sinning; what is at stake is also influencing the political authorities to cease implementing the plan. They will fear that the army will be dealt a serious blow that many soldiers will disobey. He put it flatly: "All the soldiers need to say this [that they will disobey]; it is simple. What is novel in our position is the need to inform [the authorities] beforehand so that everyone who wants to do this [dismantle settlements] will know that they will have problems and then will refrain from doing it" (Trop, 2005).

A day earlier the Association of Yesha Rabbis published a declaration which repeated that it was prohibited "for any Jew to participate or aid in any way in the dismantling of the settlements or any [Jewish] property in the Land of Israel, a land which in all its breadth is our God-given patrimony" (The Association of Yesha Rabbis, 2005). Not surprisingly, most of the signatories on the declaration had already expressed their opinion in the past regarding the legitimacy of disobeying orders in the struggle for the Land of Israel (among them Rabbis Elyakim Levanon, Dov Lior, Zalman Melamed, Moshe Levinger, Michael Hershkovitch, etc.). What stood out was the signature of Rabbi Chaim Druckman, a central leader of religious Zionist youth, Knesset member, Deputy Minister, and later an Israel Prize laureate, whose position on disobedience is complex and conditional, as we will see below. Notably, he immediately denied the authenticity of his signature and it did not appear in later publications of the declaration (Huberman, 2004).

These three publications (of Rabbis Aviner and Shapira and of the Yesha rabbis) ignited a heated debate within the religious Zionist camp regarding disobedience specifically and the democratic rule of law in general. For example, a week after the Yesha rabbi's declaration, two statements appeared rejecting the call to disobedience: the one issued by the secretariat of the religious kibbutz movement, the other by the heads of the pre-army Torah academies, both religious and secular.

The religious kibbutz declaration, despite its ostensible decisiveness in opposing the violation of state law and disobeying commands, well reflects the frustrations and soul-searching that the religious Zionist camp was experiencing. Even among those whose politics were moderately right of center, the prevalent mood was that the disengagement was being carried out in an anti-democratic manner and that it posed a danger to Israeli society. Their statement read as follows:

> We see in the unity of the IDF a necessary condition for our existence in Israel. We call upon the rabbis of religious Zionism and upon its leadership not to involve the IDF and our sons and students who serve in it in the argument that is taking place—even if they believe that the implementation of the disengagement plan is a serious and dangerous mistake . . . Our demand remains unchanged: that the decision in regard to the disengagement be made in a democratic way on the basis of the support of a majority of the people. A referendum [that has never been held throughout Israeli history] is one possibility for implementing this principle. (Reinman, 2005)

Clearly, this last sentence was not directed against the proponents of disobedience but rather as an indirect but sharp rebuke to the government of Israel that they believed was acting undemocratically. Two days later, some of the heads of the pre-army academies—religious and secular—sent letters to the Minister of Defense and the Chief of Staff in which they asked that the heads of the military establishment make clear statements denouncing disobedience in any form. They made it clear that they would continue to educate their students in this spirit. Nevertheless, they implored the security leaders not to put IDF soldiers in an emotional bind and to permit them, if they so requested, to be freed from missions that involved the evacuation of settlements (Heads of the Mechinot, 2005).

A similar position, expressed at great length and with greater impact, was that of Rabbi Eli Sadan, head of the pre-army yeshiva academy in Eli. Rabbi Sadan, one the most respected and influential figures in the religious Zionist camp, initiated the entire pre-army seminar program which has significantly affected the IDF's composition and character. Before the actual disengagement Rabbi Sadan published a special pamphlet entitled "Our loyalty to the army and the state" in which he rejected disobedience and demanded unconditional loyalty to the army and state. And yet, his arguments vacillate, perhaps even contradict themselves. He claims that when orders to dismantle settlements are given the soldier's unconditional loyalty derives from a painful place that is not entirely at peace with itself. According to Sadan, this pain should grant individuals who find evacuation orders unconscionable the right to refrain from personally implementing them. He writes:

> Our relationship to democracy determines our relationship to disobedience. *We oppose disobedience at the level of principle.* If every group announces that it will refuse to cooperate each time the decisions arrived at were against its worldview—there is no state. *But together with the aforementioned clarification and only after it has been said*, together with full recognition of the importance of preserving democracy and cultivation of the partnership between all parts of Israeli society, it should be clear as the sun to every straight thinking person *that it is impossible to order an individual, in the name of democracy, to execute something immoral that is opposed to his conscience.* This is a universal principle. In *Kfar Kassem* soldiers were found guilty for their actions even though they followed orders. *This is because no order is immune from the standards of morality, and the imperative of conscience always precedes the imperative of the government.* Every person must place each state law and every army order under the critique of reason and morality and if it is clear that the order does not stand up to this criticism he must not fulfill it. *It is not in the power of the principle of obedience to the law, even when it was passed by the majority, to free the person from the moral responsibility for the act that he does.* If you will, this is what is intended when we say 'there is no agency (*Shaliach*) for sinful acts,' because 'the words of the master and the words of the student, whose words do we obey?' [Rabbi Sadan uses here a well-known Talmudic ruling; Tractate Sanhedrin, 29a.] It does not matter who sent you, even if it was the Prime Minister himself—you are always obliged to give a full report on your action before the Creator. (Sadan, 2005) [Emphasis in the original]

It is important, to clarify just how multifaceted, some would say inconsistent, Rabbi Sadan's argument is. He sweepingly rejects ideological public disobedience "at the level of principle" but believes that a soldier's moral dilemma, when he finds himself ordered to dismantle settlements, should free him from the duty to do so. The emotional and moral price that a soldier pays in dismantling a settlement must be factored into the equation of military obedience. One must recognize that at a certain moment in the drama of obeying orders, refusal ought to be countenanced. Refusing to obey orders may well be noble and righteous, and a caring, compassionate state must make room for such exceptions to the rule. Every ethical person has his or her breaking point. It behooves a democracy, in special cases such as this, to respect an individual soldier's moral compass. Particularly a Jewish democracy, for which the Land of Israel has momentous importance, has to give way rather than insist on unconditional obedience. Notably, Sadan does not seem to be speaking of a soldier asking for special permission (that can be refused) to be relieved of a duty. Such requests do not violate the general rule of universal compliance to orders because it is the military authorities who make the final judgment. Rather, he appears to be defending the essential right possessed by individual soldiers to act in accord with their consciences.

Rabbi Ya'acov Ariel, chief Rabbi of Ramat Gan and an influential halachic adjudicator (whom we encountered in chapter 2) also takes up the question of disobedience, treating it with the typical ambiguity, even evasiveness that has often marked his attitude on the subject. In two responses to queries from October 15 and 18, 2004, he refers the questioners to his book "In the tent of Torah," part one, number 5. He refused to add a word beyond what was written there. But searching the said text turns up a rephrasing of what he wrote earlier in 1983 with a short addendum:

> In the year 1994 the genius Rabbi Shlomo Goren raised the subject once again and instructed soldiers to refuse evacuating settlements and settlers from all over the Land of Israel. So ruled as well, the geniuses Rabbi Shaul Yisraeli and Rabbi Avraham Elkanah Shapira, may he continue to live a long and good life. The conditions there [during the Oslo process] were different from Yamit. There was no doubt that at stake was the heart of the Land of Israel. And in regard to questions of saving lives (*Pikuach Nefesh*), the government admitted that it was taking upon itself risks because of the prospects of peace . . . Yet one must seriously weigh the consequences of disobeying an order; the directive to disobey an order was given mainly in regard to the evacuation of settlements and the like. (Ariel, 1998)

Concerning the Yamit evacuation, Rabbi Ariel's anti-disobedience, pro-Mamlachtiut views were quite clear. Here they tend to a certain vagueness. He avoids taking a position either for or against. This elusiveness reflects the trend, common among other leading religious Zionist rabbis, to gradually distance themselves from unconditional Mamlachtiut. As a rule, the unreserved Mamlachti positions expressed in the 1980s and 1990s have tended to become more nebulous and attenuated in the early years of the twenty-first century.

Considering the complex, at times even contorted positions of Rabbis Aviner, Sadan, Tau, and Ariel leads to the conclusion that they found themselves stuck on the horns of a religiopolitical dilemma from which they could not extricate themselves. Despite the clear prohibition against territorial concessions with its solid halachic foundation, and although their congregant's accepted their authority as rabbis, they simply could not rule in favor of disobedience. They were moved by an existential fear that in a sovereign state where disobedience becomes the common national coin, ordered social life would become impossible. They all express—each in his own way—the sense of accountability to the Jewish state, which must maintain resilient democratic institutions for the sake of its citizen's welfare and security. They each see this not merely as a pragmatic imperative but also as the necessary consequence of the state's holiness, its preeminence as a Torah value.

With the exception of a number of outlying rabbinical figures whose association with religious Zionism is dubious (and with whom we will deal at the end of this study), all the major rabbis we have discussed to this point are deeply moved by the importance—from a Torah perspective—of a state that is able to exercise ordered, predictable, law-bound authority. The critical questions for them are ones of degree: What is the appropriate and justifiable extent of disobedience? At what point are red lines crossed? When does supporting the rule of law undermine major Torah prohibitions? Which trade-offs are defensible? In a word, a "theological-normative balance" underlies the rabbis's discourse throughout; it is an inherent part of all their debates on the subject of disobedience. Even those religious authorities who speak in favor of disobedience do not ignore the imperatives that come with the sacredness of Jewish statehood; rather, they attempt to explain why striking what they perceive to be a minor blow against the rule of law does not abandon Israel to chaos and anarchy.

One very interesting development publicized at that time—which continues to be shrouded in mystery—took place in the corridors of the Knesset just before the disengagement agreement was ratified on October 26, 2004. Publicly revealed only a day after the vote was taken, it seems that senior religious Zionist rabbis signed a document to facilitate the National Religious Party's request that Prime Minister Sharon call for a referendum on the disengagement plan, to be held, notably, before the vote of the Knesset scheduled for the next day. This action, taken with the encouragement of senior figures from the Yesha Council, aimed at using the proposed referendum as a reason for the NRP not to leave the government (Alon and Mualem, 2004). The document entitled "Truth and peace loved one another" (a well-known epigram of Rabbi Uziel, the first Sephardic Chief Rabbi of the State of Israel, which expressed his support for national unity through compromise (Zechariah, 8:19)), expressed, as would be expected, intense opposition to the disengagement plan. Nevertheless, it contained significant conciliatory statements recognizing the legitimate power of the national government to decide authoritatively, even against Halacha and to give up parts of the Land of Israel:

> [We speak] out of deep distress in the face of, forbid it, a violent struggle between brothers and a profound fracture in the unity of Israel, which will be very hard to heal. We [suggest] opening a rescuing channel by holding a referendum on the Prime Minister's plan. We are certain, with the help of the God of Israel and its Redeemer, that He will give us the strength and wisdom to reach every home in Israel and to persuade in a peaceable and pleasant manner that the Prime Minister is in error . . . The decision of the Knesset approving the government's decision in regard to the disengagement will be conditioned upon its ratification in a general referendum of all the citizens of Israel. If the Knesset approves the government's decision regarding the disengage- ment without a commitment to hold a referendum, the NRP will leave the government and the coalition in 14 days. Only by the fulfillment of these conditions will the NRP be able to commit itself to stay in the coalition until the end of the term irrespective of the outcome of the referendum. (Sabato, 2005) (We thank Anat Roth for providing us with a copy of this letter.)

According to the head of the NRP, Zvulun Orlev, this letter was passed on to him in a handwritten version by Rabbi Shabtai Sabato. The call for a referendum on disengagement drew upon support from many religious circles and the letter's signatories included prominent religious Zionist rab- bis both from the pro- and the anti-disobedience schools: Rabbis Nachum Eliezer Rabinovitch, Chaim Druckman, Tzefania Drory, Mordechai Elon, Elyakim Levanon, and Shlomo Aviner, while Rabbis Mordechai Eliyahu and Avraham Shapira expressed their agreement in principle. A copy with their signatures clearly exhibited was distributed to the press. To be sure, directly afterwards Rabbis Levanon and Aviner renounced the letter, but they continued to express support for a referendum. Their renunciation derived, so it seems, from unwillingness to give their stamp of approval to the NRP's staying in the government.

In any event, there appears to have been broad agreement among the religious Zionist rabbis that a referendum, whatever its outcome, had in its power to legitimize the decision of the government. Rabbis Levanon and Aviner put it this way: "There is a national need to disperse the Knesset, to schedule new elections and to return the decision to the nation. If this will not be done, there is no escaping a referendum that will prove that the people of Israel is sovereign in its land, providing a great historic opportunity for interpersonal dialogue to clarify the truth" (Channel 7, 2004). At a later date (April 2010), Rabbi Levanon defended his position that a referendum receiving a "solid majority" (left unspecified) that validated the government's decision would go a long way toward placating the public furor. Astonishingly but guardedly he declared:

> The settlements in Judea and Samaria rest on the nation and they are the power behind it. A referendum is critical regarding the question of evacuating settlements and, therefore, if the people decide not to stand behind us, I will instruct my students to vacate. This is the halachic position and Maimonides who believes it to be so as well . . . According to my understanding and learning, the Torah says that in public issues, the position of the people is decisive. I believe in perfect faith that the people will never make such a statement but in the theoretical eventuality that they in fact do so, we will vacate. The moment that the people says with *solid majority* that it does not want us as their emissaries in these places, there is no point in our staying there. (Levanon, 2010) [Emphasis added]

The Knesset members from the Likud and the NRP did not succeed in their plan. Despite their best efforts, they were unable to induce Ariel Sharon to hold a national referendum. In a series of forceful and decisive moves that left little room for disagreement, he overwhelmed the opposition and received legislative approval for both the evacuation from Gush Katif and the reparations package for those expelled. From this moment onward an intense and widespread debate in all the educational institutions of religious Zionism erupted. The same impassioned deliberation took place in all the religious Zionists newspapers and other media outlets.

Leading senior rabbis like Rabbis Shapira, Melamed, and Lior, who supported disobedience, and, on the other side, Rabbis Sherlow and Aviner who opposed it, became deeply embroiled in this debate. Even local rabbinical leaders were drawn into it. For example, consider the case of Rabbi Yehoshua Weitzman, the head of a Hesder yeshiva in the town of *Ma'a'lot*, not at all known for hawkish views. In a series of lectures given during November and December of 2004 whose title was "On the storm over disobeying orders" Rabbi Weizman set down a nuanced, complex position that became accepted among many rabbis and soldiers of the religious Zionist camp. His halachic position was that there is no prohibition on the individual soldier to take part in evacuating settlements and settlers:

> How then to relate to the . . . case, forbid it, in which the collective decides 'to leave it [the land] to others from the Gentile nations?' Does the cancellation (*Bitul*) of the Mitzvah apply to the individual or does the problem rest with the many but not with the individual? It appears, according to the meaning of the Mitzvah, that when an individual soldier participates in it, this action is not prohibited in the way violation of the Sabbath is, because it is not he who is obligated by the Mitzvah, and, consequently it is not he who cancels it. It is the collective that cancels the Mitzvah in its decision to remove its rule over the place. It therefore seems that focusing the discussion on a particular soldier is diverting attention away from the subject at hand, which is the relationship of the collective to the Mitzvah. (Weitzman, 2005a)

Nevertheless, according to Rabbi Weitzman, the core of the discussion is not halachic but rather the emotional difficulty of a soldier with a strong Jewish identity commanded to dismantle Jewish settlements. As Rabbis Tau and Sadan had claimed, the central issue is the ability of a soldier to reconcile between his obligations to the rule of law and his loyalty to the Land of Israel. It may then be that a religious soldier with deep emotional sensitivities will not be able to take an active part in the evacuation of people from their homes. Rabbi Weitzman makes this point quite graphically:

> A soldier with these feelings, who has developed sensitivity to the plight of others—will not be able to evict a family from its home. This is not related to disobeying an order but rather to the inability to carry it out. An analogy is if a soldier receives an order to lift a tank with his two hands . . .

> 'I am sorry commander, but I cannot carry out the order.'

> 'There is no such thing as 'I can't,' only I don't want to.'

'You are refusing to carry out an order.'

'I am not disobeying an order, I just cannot.'

> It behooves us to feel that it is harder for us to take a family, parents and children and to evict them from their home than to lift a tank with two hands. This is a simple kind of moral sensitivity that is not related to this or that political view. We very much want to carry out commands and to strengthen the IDF but there are orders we cannot carry out. He who can carry out this kind of order—he must do so, but we expect of a person whose life is directed by the values of the Torah, who has developed in his heart the sensitivity and identity with the suffering of others, that he will not be able to carry out such an awful order, may it never be given. (Weizman, 2005 b)

(Rabbi Weizman's opponents would insist that he put the shoe on the other foot. What of a soldier, who faces deep emotional anguish in maintaining the occupation, for whom ruling over Palestinians in Judea and Samaria/West Bank is unconscionable? Will he/she also be able to claim "moral sensitivity" and be freed from serving beyond the Green Line?)

"Having it both ways" well describes the conflicted position of Rabbi Weizman. He teaches his students not to carry out orders but to do so without undermining the democratic rules of the game. And for those who think that Rabbi Weitzman is wary of calling for a mass refusal to carry out orders lest it undermine military discipline and unity, let it be clear that in other lectures he expressed the hope that, indeed, a great number of soldiers would disobey orders—and not only his own students. At the heart of this conflicted moral-religious dilemma lies a deep despair in regard to Israeli democracy's ability to accommodate itself to religious principles and practice. This was a common feeling for many figures in religious Zionism who tried to block the disengagement plan while remaining loyal to the normative imperatives of democracy. Rabbi Weitzman puts it this way:

> One of the heads of those opposed to the disengagement plan in the Knesset was asked what in his opinion was worse, disobeying orders or the disengagement plan. His answer was that refusing to carry out orders was worse because it constitutes 'the destruction of all the democratic rules of the game.'
>
> It is amazing to learn that there are those who relate to the conduct of life in the State of Israel as a game . . .

In football, you can play very well but if you do not score goals you don't win. The umpire decides, according to the rules of the game, who wins and it is not necessarily the better team. The 'democratic game' is the same. We play excellently; create settlements, are recruited into the army, we have won over the members of the Likud and on and on but the umpire decides this is an 'offside' and we are not counted. We are indeed the better team, but according to the rules of the game the Prime Minister is victorious. A number of ministers were fired, fundamental laws were changed, and the game goes on . . .

We are not playing! We are truly alive and we have not come to the State of Israel because the game is pleasing in our eyes. Neither is democracy a game. If you buy votes in many devious ways, this shows us you are a good player, but in no way at all does it show the truth about worthy values and leadership. (Weitzman, 2005c)

For all of his passion, Rabbi Weitzman is not issuing an immediate or practical challenge to the rule of law or democracy. Like many others on the Right and the religious Right, he rages because in his eyes Sharon was guilty of cynically manipulating power and of emptying democracy of all its content. The settlers were the better team, they occupied the moral high-ground but the rules of the game bested them. It is frustration rather than defiance that underlies Rabbi Weizman's words. Even in his exasperation at the wrong side winning, he does not go beyond bitter polemics; he does not call for soldiers to disobey orders or for other actions that violate the law. Still the subtext is clear; he hopes that there will be a collective angry reaction to Sharon's trampling of democracy. Passive resistance, or perhaps more accurately symbolic resistance on a mass scale is what he wishes for, not as a direct challenge to government authority but as an expression of frustration and lack of identity with the disengagement plan:

Every soldier with a Jewish spark in his heart will sit on the ground and recite the Psalms in tears. Is there anyone who is reading these lines who can see a person crying and reading Psalms and evacuate him? When we arrive at that terrible day, may it not come with the help of God, these will be the scenes and they are stronger than any rioting or violence. The pure truth in all its power is stronger than physical expressions of any kind. Without any tie to the question of disobedience, it is unlikely that any IDF soldier will be able to carry out an evacuation order when confronted with such scenes. (Weitzman, 2005b)

A few months later, weeks before the implementation of the disengagement plan, the journalist Avishai Ben-Chaim wrote an impassioned column decrying what he saw as a cynical hide-and-seek game on the part of the rabbis. He attempted to tear the mask off words which he saw as having double and triple meanings, words that both say and don't say, words that evaded giving explicit instructions, saying neither "yes" or "no."

> The issue is more complicated than what it seems to be. Beyond the fact that many of the yeshiva heads like Rabbi Chaim Druckman, do not express a public position on the subject, even among those rabbis who do express stern opposition to disobeying an order, there are nuances that are important to distinguish before the 15th of August [the date of the disengagement]. It is difficult for them to give explicit instructions to their soldier-students: 'implement the order,' 'evict the settlers.' Even Rabbi Sherlow explained this week that "it is difficult for him" to say to his students, 'evict.' Rabbi Drori also whispered under his breath "my students know exactly how to evict." He even declared that he who says that there is no rabbi among the senior rabbis of religious Zionism who instructs his students to evict, "speaks accurately."
>
> Rabbi Aviner is not the head of a Hesder yeshiva and stood at the head of the opponents to disobedience. He suffered countless barbs from the right wing because of his groveling and an abundance of praise from the other side because of his moderation. Rabbi Aviner explained what he thought a soldier who does not announce that he will disobey an order ought to do at the moment of truth. He said that he, for example, were he called upon to fulfill such a mission "would faint" or "tremble to the point that I could not execute the mission." Or as he summarized recently: "Refusal no! But no motivation either! There are things that without motivation are impossible such as: marriage, the study of Torah, settling the Land of Israel and the army. Faced with such a mission a soldier feels that all his oxygen has escaped, and the oxygen is Zionism, the return of the people to its land." (Ben Hayim, 2005)

Reinforcement for Ben Chaim's oblique argument came from Rabbi Eli Sadan, who, in a document published after the events of Amona (to be dealt with below), referred to the heroism of the yeshiva and pre-military yeshivot students who served in the army during the period of the disengagement, and even took part in it:

> They should be admired for their heroism. Do you know how hard it was to obey the rabbis who instructed not to break up the unity of the army when saving lives (*Pikuach Nefesh*) was at stake? Do you know how hard it is to stand in the 2nd circle or the 5th circle, to grit your teeth, to cry, and to follow the instructions of their rabbis? I testify before heaven and earth that I clarified and found that the great majority of heads of the advanced yeshivot, heads of the Hesder yeshivot and seminars ruled—do not disobey an order to participate in the 2–5th circles!
>
> Once and for all the truth needs to be told: it is painful when there is an argument between Torah greats but it is impossible to ridicule those who follow their rabbis. And it must be known—the actual discussion was not about the evictors themselves—that, we were saved from—the discussion was about those who aided in the outer circles. (Sadan, 2006)

Nevertheless, it must be added that even Rabbi Sadan, in accordance with the instructions of Rabbi Tau (discussed above) did not see serving in the first circle of the evictors themselves as legitimate according to Torah law.

And yet, outside of the rabbinical circles of religious Zionism, there began to be heard at this time clear calls for disobeying orders and for other insubordinate actions. A document published in January 2005 by the "Movement for Jewish Leadership" (a substantial radical right-wing faction within the Likud) entitled "A clarification of the obligation to disobey" was the first sign of what would become a series of unambiguous calls for nonviolent civil disobedience the object of which was to block any real chance that the disengagement would take place. The booklet, which includes almost no Torah sources, was based upon articles penned by the heads of "Jewish Leadership" and was distributed in thousands of copies throughout the country. As noted above, Moshe Feiglin—the head of the "Jewish Leadership"—advocated a broad campaign of civil disobedience as part of the struggle against the Oslo Process. He continued in this same spirit when faced with the disengagement. He declares in his article "Disobedience and draft resistance: Destruction or construction?"

> The readiness of citizens to stake out border lines beyond which they are not willing to play according to the system's rules, the readiness of citizens to violate, in extremely immoral situations,

the system's rules, this readiness, not only does it not destroy the state, it is the single guarantee to its existence . . . Resisting being drafted and disobedience in the framework of the eviction of Jews will not issue in the breakup of the army. It will make it a moral army and will strengthen its right to exist. True conscientious objection is not an opening for 'every man will do what is right in his eyes.' The objectors are the truly excellent among the soldiers. They wish to serve and sacrifice for the people and the state. Their disobedience is a lofty continuation of this sacrifice . . . In cases such as these, blind, natural obedience becomes a tool of anarchy toward which the regime is leading us . . . Soldiers with a conscience, in whom the presence of God exists, and who refuse to take part in any action of expulsion or in aiding it, will save the IDF and the state from the anarchy and destruction toward which Sharon is leading us. They will save thousands of Israelis from the march of death which began with Oslo and is gathering speed today. But above all else, they will save themselves from the tortured conscience that will upset them for the rest of their lives, if they take part in the crime. (Jewish Leadership, 2005: 11–13)

The tenor of Motti Karpel's diatribe—Moshe Feiglin's partner in the "Jewish Leadership" organization and the probable editor of the booklet—set a new standard for insurrectionary provocation and doomsday prophecies. He writes in the introduction:

The struggle is not for our homes, not for the Jewish settlement in the Gaza Strip, not for the settlement in Yesha in general and not even for the Land of Israel. The struggle is about the character of the State of Israel: will it be a Jewish state that is free or an anti-Semitic and dictatorial state . . . The struggle for Gush Katif is only the first battle in the campaign to restore the state to the people of Israel . . . The 'faith-based' community must begin to shake itself loose and to liberate itself. It must begin rising up against the Bolshevism of the Left and the ruling elites, and to free itself from the subordinate mental posture to which it has been educated . . . And more important still: the 'rules of the game' in play for the past 30 years and dictated by the Left did not allow us to stray from the rules of struggle that it dictated through the legal apparatus, the enforcement agencies and especially the media. Their victory is our acceptance of the rules. Our chance for victory in this struggle is that we will become those who determine what the rules are. Therefore, the struggle is for hegemony in the State of Israel. The indispensible condition is a spiritual shaking off of the dictatorship of the Left and the way to do this is by destroying the rules (*She'virat hakailim*), the rules of the system. Without these assumptions, it is not worth the energies, the illusions. How is this to be done tactically? . . . In the mundane world, it requires the non-violent action and refusal to obey any order to expel Jews. (Jewish Leadership, 2005: 7–8)

Although Karpel's words' immediate objective is Gush Katif, that is, vigorous civil disobedience as a means of blocking the disengagement, his more essential goal is the radical replacement of Israel's system of government. He does not reveal the details of the new system that he wishes to install, but it is clear that he attempts to exploit the opposition to the disengagement process in order to leverage a far more radical and far-reaching objective. Needless to say, he is not advocating liberal democracy. Ominously, the caption on the back cover of the booklet reads: "A little criminal—violates the law. A moderate criminal—bypasses the law. A big criminal—uses the law." To this must be added that Israel is described not only as dictatorial but is compared to the Third Reich (Jewish Leadership, 2005: 13–14, 17).

Sharon's dishonest bullying and anti-democratic use of power is manifest first, in his implementing a policy that contradicts the platform upon which he was elected; second, in his rejecting the results of the Likud's referendum; and third, in his creation of an artificial government majority by firing ministers Lieberman and Elon. These constitute a "brutal and insufferable blow to the system of government" (Jewish Leadership, 2005: 15–16). But even if these three defects could be corrected, the booklet's authors deny the authority of even a real democracy to even raise the question of evacuation:

Even a democratic majority in a national referendum cannot change this [the illegitimacy of disengagement]. A majority vote to expel entire populations is considered today a 'crime against humanity,' it is called 'ethnic cleansing' . . . The possibility of solving the Palestinian problem by uprooting a population does not exist in the dictionary of the 21st Century. Therefore, cursed be he who introduced uprooting Jewish settlements into the Israeli 'peace equation.' A society that has uprooting as part of its spirit has shallow roots in the earth, and also cannot be considered a democracy. (Jewish Leadership, 2005: 19)

This text reiterates the comparison between the evacuation of a civilian population and resettling them within the state's borders with "ethnic cleansing" and "transfer." It rejects the right of a democratically elected government to determine the state's borders and to withdraw its citizens from territories for geo-political and security reasons. Even though the evacuees' citizenship remains unchanged and even though they would receive fair compensation, Sharon's policy remains a crime against humanity. This comparison continues to be accepted by many in the religious Zionist community to this day.

A notable moment in the debate over disobedience during the disengagement which would echo long after the deed was done was the pamphlet of Rabbi Shaul Bar-Ilan, the head of the *Kollel* (a yeshiva for married students) in *Kfar Darom* (in Gush Katif) entitled "The magic button." Published by the 'Movement for Jewish Leadership' in March 2005, this document marks a watershed in religious Zionist radicalism. The pamphlet opens with a call for the total exclusion of the Jewish settlements in Gaza from the sovereignty of the State of Israel, i.e., creating a "Jewish autonomy" in Gush Katif (Bar Ilan, 2005: 5). Moreover, it contends that soldiers and police who take part in the expulsion of settlers from their homes are responsible for the financial losses incurred by those they eject. The aim of the pamphlet is clearly to encourage defiance against the sovereign authority of the State of Israel:

> The explanatory novelty of this pamphlet is in reminding [the reader] of a simple fact: the soldier who fulfills the command [to evict settlers] is in fact a person who causes monetary damage (*Motzee Mamon*) [to the settlers] . . . *The pamphlet's conclusion is therefore that because what is at stake is monetary loss, all rulings on the matter—which go beyond 'Torah law,' whatever their content—involve the abrogation of the prohibition "do not commit legal injustice." It is quite certain that as long as no such legal determination has been made, it is inconceivable that permission exists to obey orders and every soldier and policeman who participates in expelling [settlers] transgresses the sins enumerated above.* (Bar-Ilan, 2005: 6) [Emphasis in the original]

Throughout the pamphlet, Rabbi Bar-Ilan refuses to accept the standing of the State of Israel as a sovereign entity possessing the authority to

act in ways that are not the direct result of halachic rules and the decisions of a rabbinic court. He does not mention the widespread practice of
relocating people—even against their will—justified by the state's right of
"eminent domain." When the authorities decide that paving a road, erect-
ing a public structure, installing infrastructure, or establishing a military
base is necessary, expropriation of property and relocating inhabitants is
entirely legitimate. He goes so far as declaring that the arrest of a person
who refuses to comply with police orders is an act of "kidnapping." It also
falls under the category of "selling of individuals," abusing them before the
sale and contravenes the prohibition of putting people to work at hard
labor (Bar-Ilan, 2005: 11–12). Rabbi Bar-Ilan argues that the state has no
halachic status or power—in opposition to the dominant ethos of religious
Zionism stemming from Rabbi Avraham Isaac Kook and his halachic and
intellectual disciples that bestowed the state with halachic standing equal
to that of the Kingship of Israel:

> The ancient kings of Judea and Israel inherited their legal stand-
> ing from the first king of Israel, King Saul who was chosen with
> the approval of the entire people for the exalted authority that
> would be given him (Samuel: 1, 8, 11–20), *but the government
> of the Left and its priests never saw the state as a continuation of
> the ancient Kingdom of Israel.* (For this reason, they have heavy
> guilt feelings in regard to 'occupying conquered territory' and
> the 'profundity of the prohibition' that applies to ruling over
> an 'alien people'). *Even the people residing in Zion did not want,
> at the time the state was founded, to bestow upon the government
> power that was broader than what is common to advanced states in
> our time* . . . In our case, the State of Israel certainly does not
> have a binding status because of 'the law of the land is the
> law'—any more than what the British Mandate had. No one
> ever thought that the Torah gave the Mandate government the
> authority to prohibit Jews from settling in all parts of the land.
> (Bar-Ilan, 2005: 19–20)

Rabbi Bar-Ilan's most basic claim appears in the fourth "magic button" he
enumerates, which constitutes an (extra-halachic) response to his critics.

> Magic button number four: After the government's decision
> to disengage from Gush Katif and north Samaria, there is no
> longer a Mitzvah incumbent upon each individual to live in these
> areas.

[Response] There is no need to repeat that the State of Israel is not the people of Israel. The people of Israel is comprised of our fathers who have already died and our progeny who will be born in the future, those in the land and those outside it—all those whose feet stood beneath Mount Sinai. But the State of Israel is only a collection of that part of the people of Israel that now lives in the land and in a state that it shares with Gentiles—some from among righteous Gentiles and some from its most wicked. There is also no need to prove that there is no authority to any public—large as it may be—to undermine even one letter of the Torah and all that is in its power is to decide that at the present it does not have the resources to invest in this mandatory Mitzvah. Nor is it necessary to prove that the Mitzvah of settling the land falls upon each individual and is not conditioned upon the prior decision to capture this area. (Bar-Ilan, 2005: 25)

In these arguments, Rabbi Bar-Ilan deviates fundamentally from the prevalent religious Zionist view that there is an halachic linkage and continuation between the people of Israel and the State of Israel as the successor of the ancient Kingdom of Israel. For the mainstream of religious Zionists the basis of their halachic calls to disobey orders derives precisely from this principle of continuation. Drawing on this principle, the rabbis instructed—when faced with the state's refusal to fulfill the command of settling the land during the Oslo Process—that there was a halachic problem involved and refused to cooperate with the state's policy. If the State of Israel is a continuation of the ancient Kingdom of Israel, it is bound by the same laws, among them, the settling the Land of Israel. These are the teachings of the Rabbis Kook, father and son.

By contrast, Rabbi Bar-Ilan deprives the State of Israel of any halachic standing; halachically, it is void of any Jewish status. Lacking halachic standing, its authority to oversee and direct the settlement project is without basis. As opposed to the tradition of religious Zionism, Rabbi Bar-Ilan cuts the umbilical cord that ties the State of Israel with its ancient precursor. Therefore, even if the state directs that settlements be evacuated, it remains the right and duty of every Jew to continue inhabiting the land as a private person who wishes to fulfill the Mitzvah of settling the land of Israel. If the state has no halachic standing in evacuating settlements, responsibility for financial damages caused by the evacuation falls directly upon the individuals who evict (that is, the soldiers and police). Arguing that the state sent them therefore has no validity because the state has no validity.

Even though Rabbi Bar-Ilan is not one of the prominent rabbinic figures of religious Zionism, it is worth examining his position because it reflects a tendency gaining momentum among a radical minority in the religious Zionist camp. Notably, his pamphlet received warm endorsements from central figures in the rabbinical world of religious Zionism and his ideas were cited by influential figures. For example, Rabbi Avraham Shapira, former Chief Rabbi of the State of Israel, gave his support to this position:

> To the rabbi, the genius our teacher Rabbi Shaul Bar-Ilan . . . I was happy to receive the booklet "The Magic Button" you sent me that deals with the prohibition of evacuating Jews from the Katif region and other places which is based in its entirety on Halacha according to the Poskim both the earlier and later (*Rishonim ve'achronim*). May it be the will of God that this booklet opens the blind eyes of those who err in matters of Halacha. (Bar-Ilan, 2005: 2)

Rabbi Nahum Eliezer Rabinovitch is even more laudatory:

> To the rabbi, the genius, our rabbi and teacher Rabbi Bar-Ilan . . . Many thanks for the booklet, "The Magic Button" sent to me . . . In truth it requires no endorsement at all because it is full of love and splendor flowing out of the words of the sages and the halachic greats "clear, direct and true according to law" . . . And in my humble opinion preventing the expulsion decree not only will protect from all the sins involved but will fulfill thereby the performative Mitzvah unrivalled in importance which is the sanctification of God's name. (Bar-Ilan, 2005: 3)

Two letters were added to the booklet, authored by Rabbis Avigdor Nebenzahl and Zalman Nechemia Goldberg, respected and recognized scholars in the religious Zionist camp. Examining the letters carefully reveals that, oddly, they did not give their seal of approval to the contents of the booklet, did not mention the author and his essay; indeed they even expressed ideas that were essentially in opposition to those of Rabbi Bar-Ilan. Like most other religious Zionist rabbis, Nebenzahl asserted that the dismantling of the settlements was "a danger to all [the people of] Israel who are in the Land of Israel." Therefore, "they are absolutely prohibited" and "no person in Israel is to lend his hand, either directly or indirectly, to the dismantling" (Bar-Ilan, 2005: 4). But as opposed to Rabbi Bar-Ilan he understands the prohibition as applying to the state and not to individual soldiers who are responsible to those whom they damage. It is true that Rabbi Nebenzahl forbad taking part in the evacuation but this was because he saw it as aiding the state that was the guilty party; he did not speak of the individual obligations of the soldiers or police. Rabbi Goldberg gave his seal of approval to Rabbi Nebenzahl's judgments.

Beyond Rabbis Shapira and Rabinovitch, other prominent rabbis cited Rabbi Bar-Ilan and saw in his essay a worthy text that reflects the halachic reality created on the eve of the disengagement. In January 2010 Rabbi Dov Lior, arguably the most respected Halachic authority in the religious Zionist camp, answered the following question:

> Which Mitzvot and sins does a person violate when he evicts a person from his home in the Land of Israel? . . . Answer: First of all, he commits theft because he has damaged another's property—he beats another violently and then removes him from his home and destroys it. In short there are many prohibitions. One of the Rabbis from Gush Katif [Rabbi Bar-Ilan] wrote on the subject and enumerated the prohibitions involved. (Lior, 2010a)

Rabbi Zalman Melamed was even more insistent. He explicitly approved, both theoretically and practically, of the halachic conclusions drawn by Rabbi Bar-Ilan:

> Rabbi Shaul Bar-Ilan published a pamphlet in which he enumerates the prohibitions that are involved in the uprooting of Jews . . . The greatest scholars of Israel ratify Rabbi Shaul Bar-Ilan's conclusions, namely our teachers and rabbis, Rabbi Shapira, Rabbi Avigdor Nebenzahl, Rabbi Nachum Rabinovitch and also Rabbi Zalman Nechemia Goldberg who approves of Rabbi Nebenzahl's judgments. Rabbi Rabinovitch adds that he who refuses to violate these prohibitions despite the pressure applied to him sanctifies God's name and there is no greater Mitzvah.
>
> In the light of this halachic conclusion every person of Israel is obliged to resist and not to violate these prohibitions even if it involves the loss of a military career or their being fired from their work. Halacha says that a person must give up all his money and not violate this Torah prohibition, all the more so when so many severe prohibitions are involved. It is true that this demand is very difficult, but it is a straightforward Halacha. There is no authoritative scholar who believes that it

is permissible to uproot settlements even after the evil edict has already been passed. (Z. Melamed, 2005b)

These unrelenting views represent a significant escalation in the religious Zionist community's and rabbis's willingness to relate to the state in an alienated way—alienation that undermines the foundations of sovereign status of the State of Israel. Most of the rabbis who approve of the booklet and cite it are not of one mind with the assumptions of Rabbi Bar-Ilan. Closer readings of their words reveal nuances and variations. And yet, their common assumptions undercut the halachic and legal basis of the Israeli government and reject what was the common thread of the religious Zionist enterprise from its origins onward.

A short time after the appearance of the booklet, these positions began to seep even further into religious Zionist discourse (Rahat, 2005). For example, Eran Steinberg, the spokesman of Gush Katif proclaims:

> Every person, from the Right or from the Left, will, for God's sake, agree that even should a majority of 120 members of Knesset claim that it is permitted to steal and plunder, he will still not steal and plunder. Why? Just because! There are things that don't need explaining. Can someone imagine a Halacha declaring that one must remain in an army that executes such an order?! (Sternberg, 2005)

To be sure, there were those who publicly opposed Bar-Ilan's booklet, above all, Rabbi Aaron Lichtenstein (head of the *Har Etzion* yeshiva and one of the most outstanding rabbinic scholars within religious Zionist community), who ridiculed Bar-Ilan's arrogance, his ignoring the state's existence, and his claim that soldiers and policemen would be personally liable for political decisions taken by the government (Bart and Bart, 2007: 108–110).

At the same time, Rabbi Zalman Melamed and his son Rabbi Eliezer Melamed began making outright calls for soldiers to disobey orders. In the newspaper *BeSheva*, Rabbi Eliezer Melamed is reported as having spoken to secular youth; he explained that there was a built-in difference between the Left's disobedience that, in his view, was totally invalid because it obstructs the state's security, while the disobedience of the Right is merely the refusal to take part in what are only partisan political actions (E. Melamed, 2005b). His father, Rabbi Zalman Melamed, became the main spokesman for active resistance. He argued that explicitly proclaiming that one would disobey orders was part of disobedience itself and, therefore, passively avoiding taking part in the disengagement plan as a matter of personal conscience was insufficient; disobedience was a pedagogical instrument and it needed to be announced beforehand in the clearest possible way in order to effectively undermine the evacuation:

> When an order that contradicts the Torah is given and it is possible to evade fulfilling the order with various excuses, it will not do to use such excuses. One must announce: I will not violate the laws of the Torah, and for this reason I will not obey this order. This is the proper form of behavior even if there is danger in such behavior. (Z. Melamed, 2008c)

These words were written a few years after the disengagement but they faithfully express Rabbi Melamed's view (as well as those of many others) that developed and spread during the struggle against the evacuation from Gush Katif. Since Rabbi Zalman Melamed's views were very influential and were systematically developed by other settler leaders, they deserve our special, extensive attention.

Rabbi Z. Melamed's is a full-blown doctrine of proactive civil disobedience whose objective is wielding social influence—as opposed to conscientious disobedience which is a matter of personal choice limited to a specific individual As noted above, Rabbi Zalman Melamed had already advocated disobedience in the period of the Oslo Accords. As time went on, and with the recognition that Prime Minister Sharon's plan could not be stopped by conventional means, his position underwent substantial radicalization. In a talk (March 2005) entitled "Refusing an order strengthens the IDF" he returned to the words of Rabbi Tzvi Yehuda Kook: "In Judea and Samaria it will not happen without a war."

> Who loved the IDF more than my teacher and rabbi, Rabbi Tzvi Yehuda may he rest in peace? Who loved the state more than him? And precisely because of his love for the IDF and the state, my teacher and rabbi called out to the public "Do not fear," and said "There is no way to permit what is a Torah prohibition against transferring land to Gentiles, forbid it, absolutely, for all time. *Therefore it is incumbent upon every Torah sage in Israel, every man in Israel's army, to prevent and delay it with all might and main and may heaven help us.*" He also declared that one must *stand ready to sacrifice one's life against being forced to violate the Mitzvah of settling the Land of Israel, which is equivalent in weight to the entire Torah.* And he said "*In Judea and Samaria it*

will not happen without a war . . . over our bodies and our limbs."
I, as his student who was privileged to study with him and to be
near him for about twenty-five years, know with full confidence
that were Rabbi Tzvi Yehuda, may he rest in peace, here with
us he would call out to every soldier and policeman and officer
to disobey orders. And this out of his love for the IDF and the
state. (Z. Melamed, 2005a) [Emphasis in the original]

Notably, Rabbi Zalman Melamed does not claim that Rabbi Tzvi
Yehuda *actually* called upon soldiers to disobey orders. Nor does he deny
Rabbi Aviner's contention that Rabbi Kook never made such a demand.
What does emerge from his argument (in the following citation) is that the
reality facing Rabbi Tzvi Yehuda was essentially different from the one facing
Israel on the eve of disengagement. In the spirit of the many others who
used democratic arguments to justify disobedience, Rabbi Melamed writes:

The appeal to disobey orders in regard to uprooting [settle-
ments]—there is no more democratic appeal than this. Because
if the order is heard and the majority of the army will refuse to
fulfill the order—it only proves that the people is against the
uprooting and we must accept the opinion of the people. Even if
only a minority will refuse to fulfill orders—this is its democratic
right to remain loyal to its faith and we must not oblige people
to violate their faith . . . Therefore, I call . . . to act so as to
reveal the fact that the majority of the people and the majority
of the army are against uprooting Jews from their settlements,
and this by a mass petition expressing opposition to the plan
and refusal to take part in this prohibition. (Z. Melamed, 2005a)

Rabbi Zalman Melamed denies that large-scale military disobedience
would endanger the legitimacy of Israel's democratic regime. On the contrary:
He seems to see the army as a public arena in which different opinions
should be expressed, the exchange of ideas encouraged and, by extension,
autonomous actions by soldiers accepted. A soldier who refuses to obey orders
is exercising his right to freedom of thought and action. This is as radical a
form of libertarianism as can be imagined; not only does it refuse to accept
the authority of the majority; it refuses to accept even army discipline.
When the IDF leadership gives an order it is only the opening gambit in
a debate which will inexorably encourage countermoves and uncoordinated
actions. And this is as things should be. What was the prerogative of the
army leadership in setting policy, now becomes the "democratized" domain

of the many. Moreover, the right of the minority to resist includes the right to stymie the plans of the majority. The military, in Rabbi Melamed's view, is not fully subject to the authority of the democratically elected legislature and government. It—indeed, even parts of it—can express the "true" view of the nation over the head of the elected authorities. Nevertheless: Rabbi Melamed adds a caveat: "Clearly, there is nothing in my words to justify actively injuring a soldier, policeman or public official. He who does so damages the struggle against uprooting" (Z. Melamed, 2005a)

Perhaps in reaction to the Rabbis Melamed's authority-questioning teachings and to their growing influence in the religious Zionist camp, Rabbi Shlomo Aviner published a counter-argument which presents his very different conception of the army's role in Israeli democracy, especially when politically controversial issues are at issue. Among his comments is the following: "It is unacceptable to use either a military function or a military rank to advance a political cause . . . Neither the soldiers nor the officers will determine the fate of the state . . . The sovereign is the people. The people! If there is a moment of confusion, then [let there be a] referendum. It is not the army that leads the people; rather it is the people who are the leader" (Aviner, 2005b).

Returning to Rabbi Melamed: once again he is not arguing for individual conscientious objection. On the contrary, he sees a soldier's public announcement that he will disobey orders as an integral part of the refusal itself; evasiveness and blurring the lines undermines the essential objective of resistance which is to challenge the legitimacy of a government that demands evacuation. Loudly proclaimed disobedience strengthens the IDF, the State of Israel and Israeli society. Indeed, it may even be mandatory for the health of Israeli democracy. Not surprisingly, after the disengagement Rabbi Melamed attacked those rabbis who opposed disobeying orders and ridiculed their views; they suffered, he claims, from halachic timidity.

Refusal, he contends, is an essential part of democracy. He who disobeys immoral, anti-halachic orders as a matter of high principle conveys the core democratic value of individual rights, expresses the *vox populi* (Z. Melamed, 2005h). Therefore, a society in which orders are disobeyed because conscience forbids following them is a flourishing, vibrant democracy. The most essential part of their individuality is protected against the collective force of random majorities. Allowing for open dialogue, rather than enforcing laws created by an elected legislature, safeguards individual rights and. in the end, even strengthens the state's stability. In an essay entitled "Torah and democracy" he writes:

> One of the superior things about a democratic regime is that the government does not coerce the individual to perform actions

that are in opposition to his conscience. Refusal is a very healthy phenomenon from the democratic point of view which strives to give maximal individual freedom to every person and every community.

There are, nevertheless, certain basic issues about which there is no individual freedom and one of them is military service. But within the army the object is to give the individual the freedom to live according to his beliefs. Therefore, I see the phenomenon of refusal as a healthy democratic development. (Z. Melamed, 2005h: 9)

This stress on individual freedom is part of a doctrine that Rabbi Melamed consistently defended. Two years earlier he wrote:

It is a basic principle of democracy that we should not force a person to act against his conscience except for cases where there is a danger to the state. He should not be forced when [he] wishes to preserve order and law, especially when [this coercion] is exploited for a narrow political end; it is prohibited and it is improper to make this demand. The directive to evacuate an outpost is absolutely in opposition to the foundations of the religious Zionist belief and it is not a national security need that mandates forcing people to violate the foundations of their faith. (Z. Melamed, 2003a)

Needless to say, Rabbi Melamed's claims do not accord with the prevalent understanding of liberal democracy. His argument, although couched in the language of democracy, is not, his critics contend, as straightforward and simple as he would have us believe. They question whether it is authentic concern for liberal democracy and its norms that lies at the root of his motives. Rather, they see in Rabbi Melamed's arguments a flawed exploitation of democratic principles. The belief that democracy entails the right of each individual (and each soldier) to do whatever he pleases in accordance with his own values and that the majority and its military representatives do not have the right to impose its will when he acts in violation of the law, derives from the anarcho-libertarian rather than the liberal democratic tradition. His detractors doubt that Rabbi Melamed is either an anarcho-libertarian or that he is motivated by democratic ideals as they are commonly understood.

Indeed, Rabbi Melamed does not attempt to hide his only qualified and conditional commitment to democratic principles. They are not, it is clear, the main source of his ideas; he uses them as an ancillary means of defending his worldview, of speaking in ways that are likely to appeal to a wider audience than only those who are committed to Halacha. Despite his somewhat perfunctory appeals to democracy, the ultimate source of his worldview is religious faith and the supreme authority of Halacha (Z. Melamed 2005h: part 3, para. 40). Speaking to soldiers who were called up for reserve duty when the settlement evacuation was taking place, he makes clear just how secondary his democratic declarations really are. He declares:

> Even he who is called upon to aid [in executing an evacuation] must refuse and receive his punishment with love. He must utilize his democratic right—not to obey an order that violates his beliefs. I emphasized that this is democratic *not because were it not so one would need to obey the order* but because there are those in our community who fear that refusal injures democracy; for them [refusal] is a blow against the state's existence and, as an existential threat to the state, one is permitted to commit a sin for the sake of saving of lives (*Pikuach nefesh*). Therefore I added that there is here no threat to democracy; what is more, it [refusal] is part of democratic rights even though it opposes the law. (Z. Melamed, 2005c: 7) [Emphasis added]

Rabbi Melamed often attempts to conduct a dialogue between his ostensibly liberal democratic outlook on the one hand and his Torah point of view on the other. (Clearly, the latter wins.) As the following citation demonstrates once again, his reliance on democratic principles is more rhetorical than substantive. In a lecture entitled "*Tikun*" he writes:

> The democratic view that has developed in recent years is opposed to nationalism. [Democracy wishes] to wipe out the distinctions between peoples, religions and cultures and from the democratic point of view there is *no right for any individual to impose upon his fellows how to live and according to which rules they ought to act.* . . . [Hence] today a Zionist secular Jew is incapable of explaining to himself what right he has to demand this land for himself while there are others living in the land for many generations. [Neither can he explain] why his right is greater than theirs.
>   The only way to answer these questions is a belief in God—out of the knowledge that there is a Creator and he cre-ated the world according to a plan . . . At the heart of this plan

lies the people of Israel . . . Only a view such as this, which democracy does not recognize, accords with a moral and logical conception which explains that the right of the people of Israel is an essential part of this Divine plan for the sake of which He created the world and therefore the realization, that even the use of military force, and even at the price of ruling over other people that chose to live in the land, is not only permitted and justified but also mandated by this reality which is part of the historical destiny of the entire world. (Z. Melamed, 2010)

Familiarity with modern democratic discourse renders Rabbi Melamed's views quite questionable. He defends one aspect of contemporary liberal democracy but is oblivious to the other. Liberal democracy does, indeed, rest upon a universalistic image of human beings and their rights but clearly it is not opposed to the cultural and national uniqueness of peoples. Western liberal democracy is based on the concurrent validity of both these principles. As opposed to his recurrent utilization of democratic vocabulary, Rabbi Melamed is a Jewish exclusivist who believes in the superiority of the Jewish people. Hence, it is the right and duty of the Jews to rule over the Land of Israel solely and completely. No other national claims can be countenanced. Yet, despite this profoundly illiberal position, when the issue at stake is the right of refusal to evict Yesha residents, he becomes radically democratic, not to say anarcho-libertarian. He has no trouble admitting that military control over the Palestinians is anti-democratic and violates Western universal principles, but Jewish rights, he insists, override universal principles. On the one hand, democratic values are dismissed and yet, on the other, the democratic right to disobey orders is justified. The rough seams of his democratic–anti-democratic syncretism are apparent. His argumentation is well described as a squaring of the moral circle, reconciling opposites, sometimes even outright self-contradiction. Whether this is complexity or cynicism must be left an open question. Nor is Rabbi Melamed alone in this kind of strained argumentation. It regularly repeats itself in the discourse of religious Zionist spokesmen who present their opposition to the evacuation of settlers from Yesha on democratic liberal grounds while simultaneously ignoring the fact that contemporary liberal democratic theory rejects the very idea of creating settlements on the conquered land of Yesha/the West Bank.

Rabbi Melamed's anarcho-libertarian ideas go further still—at least rhetorically. He writes, for example—in opposition to his son, Rabbi Eliezer Melamed who justifies (as cited above) only disobedience of the

Right—that left-wing disobedience is as legitimate as that of the Right. He argues that noncompliance on the part of the Left also strengthens the IDF and the state.

> Even if as a result of refusing orders to uproot [settlements] there will come a counter-refusal to serve in Yesha, there is no danger to the army. On the contrary: those left wingers who refuse to serve can be freed from serving in Yesha. They will serve with motivation on the northern border and those serving in Yesha will also serve with motivation; thus the army can fulfill its role in a healthy and proper way. There is no reason to impose things upon a soldier that are against his conscience and beliefs.
>
> Of course the questioner may ask: Can an army function when the soldiers dictate to their officers where they will serve, thereby creating two armies: The Israel Defense Forces, northern section, secular and left wing, and the Israel Defense Forces Yesha Section: Zionist, religious and right wing? (Z. Melamed, 2005c: 9)

Insofar as Rabbi Zalman Melamed "answers" this question, it is as follows: the refusals on both the Right and Left are nothing more than an accurate reflection of the sharp cleavages that exist within Israeli society. Therefore, refusal will not create a cleavage; it already exists. On the contrary, he argues, it will sharpen and direct attention to the problems that cleave Israeli society and to which we do not, as yet, have a solution. In his view, the very sharpening of the extremes is likely to encourage public negotiation and discussion through which some of the problems will be resolved (Z. Melamed, 2005h). Refusal, he insists, is a means of strengthening the individual soldier's sense of identity with the army, of preventing the exploitation of the army to advance a minority political agenda, and to raise the banner of Torah within the nation (Z. Melamed, 2006j).

In short: allowing the individual soldier to refuse an order will fortify his dedication to the higher ends of the army he serves. His freedom to act in accordance with his conscience will bind him all the more tightly to the army because he will appreciate its humanity and tolerance. By contrast, when the army imposes its will and coerces him to act in opposition to his conscience, his sense of identity with the army will be seriously undermined; his motivation to fight heroically will plummet dramatically. (Z. Melamed, 2005a). Indeed, he is even prepared to broaden the boundaries of refusal to include Druze and Muslim soldiers who should not to be forced to act against their people and their co-religionists (Z. Melamed, 2005f). In fact, all value-based worldviews are sufficient reasons for refusal, so that when a soldier feels that his most precious beliefs are being desecrated, he must have the right to refuse—each according to his own worldview.

> The Left understands those who refuse to harm terrorists if their families will be hurt as well but does not understand at all the refusal to participate in removing outposts. By contrast, the Right fully understands the refusal to evacuate outposts but does not at all understand the refusal to serve in Yesha or to strike at terrorists even though their families will be hurt . . . My opinion is clear: when the order contradicts basic, deeply-rooted values that are at the foundation of the entire outlook and worldview of the one who receives the order, he has the right to refuse and it is incumbent upon the government not to force him to act in opposition to his beliefs. I want to emphasize that not every slight moral value justifies refusal but only actions that strike at foundational values. (Z. Melamed, 2005f)

Because the army is not an independent institution that autonomously enforces discipline but rather a tool meant to express and implement the state's values, it follows that values are uppermost, that values trump discipline. Rabbi Melamed believes that "the power of a society is in the spiritual content it carries; the power of the army lies in its being imbued with motivation and knowing what it is fighting for—not with blind discipline. The external framework, the discipline, has only secondary significance" (Z. Melamed, 2005f). In fact, the government's power is very restricted when it comes to executing actions rejected by substantial parts of the public (even though the government has a majority in the parliament). In a rhetorical retort to the obvious question "what will happen to a government unable to implement its policy because of mass resistance from the Right and the Left," Rabbi Melamed, returning to the libertarian strains in his thought, admits that this may be problematic but that the fault lies with the government—it should not initiate divisive policies:

> There is, indeed, a danger here, and therefore it is incumbent upon the government to take care and not to decide on actions that do not have maximal support, because this may tear the people apart. And if it does so, it carries the responsibility for all of the consequences. But it is not to be demanded or expected that a person do things that are against his beliefs. (Z. Melamed, 2005f)

Rabbi Aharon Lichtenstein recoils from what he sees as the anarchic qualities in Rabbi Melamed's thought. Relying upon the Kantian principle that individual actions must be directed by a moral vision, Rabbi Lichtenstein expresses understanding for the ethical dilemma involved in forcing soldiers to act against the dictates of their conscience. And yet, his conclusions are the reverse of Rabbi Melamed's. It is the soldier and not the government that needs to reconsider his actions:

> There is certainly good reason to argue that every person sets the moral principles that direct him and, in so doing, decides which order is patently illegal in his eyes. However, each person who champions such a basic philosophical principle must ask himself what are the practical consequences of his conception. In my view, when such a conception is applied in a political system, its meaning is the possible disintegration of the army and the nation. (Cited in Bart and Bart, 2007: 108.)

Although others repeated some of his arguments, in the end Rabbi Melamed stood by himself. As opposed to most on the religious Right who supported disobedience as an effective means to prevent evacuation, Rabbi Melamed claims that refusal to obey orders is an intrinsic good, a value in itself—whatever its practical success or failure. Uniquely, he insists upon the validity of refusal that derives from left-wing, even Muslim opinions; indeed, he accepts the legitimacy of reasons for disobedience so long as they derive from value-based worldviews. If they could be shown to be relevant to the issue, even vegetarianism or environmentalism would be valid grounds for refusal.

In the end, Rabbi Melamed's unlikely synthesis between advocating refusal, sanctifying the state and speaking the language of liberal democracy, suffered a signal defeat. It seems probable that the dissonance inherent in the syncretistic credo he preached was unworkable. How is one to assiduously protect the state's messianic standing while simultaneously accusing it of inexcusable villainy, defying the military while defending the right of the secular Left to undermine ideas that he claims are absolute and unchallengeable, to talk liberal talk while defending illiberal positions? The internal structural contradictions were too discordant for the settler camp to ingest and Rabbi Melamed's unlikely package unraveled. His doctrine became the victim of its own convolutions. The failure of his teachings became obvious a few months after the disengagement plan was executed. In the end the rabbi's teachings failed to catch on. Instead, the lofty religious status of the state overcame—even if not all cases—the halachic imperative to settle the Land of Israel. The disengagement passed with virtually no deadly violence.

Although there is much ideological communality between Rabbi Zalman Melamed and Rabbi Dov Lior, the latter is the more radical of the two—both in style and in content. Rabbi Lior's outlook tends to be of the black-and-white variety. It does not have Rabbi Z. Melamed's multisided complexity which made it difficult for many to internalize and accept. Rabbi Lior's views are especially worthy of note because many consider him to be the most prominent contemporary halachic figure in the religious Zionist camp. In radical religious right-wing circles, his leadership is virtually unchallenged. A Holocaust survivor who arrived in Israel on the ship *Exodus*, Rabbi Lior is a graduate of the Mercaz HaRav yeshiva, Chief Rabbi of Kiryat Arba, and the head of the *Nir* yeshiva in Kiryat Arba. Besides his other public functions, Rabbi Lior is among the leaders of the Association of Yesha Rabbis and of the *Tkuma* movement (the right-wing faction of the religious Bayit Hayehudi party). He moved even further rightward in the elections for the 20th Knesset (2015) supporting the *Yahad-Ha'am Itanu* party with its Kahanist coloration. Rabbi Lior supports the controversial act of ascending to the Temple Mount.

His writings include a number of volumes of responsa entitled *Dvar Hevron* (The Word from Hebron) (Lior, 2005–11), halachic essays and a voluminous number of verbal responses to queries that were prepared for publication on the internet, especially on the site "yeshiva" (www.yeshiva.org.il). Despite his halachic prominence, it should be cautioned that Rabbi Lior is not a mainstream, normative figure in the religious Zionist community. He gained much notoriety with his extreme views on Prime Minister Rabin, his attitude toward Arabs and non-Jews generally, his laudatory comments on Baruch Goldstein, his racist remarks about President Barak Obama, his describing of the European leadership as "Nazi collaborators," and so on.

Rabbi Lior's fundamental position on the halachic status of the State of Israel is similar to that held by other religious Zionist rabbis—many of them already encountered in our discussions of the Yamit and Oslo crises. Like them, Rabbi Lior sees the state as sacred although his ambivalence toward its legitimacy goes beyond what many of them—Rabbi Melamed, for example—would find acceptable. As a graduate of the Mercaz HaRav yeshiva and a student of Rabbi Tzvi Yehuda Kook, he attributes great holiness and theological centrality to the State of Israel and its institutions. Rabbi Lior sees the State of Israel as the central instrument that renders settling the land possible and settling the land he claims (in the spirit of his mentor Rabbi Tzvi Yehuda Kook) is the most important Mitzvah in the Torah. Turning Maimonides's views on their head, he argues that:

> The dwelling of the people of Israel in the Land of Israel,
> according to Maimonides, is the very basis of the people of

Israel's life. Maimonides does not mention it in the listing of Mitzvot because it is more than a specific and defined Mitzvah; it is the basis and infrastructure for the existence of the nation, the very being of our lives and for all of the other Mitzvot. Therefore, it is clear and simple that according to Maimonides there is a Mitzvah of Aliyah and it is incumbent on every Jew to settle in the Land of Israel . . . Restricting the hold of the people of Israel over the Land of Israel is like the amputation of limbs from the body . . . No health will arise from it, no purpose . . . In accordance with this, the statement of the sages is clearly understood: "Living in the Land of Israel is equal in weight to all the Mitzvot of the Torah" (*Sifri* Deuteronomy, 12). Only in the Land of Israel can the true vitality of the people of Israel be revealed. (Lior, 2009d: 4)

Hence, for so long as the state does not coerce Jews to violate their faith—as in giving up territory—it must be obeyed to the letter of the law. It should be noted in passing that Rabbi Lior is not content with halachic prohibitions against evacuation; he bolsters his position by adducing many historical, philosophical, and strategic considerations (Lior, 2008a: 3; Lior, 1984; Lior, 2002).

For Rabbi Lior, the halachic principle of "community ordinances" (*Takanot ha'kahal*) plays a major role in assessing the legitimacy of Knesset legislation. These Takanot were common in Jewish communities long before the Middle Ages. They were essentially administrative, civil, and criminal statutes organizing Jewish community life and serving its interests. Although they do not have the status of Halacha per se, they are validated by halachic authority. Takanot ha'kahal, Rabbi Lior believes, can be interpreted broadly so as to include a citizen's obligation to obey state law. Even when civil law is parallel to and different from Torah law, it can be seen as valid so long as it reflects accepted interpersonal customs, expresses the interests of the state, and upholds the principle of community welfare (Lior, 2002). Still, Rabbi Lior cautions, since the majority of Israeli laws are based upon the validity of "community ordinances," they need to be constantly scrutinized and monitored. The relevant question is: do they indeed pursue the need and benefit of society? In other words, for Rabbi Lior civil laws have no inherent democratic legitimacy or standing; their validity derives from the function they fulfill as regulators of the social and economic life of the state. Rabbi Lior's "utilitarian" position toward state law is clearly expressed in the following:

There is a rule that 'the law of the land is the law,' [which validates] everything the Kingdom legislates for the good of the citizens such as in cases of traffic law and taxes. A law that contradicts the Torah should be related to as a wicked decree; indeed at times it requires one to sacrifice one's life [rather than obey it]. Therefore, laws like traffic laws have the same force as Torah law and it is incumbent upon us to obey them. This applies to money matters as well. (Lior, 2009a: 3)

Hence, it comes as no surprise that despite his utilitarian view of Knesset legislation, Rabbi Lior, true to mentor Rabbi Tzvi Yehuda, attaches great value to the symbols of the state, to its army, and to the deep personal-spiritual ties Jews have to the State of Israel (Lior, 2009a: 5).

While Rabbi Melamed leaves no room for doubt about his unswerving loyalty to the State of Israel, even if it "sins," Rabbi Lior is less forgiving. When retreat from the Greater Land of Israel is at stake, his position is stark and unrelenting; he supports vigorous, active resistance to evacuation and refusal to obey military orders (Sheleg, 2007). Weakening the Jewish grip on any part of the Land of Israel contradicts the very essence of the State of Israel. Government laws that call for withdrawal are opposed not only to the unrivalled Mitzvah of conquering and settling the land, they fly in the face of Divine will that underlies the state and accounts for its military victories. Therefore:

All the present territorial retreats [the disengagement] are against the position taken by the Torah. A government of Israel, according to Torah law is forbidden to deliver territory of the Land of Israel to the control of Gentiles . . . Thus, anyone who supports transferring land into the hands of Gentiles in practice or even only with words transgresses the performative commandment: "And you shall take possession of the land and settle in it for I have given the land to you." (Deuteronomy, 33:53) (Lior, 2006: 5)

Although it is specifically the Jewish people rather than the Jewish state that is duty-bound to the settle the land, Rabbi Lior argues that the people of Israel is halachically identical with the State of Israel and, hence, the latter bears the same responsibility toward the Land of Israel as the former. As its representative body, the state is no less obliged to conquer and settle the land than the people. This duty falls upon the state's institutions, most notably its army. Rabbi Lior's rhetoric and halachic severity may be harsh, but in this regard at least he concurs with the vast majority of religious Zionist authorities. Like them, he declares it to be "clear and simple" that it is prohibited (in the most uncompromising sense of the term "prohibited") for the state to prevent the nation from executing its duty to conquer and colonize the land. When the eviction of Jews from their homes in the Land of Israel is at stake, elected governments and democratic principles fall by the wayside. Resistance and refusal are mandatory. Beyond his radical political theology, Rabbi Leor's political associations with Kahanists, his refusal to reject the Goldstein massacres, and his reactions to an extremist tract that dealt with killing non-Jews (more below), he was prone to particularly shrill and blunt rhetoric that placed him at the right-wing boundary of religious Zionism.

An entirely different perspective on disobedience specifically, and on Judaism in general, is that of Rabbi Yuval Sherlow. As opposed to Rabbis Melamed and Lior who are followers of the Mercaz HaRav variety of Zionism and students of Rabbi Tzvi Yehuda, Rabbi Sherlow studied in the *Har Etzion* yeshiva under the tutelage of the more dovish and liberal Rabbis Aharon Lichtenstein and Yehuda Amital. Nevertheless, he makes clear that much of his religious inspiration derives from Rabbi Avrhaham Isaac Kook (the father). Rabbi Sherlow was one of the founders (after Rabin's assassination) and remains one of the leaders of the *Tzohar* (opening or aperture), a league of modern Orthodox rabbis who attempt to make religious ceremonies and obligations more "user-friendly." He serves as the head of the Hesder yeshiva *Orot Shaul* in *Petach Tikva*. Part of his prominence in the Orthodox religious world is the voluminous number of "answers" or responsa he gave (and continues to give) to those who ask for his opinion on the *Moreshet* (tradition) (www.moreshet.org.il) and the *Kamoha* (www. kamoha.co.il) Internet sites. (One authority places the number of these responses at about 37,000).

For many, religious and secular, Rabbi Sherlow represents a courageous, semi-liberal brand of Judaism that does not recoil from expressing contentious opinions or taking divisive actions on issues that are halachically controversial. For example: homosexuality (prohibited, but empathy for those who suffer is important) sexuality (regarding older non-married women, and the question of artificial insemination), etc. He took part in the 2011 "social justice" protests, belongs to an interfaith dialogue group, supports civil marriage in Israel for those whom the official rabbinate refuses to marry, and has taken highly controversial positions on Conservative and Reform conversion (even Tzohar balked at this last opinion). Lest the reader draw the conclusion that Rabbi Sherlow flirts with "progressive" Judaism or is halachically lax, it should be made absolutely clear that he is religiously severe and politically right wing. He is associated with the rightist Habayit Hayehudi party and has, for example, prohibited women dancing (presumably at weddings, etc.) in the sight of men, and forbidden singing or listening to songs (presumably like "Amazing Grace") with a Christian character.

On the subject of the disengagement, Rabbi Sherlow has been particularly vocal, in the press, and on the Internet. Some of his responsa on the subject have been anthologized into a book entitled: *The Disengagement Responsa* (Sherlow, 2010a). As a rule, Rabbi Sherlow follows the lead of his teachers Rabbis Amital and Lichtenstein, but he differs from them in believing that the disengagement does, in fact, violate Halacha—although he refrains from expressing this view in so many words. Whatever his motives for discretion, his writings make clear that at least at the level of practice he opposed the disengagement plan for, among others, Torah-related reasons. Notably however, he did not reject, at the level of halachic principle, the feasibility of other such plans, if they were necessary (Sherlow, 2010a: 29–40).

Rabbi Sherlow repeatedly returns to his conviction that the people of Israel do not have a "right" to the land but rather have an "obligation" to preserve it in its entirety. As with many other religious Zionists, the ruling of the medieval scholar Nachmanides is cited: there is a halachic obligation that requires every Jew individually, as well as the entire Jewish community as a whole, to take over the land and to settle it. But obligations are often conditional and dependent on context. Consequently, Rabbi Sherlow desists from defining what the limits of this obligation are and to what extent one is required to preserve the land in face of internal and external exigencies. He says only that the obligation is not absolute and that under certain circumstances, moral and national considerations may override it. This position accords with his emblematic halachic approach that when "difficult questions" are involved, the various opposing interests need to be balanced; the adjudicator needs to recognize that there is no single, simple answer that is "correct."

But when it comes to disobedience, Rabbi Sherlow is adamant and decisive. It is not permitted. He gives a number of reasons for this judgment:

A. According to many Poskim the state has the authority to decide that it cannot fulfill the Mitzvah of settling the land at this time and that, strategically, withdrawing from territory advances the interests and well-being of the nation.

B. After the Knesset's decision to evacuate Gush Katif, the Jewish people have, in effect, already abandoned the territory. Disgracefully, the Knesset has, with a large majority, accepted the plan and we are permitted to respond in only one way: to do our very best to change the decision. His position is similar to that of Rabbis Tau and Aviner mentioned above, and to that of Rabbi Yoel Bin-Nun (Bin-Nun, 2005).

C. The most important issue raised by uprooting settlements is that of saving lives (Pikuach nefesh) on a national scale. Disobeying orders or not showing up for reserve duty endangers the very fabric of national life and in so doing becomes an issue of national life and death that overrides the entire Torah, even the Mitzvah of settling the Land of Israel (Sherlow, 2010).

There are, Rabbi Sherlow points out, weighty halachic authorities for whom government decisions like the disengagement are legitimate. Therefore, refusing to comply with orders as if they were patently illegal cannot be justified. Strategic positions supporting and opposing disengagement both have at least a certain degree of justice on their side. Dismissing those in favor of disengagement as if they were obtuse villains and demanding of the faithful that they resist and defy government decisions can only lead to national catastrophe. Therefore, according to Rabbi Sherlow, whether or not to obey orders—except in special cases—is not a decision to be made by soldiers:

There are many commands that it is forbidden to obey and there exists a clear red line. Nevertheless, a decision of the Israeli government determining the borders of the state is not one of them because halachically it is the government of Israel and the other echelons of political rule that are responsible for leading the people into war; they are responsible for determining what they believe cannot be [realistically] defended. I want to emphasize that in my opinion they committed a serious, fatal mistake that will exact a high price both spiritually and existentially, but my halachic position is that far worse is a torn and divided army that cannot defend its people of Israel in its land. (Sherlow, 2010a: 106)

Rabbi Sherlow presents a secondary principle to undergird his position: "A soldier is not a messenger (Shaliach) of the state. He is the instrument (Kli) through which the government pursues its actions and he must fulfill orders unless they are orders that it is preferable for the state to be dismantled rather than fulfilling them, that it would be preferable for the state not to exist with such orders" (Sherlow, 2010: 102). (As noted above, Rabbi Aviner and the heads of the pre-army religious institutions (*Mechinot*) as well as other significant figures in the religious Zionist community shared this view.) Rabbi Sherlow concludes therefore that there is no prohibition against eviction carried out by a soldier who is so ordered because he is considered only as "the long hand" of the government. This is not like the case of "agency" (*Shlichut*) in which a messenger has an independent mind and, consequently, is responsible for the actions he performs. In such cases of an independent-minded messenger the principle "there is no agency for sinful actions" applies (Babylonian Talmud, Tractate *Kiddushin*, 43a). This principle does not apply to soldiers under military discipline (Sherlow, 2011).

The re-publication of his responsa drew some very sharp condemnations. To choose only one example out of many: Rabbi Sherlow, one critic argued, deprives the individual soldier of the right to think critically for himself. The morality of an order is relegated to very distant and narrow spheres. This critic writes: "Even though it is true that it is the government's right to decide on the borders of the state, this right has limits in cases where it injures the residents of the place . . . This is democratic dictatorship that tramples the minority and its rights illegitimately" (Henschke, 2011). Whatever one's reaction to this critic's argument may be, it clearly is not the view accepted by liberal democrats. In their worldview, the range of legitimate refusal is indeed narrow and restricted, relating only to egregious cases (like the order to rape or murder prisoners or deliberately kill civilians, etc.) about which there are no disagreement. Despite the undeniable human suffering involved, this is not true of the disengagement.

A short and telling vignette brings us back to the days and weeks before the disengagement was implemented. A discussion between young people from Gush Katif about active resistance—such as blockading roads— was documented Elyashiv Reichner and it well reflects settler discourse at the time:

> LAVI: I'm opposed. Yesterday we took a youth trip to Jerusalem and we spoke to Rabbi Elon. If I understood him correctly, he told us that if the people do not want us to be here then maybe we shouldn't be here. It is for this reason that I really wanted there to be a referendum.
>
> AVITAL: If I could beat you up, I would. You want to tell me that if there were a referendum and the majority voted for the disengagement you would leave?

LAVI: Let's say, I would think about it and a lot of people would think as I do.

AVITAL: I think we are here because of an imperative of God because this is the Land of Israel and not because a government sent us or the people decided.

LAVI: But you know that the Mitzvah of settling the land is not a Mitzvah that falls upon the individual. (Reichner, 2005)

The Disengagement and Its Aftermath

As the date of the disengagement grew near, it became increasingly clear to its opponents that the plan would indeed be implemented. The settler camp that had been dealing with disengagement as a question of principle was now forced to awaken to its impending reality. Many religious Zionists who were convinced that it could not happen, that God would not allow it to happen, had no choice but to prepare for—religiously, ideologically, and logistically—what seemed inevitable. Despite voices that proclaimed "it shall not come to pass" (attributed to the former Chief Rabbi Mordechai Eliyahu), the religious Zionist leadership had to come to terms with the fact that the disengagement was already a fait accompli. Resigned and fatalistic, the religious Right's reactions to the disengagement necessarily underwent a transformation. When the Supreme Court (June 9, 2005) decided by a ten to one majority that the disengagement plan was legal, their last glimmer of hope was dashed.

The realization that disengagement would in fact take place led a number of leading rabbis to decree that serious violence must be avoided. Although symbolic resistance was justified, actions that could descend into a maelstrom of fighting and bloodshed were not. So certain were some rabbis of the case for settler restraint that they claimed, in advance of the disengagement, that even relatively moderate violent acts—such as planting dummy bombs or placing nails on the road—could not be the actions of the settler camp. For example, Rabbi Zalman Melamed argued conspiratorially that if such things did nonetheless happen, they would be the work of Shabak provocateurs (Z. Melamed, 2005c). (Rabbi Melamed was surely recalling the highly problematic actions of the rogue Shabak agent Avishai Raviv who, allegedly, encouraged Yigal Amir to assassinate Yitzhak Rabin.) Nevertheless, there is good reason to believe that Rabbi Melamed knew then, and knows today, that after the tragic case of Avishai Raviv, the Shabak, having learned its lesson, had ceased implementing such dangerous practices. Whatever Rabbi Melamed may or may not have known, he continued using the image of lurking Shabak agents. This conspiracy theory served a double purpose: it emphasized his principled opposition to unchecked violence just as it distanced the settler community from responsibility for such acts. Critics claim that he continues using this conspiratorial rhetoric despite knowing full well that actions such as these were, in fact, carried out by figures on the extreme Right in general and the religious Right in particular.

Among the indications that disengagement had come to be seen as unavoidable were the opinions expressed by Rabbi Shlomo Aviner, opinions that were quite exceptional for him. On the eve of the government's decision (August 7, 2005) to begin evacuating the settlements, he wrote:

> If the IDF evacuates settlements it is no longer worthy of the name IDF (Israel Defense Forces) . . . Blessed be the soldier who is unable, blessed is the soldier who remains a human being, who remains a Jew with a Jewish heart that they have not succeeded to destroy and that they will not be able to destroy. Blessed be the soldier who has a Jewish heart and not the heart of a terrorist . . . Only that we need to emphasize that there is here no call for disobeying orders and there is no call for rebellion. There is no political manipulation and there is no balance of terror but rather a moral, human inability of a soldier who is put in an impossible situation, in infinite difficulty, in absolute brotherly incapacity. (Aviner, 2005c) [Emphasis in the original]

It is impossible to interpret Aviner's words in any other way but as those of one who has reached the outer limit of tolerance, one who has come perilously close to calling for disobedience. In the end, his Mamlachti position triumphed and prevented him—however tested he was—from actually crossing the line.

Both spiritually and practically the "moment of truth" arrived in *Kfar Maimon* between the 18th and the 20th of July 2005. Following the security forces' success in thwarting the Yesha Council's plan to bring tens of thousands of supporters into Gush Katif, they gathered in Kfar Maimon, only a few kilometers away. The tens of thousands who came to protest found themselves surrounded by many thousands of security personnel from the IDF, the police, and the Border Guards. Despite earlier plans to breach the encircling forces and reach the Gush nevertheless, it quickly became obvious that there was no practical value to this plan: first, because it could not succeed; and second, because it would only lead to violent confrontations with the security forces. An echo of the dispirited mood that prevailed can be heard in the words of Bentzi Lieberman, then head of the Yesha Council, who replied to a group of messianic *Chabad* (a militant Hasidic group) supporters who wanted to know why the protesters did not attempt to break out and make their way to the Gush: "There are hundreds of police and Border Guards and if we break out, in five minutes there will be people with broken hands and legs on the road. We won't gain anything by it. This struggle must be handled rationally . . . Our struggle is not against the police but over the hearts of the Israeli public" (cited in Feffer, 2005).

Many, particularly in the religious Zionist community, believe that there was a prejudicial mismatch between the way the protesters behaved, which was mostly lawful, and the way they were presented in the media—mostly as violent lawbreakers. Over time this led to a bitter sense of being misunderstood, even persecuted by the country's left-wing, secular elites. The press and much of the public, they felt, failed to appreciate the enormous positive energies that were embodied in the religious Zionist community (Roth, 2011: 175–79). For most religious Zionists, the behavior of Prime Minister Sharon was deplorable and undemocratic. In an unprecedented step, he instructed the IDF to thwart the intentions of lawful, peaceful protesters to reach Gush Katif by resorting to a massive military action against patriotic citizens within the Green Line. Indeed, there were reporters (of a certain ideological stamp) who believed that this military show of force was nothing less than a media "spin" whose purpose was to paint a demonic picture of the protesters who had the temerity to confront IDF soldiers, perhaps the most highly regarded Israeli institution (Dor-Shav, 2005).

This sense of being demonized by the media, the sense that reports of the events were tendentious, was clearly accurate in some cases. (Whether this phenomenon was exceptional or common is controversial.) One such report, that of senior journalist Ben Caspit, is typically seen by the Right generally and the religious Right in particular as representative of an entire genre that vilified the protesters (let the reader decide). He graphically describes the scene in Kfar Maimon as follows:

> On the one side stood tens of thousands (in my opinion closer to 40 thousand than to 10 thousand) of variously bearded men, pregnant women, not pregnant women, babies and no end of youth fighting for the Land of Israel. On the other were 17 thousand tired policemen, worn out soldiers, weeping women soldiers, recruits, officers, religious and secular, standing guard over the State of Israel. (Kaspit, 2005)

In her doctoral dissertation dealing with the religious Zionist struggle against the disengagement plan, Anat Roth clearly and accurately presents the three factors that she believes moved the organizers to decide, in the end, not to march toward Gush Katif. It was, she underscores, a very difficult decision that entirely contradicted the original statements made by the protest's leaders as well as frustrating the passions of the demonstrators themselves:

> First, there was the fear that there would be fatalities . . . Second, that apart from Rabbi Dudkevitch [Rabbi of the Yitzhar settlement and one of the most influential rabbis of the extreme Right] no one in a leadership position believed that violently breaching the fences would stop the disengagement . . . The third reason, and the most central, is faith and value based: the holiness of Mamlachtiut that lies at the foundation of their worldview. The Halacha that the struggle for the Land of Israel is not to be conducted at any price was always present in the background but this is the first time that it stood the test of practice. From the moment that the leadership understood that breaching the fences was very likely to cause a civil war, to harm the army, the people and the state, it was clear to them all that here runs a red line. (Roth, 2011: 181)

For the great majority of the religious Zionists, even those who desperately wanted to reach and defend Gush Katif, religious principles acted as a brake upon their ideological-messianic ardor. These religious principles dictated the acceptable limits of the struggle: it was prohibited to harm the holy State of Israel, its institutional representatives and its symbols. The "theological-normative balance" was preserved despite the force used to prevent the march on Gush Katif and the palpable crisis that the protesters experienced. In the end, their commitment to the principle of Mamlachtiut prevented them from acting and sealed the fate of Gush Katif.

Nevertheless, to balance the picture, it must be said that in the course of the disengagement, other, shriller voices were heard, voices that expressed rage not only in regard to the disengagement itself and the government that orchestrated it, but also toward what was seen as the overly timid religious Zionist leadership. For example, Moshe Feiglin wrote in a burst of anger: "The Yesha Council is subjugated to Moloch. They are not bad people, but it is impossible to triumph against someone when you are not prepared to define him as the enemy . . . Every rabbi who said not to disobey is subjugated to the idol and not to the king" (cited in Shiloh, 2005).

Another radical figure who entered the fray at the very last moment and cast doubt on the legitimacy of state law was Rabbi Dr. Eliyahu Zini the head of the *Or Vi'yeshua* yeshiva in Haifa, the rabbi of the Technion's synagogue and a lecturer in mathematics. Rabbi Zini published an open letter (August 9, 2005) on his yeshiva's Internet site in which he described the evacuation from Gaza as a "crime against humanity" and tried to prove his point on the basis of the Geneva Convention (Zini, 2005a). In this letter, he carried on a passionate polemic against both the Supreme Court and the Knesset that, in his eyes, had allowed for this patently illegal action to take place. A few days after the implementation of the disengagement, Rabbi Zini published another letter in the same venue whose (windy) title was "Words spoken on Tuesday the 12th day of (the Hebrew month of) Av, the day of the brutal uprooting of Gush Katif according to the instructions given by he who autocratically stands at the head of the government of Israel." For Rabbi Zini, the Prime Minister should be labeled an autocrat because the "lovers of the land" are "the great majority of the people." In this letter Zini compared the autocracy of Sharon with that of General De Gaulle who, owing to his military glory, exercised exceptional civil authority, at times too exceptional, without heeding the people's criticism (Zini, 2005b).

Relatively rare at this time—if not actually solitary—was the voice of Rabbi Yoel Bin Nun. In an article entitled "Halachically, disobeying orders is prohibited," Rabbi Bin Nun approves of Rabbi Sherlow's position according to which the Knesset's decision to disengage had, in effect, already transformed Gush Katif into a pile of rubble. Therefore, all the actions of the army and the police lack significance; there is no power that can save this settlement even though it has not yet been evacuated.

The actual disengagement took place without the intense violence that had been predicted by many. To be sure, there was much passive resistance, scuffling, wrestling, pushing, and shoving, and also fist-fights and minor battles; some chained themselves to immobile fixtures while others threw objects at the evictors, but the worst—serious injuries or fatalities—did not occur. The scenes of disengagement were full of sound and fury and although they surely signified something, they were more theatrical and emblematic than true combat. Civil war, so often foretold, was nowhere to be seen (Roth, 2014). Dalsheim concludes that the Gush Katif settlers were considerably more moderate than the way the Left and the media portrayed them. Their most immediate concern was what their future would hold for them (Dalsheim, 2011: ch.4).

For certain analysts, the lack of serious violence derived *inter alia* from the exemplary coordination between the various parties partner to the confrontation (Alimi, 2013: introduction). First of all there was synchronization between the leaderships of the various settler groups and protesting bodies as to what constituted legitimate disobedience. More important still was the close cooperation between the Yesha Council and the security forces—the army and the police. Both the settler political and rabbinic leaderships were seen as legitimate bodies with whom it was necessary to negotiate. Being recognized as the authentic and authoritative representative of the protesting forces went a long way in containing what might have become a violent mêlée. Notably, both sides expended great efforts to make sure that the confrontation remained under control (Alimi, 2013: part 1). Roth by contrast, emphasizes, as we do, the important of Mercaz HaRav Mamlachtiut in restraining the traumatized evacuees and their sympathizers from resorting to life-threatening violence (Roth, 2011; Roth, 2014).

By and large, the rabbis did not fan the flames. The theological-normative balance proved to be more powerful than Land of Israel radicalism. Their pronouncements at the time although certainly not conciliatory were, nevertheless, not as bellicose as had been predicted. Delegitimizing the state, although it did appear at the margins, was the not the preponderant mood. The dominant feeling was one of resignation and hope nevertheless—Gush Katif had been lost but the larger war could still be won. There was also a prevalent sense that they occupied the moral high ground and that they would, despite the setback, emerge triumphant in the end. They spoke of victory through unity and love.

For their part, the security forces also acted with efficiency, restraint, and firmness—with "resoluteness and sensitivity" as the prevalent phrase had it. Emotional scenes of soldiers deeply moved by the difficult duty of evicting settlers from their homes—difficult to the point of tears—became the iconic images of the events. Even the media, often hostile to the settlement enterprise, joined in describing the evacuation as a complex and difficult emotional experience.

Parallel to the actual disengagement and directly thereafter, individuals and groups that had publicly called for active resistance and disobeying orders began a process of soul-searching and self-critique in light of the very limited number of cases in which their calls were heeded. They attempted to understand the glaring fact that their influence was so minimal. Their conclusion was clear: the scant response to their calls was a resounding public failure; they had failed to win broad public support; they had been unable to prevent disengagement and—even more seriously—there was now a precedent for evacuation from the Land of Israel without effective resistance. Those who supported disobedience only toughened their stance. They concluded that in the future only active, muscular disobedience stood a chance of preventing further evictions and expulsions. Such reactions were also the only way to restore their battered pride and to overcome their sense of bitterness. Not infrequently their soul-searching was not turned inward, that is, toward analyzing why they had failed. On the contrary, it was turned in bitterness toward those in the religious Zionist camp who had opposed disobedience.

The army's Chief Rabbi Israel Weiss, was an especial target of abuse. He had, without protest, overseen the evacuation of Jewish cemeteries, synagogues, Torah scrolls, etc. Rabbi Zalman Melamed wondered aloud, as part of the steadily growing de-legitimization of Rabbi Weiss, how he had been able to perform his military duty in opposition to the clear directives he received from his mentor, Rabbi Avraham Shapira. Moreover, Rabbi Melamed declared that there is no forgiveness for one who participated in the eviction unless he begs for pardon and compensates those who were expelled on his watch (Z. Melamed, 2005L). Few took into account the fact that Rabbi Weiss had been supported in his actions by the former Chief Rabbi Mordechai Eliyahu and by the Chief Rabbinate.

A few months after the disengagement (October 7, 2005), Professor Yehuda Eisenberg published a well-circulated article mockingly entitled "Israel Obeying Forces" (Eisenberg, 2005). He called upon the pre-military seminars to change the content of their curriculum in a way that would ensure an "appropriate" response to future orders to expel Jews from their homes. Beyond teaching Torah, "the pre-military seminars now have an important goal: to prepare students for the 'moral' side of their service. To teach them how to find their way in conflicts between law, orders and morality." Not surprisingly, Eisenberg accuses the leaders of religious Zionism who surrendered to the rule of law, to army orders and refused to resist as bearing guilt for the disengagement.

Rabbi Eliezer Melamed also pointed an accusing finger at those religious Zionists who prevaricated in the face of national crisis:

> Those who claim that it is forbidden to block roads in order to prevent the destruction of settlements and the expulsion of Jews from their land and the theft of their homes and livelihood say that the struggle lacks enough justice to legitimate demonstrations against it—as is accepted. A great weight is accorded to 'the customs accepted in the state.' In the State of Israel it is acceptable to conduct strikes in ways that seriously harm citizens, and this in order to prevent being fired from jobs or in order to get a raise in salary . . . Of course, there is no way to force the public to act contrary to its will, but moderate civil disobedience

has it in its power to force the government to compromise with its rivals. Perhaps to decide on new elections, perhaps another form of compromise. (E. Melamed, 2006a)

Although his remarks are not radical, Rabbi Eliezer Melamed seeks to undermine the voice of those who were entirely opposed to aggressive protest. We have made it clear that these very moderate voices did not constitute the majority among religious Zionist rabbis. Theirs was a relatively muted voice. What is more, they were at times forcefully set upon by their more aggressive associates. However, in the end, when the threat of serious violence arouse, it was ironically their message of restraint that influenced actions on the ground more than the militant voices of the Right.

Rabbi Aaron Trop created an image that, in the various circles of religious Zionism, became more and more current as time passed. He compared the relationship between religious and secular Zionism to the relationship between a man and a wife. He pictured their relationship as one that had deteriorated radically, to point that she was humiliated, scorned, and battered by her husband. Still, he (the husband) had the nerve to demand that she participate in the eviction from her home. Trop ends his essay with a sharply worded critique directed "inwards," that is, toward the religious Zionist leadership, both rabbinical and lay:

> Will we know how to switch discs? [rethink our assumptions] Will we know how to stop trying to please the 'lords of the land' and their distorted morality, how to cease flattering them, trying to find favor in their eyes; this is not love but surrender and groveling. We have a faith and a Torah, morality and values that are thousands of years old. Will we find the powers to go out toward our secular brothers, everywhere, in the army and the workplace, on the street and in the neighborhood with the purpose of teaching them our faith, our Torah and our values; the time has come to do so precisely because we love them. Therefore, for this reason, we need to do it with all the power we can. And no, not to wait until the Messiah does it in our place. (Trop, 2006)

How the evacuees from Gush Katif have been treated since the evacuation is another subject that demands our attention, however brief. Adding to the sense of victimhood and lending post factum justification to the cause of disobedience, the state's bungled attempts at compensating the evacuees and finding them new places of residence and sources of income cannot be overlooked. Although the government freely made promises, some Gush Katif evacuees still suffer from unemployment and the lack of permanent housing. Few would wish to argue with the assertion that they have been poorly dealt with by the government and its bureaucracy. The National Committee of Inquiry set up to examine the treatment of the evacuees had this to say:

> *The committee finds that the State of Israel failed in its treatment of the evacuees.* Studying the results five years after the evacuation reveals a very sad state of affairs: Most of the evacuees are still living in temporary trailers; the building of permanent residences in most cases has not yet begun; the great majority of public structures in the new areas where they reside have not yet been built; the percentage of unemployed among the evacuees is twice what it is among the general population; the economic condition of the evacuees is severe and there are those among them who require the welfare assistance; there are still ongoing court cases against the state in regard to the amount of compensation. We have therefore found that the job of rehabilitating the evacuees is far from over. (Committee for the Study of the Evacuees, 2010: 466). [Emphasis in the original]

One committee member, the journalist Ronen Medzini, claimed (Ynet, June 15, 2010) that the "disengagement caused the greatest harm to human rights in the history of the State of Israel." Unfortunately, sources for what has happened since 2010 are difficult to come by.

The Committee's findings make it difficult to deny that the government was less than honest in its commitment to rehabilitate the evacuees. Its callous and inept behavior only fortified the Right's (and especially the religious Right's) belief that the Gush Katif population was a victim several times over (Z. Melamed, 2006a; Uman, 2006). Indeed, many outside the narrow circle of the evacuees—friends, relatives, associates, etc.—were affected by the government's misdeeds. Perhaps the harshest expression of disappointment was that of Rabbi Yuval Sherlow, one of the most moderate voices in the religious Zionist camp. In a conference about the evacuees, Rabbi Sherlow conceded: "Had I known that five years after the expulsion the residents of Gush Katif would not yet have permanent homes, I would have called for disobeying orders" (cited in Ezra, 2010).

After the disengagement and the problematic treatment of the Gush Katif inhabitants, significant changes were refashioning the consciousness of the religious Zionist camp. This is clearly evident in the dejected words

of Rabbi Yosef Tzvi Rimon, the rabbi of South *Alon Shvut* and a senior
teacher at the Har-Etzion Hesder yeshiva. After undertaking a major, prize-
winning project to aid in the economic rehabilitation of the evacuees,
Rabbi Rimon wrote:

> I heard from an important rabbi that at the beginning he did not
> want to use the term 'expulsion' because expulsion constitutes
> a symbol for the expulsion of Jews by non-Jews, usually as part
> of pogroms, leaving them penniless. But today, after seeing the
> grim circumstances of many of the Gush Katif people in regard
> to places of residence, places of work and from many other
> perspectives, he began to call the disengagement 'expulsion.'
> (Rimon, 2006: 40)

The "theological-normative balance" was clearly wobbling. Shriller
and more bellicose voices became the rule rather than the exception. The
disengagement drama, Sharon's dubious machinations, the unfair (in their
eyes) coverage by the media, the general public's lack of appreciation for the
community's patriotism and love of country, their sense of being persecuted
by the secular Left elites, their embarrassing timidity in face of expulsion
from their homes, and the misfortunes of the Gush Katif evacuees all led
to new, more aggressive attitudes. It is to them that we now turn.

5

From the Clash at Amona (2006)
to the Price Tag Gangs (2008–2016)

The Amona Confrontation and Its Repercussions

The disengagement was executed, as noted, in relative quiet. Nevertheless, the nagging feelings of frustration, the sense of having missed an opportunity left many in the religious Zionist camp—especially among the youth—with an unresolved rage that sought catharsis (Gross, 2008). These explosive feelings were expressed a few months later in a number of sharp public confrontations between the security forces and religious Zionist youth.

It is important to pay close attention to the sentiments that prevailed among the religious Zionists youth in the aftermath of the disengagement. Many felt deep regret and disillusionment toward what they now saw as their overly "docile" behavior during the evacuation. Resistance and disobeying orders had been a sham. They had given in without a fight. The deplorable treatment of the evacuees only aggravated their sense of humiliation. Perhaps most basic was their anger toward the political, judicial, and cultural elites whom they saw as acting autocratically while masquerading in democratic garb. In their view, the elites' underlying aim was to trample the religious Zionist community underfoot. Many believed that religious Zionism and the secular Left were on opposite trajectories: while the former was growing in strength, demographics, and vitality, the latter was becoming ideologically jaded, apathetic, and morally flaccid. Secular anger, jealously, and hatred were the result of this sense of decline in the face of religious Zionist vigor. The expulsion of the Gush Katif settlers without significant pangs of conscience on the part of the ruling elite seemed to prove the point.

For religious Zionists the evacuation represented a "religious war" pitting the secular Left against the religious Right, the cosmopolitan liberals against those committed to the Torah (Roth, 2014: 423). Some in settler circles believed that the "expulsion" (the term they preferred to the tamer"evacuation") was especially problematic because it set religious

Zionism against the entire Zionist establishment. Rabbi Menahem Felix, a former Gush Emunim activist, declared that the "expulsion was not the caprice of a single corrupt and cruel leader" but rather the result of a collective design. "All the state systems were mobilized: the government, the Knesset, the Attorney General, the State Prosecutor, the judicial system, the police and the army—aided by a hostile media. They all took part in this "holy war" (cited in Roth, 2014: 421). No wonder then that alienation toward the state grew among members of the "Torah-based" camp who had, in the past, been committed to a Mamlachti worldview. Religious Zionist rabbis did all they could to preserve the foundational belief that the state possessed a sacrosanct character even if criticism of the government and its leaders was entirely legitimate. It must be said that they were only partially successful in this mission (Roth, 2014: 423–25). A crisis of leadership developed among the more radically right-wing settlers who challenged the less militant Yesha Council and its rabbis for not resisting the expulsion more forcefully, for not supporting more proactive disobedience, and for adopting an understanding relationship toward the evacuating security forces (Roth, 2014: 442–50).

The sense of being a persecuted minority was exacerbated by commonplace parallels drawn between the Gush Katif evacuation and previous historical expulsions that Jews had suffered in the Diaspora. Gush Katif was a link in a long chain. In a poem, entitled "The Ballad of the New *Galut*" written by Adam Tzachi (a *Tekoa* yeshiva graduate and son of Miriam Tzachi who filmed the evacuation from Gaza), persecuted Diaspora Jews, and Gush Katif evacuees were set side by side, with the Israeli government playing the role of the abusive Gentiles. Rendered into prose it reads:

> The place: Gush Katif; the hour: late. Most of the night has already passed and it is almost tomorrow. There is no wind outside, the air is coarse and pent up, insane and solid like the dough of despair. From the depths of the night, in the endless darkness, the dream arose of an old man running around. Screaming in every direction, his face a horror, and his painful words are heard in terror. Jews! A fire, the villainous landowner is raging; he considered and decided no stopping, no mercy. The entire town will be expelled, children and parents, infants and the old, the young men . . . The wagons await, the horses are ready, and the villainous landowner looks on as we are evicted. With raised batons, in shining helmets there are the powerful policemen who know how to hit. Your fate Jew, the fate of all Jews: shut your mouth and pick up the wanderer's stick. Do not

resist; you've learned well, the one who dares pays with pain.
The flock will look on from the distance. Callous, brute, obeying
the law. . . . (Zachi, 2005)

Both young and old penned many such works, inspired by fury and
humiliation. Galut and persecution motifs were staples. Even Holocaust
images ("sheep to the slaughter") were drawn upon (Levinger, Nir and Raziel,
2005; Willian, 2006; Cohen, 2007; Haramati, 2007; Ganz and Pines, 2008).

Similar feelings of having been betrayed by the secular elites are also
present in the writing of Rabbi Avraham Wasserman from the Ramat Gan,
Hesder yeshiva who published a few anthologies of lectures and parables
on Gush Katif. In one of them he declares:

Religious Zionism joined the world of security, settlements and
social activity only after the Yom Kippur War while the secular-
Ashkenazi Zionism had already created a state and led it in fateful
and glorious times. It was impossible to penetrate this elite. We
went to development towns that were rejected by the elite, we
joined the right wing repressed by it older brothers ("without
Herut and without *Maki*" in the words of Ben Gurion) . . . We
dreamed of redemption and leadership. But as our status rose
and our power grew, we wore a kind of striped shirt [a reference
to the biblical Joseph, Jacob's favorite, who was given a striped
shirt by his father] that was despised by our 'big' brothers. They
[the old elite] felt themselves more threatened from day to day
fearing that they would lose their hold over power and that
perhaps messianic ideas would lead the state to madness. Love,
persuasion, reason and talk of national responsibility did not help.
The struggle is over inheriting the leadership—they dried us out
leaving us with minimal protection in the face of the enemy
and afterwards as well when we were sold to the Ishmaelites for
the price of a pair of shoes and even less, no one came to our
aid . . . despite the fact that we were a majority who opposed
these criminal acts. But our evictors allowed us to cry and to
drink. The seed of destruction of our brother Joseph sprouted
here anew and smashed Gush Katif and northern Samarai, created a deep rift within the people and encouraged our enemies to
fight against us all the more forcefully. (Wasserman, 2007: 5–6)

These harsh images of having been sold to the enemy, the recreation
of the Joseph story, express the distress that consumed many within religious

Zionism on both sides of the Green Line. They felt that the state—and even worse, its citizens—had turned their back on them, and, in the all-too-readily employed image (one whose historical origin is in the infamous *Dolchstosslegende* used by the Nazis), "stabbed them in the back." The harshness of Rabbi Wasserman's parable likely does not represent the majority of the religious Zionist camp or even the voice of the evacuees from Gush Katif. (He lives in the up-scale town of *Givatayim*.)

Another fascinating personality whose outlook was transformed by the disengagement was Rabbi Shmuel Tal, the head of the Gush Katif yeshiva. Although he continued to believe that Israel was the "beginning of redemption," he rejected Zionism as a secular movement and denied that the State of Israel had a religious Mamlachti status. Moving closer to the Haredi camp, he rejected the secular media and the universities as enemies of Torah Judaism. Israeli Independence Day should not be celebrated; Jerusalem Day with its more obvious religious resonance should take its place. He instructs his students to wear *Tfilin* (phylacteries) for as long as they are studying in the yeshiva. Because of modesty issues, he advises those of his students who chose to be conscripted into the army to serve in the *Nachal Heredi* program which has no contact with women soldiers. Not surprisingly, he was an energetic supporter of disobedience.

On the other hand, consider the moderate, conciliatory tone of Rabbi Yehuda Zoldan, himself a resident of *Neve Dekalim* in Gush Katif:

> The struggle had a positive side. I was of course against the disengagement, but it transmitted a great positive message as well: for settling the Land of Israel, for heroism and resoluteness of the people for its land, for a proud national posture . . . The efforts to explain, the straight talk, even if they did not succeed for the moment and we were expelled from our homes, did not happen in vain. We learned about ourselves that it is possible, that we can explain what Torah is and what is our purpose here in this place—at different levels and for different ages. This was not enough because the many listeners generally heard different things more loudly and more often and therefore we were a drop in the sea. But there are many such drops, may they only deepen, grow, influence and shape a different consciousness. (Zoldan, 2006: 77–78)

One powerful source that strengthened the discourse of disobedience and sharpened the ideological and Torah-based calls for active noncompliance with government directives was the *Kommemiut* movement set up at the time of the disengagement by the students of Rabbi Tzvi Yehuda Kook— such as Rabbis Dov Lior, Zalman Melamed, Elyakim Levanon, David Chai Hacohen, and others. The movement began by disseminating Portion of the Week leaflets in synagogues called Kommemiut as well as a monthly named *Kumi Ori* (Rise up and Awake). Leaders of the movement returned to the claim that at stake was a struggle between the forces of light represented by the religious Zionist camp, and the forces of darkness incarnated by the secular Left who wish to destroy every iota of Israeli Judaism.

These rabbis integrate a classic Mamlachti vision of the state with what might be called moderate "post-Mamlachti" ideas. The familiar Mamlachti paradigm of the state's holiness remains, but they insist that there is a marked distinction that must be drawn between the state and the government (Mozes, 2009: 111–13). Speaking of possible future evacuations of settlements, the Kommimiut movement argued that it imperative to create a "balance of terror" that will deter any such future withdrawals. This concept of deterrence was critical for the clash at Amona.

Nevertheless, pointing to the rage and frustration following the disengagement is insufficient. There was also a change in government leadership. It was not merely a change in the ruling party but a change in the personalities who stood at the helm of government. Although Ariel Sharon, in their view, betrayed them, he was nevertheless an admired military hero and the moving force behind the building of the settlements. In spite of the disengagement, his earlier reputation stood him in good stead. As opposed to Sharon, his successor as Prime Minister, Ehud Olmert lacked these credentials. Beyond this, his public behavior toward the settlers and the religious Zionist community as a whole was perceived as less than empathetic.

There were three major episodes that intensified the sense of alienation between the religious Zionists and Prime Minister Ehud Olmert: first, the Amona events, second, Olmert's call for what came to be known as the "Realignment (or "Convergence") Plan" which would have evacuated many settlements and moved their residents into larger settlement blocs, and third, the events of the "House of Controversy"/"House of Peace" in Hebron.

The clash at Amona represents a fault line in religious Zionist-government relationships. Amona was originally founded in 1997 as an eastern neighborhood of the veteran settlement *Ofrah* and it was the largest "outpost" in Judea and Samaria/the West Bank. The complex approval procedure and the transfer of ownership over the lands were, the settlers claimed, bureaucratically stalled for years and hence was never officially authorized. Incongruously, however, as with many other unauthorized settlements, various government offices invested heavily in Amona, setting up much of its infrastructure. For example, the Ministry of Housing invested large sums in preparing the land for the building of permanent housing (Sasson, 2004). These structures were in the course of being built when in 2000 an injunction to stop construction was issued by the judiciary. In spite of this injunction and other injunctions that were issued thereafter, the residents continued building. They claimed that they were being discriminated against and that there was an unfair and unequal enforcement of the law for political reasons. The fact that the government had substantially invested in the creation of the settlement strengthened their argument. The construction of permanent housing was accelerated in 2004 and completed in 2005. Repeated petitions by the "Peace Now" movement arguing that Amona was built on private Palestinian land were submitted (the owners were not located and were not a party to the petitions). This led in the end to a Supreme Court injunction to the Minister of Defense Binyamin Ben-Eliezer to execute the demolition of the structures. In line with a request made by the government, the demolition was delayed until after the disengagement.

In January 2006, a few months after the retreat from Gush Katif, plans for the demolition began. Much has been written about the preparations made by the Israeli government and the security forces before the Amona evacuation. Indeed—momentarily jumping ahead of ourselves—a parliamentary committee was set up to study the preparatory measures taken prior to the events. First, a number of attempts were made to reach an agreement that would include the evacuation of the permanent structures or their demolition by Yesha operatives themselves—but these were rejected by the government. Why these options were set aside—as is so often the case in such charged issues—is the subject of controversy. There are those who argue that the security forces rejected the proposals because they judged them to be unworkable. Others believe there were more sinister forces at work, to wit, that the government deliberately planned for a confrontation in order to enhance its power of deterrence against the settlers. From the other side, there is also reason to believe that certain elements within the settler leadership, for their own deterrent purposes, also wanted a confrontation although with only limited violence and without dramatic, far-reaching consequences (Arnon, 2005; Amitai, 2006).

On the morning of Wednesday, the 1st of February 2006, police and army forces numbering a few thousand were deployed in Amona facing a similar number of youth (mostly religious Zionists) who had earlier reached Amona and barricaded themselves into the permanent structures marked for demolition. Any attempt to sketch an accurate picture of what happened in Amona is compromised by the enveloping fog of battle. Facing the parliamentary investigative committee set up to scrutinize the events, the security forces provided an only partial and unclear account of what had transpired. On the other side, the account given by the demonstrators is naturally suspect of being biased and self-serving (Roth, 2011: 249–65). It is therefore imperative to deal with those facts about which there is little controversy: there were more than 200 wounded who required hospitalization, about three-quarters of them demonstrators. Harsh crowd dispersal tactics were employed—most notably horse-mounted charges by the police into the midst of the protesters. Video clips show police beating demonstrators with truncheons even when they were lying on the ground. Some testified that young female demonstrators who did not pose a direct threat to the security forces were evicted forcefully, without care for their modesty or physical well-being. Many public figures were injured in the course of the events, including two Knesset members. Moreover, the level of coordination among the deployed forces—the police, the army, the political echelon—was flawed and led to serious operational failures. The totality of these malfunctions and the grim consequences of the clash led even left-wing organizations to appeal to the legal authorities demanding that the use of exaggerated force in Amona be investigated (B'Tselem, 2006).

There can be no doubt that the Amona episode was problematic, both operationally and in terms of demonstrator violence. But there were legal difficulties as well. Before the evacuation, it was said that announcements had been made that Amona and its permanent structures were a "closed military area" and that the demonstrators were guilty of unlawful assembly. However, it appears that no such announcements were, in fact, made. According to Israeli law, both of these announcements—a "closed military area" and "unlawful assembly"—must be made before forcible eviction of protesters becomes legitimate. The Knesset investigative committee determined that the IDF and the police had not made the necessary announcements and hence their activities were unlawful. Professor Emanuel Gross (a well-known, often-interviewed criminal law expert) told the committee:

> The penal code explicitly states that it is necessary to announce, how to announce, etc., which is to say, that it is insufficient to assume that he [the demonstrator] simply knows of it or anything of the sort. Neither must we see this as simply a formal issue. It is necessary to inform so that it be clear to the relevant individuals that this assembly is indeed seen by the police as an unlawful assembly . . . Until this pronouncement is made there is nothing that prevents the public from being there. (Parliamentary Inquiry, 2006: 22)

Nonetheless, on the other side, it is impossible to ignore the many illegal actions committed by protesters against the police, the Border Police, and the soldiers. Among others criminal acts, they threw stones, cinder blocks, iron bars, and water mixed with paint from the building's roofs and forcibly resisted arrest. Discussing the issue of violent protestor behavior leads inevitably to the question: was the violence planned and initiated by the protesters or can it be ascribed to hotheaded behavior triggered by the disproportionate violence directed at them by the security forces?

Testimony from all sides emphasized the unprecedented ferocity of the confrontation. An emergency room doctor at the Hadassah *Ein Kerem* hospital said that in his twenty years of practice he had never seen anything the likes of this kind of violence. It was miraculous, he added, that there were none more seriously wounded. The chief of the Border Police claimed that the violence at Amona went beyond anything he had seen. He claimed that the police were genuinely in fear for their lives (Pedhazur and Perliger, 2009: 135–37).

Based upon many witnesses—notably that of Yuval Diskin, then the head of the Shabak—the Knesset committee concluded that a relatively small and extreme minority of the protesters had incited the violence.

The Amona events reveal yet another deterioration in the ability of Yesha leaders to control parts of their youth as well as the dangerous tendency, which only grows and grows, of tens of protesters to use harsh violence against the security forces. The head of the Shabak and the army's Chief of Staff on the one side, and some of the heads of Yesha on the other painted a worrying picture of the rise of bitterness and violence between part of the youth and the police and army, of radicalization, of a certain loss of leadership, restraint, monitoring and control by public leaders.

Yesha leaders tried to moderate the struggle in the spirit of the disengagement's passive resistance. Yet the head of the Shabak said the protestor's preparations pointed to the violent confrontation they were planning. About 100 youths and adults—mainly residents of radical settlement Yitzhar—hoarded rocks, timber etc. for the clash. Neveretheless, Yesha leader's effective appeals to avoid violence led to the departure of most of the radical group. "The feeling of this group was that there would only be a mild struggle and that the pressure of the Yesha Council was working against them and therefore they left the place in the afternoon." Before leaving however, they caused considerable damage: vandalizing mechanical equipment, storing cinder blocks on roofs and spreading motor oil and Ninja tacks on the entrance path to Amona. These were the same people, Diskin declared, who were responsible for cutting down Palestinian's olive trees. They also were the same people who threatened and injured the homes, families and cars of soldiers who took part in the evacuation. Among those who barricaded themselves and resorted to violence, there were those who refused to accept the authority of the Yesha Council—a phenomenon with intimations for the future.

The committee believes that a part of the young people who barricaded themselves do not distinguish between the legal right to protest or to indulge in calm passive resistance—and between violent resistance to government decisions and/or to the rulings of the courts, with the aim of revoking them or, regretfully, disrupting them. The claim that the resistance to the disengagement failed because it was too moderate is an example of this kind of misunderstanding; as if there is a possibility that a certain group will disrupt or prevent government decisions in a democratic state. The pronouncements and placards about war in Amona are witness to this dangerous line of thinking. (Parliamentary Inquiry, 2006: 22)

Although illegal, violent behavior against the security forces did not represent the mainstream of the religious Zionist community or even of the protesters themselves, it must be noted that within the rabbinical-spiritual leadership of the settlers in Judea and Samaria very warlike voices were being heard—and not only at the margins. For example, Rabbi Zalman Melamed argued that it was legitimate for the protesters to resort to violence in order to protect themselves (Z. Melamed, 2006f; Z. Melamed, 2006g). Rabbi Lior went further still: not only was violent self-defense permitted, it was allowed in order to protect a comrade. He therefore allowed the throwing of stones and cinder blocks from the roofs when horse-mounted policemen attacked the protesters (Lior, 2006a; Lior, 2006b; Lior, 2006c). He writes:

There were young people on the roofs who saw horses trampling girls below. How is one to act under such circumstances? Why are the blows that we received not the subject of discussion? . . . We must resist for the sake of heaven . . . This is rage in God's name and that is a healthy thing. After they push us into such a situation, we express our opposition and cannot reconcile ourselves to sinful actions. We are being forced to be zealots in the name of God. (Lior, 2006f: 70)

Similarly he declares: "It is certain that according to Torah law a person may oppose with force any kind of violence aimed at expelling him or destroying his home. Also, to come to the aid of comrades in such cases. He who damages or destroys should be related to as a wicked person with all the implications that derive from this" (Lior, 2006c).

Rabbi Yisrael Ariel, who opposed all forms of active violent resistance in the Yamit evacuation, underwent, as did much of the religious Zionist community, a process of growing radicalization. In an essay entitled "The lovers of Amona, the lovers of God," he declares:

> The right of an individual to defend his home and his property is a basic right that is rooted in verses of the Torah. Moreover, the Torah permits the home-owner to prevent the entrance of a person who breaks into his home, even while exercising force . . . Therefore, a soldier who breaks into a person's home, even if he received an order to do so, is considered like a common brigand . . . The phrase 'it is forbidden to raise your hand against a policeman,' is true only in so far as the policeman obeys the Mitzvot of the Torah and of justice. (Ariel, 2006)

Both Rabbi Lior's and Rabbi Ariel's articles appeared in the *Kumi Ori* periodical published by the Kommimiut movement that based itself on the teachings of Rabbi Avraham Shapira and Rabbi Tzvi Yehuda Kook. Its fourth number, from which we have just cited, was dedicated to Rabbi Tzvi Yehuda and its closing section was entitled *Si'ach Locahmim* (fighter's talk) (mockingly recalling a similarly named "humanistic" discussion between soldiers after the Six Day War). A panel of youth who had taken an active part in the Amona resistance discussed with unrestrained bitterness their experiences during the evacuation. Yet, the volume's tone was not homogeneous. In the same volume there appeared a conciliatory essay of Rabbi Mordechai Grinberg, head of the prestigious *Kerem Be'yavneh* Hesder yeshiva that called for love of the straying souls in the spirit of the teachings of Rabbi Tzvi Yehuda (Greenberg, 2006: 46–52).

At much the same time, Rabbi Eliezer Melamed wrote his "Amona Responsa" in which he denounced media condemnations of the Amona resistors:

> The frenzy of the self-condemnations is a serious error. For example, the condemnation of youth accused of throwing rocks and cinder blocks. There was one youth who saw a policeman

hitting his 15 year old friend with a truncheon as he lay on the ground helpless. He lifted a block and lightly hit the helmet of the policeman. The policeman fell and stopped the beating. Is it right to condemn this young person who perhaps prevented murder? Every such condemnation that is heard in the media serves as fuel for hatred and the intensification of violence against loyal Jews and precious youth. (E. Melamed, 2006a: 2)

The Yesha Rabbinical Committee led by Rabbi Lior went further still; they threw restraint to the wind, borrowing phrases from Scripture that speak of active resistance. Anticipating the destruction of the permanent structures in Amona they proclaimed: "We must stop by whatever means the persecution of Jews and the sale of our holy land, to stand together for the salvation of the soul of Israel. We are faithful to the words of Rabbi Tzvi Yehuda Hacohen Kook that over Judea and Samaria there will be war" (The Association of Yesha Rabbis, 2006).

Rabbi Joseph Badichi, one of Rabbi Tzvi Yehuda's acolytes, who authored *Geulat Or Hatzvi* (Jerusalem, 2005) a compendium of Rabbi Kook's works, referred to Rabbi Tzvi Yehuda's confrontational phrase ("there will be a war") as a "legal ruling" (Badichi, 2006). About a year after the evacuation of Amona, Rabbi Yaacov Antman of the settlement Yitzhar, in an essay entitled "Redemptive *Mamalachtiut*," attempted to clarify the background to Rabbi Kook's combative words. They derived, he claimed, from the sense of power the rabbi felt in view of his disciples and followers who were working unstintingly to settle the Land of Israel. Rabbi Antman concludes: "a king who feels the vitality and health of the people of Israel coursing through its national fabric, declares war. War that includes self-sacrifice and the willingness to be killed" (Antman, 2007).

Emanuel Shiloh, the editor of the *BeSheva* newspaper, made this shift of perspective clear when wrote a week after the Amona evacuation:

The believing community emerged from Amona physically battered but strengthened ideologically and morally. The resolute and combative line has become the dominant one while the 'moderate' voices lower their volume. At the end of a half year of post-mortem discussions it is evident that the tough position has struck deep roots in the hearts of the public in general and in the hearts of the committed youth in particular. Most of the young people who experienced the events of Amona only became more invigorated and answer 'certainly' when asked will they come to the next confrontation. If until now we spoke of the 'spirit of Gush Katif,' from now on we should, perhaps speak about the 'spirit of Amona.' (Shilo, 2006)

For many in the religious Zionist community the events of Amona became a "collective healing," a reinforcement of their own positions and a preparedness to stand up to even brutal violence in defense of their worldview. They felt that the event had tempered them, grounded them in preparation for what was to come. It had restored their pride lost in the disengagement's passiveness. Notably, Shiloh does not mention specific leaders of the religious Zionist community and for good reason. One of the consequences of Amona was a general weakening of rabbinic and communal authority among the extreme wings of religious Zionism. In their zealotry, the protesters had left the rabbis behind. Shiloh clearly supports the approach, prevalent after Amona, that a new readiness to violate the law had taken root and that all those who opposed the Greater Land of Israel vision would be resisted with all might and main.

One can catch a vivid glimpse into the chasm that had opened up between the young and the adult generations in the aftermath of Amona in an anonymously published dialogue entitled "I seek my brother: A real conversation between a father and his daughter":

Father: My daughter returned from Amona, shocked, battered and hurting . . . She who spoke proudly about the nation and the land and about the Israel Defense Forces and about her will to serve as a combat soldier . . .

Daughter: . . . But after the fourth day, the army—not the defense army but the army of Nazis, with Special Forces police beating mercilessly, throwing children out of windows as if they were objects.

Father: My dear daughter, no, not Nazis my darling, they are our brothers together with the army and the land . . . after all we do not have another country . . .

Daughter: Stop being so Mamlachti; Mamlachtiut died a long time ago!!! You don't understand that it is Mamlachtiut that is killing you . . . And don't you dare call any Special Forces Police or Border Patrol operatives or any of their like . . . my brothers . . .

Father: But not Nazis, no, grandpa lost his entire family in Auschwitz, not Nazis . . .

Daughter: Dad, I remember but I am not burdened with difficult Holocaust memories; I am a Jewish girl from the Land of Israel, a healthy girl from the Jewish people in its motherland, and what I saw, experienced and pained did not remind me of the Holocaust but reminded me of the Jewish police in the ghetto in the service of the Nazis, sending children to perish. (Under the initials Shin Mem Chet, 2006)

Although this text is exceedingly harsh, it does represent voices of *some* young people who returned from Amona—children who had gone there with strong Mamlachti commitments. They were a minority but a vehement minority. Nevertheless, although the "theological-normative balance" suffered a grievous blow, the mainstream of religious Zionist youth remained loyal (if a bit more guarded) to Mamlachtiut and continued to reject unrestrained disobedience. In religious educational institutions as well as in the religious community in general, the state, for the most part, retained it holiness, its singular religious, historical, and national status. And yet, a sea-change took place in Amona. Its effects will be studied in what follows.

As opposed to the belligerent rabbinical voices mentioned above, even in the Amona period there were still noteworthy religious Zionist figures that sought moderation and urged the youth to avoid confrontations with the law and its representatives. One such example was a pamphlet issued by Rabbi Eli Sadan, the head of the pre-military seminar in *Eli* which was signed by a large number of leading religious Zionist rabbis including Rabbis Yaacov Ariel, Chaim Druckman, and Tzfania Drori and supported by others such as Rabbis Aryeh Stern, Eliyahu Blumenzweig, and David Stav. Entitled "Our path at this time," the pamphlet appeared in the turbulent period following the Amona events. It attempts to set down a worthy Mamlachti line of thought and action that opposes violence toward the security forces and preaches reconciliation to majority decisions passed by the public's elected representatives. In paragraph 7 of the pamphlet the rabbis assert: "Our loyalty to the state and the army is not an additional or separate matter, forbid it, but draws entirely upon and receives its value from the Mitzvot of the Torah." In the pamphlet's only reference to disobedience, the authors write:

Consequently, if we are informed in the name of the state or an army order to violate a Torah prohibition, even the least important, we will not be willing and we will not heed. Indeed, this is the very partnership to which we all agreed—the state does not have the power to tell the individual to act against his faith and his conscience but the individual or a minority group cannot impose its views and will on the public. And general state matters will be run by a majority according to the parliamentary system. As a result, it does not even occur to us to act in a bellicose way in order to impose our opinions upon the general public. Not on the subject of Torah and Mitzvot and not on the subject of the Land of Israel. Rather we will do all we can to bring the nation closer to our Torah and hence we will advance all together. (Sadan et al., 2006: 1–2)

This shrewd formulation was meant, so it appears, to make signing the document palatable both for rabbis who rejected civil disobedience and for those who were prepared to support passive disobedience—such as Rabbis Aviner and Sadan. Nevertheless, the formulation the rabbis chose makes clear that even if it may be acceptable for an anguished individual soldier to disobey an order on the private and local level, it is unacceptable to call explicitly for the use of force to thwart a majority decision. The pamphlet's text offers a subtle compromise that many could accept: expressions of personal moral distress ought to be balanced against the national responsibility to obey the law (Wolf, 2006; Friedman, 2006). The balance is indeed delicate: understanding for individual conscientious objection as opposed to a clear rejection of major civil disobedience.

The Sadan pamphlet received its share of criticism. Rabbi Eliezer Waldman from the Kiryat Arba Hesder yeshiva, made this mordant observation:

May the heavens tremble, how can it be that there is not here a cry for loyal and committed Jews, the settlers of Judea and Samaria, to resist with all possible strength, in order to prevent the additional crime of expelling tens of thousands of Jews from Yesha and the transfer of the mountainous lands to the enemy—it can only be the continued ignoring and silencing of the words of our teacher and master Rabbi Tzvi Yehuda of blessed memory . . . 'There is no permission whatever to [violate] this Torah prohibition against the transfer of our lands to the Gentiles, forbid it, for all time and absolutely, and therefore there is a responsibility on every person of Israel and on every Torah sage in Israel and on every military man in Israel to prevent, delay it with all his strength, and may heaven help us.'

> And is there not in these words [of Rabbi Sadan's pamphlet] the abandoning of loyal brother settlers to the evil edict of an irresponsible government that lacks Zionist faith?. . . . (Waldman, 2006: 16–20)

In the years following Amona, the conciliatory, anti-violence approach was pushed further to the sidelines; it was no longer the default policy of the religious Zionist camp. This change did not derive from an abrupt, one-time pronouncement, or from an explicit policy shift initiated by the religious Zionist rabbinical leadership. Discipline and restraint gave way to violence in small but visible steps. With the passage of time, the radicalized youth broke free from their erstwhile mentors leaving them unchecked by the usually more circumspect leadership of the rabbis and prominent communal figures. Anarchist elements grew up at the borders of the religious Zionist movement, elements for whom even arch-radical rabbis were no longer authorities. Roiling anti-system currents surged at the margins. It is difficult to determine whether these developments were the natural outcome of frustration in the face of unachievable messianic goals or the result of the mishandling of the Gaza disengagement and especially the Amona eviction. The more pressing question relates to the anarcho-violent tendencies that appear to be gaining momentum. Has a new outlying but entrenched settler culture, with its own vocabulary, rules of conduct, and value hierarchy struck root? Or are the perpetrators of criminal, sometimes terrorist acts, wild weeds, rotten apples that do not reflect on the majority of law-abiding settlers? We return to this subject at the end of this chapter.

In the Aftermath of Amona

About a year after the Amona clash, and following the Second Lebanon War a number of Yesha leaders gathered for a critical debate about the political way forward. Nadav Shragai (the Haaretz newspaper's reporter on the settlement project) describes the debate in an article entitled: "They are sick of the state" (Shragai, 2007). He argues that for many of the participants, the Amona events constituted an ideological fault line that affected the commitments of the religious Zionist youth, the young adults among the settlers and even their sympathizers within the Green Line. For many of them, the state and its institutions were no longer sacrosanct, its authority no longer self-evident. Thwarting the state often became more of a priority than obeying it. Amona, some argued, was a powerful warning to those who advocated further evacuations. Uri Ariel (later a government minister), a figure whose loyalty to the state cannot be questioned and who did not call for the violation of law, said in this debate:

> The fact that since Amona not even a single outpost was uprooted, despite the continuing pressure of the extreme Left organizations and despite the will of the Defense Minister, derives directly from the fact that the struggle in Amona presented an intolerable Price Tag to the army and the police . . . The army and police establishment recoiled from the appalling consequences of the hundreds of wounded and from the shock that stunned even the most compromising in our camp. Above all, the establishment feared that Amona would sear alienation and the sense of persecution into the national religious consciousness. (Shragai, 2007)

This was one of the very first times the moniker "Price Tag" was used in the context of the struggle for Judea and Samaria. In the future, this phrase would be given a far more menacing significance. For Uri Ariel, Amona was an "educational" experience that pitted the settlers against the "establishment." But while Ariel speaks in relatively temperate terms about the relationship between "our camp" and the state, Rabbi Aaron Trop, very much in character, goes considerably further.

> The Amona ordeal sharpens the question of loyalty and the source of authority. The expulsion from Gush Katif and the Amona pogrom force us to look straight at reality, to stop fooling ourselves and our children by saying that there is no contradiction between our loyalties—because we see with our very own eyes that there is a contradiction . . . The participation of kippah-wearing slaves bearing [army] ranks in the expulsion and the pogrom, and the proud stance of the marvelous youth in Amona against the brutal troops teaches us of the two paths within religious Zionism. The youth observes, sees and learns from this observation to re-adjust its relationship to Halacha and to the ruling institutions. (Shragai, 2007)

By contrast, Bentzi Lieberman, head of the Yesha Council during the disengagement, sees the events of *Kfar Maimon*—when violent action and a mass illegal breakthrough to Gush Katif was prevented by the Yesha leadership—as the defining moment because "in Kfar Maimon the Yesha Council announced before the nation and the world that settlement without the [support of] the people and without Israeli society—has no basis" (Shragai, 2007).

In addition to the traumatic and defining qualities of the Amona clash, two other radicalizing events need to be mentioned. In August 2006, at the height of the Second Lebanon war, Prime Minister Olmert was cited as saying in an interview with the Reuters news agency that victory in the war would bolster the momentum of the "convergence" plan whose intent it was to disengage unilaterally from much of Judea and Samaria—as had been done in Gaza—while leaving in place two major settlement blocs that equaled some 2 percent of the area of the West Bank.

As might be expected, his comments earned fiery condemnation from the Right. Indeed, some members of his own *Kadima* party joined in denouncing the plan. What is important for our purposes is that Olmert's words triggered some extreme although marginal statements in the religious Zionist community to the effect that if these were the Prime Minister's intentions, participation in the (Lebanese) war effort should be halted, orders should not be obeyed, and soldiers should not report for reserve duty. The most prominent example was that of Shoshi Greenfeld, then a reporter for the *Makor Rishon* newspaper, whose brother had been killed in the war. Greenfeld ejected the Chief Rabbi of the IDF, Rabbi Yisrael Weiss (who opposed disobedience), from her brother's funeral. She herself delivered an emotional eulogy whose central purpose was to encourage soldiers not to cooperate with the state's institutions and with the security forces. "Speaking" to her brother, she said:

> In your last telephone conversation I told you: do not become cannon fodder; Olmert said that the campaign provided leverage for the convergence; come home, you have an historic opportunity to refuse so that the pogrom of Gush Katif does not return to your home, to Michmas . . . This is a war for absolutely nothing. For the sake of the state's ruling elites a crime is being committed, I told you, please do not go, I pleaded . . . And what does Olmert care? Or the dictators? They know that they will not be the ones to pay the price of these crimes. Their sons refuse to serve. In the end you came back, my brother, cannon fodder in a coffin in a war for absolutely nothing or for the peace of convergence. (Greenfeld, 2006)

To be sure, Greenfeld was and remains a relatively solitary voice in the religious Zionist chorus. Moreover, one cannot ignore the personal animus, the intense grief that lay behind her words. Not surprisingly, she was roundly criticized by other grieving families from the religious Zionist community. Still, her calls were heard and absorbed by some marginal elements. The first was Avi Avalo resident of Efrat and an activist in the "Jewish Leadership" movement. Avalo responded to Olmert's comments by abandoning his unit in Lebanon and setting up a protester's tent opposite the Prime Minister's office in Jerusalem. And yet, despite his defection in the midst of war, he did not earn the rebuke of the community in which he lived. A not insignificant number of religious Zionist activists even accorded him a media platform from which to trumpet his views (Channel 7, Katif.net, and others). There were those who expressed deep sympathy for his actions like Eran Steinberg, the former spokesman of Gush Katif (Sternberg, 2006).

Nevertheless, despite the game-changing comments of Prime Minister Olmert connecting the Lebanese war with his convergence plan, the calls for disobedience remained relatively muted. To be sure, there were important exceptions. At least three public organizational initiatives took place within the religious Zionist camp: to publish a censuring petition, to dispatch a stinging letter to the Chief of Staff, and even to warn about (an unheard of) strike in the IDF (Avraham, 2006; Asenheim, 2006; Weiss and Haddad, 2006). Still, these reactions were quite different from those associated with the battle at Amona where the unraveling of the tie between sections of religious Zionism and the state was patently visible. In the end, with the IDF fighting in Lebanon and with Hezbollah rockets raining down on Israeli cities, the protester's hostile intentions were blunted; the "theological-normative balance" continued to hold.

Another confrontation of a very different kind took place in the course of 2008 in the A-Ras neighborhood in Hebron. The status of the "Brown House" (or the "House of Peace" as its residents called it—Rabbi Yitzchak Ginzburgh wanted to call it the "House of Truth and Peace") was mired in legal controversy: had the house been legitimately purchased by representatives of the Jewish settlement in Hebron or had it been occupied illegally? In March 2007 more than a hundred settlers entered the house to exercise their legal right—so they claimed—to inhabit the building that had been duly purchased. On the other side, the building's Arab inhabitants appealed to the Supreme Court demanding that the property be returned to them. Intensive legal discussions led to the court's directive that the settlers vacate the building pending clarification of the facts (Shragai, 2008c).

A large conference of rabbis held in Kiryat Arba against the background of the court's decision issued a manifesto appealing for many to "come to the House of Peace and to block the expulsion with their bodies." Nonetheless, the manifesto did not call explicitly for violent resistance. Neither did it directly encourage soldiers to disobey orders (Etzer, 2008).

The building's settler inhabitants showed no such restraint. In the weeks leading up to the evacuation of the house, extreme right-wing groups gathered in the building, most of them young people who did not recognize the authority of the Judea and Samaria settler leadership and acted with great violence, verbal and physical, against anyone they saw as an enemy. The settler leaders denounced these acts of violence—especially noteworthy were Danny Dayan, the head of the Yesha Council, Yisrael Harel, Aryeh Eldad, and others. Still, we need to add that this denunciation took place very late in the day, only just before the evacuation took place. By then circumstances had already deteriorated into anarchy. The violent actions of the house's occupiers and of others who came to support them included physically harassing the Arabs of Hebron and its vicinity as well as vandalizing Moslem cemeteries. There were also a number of violent encounters in which the Israeli security forces in the city were attacked. Enraged by their actions, Yisrael Harel, a sympathizer with the settler cause, wrote in the *Haaretz* newpaper:

> These thugs who are running riot and damaging people and property do not protect the settlements as they and their defenders claim. The opposite is true: They envelop the cause in stench, weaken its status and its strength. There are those who suspect that there are provocateurs among them . . . In pulling up from the roots those who rise up to destroy it, the Yesha settlers will regain their honor, their morality, the justice of their path and its momentum. (Harel, 2009)

Nadav Shragai, another *Haaretz* journalist who is close to the settlers and regularly documents their motives and policies chose to make an emotional personal statement; he aimed harsh words at "the heads of the Yesha Council, the rabbis, the educators and the parents" for their inexcusable forbearance. After detailing the crimes, both legal and moral, that he had witnessed in the occupied house he wrote:

> This is not a searing into consciousness but a fire in consciousness. The thousands you planned to bring to the 'House of Peace' did not come, because you had already fixed in your consciousness that what was at stake was a 'fire' and not a 'searing.' This fire does not consume only fields of thorns and Palestinian groves, but 'burns down the club' in its entirety, the beautiful, moral and just settlement project that you have established, as in 'let my soul perish together with the Philistines.' (Shragai, 2008d)

Despite Shragai's allegations of forbearance, Danny Dayan, the head of the Yesha Council, had in fact sharply attacked the violence of the house's inhabitants two days earlier. In an interview, he expressed himself with unprecedented harshness against Daniella Weiss, a leader of those occupying the house.

> Daniella Weiss and her ilk have become a strategic danger to our hold on Judea and Samaria. Pure and simple. In the Israeli public mind, she turns Yesha into a kind of 'wild west' that no normal person wants to have as part of his country. After the catastrophes brought on Israel by the disengagement and the retreat from southern Lebanon, there was a consensus in public opinion that it was forbidden to retreat from Judea and Samaria. Olmert had to shelve his convergence plan.
>
> Because of people lacking reason such as this, who, although they are a negligible minority, determine with their actions the image of us all . . . The argument that the struggle over Gush Katif failed because we did not employ enough force, because we did not create 'a balance of fear' is ridiculous. It failed because there were not enough fingers in the Knesset, because we did not have enough support in the public and, therefore, the politicians did not fear the punishment of the voter if they supported the disengagement. On the eve of the elections, Weiss and her friends are determining that we will have yet fewer fingers in the Knesset, even less public support. (Weiss, 2008b)

Like Danny Dayan, Chanan Porat, one of the fathers of the settlement movement declared:

> Our line is that we have love and it will triumph and that we do not cross red lines. This is a deep and decisive line. In the religious Zionist community, the youth is 99 percent [that is, almost perfect]. We have groups, the danger from whom I do not dismiss, but it is important to see them in proportion . . . They [the 'hilltop youth'] distort this concept so I say 'accursed be their rage for its ruthlessness and their wrath for its ferocity' (Genesis, 49:7) . . . We must be very decisive practically in differentiating ourselves from this line. And I believe that we have the ability to contend with it even though it is a difficult contention. (Porat, 2008)

Nonetheless, the "99%" pure argument of Porat, can be challenged. It is impossible to escape the fact that on the eve of the evacuation from the occupied house a number of elected officials made equivocal statements about reacting violently to the evicting security forces. Among them was MK Uri Ariel who said: "There is no need to hit, but if someone hits us, we will defend ourselves." Malachi Levinger, head of the Kiyat Arba-Hebron Council admitted that the leadership did not have control over all those barricaded in the house. "Like a person who is defending his house we will act, I hope, without violence. We do not have control over all the people on the ground. I fear violence in the event of an evacuation. Like Amona where justice was not done, the same holds here as well. Therefore, the reactions are not under our control" (Weiss, 2008a). Much at the same time, in a public conference held in Kiryat Arba, a bitter argument broke out between Rabbi Shalom Dov Wolpe (a Chabad-Lubavitch adherent and radical right-wing activist) and Rabbi Eliezer Waldman (also at the right wing of the settler spectrum) on the subject of the Brown House. Nadav Shragai describes the confrontation as follows:

> In the conference, Rabbi Shalom Dov Wolpe from the Organiza-tion of the Rabbis of the Land of Israel remarked that "the State of Israel in its present form is today an enemy of the people of Israel and the Land of Israel. We will defeat the internal enemy which is at present the State of Israel." Rabbi Eliezer Waldman who rose to speak after Wolpe responded sharply: "The State of Israel is not the enemy of the people of Israel. It is ours, of every single Jew. Stop this nonsense. We are fighting against those who want to impose a lie and warped law upon us, against those who have disengaged from Judaism, from Zionism and from the Land of Israel, against those who have ceased believing in the natural justice that the Land of Israel belongs only to the people of Israel." After Waldman's words, Wolpe retracted his statement and said that they were directed against the govern-ment of Israel and not the State of Israel. (Shragai, 2008b)

A careful reading of Rabbi Wolpe's writings and statements puts his retraction into question. He does indeed believe that the State of Israel is a dangerous enemy of the people of Israel. (He later headed the "Jewish Authority in the Land of Israel" that saw itself as the genuine representative of the people of Israel as opposed to the Jewish Agency and the govern-ment of Israel). He repeats this position again and again. For example, when accused by Rabbi Yoel Bin Nun of having totally despaired of the State of Israel he responded: "A wonderful definition, well said Rabbi Bin Nun . . . ! Indeed, we have despaired of the state that destroys the Land of Israel and is set to establish a center of terror in the heart of the Land of Israel" (Wolpe, 2011).

At the same conference on the eve of the evacuation, Rabbi Zalman Melamed remonstrated against the hostile ruling of the courts. As a matter of principle, he asserted:

> Laws whose origin are in falsification are not considered laws. From here we call out to the soldiers of the IDF saying that we love the IDF very much and wish to protect its strength and its wholeness . . . What will protect us is the greater the number of soldiers who avoid cooperating with the expulsion of Jews from their homes. Had soldiers refused, there would not have been given—even in the Lebanon war—such warped commands that caused so much damage. (Weiss, 2008a)

All this was said before the violence of the house's occupiers reached its peak. Still, even after the violence escalated and until the actual evacuation there was almost no reported condemnation by the rabbis of these thuggish actions. The single exception was Rabbi Shlomo Aviner who, in his weekly column in the newspaper *Ma'ayanei Hayeshua*, wrote an article entitled "Have you raised your hand against a soldier?" that expressed deep shock over the very idea of resorting to violence against the security forces who represent the people of Israel and sacrifice themselves for the sake of the land. On the other side, Rabbi Dov Lior, while not justifying the damage to Arab property, argued—true to accusations he had made before—that it was the work of provocateurs and refused to denounce their actions. He called the evacuation of the Hebron house a profanation of God's name but refrained from using this appellation to describe the house's occupiers (Lior, 2009f).

On December 4, 2008, a year and a half after they occupied the house, the Jewish inhabitants were evacuated with a great show of force in which roughly twenty of the occupiers and members of the security forces were injured. The political and spiritual leadership that sponsored the violent actions of the occupiers were, for the most part, recognized figures on the extreme militant side of the religious Zionist camp. But it must be added that many in the central leadership of religious Zionism and on the Israeli Right did, if a bit late, condemn the actions of the occupiers of the Brown House.

Probably the most radical of the all the settler rabbis, Rabbi Yitzchak Ginzburgh (see below) in a well-publicized gathering less than two weeks prior to the eviction, sketched before those assembled the guidelines that should be followed when the actual evacuation took place. His writing is disingenuous and deliberately evasive but an exhaustive reading of his texts leaves no doubt about his glorification of revenge and violence (see Ben-Horin, 1995; Moses, 2009: 75–78; Yifrach, 2014). He spoke glowingly of the "heroism" involved in disobeying orders:

There are a number of levels to disobeying an order: he who refuses to evacuate when it is so ordered, he who says that he cannot be a partner to an army that evacuates and even more so he who refuses to be drafted. He [the third] says that he wants to serve the people of Israel but not in this army . . .

In order to intensify the awareness and the readiness of soldiers to disobey orders, when necessary, we must also act in happiness—to go into the IDF's bases, many comrades together, to dance (to give out jelly doughnuts with a note inside about disobeying orders . . .) And all kinds of cute things including a bit of humor at the expense of the system . . .

What we have been told is eternity and majesty. Eternity is for all eternity; there must be something of eternity in triumphant actions. Even disobeying an order, as in Gush Katif, is heroism, it is non-identification and it is very important—but it did not reveal itself as an entirely triumphant force. We need something else that is triumphant, something active . . . to arise and do something, arise and do . . .

Anything that disrupts here—especially at the hour of truth—any action that can disrupt the state—this is part of the sphere of eternity. It is for all eternity. We can already see that these things work. We must be careful to do this wisely, with reason and to pay attention that it is without physical violence—there is no need for any physical violence . . . He who has brains can disrupt the entire state without violence. This thing is eternity. In regard to the Arabs as well, head to head, violence is unnecessary; there are many things that can be done in order to encourage them to get out of here. (Ginsburgh, 2008)

With the unfolding of events surrounding the Brown House, a visible fissure opened between the mainstream of the religious Zionist camp on the one hand and militant settler groups on other. When faced with eviction, the main camp of religious Zionism stayed, for the most part, within the constraints of the law—although at the level of rhetoric they flirted with illegality, sometimes even violence. The militant settlers, on the other hand, openly advocated and participated in illegal and violent actions. When the worrying scope of resistance to the security forces became clear, when a variety of conspicuous violent deeds were committed—already referred to at this time by the term "Price Tag"—many in the religious Zionist camp explicitly and unequivocally distanced themselves from the perpetrators and their actions. Some did their best to minimize the phenomenon. And yet, it must be said that the influence of those with a non-Zionist outlook (like Rabbi Ginzburgh) was on the rise. These views found a receptive audience, especially among the youth for whom the sense of powerlessness during the disengagement and the violence of the Amona events remained open sores. The delicate "balance" that had been preserved until this time was being upset. Mamlachtiut was more and more on the defensive.

There were those who expressed deep concern about the direction events were taking. For example, it is worth citing the words of Rabbi Yossef Weitzen, rabbi of the *Psagot* settlement who was clearly alarmed by the violent acts committed in the militant settlement *Migron* during the Independence Day celebrations in 2008. At the time, the heads of the Yesha Council were in Migron, attempting to hammer out an agreement about the unauthorized outposts when young thugs from the settler's militant wing roughed them up. Rabbi Weitzen compared them to the most extreme ultra-Orthodox group that does not recognize the state and indulges in violence.

> In any event, to my great sorrow, I believe that what took place on Independence Day is not only a local action. For a long time already, I have felt that basic things in which I believe are not internalized in our community. As a general heading I would say that part of our community is going in the path of the Neturei Karta [the most radical anti-Zionist sect in the Haredi community]. Neturei Karta does this in regard to the observance of Mitzvot and honoring the Sabbath and we do it in regard to the Land of Israel. (Weitzen, 2008)

The Status of State Institutions during the "Price Tag" Period

In the last decade there have been many skirmishes, acts of violence, arson even murder (often by individuals who have parted ways with religious

Zionism) but these have been largely local, independent initiatives rather than the work of well-organized groups. Still, a number of very significant developments require our attention. Some of these events and transformations have received only passing coverage in the media.

1. The removal of the *Har Bracha* yeshiva from the "Yeshivot Hesder" category following the refusal of yeshiva's head, Rabbi Eliezer Melamed, to condemn right-wing political protests by IDF soldiers in uniform.

2. The investigation of a number of rabbis regarding the book *Torat Hamelech* (The King's Law), most notably Rabbi Dov Lior.

3. Much-publicized confrontations that took place about women singing at IDF ceremonies. Although this subject is not strictly part of the Land of Israel discourse, it is not entirely separate from it either.

4. Most important: A long series of violent "Price Tag" attacks that have been directed against Arabs and their property— especially cutting down olive trees and torching cars. Mosques and churches have been vandalized and set on fire both in the West Bank and inside the Green Line. There have also been brazen attacks against the property and soldiers of the IDF. Most recently, the group—actually an anarchic congeries of individuals—has turned to outright terrorism.

5. In late 2009, conspicuous political protests by IDF soldiers on active duty took place.

These virtually unprecedented acts provoked a wide range of intellectual and rabbinic responses. First (October 23), a number of soldiers from the *Shimshon* regiment of the *Kfir* brigade unfurled banners during the initiation ceremony at the Wailing Wall reading "Shimshon does not evacuate *Chomesh*" (a settlement in the West Bank). These soldiers were dismissed from the brigade and sentenced to twenty days in a military prison. Their act set off a series of chain reactions both in the IDF and in the religious Zionist community.

A few weeks later twenty-five reserve officers and soldiers from the same brigade sent a letter that condemned the IDF's stern reaction to the demonstrating soldiers. They supported the soldiers' protest and demanded that the brigade not participate in any evacuation activity. Shortly thereafter, six soldiers from the *Nachshon* regiment raised a banner on the roof of a military building on which it was written "Nachshon does not expel either." These soldiers were sentenced to twenty to thirty days in military prison. A week later, a placard was found in an army base in the Jordan Valley saying "Kfir doesn't expel Jews."

Among those who participated in these actions there was a student from the *Har Bracha* Hesder yeshiva. Rabbi Eliezer Melamed, the yeshiva's head, adamantly refused to condemn his behavior. The rabbi's calls to disobey orders under certain circumstances did not ingratiate him with the military either. In the end (2010), the Chief of Staff, General Gabi Ashkenazi recommended to the Minister of Defense Ehud Barak that the special Hesder arrangement with the yeshiva be terminated. This took place a few days later following a particularly bitter exchange between the parties to the dispute. (The Har Bracha yeshiva was readmitted to the Hesder program in 2013.) Although the Union of Hesder Yeshivot fought against the expulsion of Har Bracha, a large majority of the Union's rabbis opposed political protests in the IDF and rejected Rabbi Eliezer Melamed's support for the demonstrating soldiers. Nonetheless, these rejections were quite often stammered or inaudible; there were very few rabbis in the Hesder movement who publicly condemned Rabbi Melamed and his faction. In particular the Union of Hesder Yeshivot firmly supported Rabbi Melamed's right to express his opinion freely. In a flyer printed at the time they asserted:

1. All the heads of the Hesder yeshivot firmly oppose any protest within the IDF. Because of the will to preserve the cohesion and unity of the IDF we once again express our appreciation of the security system, of the IDF and of its officers who are engaged in the holy work of preserving and protecting the State of Israel and its residents.

2. Out of responsibility for the cohesion of the IDF we once again demand that the security system avoid involving IDF soldiers in tasks that have a civilian character.

3. For these reasons we call for a dialogue with the IDF and for the renewal of the glorious tradition in which decisions affecting Hesder are made in a coordinated and understanding way. The decision of the Ministry of Defense to cancel the Hesder framework of the Har Bracha yeshiva is grave and creates a serious tear in the fabric of the IDF and the people. The Union will do all it can to return the situation to its former status in all that relates to the Har Bracha yeshiva.

Rabbi David Stav, spokesman of the Union of Hesder Yeshivot added:

> Appreciation of Rabbi Melamed was expressed during the meeting and all, *all* members of the Union wish to see him as indivisible part of the Union. For his part, Rabbi Melamed expressed the will to act according to the rules of the heads of the yeshivot and in this way to renew the honorable and practical dialogue with the heads of the security system. (Union of Hesder Yeshivot, 2009)

Leaders of the Hesder yeshivot were under heavy pressure to support Rabbi Melamed and to oppose the sanctions imposed by the IDF. The firm yet dialogue-seeking character of the Union rabbi's document and of Rabbi Stav's comments reflected their conflicted convictions.

These complex attitudes, as well as the resolute opposition of most yeshiva heads to political protest in the army, were clearly expressed in an angry letter that Rabbi Yuval Sherlow (the head of the Hesder yeshiva in *Petach Tikva*) addressed to his students at the time.

> Recently, some of the participants in the dispute took it upon themselves to decide what other rabbis, me included, should believe in regard to the declaration that 'we are all Rabbi Melamed' and to the effect that most of the yeshiva heads support this but are embarrassed to express their position out loud. I see in these things first and foremost a lie . . . However, there is here something far more serious and it is the attempt to impose upon the public and the Torah-based discussion one and only one position that I, of course, believe is incorrect. Even more: it is very damaging. (Sherlow, 2010)

As opposed to Rabbi Sherlow's moderation, Rabbi Melamed's militancy received support from an unexpected source. Rabbi Chaim Druckman, the head of the *Bnei Akiva* yeshivot who was also in charge of the IDF's conversion program lent his voice to the more combative faction. One of the more temperate leaders in the religious Zionist rabbinic world, Rabbi Druckman set off a storm when he ruled that refusal is a legitimate last resort when a soldier receives an order to evacuate settlements. According to Rabbi Druckman, a soldier who receives such an order must act with restrained strength and take no part in fulfilling the command. If all other options have failed, there are times when no other choice remains but disobeying orders (Druckman, 2010).

Returning to the issue of political protests in the army, it must be added for the sake of fairness that Rabbi Melamed's sympathy for the protesting soldiers was not wholehearted. He elucidated his own equivocal position as follows:

> Had they [the protesting soldiers] consulted with me it is prob-able that I would have recommended avoiding it because it is only when they coerce a soldier to aid in expulsion that he must refuse, but there is no necessity for him to protest, certainly not at the swearing-in ceremony . . . But after having done what they did with self-sacrifice for their nation and homeland I respect their actions and recognize the usefulness that arises from public protests such as these. We are talking about soldiers with very high motivation and as their kind multiplies in the people and in the IDF, our situation will be better. (E. Melamed, 2009)

Rabbi Melamed earned the enthusiastic support of Rabbi Nachum Eliezer Rabinovitch, head of the Hesder yeshiva in *Ma'aleh Adumim*, who unre-servedly denounced using the army for what he saw as "political" purposes.

> Had we not been afraid in the period of the expulsion and there would have been a readiness among the yeshiva heads to insist upon the democratic principle, not to speak of the basic Torah principle, it would have been possible to prevent it . . . In no democratic country in the world do they use the army against citizens . . . Only in dictatorial states is it accepted that the dictator use the army to do his bidding. But in democratic states the army is consecrated for one thing only—to protect the state. So it ought to be and this is what is written in the ethical code of the IDF. (*BeSheva*, 2009)

Rabbi Lior once again took the more radical position. He unambigu-ously called for protests to take place in the army and compared these protests to the *'Aliya Bet'* project against the British Mandate (Lior, 2010b).

Protesting Hesder yeshiva students are not marginal figures in the religious Zionist community. Indeed they, like Hesder students in general, are counted among the more normative role models for civil-religious behavior. Beyond their readiness for self-sacrifice, they are seen (as opposed to the Brown House militants) as disciplined, serious young men who are subject to rabbinical authority as well as to the laws of the state. It is not surprising therefore that the army protest movement proved to be short-lived and limited to a few soldiers. Despite fears to the contrary, it did not become a widespread phenomenon. In fact, about two years later, when an infantry company made up entirely of students from the *Elon Moreh* yeshiva headed by Rabbi Elyakim Levanon (whose position on democracy, disobeying orders, the rule of law, and army protests can hardly be called "liberal") was chosen as the best company in the brigade, the rabbi was delighted. He declared that "The spirit they received in the Elon Moreh yeshiva is the same spirit that accompanied them in the army as well. As students in the yeshiva they are taught to give their all in everything: in soldiering, security, mutual aid, the love of Torah and care in the performance of Mitzvot" (Pioterkovsky, 2011).

Among Rabbi Levanon's students—even those who in the last resort would disobey orders—there is little evidence of their turning to violence, either verbal or physical, toward ideologically hostile fellow soldiers, toward security forces who do not always act as they deem fit—even, it would appear, toward Palestinians. Despite the ideological traumas we have detailed and although there was much overheated militant rhetoric, the hard core of yeshiva students has remained law-abiding. For the most part they have internalized the message that the State of Israel and the IDF are holy, the corollary to which is that they must be honored insofar as possible. In principle, the discourse of disobedience has an uneasy place in this worldview but, as this chapter tries to demonstrate, the balance between the state's authority and that of Halacha and the Land of Israel has been shifting of late. The balance continues to hold but, *at least* at the margins, radicalism is eating away at the cohesion and integrity of the IDF and of the state.

Torat Hamelech and Rabbi Dov Lior's "Ambush"

In their book *Torat Hamelech* (The King's Law) its authors, Rabbi Yitzchak Shapira and Rabbi Yosef Elizur, both from the *Od Yosef Chai* Yeshiva, in the radical settlement Yitzhar and disciples of the Rabbi Yitzchak Ginzburgh, study the "proper" behavior of Jews toward Gentiles and under what circumstances killing them is permissible. (After an attack on an army base traced back to yeshiva students, the Od Yosef Chai yeshiva was closed down in April 2014 by the IDF and transformed into a military base. As of the spring of 2015 it still serves to house a unit of the Border Guard police).

Torat Hamelech is a learned treatise based on many scores of traditional sources and, although it surely lies on the periphery of halachic debate, it would be disingenuous to claim that their arguments are entirely outside the realm of Torah-based discourse. It received the stamp of approval by leading radical halachic authorities such as (not surprisingly) Rabbis Lior and Ginzburgh; but it was also endorsed by Rabbi Yaacov Yosef (son of Rabbi Ovadia Yosef) who recommended that the authors receive the Israel prize, Rabbi Meir Mazoz an important Posek and so on. The *Kikar Shabbat* Internet site reports that more than fifty rabbis of the religious Zionist community endorsed the book as well without, it needs to be added, mentioning them by name. It must be made clear that the vast majority of rabbinic scholars condemned the book as entirely distorted; some even insisted that it be burnt.

Why did the book create such a storm of debate and protest? Learned treatises are usually not the stuff of intellectual tempests. Indeed, its complexity and very detailed argument prevent anything but the briefest summary. *Inter alia* the book claims that killing a Gentile is a lesser offence than killing a Jew; that a Jew who kills an innocent Gentile at a time of violent conflict does not deserve punishment; the prohibition against killing Gentiles does not derive from the value of their lives because their human legitimacy is inferior; any Gentile who poses a threat (in the broadest sense) to the Jewish people may be killed; Goyim who do not observe the seven Noahide laws may be killed; he who verbally weakens the Jewish Kingdom is a Rodef who may be killed; if enemy soldiers have mixed with a civilian, innocent, Gentile population the latter may be killed; as to killing babies and children, it may be claimed that they should be harmed (*Lifgoa*) if it is clear that they will grow up to be our enemies; the children of a wicked king (read: leader) can be killed in order to put pressure on him and so on.

In the spirit of these radical pronouncements (although it does not directly belong to the discourse of disobedience we are following), it must be added that at very much the same time (December 2010) a halachic ruling was signed by fifty city and town rabbis, most of whom were civil servants, prohibiting renting or selling homes to Arabs, which action could be punished by excommunication or banishment (*Niydui*). They included the rabbis of substantial towns and cities such as *Rishon Le'Zion*, *Ashdod*, *Herzlia*, *Rosh Ha'ayin*, *Ramat Hasharon*, *Kfar Sava*, etc.

Because of the charge that Torat Hamelech was guilty of incitement, the Attorney General conducted an investigation into the book's authors and endorsers (Mashiach, 2011). Handcuffed, the book's main author, Rabbi Yizchak Shapira, was interrogated by the police. So was Rabbi Yitzchak Ginzburgh, who broke into song and dance when his interrogation was over. The high point of this affair was undoubtedly the summons for questioning issued to Rabbi Dov Lior in February 2011 because of the endorsement he gave to the book. He refused to present himself to the police. Two main reasons were given for Rabbi Lior's decision not to respond to the warrant:

First, he believed in the right, indeed the duty of every rabbi to express the Torah-truth as he saw it without fear of intimidation. Second, the enforcement in this subject was, in his view, entirely selective, that is, prejudicial to right-wing activists as opposed to the seemingly free tongues of the spokesmen of the Left who de-legitimized the state and yet enjoyed the protection of the law on the basis of the principle of freedom of expression.

Rabbi Lior was "ambushed" by the police in Jerusalem and held for a number of hours of interrogation. Angry denunciations from the religious Zionist community and outside it were heard. Even many not associated with Rabbi Lior's views raised objections. Figures on the Right saw it as a blatant attempt to silence selectively right-wing rabbinic opinion. For example, the two Chief Rabbis posted an announcement saying that "we are distressed and pained about the grave blow to the honor of an important rabbi and judge, among the greatest of Israel's rabbis and a leader of the religious community" (Nahshoni, 2011a). Rabbi Chaim Druckman and the *Tzohar* rabbis (a relatively liberal Orthodox organization) declared that the police and the Attorney General had "crossed a black line"; they do not enforce the same rules on intellectuals who speak for the Left. The upshot of these critiques is well expressed by the right-wing journalist Moti Ovadia:

> The arrest of Rabbi Lior in [the] middle of the street caused politicians and even many rabbis—among them those for whom Kiryat Arba is not at all their holy grail [sic]—to condemn the police and to come together in joint protest. The entire episode took no longer than a few hours, but the effect far surpassed it. Many hundreds of young people who went to the major intersections, disrupted traffic and did not fear to be arrested and even to suffer blows from the police force.
>
> Rabbi Dov Lior will be hoisted on the shoulders of many in religious Zionism in the coming days, among them those who were hurt by the 'offense against the honor of Torah,' others enraged by the offense against a 'serving rabbi' and also those who see in it only an offense against religious Zionism. No one has any doubt that what the police did today, it would not dare do to any Lithuanian 'Torah sage' or supporter of Shas. (Ovadiah, 2011)

This case reinforced the feeling—common among the religious Zionist youth at least since the disengagement and Amona—that their camp was being selectively persecuted and that the law was being unfairly enforced. In their view, this was another case of left-wing elites exploiting government institutions in order to further their partisan political agenda. In spring 2012, the Attorney General dismissed the case: he ruled that the book was halachic discourse that did not *actively* incite to violence and that it was covered by the right to "free speech."

Women Singing in the IDF

This issue grabbed headlines on the 5th of September in 2011 when nine soldiers from the IDF Cadet School left a "legacy of battle" (*Moreshet krav*) ceremony when a number of women soldiers appeared on stage to sing. For them, halachic restrictions prohibited men from listening to women singing. Although the matter had been coordinated with their staff officer, the regiment commander demanded that they return to the event. After they left for a second time, it was decided to try them before a military tribunal. Some of the cadets apologized and, consequently, were reinstated in the course, while those who refused to apologize were dismissed. The issue triggered great interest in the Israeli public: among the secular communities, this was yet another example of religious obscurantism. In the *Hesder* yeshiva world and the religious pre-army seminars, by contrast, the issue raised hackles because of what they saw as lack of sensitivity to the cadet's religious beliefs. After all, they claimed, this was relatively minor issue and the army's unwillingness to defer to the soldiers' religious conscience could not be justified by the country's larger strategic interests. For many religious Zionist soldiers, this was yet another stage in the alienation of the IDF from Jewish values and religious Zionism (Cohen and Susser, 2014).

It is true that women had sung in IDF ceremonies for years without objection by the yeshiva students—it seems not to have bothered them religiously or they found wily methods of getting around it. From their point of view what rankled was the army's unwillingness to accept the religious explanations of the cadets and the haste and seeming enthusiasm with which they were dismissed from the course. Rabbinic reactions to the army's policy varied. Some were extremely critical. Among the critical reactions in the religious Zionist camp that of Rabbi Elyakim Levanon stands out. Not surprisingly, Rabbi Levanon had also supported some degree of disobedience in the confrontation between religious soldiers and the state's enforcement agencies.

In an interview on the *Kol Chai* radio station on the 17th of November 2011, Rabbi Levanon attacked the conclusion of the special committee that had been set up by the Chief of Staff to deal with the subject of women singing in the army. The committee determined that religious soldiers were obliged to take part in official ceremonies in which women sang. On the other hand, they were to be accommodated when the event was not an official one. Reflecting the growing severity of religious demands (*Chumrot*) and the increasingly toxic relationship between the army and rabbinical authorities, the debate quickly got out of hand. Rabbi Levanon did not mince words. He said that he and many other rabbis would direct their students to leave events in which women sang, whatever the consequences. In the course of the interview he declared:

> People do not understand the Halachic mess they have gotten themselves into. They are hastening the situation in which rabbis will be forced to direct soldiers—you must leave such events even if you will stand before a firing squad and they will shoot you dead . . . If the IDF accepts the recommendations of the committee whose upshot is that religious soldiers will need to be present when women sing I say circumspectly that there will be many rabbis and Poskim who will issue the directive that a soldier needs to sacrifice his life and leave the event . . . This is all clearly harassment of religious soldiers . . . I sincerely hope that there will be there some wise people who will avert this horrible step, but if not—we will not have a choice . . . I will tell anyone who asks me not to be conscripted any longer. (Levanon in a radio interview to Kol-Chai Station, Nov. 17, 2011)

Although the subject of women singing is indeed minor and does not directly impinge upon defending the integrity of the Land of Israel, it is hard to avoid the feeling that Rabbi Levanon's denunciation of the committee's decision is related to his conditional support of disobedience against the evacuation of settlements. It seems that the support of disobedience in regard to the Land of Israel does not stop there. Radical positions beget more radical ones. In any event, these comments of Rabbi Levanon generated deep antagonism not only in the general public but among various rabbis as well. His unrestrained statements against the IDF, his unambiguous declaration that under certain circumstances he would direct his students not to be drafted were far from being accepted either by the public or by the rabbis (Roth, 2011; Nahshoni, 2011b).

To be sure, the Union of Hesder Yeshivot, without expressing their opinion on the subject of women singing itself, conveyed its support for the cadets who were dismissed and demanded that the IDF not repeat such actions again in the future. But they preferred to lower the flames and open a dialogue with the army. The storm following Rabbi Levanon's comments erupted mainly in the general Israeli media. "Exclusion of women" (*Hadarat nashim*) became a much-repeated catch-phrase and many related issues of female "modesty" were given great attention. For example, the separate seating on Haredi-utilized bus lines and the actions of Haredi extremists in *Beit Shemesh*—spitting on a school girl for allegedly not being sufficiently covered up—became *causes célèbres*. Here too many in the religious camp felt victimized; they saw the media campaign as directed against Torah-observing Jews with the intent of vitiating their influence on Israeli society.

But conciliatory, democracy-supporting voices were also heard. Rabbi Eli Sadan spoke for a large constituency, both rabbinical and lay, when he emphasized the critical nature of democracy for the Zionist project and the need to find ways for the religious and the secular to live together harmoniously—especially in the period after Amona. In a booklet on democracy and discipline in the military he writes:

> The great miracle of the cooperative movement toward the creation of the Jewish State could not have taken place without the democratic system of government. I know that there are those who wish to insert into this word wide-ranging meanings to which we need not agree but the fundamental meaning of democracy in Israel is the ability of many people to work together for the greater glory of the State of Israel because each of them has agreed that there would be elections and that the elected representatives . . . will decide on the path of the State of Israel and that every citizen will be obligated by these decisions . . . The consequence of this is the strengthening of the Knesset, the government and the agreement that the state will act according to their decisions, even when they are unacceptable to us! . . .
>
> According to the rules of the General Staff, a commander does not have the right to order a soldier to perform an action that contradicts his religious beliefs. And if he does so it is the right for the soldier to disobey orders. But the question 'what is the judgment of Torah'? (*Da'at Torah*) is not given to each and every soldier according the school from which he comes but to the chief rabbi of the place (*Mara de'atra*) which is the military rabbinate. (Sadan, 2012: 9–12)

Rabbi Sadan's position represents the "theological-normative balance" at work. He seeks to prevent the tensions between religious Zionism and the secular institutions of the state from undermining their necessary coexistence. For the many religious Zionists who follow in his path, those who exacerbate the struggle and contribute to the internal split in the people "reveal the source of impurity that exists in them!" (Sadan, 2012: 17).

Parallel to Rabbi Sadan's booklet, at the beginning of 2012, a new religious Zionist movement, *Beit Hillel*, was founded in order to advance what they saw as the vital covenant between religious Zionism and the rest of the citizens of the state and its institutions. (Full disclosure: one of the authors is among its founders.) This movement, which has more than a hundred rabbis and tens of women teachers of Torah, is comprised mainly of graduates of schools in which the influence of Rabbi Tzvi Yehuda Kook is weaker than the more peace-seeking ideas presented by Rabbi Sadan. The movement's platform deals, among other things, with the relationship between Torah and democracy. Although proximate to Rabbi Sadan's position, Beit Hillel is based upon a deeper internalization of democratic ideals (although clearly not the "Jewish democracy" proposed by Rabbi Tzvi Yehuda). Because the group's platform is of great importance, we cite it at length.

> We think that one ought not to violate the state's laws even when there is ideological disagreement with actions carried out by the law enforcement agencies. We believe that citizens have the right to protest, but in all cases this must be done within the borders of the law and without the resort to violence of any kind. The directives of law cannot, of course, overpower the directives of Halacha. But one must try to minimize these potential clashes rather than intensifying them.
>
> As part of the respect for the institutions of Israeli democracy we recognize the decisions of the Israeli courts. Nevertheless, we long for the renewal of Jewish Law but parallel to this hope we see in the legal system a vital instrument for the preservation of state law and insuring peace in the land . . .
>
> The democratic system places great store on individual rights including the rights to life, security, liberty, equality and respect. We believe that these values accord with Jewish ethics and support the preservation of these rights for all citizens of Israel without distinction of gender or sector . . .
>
> For the Mitzvah-observing soldiers, service in the IDF presents a significant meeting place for Halacha and democracy and not infrequently it is liable to create problematic points of friction. Our starting point is that service in the IDF is both an obligation and a right and that the army should take prudent

steps to minimize confrontations and points of friction. We distance ourselves from any possibility that there be secular coercion upon soldiers who want to observe Halacha and the religious way of life as received from their teachers.

At the same time we think that in the context of Halachic rulings it is important to relate to basic Jewish values such as preserving the unity of the people and being mindful of the respect owing to all of humanity. These values must be considered as serious factors that should, in cases of conflict, lead to basing oneself on the more lenient sides of Halacha. We place our trust in the Chief Army Rabbi and in the army's rabbinical system that are responsible for providing solutions to halachic problems in the IDF and empower them in the holy work they perform. (Beit Hillel, 2012)

These words represent positions to which many in the religious Zionist community would happily affix their signature. Nevertheless, as has been repeatedly noted, these views are also under significant and growing pressure from the less liberal branches of the religious Zionist communities. Much of what has been discussed in this chapter details various aspects of this militant, rightward move. The next section however presents what is the most threatening recent development in the religious Zionist world: the rise of vigilante violence, and, at the fringe, outright terrorism.

Vigilante Violence and the "Price Tag" Gangs

Special attention must be given both to the "Price Tag" (*Tag Mechir*) phenomenon and to the militant "Hilltop Youth" (*No'ar Hagva'ot*)—although some of the latter are no longer youths. There can be no doubt that the most radical and violent vigilante behavior belongs to the marginal settler group that goes under the name: Price Tag. They appear to be a loose congeries of disaffected, frustrated, often psychologically troubled youth who see it as their duty to take revenge upon Israel's enemies, to exact "payment" for their perfidy. Especially worrisome are the forgiving attitudes adopted toward them by substantial parts of religious settler leadership. Not only do they refrain from forcefully combating the Price Tag phenomenon, they relate to it with a certain degree of forbearance, even understanding. Neither do the state authorities pursue these criminal elements with anything near the energy they expend in bringing Arab terrorists to justice. Indeed, most often these defacers, vandalizers, and terrorists escape apprehension by the police even though, in some instances at least, their identity is not terribly difficult to reveal.

Price Tag exploits began in 2008 as a means of diverting the security forces' attention away from dismantling settlements. Soon their actions became more violent; they retaliated against the security forces for every attempt to harass them or to impose the law in ways they found unacceptable. Most often, however, the object of their revenge was Palestinian militants who attacked settlers. Feeling vulnerable, parts of the settler movement saw the Price Tag strategy as legitimate. Although most of the vandals are teenagers, it must be noted that a number of radical rabbinical figures are associated with their actions. Nadav Shragai mentions Rabbis Ginzburgh, Dudkevich, and Yitzchak Shapira of the Od Yosef Chai yeshiva (Joseph still lives) in the Yitzhar settlement as the spiritual mentors of the Price Tag gang (Shragai, 2008a). Shragai writes:

> The settler establishment and the great majority of the Yesha rabbis are reserved in regard to [Price Tag's] behavior. Some like those from the Dolev settlement and the head of the Benyamin Council, even condemned the group in strong language. Most settlers do not take part in their activities but the youth who are identified with it, accepts its strategy as a creditable way to deter the security forces and the Palestinians from harming Jews. (Shragai, 2008a)

The Rabbi with the greatest influence over the Price Tag gangs is Rabbi Yitzchak Ginsburgh. Rabbi Ginzburgh espouses violent extremist positions that are a blend of Kabbalist Chabad-Hasidic ideas, virulently anti-democratic views, racism, and messianic fervor sanctifying the vital, natural, unbridled expression of religious enthusiasm. Vengeance against the enemies of Israel, the Goyim, falls into this last category. Ginzburgh's exclusivist (not to say xenophobic) views that distinguish between Jewish and Gentile blood are perhaps found in their most concentrated form in the book Torat Hamelech (The King's Torah) discussed above. To recap: the book deals with Dinei Nefashot (issues involving life and death) between Jews and Gentiles and was published (2009) by two of Ginzburgh's students, Rabbis Yitzchak Shapira and Yosef Elizur. The book, as will be recalled, takes up the Halachot that pertain to killing non-Jews during peacetime and in times of war (Shapira, 2009). Following the public outcry caused by the book, a police investigation was launched in the course of which Rabbis Ginzburgh and Shapiro were interrogated. In the end, the Attorney General closed the investigation without indicting the authors or their mentor because, in his view, the book was written in a factual, scholarly manner and did not explicitly call for violence.

Like Rabbi Meir Kahane, Rabbi Ginzburgh is fixated on the value of Jews taking revenge against non-Jews. Vengeance, Ginzburgh tells us, is a natural, healthy response that vents deep existential needs and is a key to mental well-being. When it is prevented from expressing itself, the natural, existential basis of life is lost. Therefore, the Torah's approach to revenge is that "the way of the world comes before Torah" which in Ginzburgh's eccentric interpretation means that revenge is permitted when, for example, an individual whose relative has been murdered kills the murderer so as to "redeem his blood." The violation of Jewish honor is another cause for violence. Since Jewish honor is the honor of God, Jewish revenge is the revenge of God (Ginzburgh, 2000: 79–82). Still, praiseworthy revenge is limited to those whose motives are impersonal and whose actions derive solely from the noble desire to rescue Jewish public honor. Authentic revenge is, in essence, spontaneous and self-sacrificing but it is nevertheless complex and demands a sense of proportion and recognition of boundaries (Ginzburgh, 2000: 84).

The legitimacy of revenge underlies Ginzburgh's unequivocal sympathy for Baruch Goldstein's massacre in Hebron's Tomb of the Patriarchs. He made no attempt to hide his admiration for Goldstein. Ginzburgh's essay *Baruch Hagever* provides a justification for the massacre. The title (as we noted earlier) conveys the message: *Baruch* = Blessed be the *Gever* = man, i.e., the real man. (Ginzburgh disfigures Jeremiah's declaration: "Blessed be the man who puts his faith in God" 7:17). Published soon after massacre in the Tomb of the Patriarchs, the essay created a great public stir. Ginzburgh claims that Goldstein's mass murder should be understood as incarnating five distinct virtues: the sanctification of God's name, the saving of lives, revenge, the eradication of evil and the struggle for the Land of Israel (Ginzburgh cited in Ben-Horin, 1995: 20).

Price Tag bands do not seem to form a hierarchical organization but rather are made up of individuals and small cells that are, so it is often claimed, difficult to trace and apprehend. (In this regard they differ from the Jewish Underground of the 1980s that was more organized and disciplined. Moreover, the Underground was composed of adults while the Price Tag militants are often under the age of twenty). Their tactic of remaining silent, and refusing to answer questions has also added to the difficulties faced by the security organizations. The fact is that since 2008 there have been at least fifteen arson attacks against mosques and only a handful of the perpetrators have been caught. By contrast, in June 2015 two young men were charged (and admitted) setting fire to the Loaves and Fishes church near the Sea of the Galilee.

Nevertheless, far more central rabbinical figures in the militant right-wing of the settler movement, those often spoken of as national ultra-Orthodox (*Hardeli*)—such as Rabbis Dov Lior and Zalman Melamed—refuse, on principle, to condemn the "Price Tag" phenomenon, pleading ignorance of their actions and claiming that the perpetrators are probably *Shabak* provocateurs. Still, most mainstream religious Zionist rabbis explicitly and energetically reject the actions of the Price Tag group as not only unacceptable, but as harmful to the future of the Jewish settlement project.

From 2011–2012 onward, a major escalation in Price Tag's violent activities took place. (The United Nations reports a fourfold increase in vigilante vandalism and attacks against Arabs in recent years.) First of all, their attacks have spread and now include Arab citizens of Israel living within the "Green Line." Mosques and churches in the Galilee have been torched. Second, in a number of cases, Price Tag's attacks have been directed against IDF soldiers and bases. An army base in Samaria was badly vandalized—tires were slashed, electric cables were cut, and graffiti reading the brigade commander is "bad for the Jews" was scrawled on the walls. A cinder block was thrown at the deputy brigade commander causing physical injury. Particularly offensive and often picked up by the international media is the practice of Price Tag hooligans to chop down Palestinian olive trees, some planted by their current owner's ancestors many decades ago. The security forces claim that they have great difficulty in indicting the perpetrators because evidence of their crimes is difficult to come by. When arrested, they remain entirely silent. Nevertheless, the lack of indictments has also been attributed to reluctance to confront the Price Tag perpetrators and by problems involved with the *Shabak* investigating Jewish youth. In June 2013, with matters getting badly out of hand, the government's Security Cabinet authorized the Minister of Defense to declare Price Tag "a non-permitted [*Bilti Muteret*] association" which would, it was hoped, provide the security forces with more adequate tools to prosecute the group and control their activities (Breyner and Tibon, 2013). Indeed, the head of the opposition, Eitan Kabel, proposed a law (2014) that would outlaw Price Tag as a "terrorist organization" and impose severe punishments on their violent activity. As of early 2016, the bill has not progressed since then.

The "Hilltop Youth" live in illegal farms and isolated outposts located deep within heavily populated Palestinian areas. (It should be noted, if only in passing, that about 100 illegal outposts exist, many founded during non-Likud governments—some on private Palestinian property, some in violation of Supreme Court decisions). Often the Hilltop Youth put great emphasis on blending into the natural surroundings of Samaria, that is, returning to nature, consuming only natural foods, riding horses, and the like. Inevitably, there are repeated clashes between the outpost dwellers and the encircling Palestinian population. These isolated settlers often harass their Arab neighbors by preventing the olive harvest, destroying property, and employing physical abuse (Lavie, 2003). Shlomo Fischer argues that violence is part of their ethos of returning to the soil:

> I believe that the violence which is part of the lives of the hilltop settlers results not only from their circumstances. It is not only that they live in proximity with a hostile population that forces them to incorporate violence into their hilltop life's routine. In my view, violence is part of their ethos. The fact that all the hilltop settlements are located deep inside the territory populated by Arabs makes it clear that this not merely happenstance but a deliberate choice. These settlers planted themselves 'in the face' of the Palestinians in order to show 'who's the boss,' who are the real owners and controllers of the land. Therefore, they do not try to avoid confrontations; they even provoke them. It seems to me that the appeal of violence is also bound up with the hilltop settlers' sense of union with the soil itself, with nature and its staying power. This bond is explicitly expressed in the writing of Rabbi Ginzburgh. (Fischer, 2007b: 444)

A worrisome portrait of Price Tag appears in an essay of Shabtai Bandet from mid-August 2015 (Bandet, 2015). According to the United Nations Office for the Coordination of Humanitarian Affairs, in the course of 2014 about 330 "hate crimes" were committed in the West Bank, excluding Jerusalem. But only in rare cases were indictments issued because of the difficulty of gathering conclusive evidence and because of the suspects' obstinate policy of remaining silent. Neither is it easy to prove that racist motives were involved in attacks against property. Moreover, in most cases minors were involved and the courts treated them leniently. For their part, Israeli human rights organizations claim that the state does not do nearly enough to deal with these hate crimes. Not infrequently, they claim, IDF soldiers stand aside and do not interfere with their violence. Police investigations, they report, are half-hearted and ineffective. It is also argued that the Hilltop Youth, who have often dropped out of standard educational institutions and are no longer under their parents' control, receive little or no instruction in civics or even in consensual religious ideas that might constrain their unbridled violence.

Price Tag of course has no political representation in the Knesset. Nevertheless, the *Yahad—Ha'am Itanu* party list, which received more than 3 percent of the vote in the 2015 elections and barely missed passing the electoral threshold of 3.25 percent, contains personalities who refrain from condemning their actions. The same can be said, as we shall see, of some leading halachic authorities like Rabbi Dov Lior who rejects "apologizing." Indeed, in the run-up to the evacuation of the Brown House, Rabbi Eliezer Melamed spoke of Price Tag methods as "very effective" (E. Melamed, 2009).

For the sake of balance and proportion, it must be added that Arab violence against settlers—including terrorist murder—continued apace as well. Sympathy for these actions is, arguably, greater among the Palestinian population (certainly within Hamas and Hizbollah) than Price Tag violence is among Jewish Israelis, even among the settlers. It is nevertheless true that Price Tag sympathizers see their violent actions as legitimate revenge. In this tragic circle of violence, both the settlers and the Palestinians present self-congratulatory narratives.

Violence-driven messianism is usually more theologically muddled than religiously systematic. It has transformed what was a marginal group of bizarre hooligans into a criminal phenomenon that can no longer be ignored, one that appears to be slowly seeping into the outlying (and not so outlying) regions of religious Zionism. What is clear is that the Yesha leadership is helpless in the face of their violence. Many, even in the religious Zionist camp, believe that the Yesha leadership consciously chooses not to do what it must in order to foil their activities because they serve their end of effectively intimidating Palestinians. Even though it is quite clear that the Price Tag activists have grown in number, influence, and fanaticism, it may well be that the real danger lies in the circle of passive sympathy for them that is far larger than the relatively small number of perpetrators themselves.

Overt rabbinical support for Price Tag attacks has been relatively scarce and usually elliptical. Apart from Rabbi Ginzburgh, unconcealed expressions of sympathy are rare. Even those who sympathize with them are very careful not to overstep the boundary of the law. Because their texts and lectures are carefully scrutinized by the legal authorities checking for "incitement" and for supporting an "illegal organization," these rabbis tread cautiously. They choose their words with great care.

As opposed to Rabbi Ginzburgh, the moderate and Mamlachti Council of Binyamin Rabbis harshly and consistently condemned all manifestations of violence, most especially when they are directed against the IDF and the members of the Yesha Council. Such was the case when they denounced violence against the heads of the Yesha Council who were negotiating an agreement about the status of unauthorized outposts (Binyamin Rabbis Council, 2009b) and later when the first acts of violence against the IDF (September 7, 2011) were reported. They wrote:

> Following the attempts at arson tonight and following the appeals directed to them [the arsonists] by some of the residents of Binyamin, we wish to declare our clear position toward actions that are called 'Price Tag.'
> First of all, we do not know who stands behind these actions and there is no reason to cast aspersions until the matter is clarified. These actions are forbidden both according to law and according to Halacha. In our view, and in the view of many, not only do they not at all help in strengthening the settlements and their development but cause profound damage to the entire struggle for Yesha and for the Land of Israel in general, and endanger the lives of citizens. Especially grave are the recent actions against army property and against the mosques, not least because they are likely to cause the shedding of Jewish blood.
> We know very well the difficulty of confronting the injustice of destroyed houses and the crimes of slander and abandonment directed at large parts of the settlements; nevertheless, and despite it all, it is absolutely prohibited to be drawn into these kinds of actions that are liable to 'play into the hands' of those who are encouraging the destruction of settlements. (Binyamin Rabbis Council, 2011)

Also worthy of note is that although many of the signatories to this declaration condemned the entire policy of evacuations, they make no mention of disobeying orders (Binyamin Rabbis Council, 2009a).

As we have come to expect, Rabbi Zalman Melamed takes a more provocative position. It will be recalled that at the time of the disengagement he refused to condemn violent actions on the grounds that they were committed by Shabak provocateurs (Z. Melamed, 2005c). In regard to the Price Tag bands as well, he avoids condemning violence as a matter of principle. He affirms that:

> It is not my way to deal with condemnations about unworthy actions that are done by public figures or rabbis or young people.

These condemnations, I believe, do more harm than good. We must increase the unity of Israel, especially in the religious community and for each of us to see the virtues of his comrade. (Z. Melamed, 2012)

In fact, Rabbi Melamed even condemns the condemners. He who condemns, the rabbi declares, strengthens "the claims of those who believe we are illegitimate." He protests that whoever is responsible for these acts, they are not related to him or to his students. Hence he is not required to condemn them or take responsibility for their actions (Z. Melamed, 2012).

Like Rabbi Zalman Melamed, Rabbi Dov Lior attributes Price Tag violence to provocateurs (Lior, 2010a). When asked about Price Tag actions, he prevaricated. The question posed to Rabbi Lior was spelled out simply and clearly: how did he react to Price Tag activists who say that "as a response to the evacuation of outposts we strike at Arabs and their fields randomly"? Rabbi Lior answered: "It is difficult for me to answer that because I don't know why they do this and what their purposes are, and I am not up to date about it" (Lior, 2009f).

The head of the ultra-nationalist National Union Party Yaacov Katz (aka Katzaleh) responded to the rampage on the army base and the damage done to military equipment by pointing an accusing finger at the Shabak (Katz, 2011). In the same spirit, Rabbi Yehoshua Shmidt head of the Hesder yeshiva *Birchat Torah* in the *Shavei Shomron* settlement and its communal rabbi declared: "Among the youth in Samaria, there are [outside] instigators on the loose who initiate these violent actions; they are the ones responsible for raising their hands against IDF soldiers" (Nir, 2011).

The refusal to condemn the attack on the army base and the life-endangering blow suffered by the deputy brigade commander comes through clearly in the exculpatory words of Bezalel Smortrich, currently an MK for the religious Zionist *HaBayit Hayehudi* party. In an article entitled "What in the blazes do we have to do with Peres?" he attacked the rabbis and the members of the Yesha Council who came to President Peres the day after the army base rampage to express their anger and shock. Smortrich writes:

I find it difficult to understand the response of the adults to the misdeeds of the youth this week. I find it difficult to understand what this has to do with education. The serious and especially sad attack against IDF soldiers this week was carried out by teenagers whose immense and bottled-up rage and frustration burst out uncontrollably and dreadfully and led them to prohibited quarters. Do you, when this happens to your students in the yeshiva, send them to the 'iron hand' of the Shabak, the police and the military tribunals?! Is this the way to deal with dispirited youth? And let it be clear, when I say dispirited I do not refer to something negative. I refer to idealistic youth with high and pure aspirations, with enormous powers and marvelous intentions who, precisely because of all of this, find it difficult to cope with the complexity of life, with the untrammeled lie that is dominant all around them, the abuse and cruelty of the system that is entirely mobilized against them and against all they hold dear and good. (Smortrich, 2011)

Despite Smortrich's backhanded exonerations, the attack on the army base led to almost wall-to-wall condemnations in all quarters of religious Zionism (Amrousi, 2011). Rabbi Professor Daniel Herskowitz, then the head of the HaBayit HaYehudi party and the Minister of Science and Technology, was cited as saying: "Tonight a red line was crossed. We must eject from amongst us those wild growths that in the name of the holiness of the soil are prepared to profane the name of heaven and to employ terrorist methods against IDF soldiers." Similarly Uri Ariel from the far-right National Union party declared: "Breaking into the base and the vandalizing of IDF property are extremely deplorable. I condemn the rioters who participated. At stake is an event that must not recur in any way or form and I expect the legal system to deal with this phenomenon urgently and with a strong hand." (Altman and Shumpalbi, 2011)

Most severe in condemning Price Tag's actions was the former Chief Rabbi of the IDF, Rabbi Itamar Ronsky among the founders of the settlement *Itamar* and the head of its yeshiva who said: "It is impossible for things to continue. I say something from my guts: If this reality will be dominant here, I have no place here any longer; I will not stay in this place. If the riots continue and this will become the reality, my place will not be among them and I say this as someone who has lived here tens of years" (Atali, 2011).

The peak of the Price Tag terrorist actions was an arson attack (August 13, 2015) on an Arab home in the village of Duma near Nablus (Shechem). An infant and his parents were burnt alive. Others were critically wounded. Graffiti scrawled on the walls read: "Revenge" and "Long live the Messiah King." This was not the first arson attack against Palestinian homes but, remarkably, almost none of the others ended in fatalities. The execrable exception was the abduction and burning alive of Mohammad Abu Khder in Jerusalem (July 2014) in retribution for the murder of three

Jewish youths. In this case, the perpetrators were apprehended, admitted to the crime, and recreated their actions for the police.

In a detailed column in the *Haaretz* newspaper (August 7, 2015), Chaim Levinson reported that an especially extreme faction of Jewish militants had organized around the personality of the twenty-four-year-old Meir Ettinger, the grandson of Meir Kahane. (The police banned him from entering Judea Samaria for a year and Jerusalem for six months). This group included some veteran Price Tag activists and they supported violent anarchist action against the state, the purpose of which was to cause the collapse of the State of Israel though subversive, destabilizing actions against Arabs. Levinson recounts that these young people came from all parts of Israel, committed violent deeds from about sixteen onwards and ceased when they married at about the age of twenty-one (Levinson, 2015).

Ettinger himself, who was labeled "the number one objective" of the Shabak's investigations, dropped-out of his yeshiva studies and began wandering around the various hilltop settlements. He was put under house arrest for collecting information on the movements of IDF units. After twice violating the terms restricting his movements, he was jailed for six months. The time in jail only radicalized his views. In 2012, he identified himself with the extremist Yitzhar settlement and the views of its rabbi, Yitzchak Ginzburgh, most especially, the aim of re-founding of the biblical Jewish Kingship. But this too became insufficiently radical for his tastes and he began to plan the "revolt"—the name of the document that was discovered by the authorities—that no longer heeded the authority of even the most radical rabbinic figures but was entirely anarchic and unstructured (Levinson, 2015). In an interview (February 1, 2016) for Channel 7, his wife, Moriah Ettinger, declared that "all his ideas are based upon discussions with Da'at Torah authorities, especially with Rabbi Yitzchak Ginzburgh from whom he draws his ideas and for whom he attempts to be a mouthpiece" (Elior, 2016).

Following the arson in the Duma village, Ettinger was arrested and "administratively detained" for half a year. Despite the democratically dubious practice of administrative detention (that is, detention without trial), the authorities were convinced that Ettinger was involved in incitement and violent acts and decided that administrative detention was the best option. (There are hundreds of Arabs suspected of terrorist activities being held without trial as well.)

On December 24, 2015, Israel's Channel 10 TV station showed a 25-second video clip, filmed at a wedding that took place several days earlier. The clip shows a room of jumping, dancing men wearing white skullcaps, many with the long sidelocks. Some of them are brandishing guns and knives. Two of them appear to be stabbing pieces of paper they hold in their hands, which the television station identified as pictures of an eighteen-month-old child, Ali Dawabsheh, who was incinerated in the Duma attack (Hadid, 2015). The clip elicited furious condemnations from both the Left and the Right. Prime Minister Benyamin Netanyahu condemned the video: "The shocking pictures that were broadcast this evening show the true face of a group that constitutes a danger to Israeli society and to the security of Israel."

The suspects in perpetrating the Duma arson were arrested in January 2016. They were linked to the *Tag Mechir* gangs. Twenty-one-year-old Amiram Ben-Uliel was indicted on three counts of murder (the infant and his parents) and a minor involved in the arson was also charged. According to the indictment, they perpetuated the act as revenge against the earlier murder of Jewish settlers. Ben-Uliel, it was charged, deliberately searched for a house in which there inhabitants rather than an abandoned structure. He threw the Molotov cocktail into the bedroom where the home's residents slept and escaped on foot. Simultaneously, charges were leveled against others suspected of torching Arab and Church property (Levinson and Ravid, 2016).

Extreme right-wing activists complained that the state had used torture to bully the suspects into confessing their crimes. The Price Tag prisoners, they claimed, were appallingly abused by their interrogators. But public opinion clearly supported "taking the gloves off" after the Duma murders. Minister of Education Naftali Bennet, the most dominant political figure in religious Zionism, took a clear stand that supported toughening the methods used in dealing with Price Tag terror. They had challenged the authority of Israel as a sovereign state and everything within the law should be done to apprehend and punish them.

Notably, in the half-year since "cracking" the Duma case, there has been a sharp decline in Price Tag terrorism. The new judicial and investigative powers granted the Shabak (including what is often spoken of as applying "moderate physical pressure") appear to be broadly supported by the public—both Left and Right—and, what's more, quite effective—at least at the time these lines are being written.

The blog-response of Meir Ettinger to the jailing of the two Price Tag arsonists is worth citing. It was posted on July 30, 2015:

To the protests about the Land of Israel must be added a serious protest again the great sin of the State of Israel that permits the existence of idolatry, of many churches and monasteries, in the Land of Israel.

The sound of their ringing bells mixes with the many evening sounds of Torah and prayer that exist, thank God, in the holy land. Double the protest is required when the State of Israel piles sin upon sin and not only does not fulfill the duty and Mitzvah for which we received this land, but it also arrests and detains in prison the two lads suspected of torching the church . . .

The truth must be told: there is no terror organization but there are many, many Jews, far more than what is thought, whose value priorities are absolutely different than that of the Supreme Court or the Shabak; the laws to which they are committed are not those of the state, [they are] far more eternal laws . . .

To our sorrow, the media almost in its entirety are mobilized to present what democracy has to say but the Jewish side is barely heard by people of Israel. We must go out and present our case 'to reach every Jew with a Jewish side' with the story of Yehuda Asraf and Yinon Reuveni [the arsonists held in custody] because the time has come to break down the prison wall of our souls, to fear only God and begin to loudly speak 'Jewish.' (Ettinger, 2015)

One week later (August 6, 2015) Benzi Gopstein, head of the far-right, anti-assimilation association *Lehava*—two of whose members had torched a bilingual (Hebrew-Arabic) school in Jerusalem in June 2014—outdid Ettinger in his forthrightness. (Note that Ettinger, trying to avoid the charge of "incitement," pulled back from saying in so many words that Israel ought to destroy churches; instead he wrote obliquely that Israel "does not fulfill the duty and Mitzvah for which we received this land"). Speaking at a panel discussion that was recorded, Gopstein affirmed the duty to eliminate "idol worship" in Israel. He cited Maimonides on the subject and insisted that "idol worship must be destroyed." This commandment, he declared, was still valid. Asked if this meant destroying churches, Gopstein answered in the affirmative. When warned by a fellow panelist that his words were being recorded, he said "I'm prepared to sit in jail 50 years for it." He asked: "is there even a question [in this matter]?" (Gronich, 2015). Not surprisingly, the Catholic Church in Israel turned to the Attorney General and demanded that Gopstein be charged with incitement.

Conclusions

In 2001, Dov Schwartz tellingly diagnosed the decline of religious Zionism in the eyes of the general public and, more critically in its own eyes. This decline, he argued, divided religious Zionism's leadership into two factions. First, there were those who believed that the "solution" was *Tikkun* in the sense of "metaphysical repair of the world" and, second, there were others who argued that the "solution" was to be found in *Tikkun* in its "halachic-practical" sense (Schwartz, 2001b: 129–30). Schwartz believes that metaphysical *Tikkun*, which derives from Rabbi Tzvi Yehuda's worldview, finds itself on the defensive. He writes:

> Directing accusations against the National Religious Party for its being dragged into the idea of the Greater Land of Israel and its ignoring social problems has already become quite fashionable. Rabbi Tzvi Yehuda Kook's circle is directly responsible for the rise of the theological dimension of Gush Emunim and this idea unfortunately gained control over the religious community in the 1970s and 1980s. This direction is seen as somewhat of a failure. (Schwartz, 2001b: 130)

Has the theological direction of Gush Emunim indeed failed? Our work has focused upon the Gush's theological contention that the Greater Land of Israel is the single portal through which salvation can come to the people of Israel. Parallel to this theological-metaphysical Tikkun, a dramatic demographic and geographical revolution has taken place which brought hundreds of thousands of settlers to Judea and Samaria/the West Bank. In many cases, this "on the ground" revolution was directly associated with the program of metaphysical Tikkun, in other cases it was driven by more mundane motives. Settlers—both those with metaphysical objectives and to a lesser degree those drawn to Judea and Samaria/the West Bank by practical "quality of life" considerations—experienced moments of euphoric success (the extraordinary flourishing of the settlement project) as well as traumatic crises such as the disengagement, Amona, and so on. Considering the more than 350,000 to 400,000 settlers in the West Bank (not including East Jerusalem) and their high fertility rate (more than 5 percent) it is difficult to conclude that the settlement project in the Greater Land of Israel has failed.

What has perhaps failed—or more accurately is in the process of failing—is the Yesha leadership itself. Beginning with the disengagement, through the weakening of the Yesha Council and the fragmentation of religious Zionist rabbinate and ending with the crisis of leadership to which we are witness in the second decade of the twenty-first century, classic Mamlachtiut appears to be on the defensive. And yet, one cannot doubt that the settlement project, whatever its difficulties, continues to have very many "soldiers." Even if the actual fulfillment of the Greater Israel vision seems farther than ever, given the internal and international pressures on the state and the doubts of many within the settlement movement itself as to its feasibility, the settlement project cannot be judged as anything but a practical "success."

The teachings of Rabbi Tzvi Yehuda Kook represent the intellectual fount from which both the Mamlachti and the disobedience-supporting schools spring. This common source attests to the great power of Rabbi Tzvi Yehuda's ideas more than thirty years after his death. Indeed, they still define much of the character of the religious Zionist settlement project in theory and in practice (Hoch, 1994: 244–61). Both those who support disobedience and resistance as well as those who adopt a more Mamlachti stance regularly cite his words as "proof texts" for their policies.

The two schools have much to base themselves on. On the one hand, Rabbi Kook was at great pains to glorify the state as the vehicle of redemption and the herald of the messianic era. He heaped superlative upon superlative in describing the pivotal role of the State of Israel in the Divine eschatological drama. On the other hand, he could not have been more critical toward state policies that sought to evacuate Jewish settlements. His talk of "war" still resounds in some settler circles. It is no wonder then that a complex, discordant mixture of declarations and acts are associated with his name.

Although the two streams that flowed from his teachings found their different voices only after his death in 1982, the theological-practical dissonance in his thought itself is difficult to miss. Even the "theological-normative balance"—which sometimes agitated him profoundly—is common to both schools, with each striking the "balance" in a different way. With the exception of extreme elements that appear to be proliferating rapidly at the perimeters of the settler community, even those with a lukewarm attitude toward Mamlachtiut have avoided, at least until now, denying the deep tie between the State of Israel and religious deliverance. To be sure, some of them give vent to their frustrations with intense, at times violent protests against government policy, but still they refrain from throwing out the baby with the bathwater.

At least since the disengagement, fissures between the two schools have become considerably deeper and have led to harsher adversarial relations in regard to what the proper "balance" between theological imperatives and practical politics ought to be. Without the unifying voice and moral stature of Rabbi Kook, what had been a consolidated Gush Emunim ideological credo began to unravel. Until his death, he preserved the tie between religious Zionism and the secular political leadership but in his absence this relationship became more tenuous. Under the aura of his authority, even the most radical did not dare question the lofty religious status of the state and the importance of honoring its institutions.

This is no longer the case. Not only do the leadership circles of the settler community suffer from fragmentation and ideological discord, post-Mamlachti factions have expanded and violent gangs subject to no authority spread mayhem both inside and outside the Green Line. It becomes increasingly difficult to dismiss them as rootless, bizarre hoodlums without any sources in the settlement project. They have not fallen out of the blue. Understanding them and their modus operandi requires paying close attention to the context of settler messianic zeal and the rightward trajectory of Israeli politics. They cannot be dissociated from the long list of democracy-undermining statements, ideologies, legislation, etc. that have swept over Israeli public life in the past decade (Fuchs, Blander and Kremnitzer, 2015).

It is no secret that friction between certain elements in the settler population and the security forces has become more common and more intense. Evacuation of unauthorized outposts, even the demolition of a half-built structure can erupt into a pitched battle. Memories of the disengagement and of Amona are not easily expunged. The settler's nightmare scenario of a major pullback from Yesha, although highly unlikely in the near future, continues to gnaw at the back of their minds. Despite their political successes since Amona, a residual siege mentality persists. Whether they are justified or not, feelings of being persecuted by the media, the courts, and the secular elites give credence to the not uncommon sense that their backs are up against the wall.

In a study of the religious-secular impasse at the start of the twenty-first century, Asher Cohen and Bernard Susser (Cohen and Susser, 2000:

chapter 6) argued that the "the politics of accommodation" which had been the basis of the stabilizing "status quo" agreement between the religious and the secular communities was in the process of attenuation. A strident "all or nothing" political style was taking its place. The Israeli political system was steadily moving from accommodation to escalation. Their research dealt mainly with the classic religion-state issues such as Sabbath observance, marriage and divorce, "who is a Jew?" the dietary laws, etc., rather than with issues related to the Land of Israel. Nevertheless, parallels can be drawn.

Cohen and Susser's study ends with a question about those Israeli Jews who consider themselves "traditional" to one degree or another. (Depending on the criteria for "traditionalism," their numbers range from a quarter of Israel's population upwards). They observe some halachic commandments some of the time. While they feel a certain proximity to the religious tradition in general, they are hardly meticulous about details. Although this large population of "traditionalists" does not see itself in "either-or" terms—as either fully secular or entirely religious—with the escalation of religious-political conflict, the dichotomous view is nevertheless gaining traction. More often than not, it frames inter-personal anticipations and stereotypes. The stark equation: religious equals Right vs. secular equals Left, although certainly vastly oversimplified, has struck deep roots in the public mind. This applies not only to the religious issues that Cohen and Susser study; it has become increasing true in the battle over the fate of the West Bank/Judea and Samaria.

Our research bolsters Cohen and Susser's conclusion. Scrutinizing what has taken place since the 2005 disengagement, one can hardly doubt that radicalization and disaffection on both sides has grown significantly. Parts of the religious Zionist community have undergone a process of growing alienation from the State of Israel and its institutions. Post-Mamlachti positions are far from the rarity they once were. Neither are the justifications for disobedience. It is entirely conceivable that certain government directives such as a significant retreat from Yesha could trigger large-scale disobedience and aggressive resistance. Speculation about numbers and percentages is, of course, fruitless; but saying that these numbers would be "unprecedented" does not go beyond the borders of responsible political forecasting. Yet, although radicalization has clearly taken place, we continue to believe that for the "silent majority" of the religious Zionist settler camp the Mamlachti faith in the state's holiness generally prevails, or in the terms we have been using, the "theological-normative balance" continues to hold.

From the Gush Katif disengagement and the shabby treatment of its evacuees, through the traumatic events at Amona, the evacuation of the Brown House in Hebron, the expulsion of the Har Bracha yeshiva from Hesder union, Olmert's "convergence" plan, the women singing issue, the much publicized arrest of Rabbi Dov Lior, the demolition of outposts and illegally built homes etc., the religious Zionist community has undergone a distinct change of mood and direction. As counter-intuitive as it may sound with the Right so firmly ensconced in power and likely to remain so for the foreseeable future, some on the religious Zionist Right remain under the shadow of the string of painful events mentioned above. Although usually falling under the radar of the secular community, certain circles in the religious Zionist camp continue to believe that they are victims who have been set upon by the entrenched liberal media, academia, and the judicial elites. But a new consciousness is growing parallel to old one—even overwhelming it. Increasingly, the sense of constituting the "new elite" that is displacing the veteran secular Ashkenazi establishment is striking roots in the religious Zionist consciousness. Without "psychologizing" these dissonant perceptions, it can be said nevertheless that neither is unchallenged or entirely consensual.

It is cuttingly ironic that in the second decade of the twenty-first century much of the Center-Left and Left feel a sense of alienation and despair that is equal and opposite to that of religious Zionism during the Oslo Process and the Disengagement. Probably since the Rabin assassination but certainly since Netanyahu became Prime Minister in 2009, the liberal media and its mostly secular constituency have expressed exasperation at the growing influence of the Right and the religious in the public sphere. In the eyes of secular liberal-left circles, the Right, often spearheaded by religious Zionists, has exacerbated an already problematic "occupation," blocked every avenue to peace with the Palestinians, transfigured Israel into a pariah state in the international community, and amplified the Jewish character of the state at the expense of its democratic identity. Some have spoken of the country's political and religious trajectory as nothing less than a tragic drama leading to catastrophe. The "two-state" solution, the centerpiece of Center and Left's political program, has been pronounced "dead" by many respected analysts. The dramatic expansion of settlement activity—especially locating settlements so as to prevent the establishment of a contiguous Palestinian State—promotes a sense of helplessness and hopelessness on the Center-Left continuum of Israel's political spectrum. Far from being victims, secular liberals see the religious Right as riding a triumphalist wave, as the "lords of the land." Indeed, in the 2015 elections it became painfully clear that the Jewish Center-Left and Left represent little more than one-third of the Israeli electorate—40+ of 120 Knesset seats. The old version of the Zionist dream, they lament, is slipping through their fingers.

Although it is quite clear that a major evacuation from Judea and Samaria/the West Bank seems at present a far-fetched scenario, we cannot avoid asking these questions, hypothetical though they may be: What if political trends take a sharp turn, undergo a seismic shift, and withdrawal from Yesha becomes a real option? What if, in the context of a peace agreement—whether imposed from without, or following a dramatic leftward shift in public opinion—the government decides to withdraw from large swaths of the West Bank? Would the "balance" continue to hold? Taking into account that an evacuation of this kind would be many times the magnitude of Gush Katif, would the religious Zionist community continue to respect the state and its democratic decisions?

It requires no prophetic powers to predict that for parts of the settler youth a major evacuation would constitute a casus belli. Those who grew up in Yesha settlements and know no other home or way of life (many of them second- or even third-generation settlers) would see expulsion as an unendurable personal tragedy and an intolerable violation of their religious faith. For them settling the Land of Israel is the be-all and end-all of the religious Zionist enterprise and dismantling large parts of the settlement project would provoke unprecedented reactions. Unless some utterly unforeseeable transformation in the religious Zionist settler community takes place, disobedience and violence can surely be expected.

Survey research confirms these impressions. In 2010, the respected pollster Minah Tzemach reported that the percentage of religious Zionist youth between the ages of 15 and 18 who justified disobedience if settlements were evacuated stood at 38 percent, which was double the number among Haredim and traditional Jews, which was 19 percent. For secular youth, the percentage was 15 percent. As the cohort ages—between 21 and 24 years of age—the numbers change rather substantially: disobedience is supported by 33 percent of the religious Zionists, 29 percent among Haredim, and 20 percent of the traditionalists. For the secular, the number drops to 9 percent. When asked about refusing to serve in the West Bank only 1 to 5 percent showed any sympathy (Zemach, 2010: 57). Apart from the astonishingly high numbers of those who support insubordination if settlement evacuation were ordered, what stands out in Tzemach's survey is the number of Haredim above the age of twenty-one who report they would resist. A growing convergence between Haredim and the national religious seems apparent.

Four years later the Israel Democracy Institute conducted a similar survey. When religious Zionist young people were asked whether a soldier who opposes a government decision to evacuate settlements "should disobey orders?" 23 percent agreed fully and 17 percent tended to agree. The more their self-identification tended to the Haredi Leumi or Haredi, the percentages of those who justified disobeying orders rose. Also correlated with support for insubordination was the degree of importance the respondent attached to the authority of the rabbis (Herman et al., 2014: 145–46). Particularly striking is the very high percentage of those who supported disobedience among pre-army religious seminar graduates: 35 percent were entirely in favor and 29 percent tended to be in favor. These statistics are of special importance because these young people are slated for combat duty and for officer courses. Students in the Hesder yeshivot are less radical in their beliefs: 22 percent answered that they would definitely disobey while 17 percent said that they would likely disobey. They too are slated for combat units and officer positions (Herman et al., 2014: 148). The long-lived taboo against insubordination has clearly been broken.

Nevertheless, it would be hasty to dismiss the stubbornly enduring power of religious education that stresses honoring the state and its holy character. Even faced with the "unthinkable," disengaging from the state might well be "unthinkable" as well. It would be tantamount to renouncing more than a century of religious Zionist history. Although certainties are few, what seems to be the most likely eventuality is a profound rupture within the movement. The more zealous on the religious Right might well abandon their erstwhile Zionist loyalties and reject Mamlachtiut as an anachronism. Long-established practices such as rallying to the Zionist flag, actively contributing to the state's welfare, cooperation with secular Zionism out of a sense of a common fate, military mobilization to protect the state, etc., would probably suffer grievous blows.

Doubtless, even the more mainstream Mamlachti factions of religious Zionism would undergo a shocking trauma. Opposition to violence and disobedience would likely weaken considerably. The ideological and emotional readiness to serve in front-line combat units would be sorely tested and considering the growing presence of religious Zionist soldiers among the ranks of the low- and middle-level officer corps, this threat looms especially large. Were a major evacuation to take place, the sense of being besieged victims, so powerful after the disengagement and the Amona debacle, would almost certainly reappear and with a vengeance. What can be said with confidence is that the response to a major evacuation would far surpass, in violence and resistance, the relatively mild settler reaction to the disengagement from Gush Katif.

From the day the religious Zionist movement was founded it was dogged by the question of its relationship with secular Zionism. For most of the twentieth century until the rise of Gush Emunim in the 1970s religious,

Zionism resigned itself to the seniority of the secular Zionist leadership led by the Labor movement. But the growing ideological activism of the religious Zionist community that erupted after the euphoria of the Six Day War and the growth of a generation of enthusiastic yeshiva students has altered the equation. Paired with the decline of the Labor movement, these factors prepared the ground for the fraying of the "historical covenant" between the Labor movement and the religious Zionists. Displacing this "historical covenant" is religious Zionism's alliance with the Right and a less dramatic but nevertheless important proclivity to draw closer to parts of Haredi world whose right-wing views are increasingly converging with their own.

And their sense of triumphalism is difficult to miss. From the rise of Gush Emunim onwards the leaders of religious Zionism have insisted on becoming not only, as the phrase goes, "kashrut supervisors in the train's dining car" but the conductors of the train's engine. To be sure, the Likud has been the driving force since the reversal of 1977. Nevertheless, on the ground, it is the religious Zionist youth with their messianic vision that has energized the settlement project and set much of the agenda of Israeli public life.

Already in its earliest stages, there were confrontations with state authorities but the rules of the democratic game were, for the most part, observed. Although some figures in the religious Zionist camp adopted behavioral norms that did not accord with the rule of law, during these early years, and despite their tendency to "elasticize" the law and even to bend it outright, the settler leadership saw their project as expressing the Zionist consensus despite the electoral majorities that rejected their agenda. Moreover, they understood their actions—even when contravened the law—as consistent with legitimate Western ideas of civil disobedience. Whether their efforts fortified the state and its values is, of course, a matter of opinion—at times of polar opinions. What cannot be in doubt is that despite the self-understanding that they were acting within the bounds of political legitimacy, from the start a certain degree of "illegalism" was structured into their project.

The dilemma we have been exploring in this study concerns the tension between two poles of religious Zionism. Although both share some important intellectual traits (derived from Rabbi Tzvi Yehuda), they differ basically in their politicoreligious priorities. One pole centers upon the obligation to the sacrosanct State of Israel, its laws and its law enforcement agencies. The other pole focuses on the imperative that religious Zionists settle all parts of the Land of Israel, especially those beyond the Green Line. The latter also hold an uncompromising dedication to Halacha as interpreted by different religious Zionist rabbis. These two poles of commitment make for a tension that is constitutive of contemporary religious Zionism. It is too early as yet to make definitive statements, however, it does appear that those who question Mamlachtiut are becoming bolder and more visible. The great majority who, in the past, conceived of Israel as "the throne of God in world" seems to be in the throes of a critical identity crisis. To some extent at least they express reservations about the rule of law and the state's being the vehicle of religious deliverance. They are no longer the unchallenged consensus. Acrobatic distinctions between a heretical government and the holy state can go only so far; at some point, blurring of the lines seems inevitable.

In other words, the "theological-normative balance," which we have discussed over the course of this study, is no longer beyond challenge. Our central claim that there are self-balancing forces that encourage most of the religious Zionist camp, most of the time, to obey the law and to accept established social-political norms, even when they contravene their cherished religious principles, is developing a still small but increasingly strident opposition. The "theological-normative balance," which has acted to curtail anti-system disobedience in times of serious ideological crisis is showing signs of wobbling. Its future seems uncertain. The balance's efficacy, which derived from the countervailing powers that created an equilibrium between the rule of law and the Greater Land of Israel, was badly shaken by the disengagement from Gush Katif and Amona. Very notably, this weakening of the "balance" is currently "camouflaged" by the sharp rightward swing of Israeli politics that renders balance-threatening policies (in the foreseeable future at least) quite unlikely.

Nevertheless, as we have often insisted, the "balance" remains the prevailing orthodoxy to which most religious Zionists adhere—despite the spirited challenges to its contemporary relevance. Therefore, religious faith which can easily become an adversarial, anti-system force leading to frontal confrontations with the state and its laws has acted in the Israeli case as a braking system that prevented crises from spilling over into mass religious defiance. In regard to the Greater Land of Israel problem—a non-negotiable issue for many in the religious Zionist camp—the "theological-normative balance" has acted as a moderating factor in the Torah-state confrontation because of the religious qualities of the state itself. Rhetoric, radical though it may be, has not in the main led to radical action. There is often a "disconnect" between principles loudly enunciated and the restraint that prevails in practice.

As we noted in the introduction, the three authors approached this study with a feeling of great apprehension in regard to the changes that were transforming the State of Israel in general and religious Zionism in particular. Although our ideological commitments often differed sharply from one another, we were united in our concerns for the welfare of Israel as a Jewish and democratic state. Hence, our object has gone beyond presenting a factual report on events and opinions. We have aspired to focus on the complexity, the paradoxes, and the internal balances that characterize religious Zionism—specifically in regard to the collision between the Land of Israel issue and the authority of state law. No less, we have attempted to call attention to the increasingly fragile modus vivendi that has characterized the relationship between religious Zionists and the state over the course of the past decades.

In a recent study, dozens of individuals from the religious Zionist camp—ranging from *Hardeli* to (what is termed) "bourgeois" religious Zionists—were interviewed. The findings (which accord with those of Mina Tzemach and the Israel Democracy Instituted cited above) strongly suggest that there has been a growth in the support for violent struggle, just so long as it does not involve "hard" violence, that is, the use of firearms. Disobeying orders when commanded to evacuate settlements was supported by a large cohort. What is most significant is that these tendencies characterize even those groups that support a Mamlachti position and even those spoken of as the more moderate religious "bourgeoisie." One of the study's paradoxical conclusions is that there is a rise in the correlation between the growing support for conscientious objection and the degree to which the respondent relied on democratic justifications for disobedience (Mozes, Helinger and Rynhold, 2014).

One of our conclusions is the importance of continual dialogue between the settler community and the state's elites and leadership. Such dialogue is especially vital in order to moderate sharp clashes that are liable to erupt in the event of dismantling outposts and especially in the case of further evacuations from Judea and Samaria. Lacking such dialogue, parts of the religious Zionist community are likely to feel themselves outside of Israeli power decision making process—with dangerous consequences. Cynics will shrug their shoulders and discount the effectiveness of dialogue. It is indeed an open question whether such dialogue can moderate what is, on the one hand, an absolute commitment to the Land of Israel and, on the other, the claim to the full authority of a democratically elected government to make decisions. In any event, as noted repeatedly, with the Right firmly "in the saddle" this is not, at present, an urgent question.

What kind of majority would be necessary were the issue of evacuation brought to a vote either in the Knesset or in a national referendum? The religious Zionist position here sharply conflicts with that of secular liberals. For the settlers and their religious Zionist supporters a solid Jewish majority would be critical. (Ironically, included among the Jews would be immigrants from the former Soviet Union who are not considered Jewish by religious Zionists, perhaps even the Druze.) The argument is that such a Jewish majority—and only such a majority—could legitimize the uprooting of tens of thousands of Jewish settlers from Yesha. By contrast, a majority that relied on Arab votes would create an explosive situation that would make retreat a nightmare. So much is certainly true. However, from the liberal democratic point of view, the demand for a substantial Jewish majority would undermine the very basis of Israel as a democratic state. Political considerations cannot override the basic democratic principle that grants equal rights to all citizens. Requiring a Jewish majority is in such stark opposition to the most basic liberal Western principles that it would create nightmares of its own.

The three authors feel differently about the ability, at this stage, for a true discourse of mutual respect to develop between the competing ideological elites. One point of view is that the militancy of both sides and the incompatibility of their agendas render this unrealistic. It is entirely possible that dialogue could make a difference of degree and tone, but the issues involved are too deep-seated for even frank, respectful conversation to overcome. For both sides, the very character of the Zionist project is at stake. From this more pessimistic point of view, a more wrenching denouement is the likelier outcome. The two others believe that the Zionist vision can be preserved, despite these rifts, and that dialogue is the most effective means to go about it. But even the more optimistic among us are convinced that a basic self-critique of religious Zionism is imperative; how is disobedience, especially violent disobedience to be discouraged? At a minimum, such a partial rapprochement would necessitate determined actions to uproot the criminal "Price Tag" groups and the extreme "Hilltop Youth"—to denounce them without stammering or hesitation.

Reestablishing the "theological-normative balance" is therefore critical. On it rests the stability and wellbeing of Israel as a Jewish and democratic state. Is it possible to retain the kind of common commitment to the welfare and flourishing of the state and its citizens that can overcome the centrifugal forces that threaten to undermine its viability? Can the center hold?

Appendix 1

It is known that since the signing of the Oslo agreement the number of those killed in attacks has grown threefold from what it was during the years of the Intifada. And the more this evil government concedes to the Arabs so the attacks in all parts of Israel grow, especially toward the residents of Yesha, and there is scarcely a village that doesn't have individuals who have been murdered or severely wounded.

And now, with the implementation of the Oslo Agreement and granting ruling powers to the Palestinian Authority over territories and roads, the danger has grown greatly. Terrorists can prepare for attacks in the autonomous areas with impunity. The Israeli government equipped them with rifles and they fire upon the cars of soldiers and civilians, and there is no end to it. Their daring increases . . . Today about 90 percent of the cases of firing in the Gaza area, is done by weapons supplied to the Palestinian police by the government of Israel . . .

And if, until the agreement in Gaza and Jericho, the ministers of the government could claim in good faith that the Palestinian police would battle against terror and that Gaza and Jericho would serve as a test case for the entire agreement, now, after the bitter reality proves otherwise, still this evil government strives to continue applying the agreement throughout Judea and Samaria. Not only this, but they free terrorists from jail and these terrorists are involved with terror attacks and murder . . .

Men and women, settlers in Yesha and other parts of the land have turned to us, with their lives at stake, and asked: what is the law in regard to this evil government and to he who stands at its head:

A. Can they be reckoned as accomplices to acts of murder committed by the terrorists because they, in their policies, are responsible for the strengthening of their [the terrorist's] power and for equipping them with arms, and giving permission to Palestinian policemen to enter

Gaza and Jericho? And if they say that we did not know that it would be so, and, in fact, they promised at the time of the signing of the agreement that from now on peace would reign and the attacks would end and the PLO would take care of Hamas without the [intervention of the] Supreme Court etc., they were warned again and again by all the representatives of the settlers and heads of the opposition not to place their trust in murderers and their words. Therefore the question arises: can the members of the government be considered accomplices to the acts of murder that were committed and if, according to Halacha, they ought to be put to trial, what are the appropriate punishments if they are found to be accomplices to murder.

B. And of course we know that there are many sides to the problem; on the one side the government is authorized to act for the good of the people as it sees fit. But, on the other side, perhaps halachic law changes in regard to a government that does not have a Jewish majority and rests upon the Arab votes (and according to what has been publicized, they colluded with anti-Semites against the Jewish majority).

C. All this regards the murders that have already been committed, but the more difficult question is, according to Halacha, what would be the ruling on the government in the event that it continues to implement the said agreement in Judea and Samaria? In regard to an individual who commits an action that endangers the security of another individual there are authorized rulings . . . But what needs to be clarified is what is the law regarding elected officials who commit such acts in the framework of performing their duties? And also what is the ruling in regard to 'delivering' (Mesira) done unintentionally, out of blindness and ignoring the facts as well as the opinion of the Jewish majority?

And even if the definition of this act is 'delivering' (Mesirah), clearly it is unacceptable that everyone be authorized to kill and attack the heads of the public, because there is no greater damage to the general welfare of the public than such chaos in which every man does what seems right in his eyes; as our sages of blessed memory say: "Pray for the welfare of the government, for were it not for the fear thereof, men would swallow each other alive." So it seems that we cannot apply the rule of individuals to the government. Nevertheless, perhaps the sages of Israel and the heads of the public need to warn the Prime Minister and the government ministers that if they continue to deliver the residents of Judea and Samaria to a government of murderers, according to Halacha it will be necessary to put them on trial and punish them according to the law of a 'deliverer' (Moser). This is especially so since the government itself equipped them with arms and money to pay for their services.

D. Are the heads of the army who were also complicit in the designing of the said agreement to be considered accomplices to sin since the government relied upon them as experts in the matter of security and they did not warn the government about the murderous, dangerous consequences of the agreement—are they partners in responsibility? Or, perhaps, because it was not they who decided, responsibility does not rest with them?

E. If according to Halacha it is possible to punish them in a court of law, is it the responsibility of every man of Israel to act in order to bring them to justice, in a religious court, or, failing that, in a secular court?

F. Is it incumbent upon the leaders of the public, rabbis and activists to warn the Prime Minister and his ministers, in this difficult hour, that if, after the bitter experience with the agreement in Gaza and Jericho, they continue to implement it throughout Judea and Samaria it would be necessary, according to Torah law, to apply the Jewish Halacha [and to put them on trial] under the category of one who 'delivers' (Moser) Jewish souls and their property into the hands of Gentiles?

And let the rabbi [those to whom the query was sent] not say that this is an unworthy question, because it is no longer possible to silence the question that bursts out of pained hearts of Jews in Israel and the Diaspora and there are many who deal with this subject with great seriousness. And also orphans and bereaved parents that were harmed by the terrorists have turned to us with this question, and the voice of our brother's blood calls out to us from the ground. Therefore we turn to the venerable rabbi and ask that he give us a clear answer in this matter.

It is known to us that the very involvement in this question is liable to awake, forbid it, a severe dispute among the people, but in light of the reality on the ground, we fear and are anxious that the situation will worsen so badly, forbid it, until questions of this sort will become a public matter and in the hearts of the injured, feelings of vengeance will arise and each man will do what is right in his eyes.

And since the question is so large and difficult and touches upon the entire nation, we hereby turn to the chief sages of the generation, the eyes of the community, that they instruct the people the straight path on which they ought to go. And although, sadly, the government does not heed with proper respect to the voice of Torah, still there is no doubt that a halachic ruling from the great Torah scholars will have great influence in heaven as on earth. (E. Melamed, 1995, in Forum Erez Moledet, 2008).

Appendix 2

In the month of Tamuz 5755 [July 1995] after the minority government's [Rabin's government supported from the outside by Arab MKs] decision to vacate army bases in Yesha, the question arose among soldiers: were they required to implement the decree or should they disobey orders and refuse to take part in the evacuation? I communicated with the Rabbi, the Great Avraham Shapira may he live a good and lengthy life, head of the of the Mercaz HaRav yeshiva and [former] Chief Rabbi of Israel and according to his request I convened a meeting of a number of prominent rabbis, representatives of the Union of Rabbis for the Jewish People and the Land of Israel. At the end of the meeting a ruling was published.

Halachic Ruling in the Matter of Disobeying Orders

Following is the ruling given in the past by the Chief Rabbinical Council and other rabbis in regard to the prohibition of vacating parts of the Land of Israel and the Golan, we were asked if it is permissible to vacate a military camp or a military facility that is located in an area populated by Arabs in the territory of the Land of Israel.

We hereby determine that the Torah prohibits vacating army bases and transferring them to the control of Gentiles because it violates a 'performative' Mitzvah (*Mitzvaht a'seh*), places individuals in jeopardy and endangers the existence of the state.

A. It seems obvious that in regard to an area which the IDF controls, the Mitzvah of settling the Land of Israel applies, as Nachmanides wrote— this includes [the obligation] 'to conquer it and not to leave it in the hands of any nation but our own.' And in an area from which the IDF retreats 'the burden of the nations' applies—which means violating the aforementioned [performative] Mitzvah. In addition, today it entails

277

endangering lives of Israelis as well as a threat to the existence of the state, and this involves 'neither shall you stand idly by when the blood of your neighbor is in danger' (Leviticus 19:16).

B. Even an army base is a Jewish settlement in all regards. Its uprooting and abandonment to Gentiles involves the uprooting of a settlement in the Land of Israel which is prohibited according to [Jewish] law.

C. Therefore in answer to the query, it is clear and simple that it is prohibited for any Jew to take part in any action that aids in evacuating a settlement, camp or facility, as Maimonides rules (The Laws of Kings 3:9). For even if a king orders that we transgress the Torah we are not to obey him.

D. The IDF has never put soldiers in a position where they needed to act against their religious, moral or national conscience. We call upon the government and the army leadership not to place soldiers in a position where they will need to waver between their loyalty to the values around which they have built their lives and army commands.

E. We appeal to the government and he who stands at its head not to lend their hands to splitting the nation and the IDF, and to strengthen the unity of Israel in this difficult hour.

a. In an appendix to the ruling the rabbis wrote:

> The IDF is precious and holy in our eyes, and it is what its name says—its function is to defend the Land of Israel and to protect the nation's life and not to act in ways that are the opposite of its mission and that endanger Jews. Beyond the ruling that forbids vacating territories in the Land of Israel, half the nation is against this agreement; views are divided including the views of the army's officers. It is not moral to impose upon soldiers actions that violate not only their religious but also their national and moral conscience. Demanding this of them is a moral crime and it is not legal. We hope that the army's officers will allow every soldier to act according to his religious conscience. "May God give strength to his people; may God bless his people with peace." (E. Melamed, 1994)

Appendix 3

In answer to your question on the Torah point of view in regard to participating, in the context of army reserve duty, in evacuating lands and buildings in Yesha and the Golan we hereby make our view known: Since it was already ruled by most of the rabbis in Israel that there is a prohibition against evacuating territories in the Land of Israel and transferring them to Gentiles, according to Nachmanides's writings (also recently so ruled in a conference attended by more than a thousand rabbis and Yeshiva heads) and also so ruled by the previous Chief Rabbinate and the Council that preceded it, [we declare] that as in the case of all Torah prohibitions, it is forbidden for Jews to take part in any action that aids in such an evacuation, as Maimonides ruled (Laws of Kings, chapter 3) that even if the king commanded transgressing a law of the Torah, he is not to be obeyed (cited by Shochetman, 1995: 75).

Appendix 4

A. The Oslo B Agreement that the government is preparing, is opposed to the Torah for three reasons:

1. Transferring parts of the Holy Land to non-Jews is forbidden by a Torah prohibition that is severe and absolute.

2. The IDF's retreat from the cities of Yesha and transferring responsibility for their security to foreign forces involves putting them [Jews] in mortal danger (*Hatarat damam*) and the abandoning of Jewish souls.

3. A messenger cannot do otherwise than the will of he who sends him, and the majority of the Jewish people in the Land of Israel and all the more so in the Diaspora have not given this minority government the authority to decide in these essential and fundamental and that decide its fate.

B. Therefore, according to [Torah] law, it is forbidden to sign this agreement. The Chief Rabbinate of Israel has long ago so ruled as has the Council of Torah Sages.

C. This conference warns that the hasty and frightened actions of the government of Israel in regard to the agreement may trigger, forbid it, a split in the nation both in Israel and in the Diaspora.

D. We hereby make this important announcement: that if, forefend it, the government signs the Oslo Agreement, this signature has no value. And every government that represents the Jewish people should not pay attention to this agreement.

E. This conference protests against the government: its ignoring the bloodshed since the agreement, its ignoring the manifestations of hatred toward Jews, its ignoring the many declarations by the head of the PLO, as heard on cassette recordings, that demonstrate for all to know that he [Arafat] is not interested in real peace. There is no saving of lives here only the endangering of lives. This is not the longed for peace that everyone wants . . .

F. This conference affirms the decision of the rabbis, sages of Israel, that it is forbidden for all Jews, including soldiers, to participate in actions to evacuate Jews or military bases from their place, and that this is not permissible—not because of orders, not because of ties of friendship as they may be. The IDF is supposed to defend the borders of the country and the lives of Jews and not to evict them, and it is what its name says: the Israel Defense Forces (The Association of Yesh'a Rabbis, 1996: 1).

References

Alimi, Eitan. 2013. *Between Engagement and Disengagement Politics—The Settlers' Struggle against the Disengagement Plan and its Consequences.* Tel-Aviv: Resling. (Hebrew)

Almond, Gabriel A., Scott R. Appleby, and Sivan Emmanuel. 2003. *Strong Religion: The Rise of Fundamentalism around the World.* Chicago: University of Chicago Press.

Alon, Gideon, and Mazal Mualem. 2004. "Netanyahu, Livnat, Naveh and Katz Retreated at the Last Moment—The Disengagement Plan has been Approved by a Majority of 67 MKs, *Haaretz* (October 17, 2004) (Hebrew)

Altman, Yair, and Atilla Shumpalbi. 2011. "Netanyahu: We Should Act Against IDF Attackers; Livni: It's your Fault," *Yediot Aharonot* (December 13, 2011). (Hebrew)

Amitai, Oren. 2006. "LeGeulat Yerushalayim HaKedoshah," (Toward the Redemption of the Holy Jerusalem) *Ma'ayanei HaYeshu'ah* (Kislev 5766; December, 2005). (Hebrew)

Amitai, Yotam, and Hadas Minka-Brand. 2010. "Now and in the Other Times: Motivating Subordinates to Perform Tasks Involved in Public Controversy," *Maarachot* 429: 12–21. (Hebrew)

Antman, Yaakov. 2007. "HaMamlakhtiyut haGoelet," (Redeeming Statehood), *Komemiyut* (19 Adar 5767). (Hebrew)

Amrousi, Emily. 2011. "A Gang of Leaderless Outlaws," *Yisrael HaYom* (December 7, 2011). (Hebrew)

Aran, Gideon. 1985. *The Land of Israel between Religion and Politics: The Movement to Stop the Withdrawal from Sinai and its Lessons.* Jerusalem: The Jerusalem Institute for Israel Studies. (Hebrew)

Aran, Gideon. 1987. *From Religious Zionism to Zionist Religion: The Sources of Gush Emunin and its Culture.* PhD dissertation, Jerusalem: The Hebrew University (Hebrew)

Aran, Gideon. 1991. "Jewish Zionist Fundamentalism: The Block of the Faithful (Gush Emunim) in Israel." In *Fundamentalism and the State: The Fundamentalism Project,* vol. 2, eds. Martin E. Marty and Scott R. Appleby. Chicago and London: University of Chicago Press, pp. 265–344.

Aran, Gideon. 2003. "From Pioneering to Torah Study: Background to the Growth of Religious Zionism," in: Avi Sagi and Dov Schwartz (eds.), *A Hundred Years of Religious Zionism*, vol. 3. Ramat-Gan: Bar-Ilan University Press, 31–71 (Hebrew)

Aran, Gideon. 2013. *Kookism: The Roots of Gush Emunim, Jewish Settlers' Sub-Culture, Zionist Theology, Contemporary Messianism*. Jerusalem: Carmel. (Hebrew)

Ariel, Yaakov. 1983. "Disobeying an Order due to a Mitzvah or a Moral Consideration," *Techumin* 4: 173–79. (Hebrew)

Ariel, Yaakov. 1998. "Hafarat Pekudah miShum Mitzvah," (Disobeying an Order Because of a Divine Comandment), *Shut beOhala shel Torah* (In the Torah's Tent Responsa). Kfar Darom: Institute of Torah and Land, section 5. (Hebrew)

Ariel, Yaakov. 2004. "Seiruv li'Fkudat Pinuy," (Disobeying an Evacuation Order). *Yeshiva* website (30 Tishrei 5765). (Hebrew)

Ariel, Yisrael. 2006. "Ohavey Amona, Ohavav shel Makom," (Lovers of Amona, Lovers of God), *Kumi Ori* 4, 30–31. (Hebrew)

Arnon, Noam. 2005. "A Speech in the Congress of Leading Youth," *Founding Conference of Komemiyut* (December 22, 2005). (Hebrew)

Assenheim, Omri. 2006. "Lieutenant Amihai Merhaviah RIP from the Eli Settlement, who was killed Last Week in Bint-Jbel, was Suspended for a Year from Operational Command Due to a Letter of Protest He Sent to the Chief of Staff," *Maariv* (August 4 2006). (Hebrew)

The Association of Yesha Rabbis. 1992. Public Statement on the Government's Decisions regarding Settlement Evacuations. *The Association of Yesha Rabbis Bulletin 2*. (Hebrew)

The Association of Yesha Rabbis. 1995. "The Announcement of the Association of Yesha Rabbis (Majority Opinion)," *Nekuda* 27. (Hebrew)

The Association of Yesha Rabbis. 1996. "World Rabbis' Union for the Land of Israel and the Jewish Nation's Announcement," *Bitaon Va'ad Rabanei Yesha* 28. (Hebrew)

The Association of Yesha Rabbis. 2002. "A Declaration and a Call for Military Disobedience at a Meeting held at Havat Gilad" (8 Heshvon, 5763; October, 2002). (Hebrew)

The Association of Yesha Rabbis. 2004. "A Publication Containing 60 Signatures of Rabbis Calling on Soldiers to Disobey Orders." (Hebrew)

The Association of Yesha Rabbis. 2005. *Declaration for Disobedience*. (Hebrew)

The Association of Yesha Rabbis. 2006. *An Announcement* (2 Shevat, 5766; January, 2006). (Hebrew)

Athaly, Amihai. 2011. "If the Harassment of IDF Soldiers Continues—I will Leave Judea and Samaria," *NRG* (December 14, 2011). (Hebrew)

Aviner, Shlomo Hayim haCohen. 1982. "Ve'Lo Shikarnu biVritecha" (We did not Lie upon your Covenant), *Artzi* 1, 38–39. (Hebrew)

Aviner, Shlomo Hayim haCohen. 1983. *'Am kaLavi* (A Nation Resembling a Lion), vol. 2. Jerusalem. (Hebrew)

Aviner, Shlomo Hayim haCohen. 1986. *Rosh haMemshalah* (The Prime Minister). Beit-El: Hava Books. (Hebrew)

Aviner, Shlomo Hayim haCohen. 1990a. *MiKedem leVeit-El* (East of Beit-El), vol. 1, Beit-El: Sifriyat Beit-El. (Hebrew)

Aviner, Shlomo Hayim haCohen. 1990b. *Shut Intifadah* (Intifadah Responsa). Beit-El: Sifriyat Beit-El, 1990. (Hebrew)

Aviner, Shlomo Hayim haCohen. 2002. '*Am veArtzo* (A Nation and its Land), vol. 2. Beit-El: Hava Books. (Hebrew)

Aviner, Shlomo Hayim haCohen. 2005a. "HaTzava haZeh Hu Shelanu" (This Army is Ours) *Be'Ahavah uve'Emunah* (15 Tishrei, 5765; September, 2004). (Hebrew)

Aviner, Shlomo Hayim haCohen. 2005b. "Hafsiku le'Forrer et Tzaha'l" (Cease Fragmenting the IDF), *Be'Ahavah uve'Emunah* (10 Adar, 5765; February, 2005). (Hebrew)

Aviner, Shlomo Hayim haCohen. 2005c. "Tzahal lo Yachol?" (The IDF Can't?) *Be'Ahavah uve'Emunah* (1 Av, 5765; August, 2005). (Hebrew)

Aviner, Shlomo Hayim haCohen. 2008a. "Lo Elekh laTzavah!" (I will not Enlist to the Army), *Be'Ahavah uve'Emunah* (10 Adar, 5768; February, 2008). (Hebrew)

Aviner, Shlomo Hayim haCohen. 2008a. "Mashber haTzionut haDatit" (The Religious-Zionist Crisis) *Be'Ahavah uve'Emunah* (29 Adar, 5768; April, 2008). (Hebrew)

Aviner, Shlomo Hayim haCohen. 2009a. "Le'Taken et haGeirush min haGush" (To Correct the Expulsion from Gush Katif), *Be'Ahavah uve'Emunah* (5 Tishrei, 5769; October, 2008). (Hebrew)

Aviner, Shlomo Hayim haCohen. 2009b. "Heramtem Yad 'al Hayal?!" (Have you Raised your Hand against a Soldier?!), *Be'Ahavah uve'Emunah* (17 Hesvan, 5769; November, 2008). (Hebrew)

Aviner, Shlomo Hayim haCohen. 2009c. "Ahdut haMahane" (The Unity of the Camp), *Be'Ahavah uve'Emunah* (2 Kislev, 5769; November, 2008). (Hebrew)

Aviner, Shlomo Hayim haCohen. 2011. "Seruv Pekudah ve'Halah" (Disobeying an Order and Onwards), *Be'Ahavah uve'Emunah* (1 Adar, 5771; February, 2011). (Hebrew)

Avraham, Ruth. 2006. "Reserve Soldiers: We will get Even at the End of the Fighting," *Arutz 7* (August 2, 2006). (Hebrew)

Arutz 7 (Editorial). 2004. "Rabbis Eliyahu and Aviner: We Didn't Sign," *Arutz 7* (October 27, 2004). (Hebrew)

Badihi, Yosef. 2006. "HaPo'alim 'Im El," (Those Who Act with God) *Yeshiva* website. (Hebrew)

Badihi, Yosef. 2007. "Me'Oro," (From His Light) *Kumi Ori* 16, 39–51. (Hebrew)

Badihi, Yosef. 2008. "Mi la'Hashem Elai," (Who is on the Lord's Side? Let Him Come with Me). *Arutz 7* (January 31, 2008). (Hebrew)

Badihi, Yosef. *Geulat Or Hatzvi* (The Redemption of the Deer's Light). Jerusalem. Self-published.

Bakshi, Roni. 2007. "The Struggle that Never Erupted," *Be'Sheva* (August 12, 2007). (Hebrew)

Balázs, Gábor. 2013. "The Conflict of Conscience and Law in a Jewish State," *Shofar* 31, 2: 118–36.

Bar-Ilan, Shaul. 2005. *Kaftor ha'Pele* (The Magical Button). Jerusalem: Manhigut Yehudit. (Hebrew)

Bareli, Avi, and Nir Kedar. 2011. *Israeli Republicanism*. Jerusalem: Israel Democracy Institute. (Hebrew)

Bart, Shaul, and Yitzak Bart (eds.). 2007. *In the Storm of Eviction*. Tel Aviv: Miskal. (Hebrew)

Bedau, Hugo Adam, 1991. "Civil Disobedience and Personal Responsibility for Injustice," in *Civil Disobedience in Focus*. London: Routledge, 49–67.

Beit Hillel. 2013. "Platform," *Beit Hillel* website.

Belfer, Ella. 2004. *A Split Identity: The Conflict between the Sacred and the Secular in the Jewish World*. Ramat Gan: Bar-Ilan University Press. (Hebrew)

Ben-Eliyhau, Hen. 2006. "Or? Eyzeh Or?" (A Light? What Light?) *Jewish Leadership* website (9 Tamuz 5766). (Hebrew)

Ben-Hayim, Avishai. 2005. "Beginning of Sabbath: When the Rabbi Says No, What does he Mean?" *NRG* (July 7, 2005). (Hebrew)

Ben-Horin, Michael (ed.). 1995. *Barukh haGever: Sefer Zikaron laKadosh Dr. Barukh Goldshtein HYD* (Blessed is the Man: A Memory Book to the Holy Dr. Barukh Goldstein, May God Avenge his Blood). Jerusalem, Golan Heights: Shalom 'al Yisrael. (Hebrew)

Ben-Shlomo, Yosef (1990). *Poetry of Being: Lectures on the Philosophy of Rabbi Kook*, trans. Shmuel Himelstein. Tel-Aviv: Mod Books.

Be'Sheva (editorial). 2009. "Why Shouldn't Rabbis Be Granted Academic Freedom?" (December 7, 2009). (Hebrew)

Bick, Etta, 2007. "A Clash of Authority: Lay Leaders and Rabbis in the National Religious Party," *Israel Affairs* 13 (2), 401–17.

Bin-Nun, Chemi (2015). *Civil Disobedience: The Israeli Experience*. New York: Paragon House.

Bin-Nun, Yoel. 2001. "An Interview with Rabbi Yoel Bin-Nun," in: Rubik Rosenthal (ed.), *A Rift: Israeli Society between Rupture and Fusion*. Tel Aviv: Yedi'ot Aharonot, Sifre' Hemed, Histadrut haMorim be'Yisrael, 65–86. (Hebrew)

Bin-Nun, Yoel. 2005. "Mi'Bhina Hilkhatit Asur Lesarev," (Halakhically it's Forbidden to Disobey), *HaTzofe* (August 12, 2005). (Hebrew)

Binyamin Rabbis Council. 2009a. "On Methods of Managing Disagreements and Disputes Within our Sector," *Binyamin Region Council* website (1 Elul 5769; August, 2009). (Hebrew)

Binyamin Rabbis Council. 2009b. "A Call to Prime Minister Netanyahu and His Cabinet Members," *Binyamin Region Council* website. (Hebrew)

Binyamin Rabbis Council. 2011. "Price Tag Attacks are Forbidden," *Arutz 7* (October 3, 2011). (Hebrew)

Bleicher, Moshe. 2011. "U'Deror Ken Lah," (The Sparrow Has Found a Nest) in: Netanel Elyashiv (ed.), *U'Kra'atem Deror baAretz* (Proclaim Liberty throughout the Land). Eli: Machon Binyan Torah, 74–96. (Hebrew)

Breyner, Joshua, and Amir Tibon. 2013. "The Government: Price Tag: Illegal Association but not Terror," *Walla* (June 16, 2006). (Hebrew)

B'Tselem. 2006. "B'Tselem: Investigate Excessive Force in Amona Demolitions," *B'selem* website, http://www.btselem.org/hebrew (February 2, 2006).

Cavanaugh, William T., and Peter Scott. (2007). "Introduction," in Peter Scott and William T. Cavanaugh (eds.), *The Blackwell Companion To Political Theology*. Malden, MA: Blackwell, 2–4.

Coalition of Rabbis for the Israeli Nation and Land. 2008. "An Opinion for Disobedience," *Komemiyut* (25 Sivan 6768; June, 2008). (Hebrew)

Cohen, Asher, and Bernard Susser. 2000. *Israel and the Politics of Jewish Identity: The Secular-Religious Impasse*. Baltimore, MD: Johns Hopkins University Press.

Cohen, Asher, and Bernard Susser. 2000. "Women singing, cadets leaving: The extreme case syndrome in religion-army relationships," in *Civil Military relations in Israel: Essays in Honor of Stuart A. Cohen, Elisheva Rosman-Stollman and Aharon Kampinsky*), Lanham, MD: Lexington Books.

Cohen, Itamar. 2004. "Al Pekuda Lefanot Yishuvim" (On an Order to Evacuate Settlements). *Magen Shaul—Nokdim Mechinah* website. (Hebrew)

Cohen, Shimon. 2011. "The 'Exclusion of Women' Campaign: An Incitement against Religious People in Disguise," *Be'Sheva* (December 14, 2011).

Cohen, Stuart. 2007. "Tensions Between Military Service and Jewish Orthodoxy in Israel: Implications Imagined and Real." *Israel Studies* 12, 1: 103–26.

Cohen, Yaniv. 2007. "A Lamentation to Katif: Poems from a Different Perspective," Karnei Shomron: Y. Cohen. (Hebrew)

Commission of Inquiry, 1994. *Commission of Inquiry—Massacre at the Tomb of the Patriarchs in Hebron*. Chair: Justice Meir Shamgar. Jerusalem. (Hebrew)

Dalsheim, Joyce. 2011. *Unsettling Gaza—Secular Liberalism, Radical Religion, and the Israeli Settlement Project*. New York: Oxford University Press.

Dalshheim, Joyce, and Assaf Harel. 2009. "Representing Settlers," *Review of Middle East Studies* 43 (2): 219–38.

Din ve'heshbon. 1994. *The National Inquiry Committee for the Massacre in the Cave of the Patriarch in Hebron*. Jerusalem. (Hebrew)

Don Yehiya, Eliezer. 1980. "Stability and Change in a Political Camp Party: The Young Turks of the NRP," *Medinah Mimshal Ve'Yahasim Beinle'umiyim* 14: 25–52. (Hebrew)

Don Yehiya, Eliezer. 1987. "Jewish Messianism, Religious Zionism and Israeli Politics: The Impact and Origins of Gush Emunim." *Middle Eastern Studies* 23: 215–34.

Don Yehiya, Eliezer. 1992. "The Negation of Galut in Religious Zionism," *Modern Judaism* 12 (2): 129–55.

Don Yehiya, Eliezer. 1997. *The Politics of Accommodation: Settling Conflicts of State and Religion in Israel*. Jerusalem: The Floersheimer Institute for Policy Studies. (Hebrew)

Don Yehiya, Eliezer. 2003. "The Book and the Sword: Nationalist Yeshivot and Political Radicalism in Israel," in Avi Sagi and Dov Schwartz (eds.) *A Hundred Years of Religious Zionism*, vol. 3. Ramat Gan: Bar-Ilan University Press, 187–229. (Hebrew)

Don Yehiya, Eliezer. 2004. "Leadership and Policy in Religious Zionism: Chaim Moshe Shapira, the NRP and the Six Day War," in Asher Cohen and Yisrael Harel (eds.) *Religious Zionism: The Era of Change—Studies in Memory of Zvulun Hammer*. Jerusalem: Mosad Bialik and KKL, 135–70. (Hebrew)

Don Yehiya, Eliezer. 2008. *Crisis and Change in a New State: Education, Religion, and Politics in the Struggle over the Absorption of the Mass Immigration to Israel*. Jerusalem: Yad Ben-Zvi. (Hebrew)

Dor-Shav, Eitan. 2005. "A Sigh of Relief in the 'Ranch Forum,'" *Maariv* (July 18, 2005). (Hebrew)

Drori, Zefaniah. 2007. "Readies with Rabbi Zefaniah Drori," *NRG: Judaism* (January 9, 2007). (Hebrew)

Drucker, Raviv, and Ofer Shelah. 2005. *Boomerang: The Failure of Leadership in the Second Intifada*. Jerusalem: Keter Books. (Hebrew)

Druckman, Hayim. 2005. "Geula Rishona u'Geula Aharonah" (First Redemption and Last Redemption). *Yeshivat Or Etzion* website. (Hebrew)

Druckman, Hayim. 2000. "An Interview with Rabbi Druckman," *Olam Katan* (23 Tevet, 5770; January, 2010), 4–5. (Hebrew)

Dudkevitsch, Dudi. 2011. "Rabbi Dudkevitsch: 'Price Tag' Actions do not Follow the Path of the Torah," *Kipa* website (December 12, 2011). (Hebrew)

Dworkin, Ronald, 1985. A *Matter of Principle*. Cambridge, MA: Harvard University Press.

Eisenberg, Yehudah. 2005. "Tzeva haTziyut le'Yisrael," (Israel Obedience Forces) *HaTzofeh* (October 7, 2005). (Hebrew)

Elior, Rachel. 2016. "Drinking from Rabbi Ginsburgh's Water," Haaretz-Books, April 8, 2016). (Hebrew)

Elitzur, Itay. 2008. "Mi'Shulchanah shel Komemiyut" (From Komemiyut's Table) *Komemiyut* (25 Sivan 5768; June 2008). (Hebrew)

Elizur, Itay. 2008. "MiShulchana shel Kommemiyut" (From Kommemiut's Table), 22 Sivan, 5768; June, 2008). (Hebrew)

Elitzur, Uri. 2005. "Is she a Leftist?" *Be'Sheva* (March 11, 2005). (Hebrew)

Elon, Menachem. 1994. *Jewish Law: History, Sources, Principles* (4 vols.) (Bernard Auerbach and Melvin J. Sykes, trans.). Philadelphia and Jerusalem: Jewish Publication Society, 1994.

Epstein, Alek. D. (1999). "In Search of Legitimacy: Development of Conscientious Objection in Israel from the Founding of the State to the Lebanon Campaign," *Israeli Sociology* 2: 319–54. (Hebrew)

Ettinger, Meir. 2015. In Meir Ettinger Blog, *The Jewish Voice*, July 30, 2015. (Hebrew)

Ezer, Ornit. 2008. "The Struggle on the 'House of Contention begins,'" *Arutz 7*, July 16, 2008). (Hebrew)

Ezra, Hezki. 2010. "Rabbi Sherlow: I Would Have Called for Disobeying an Order," *Be'Sheva* (February 16, 2010). (Hebrew)

Federbush, Shimon. 1952. *Mishpat ha'Melukha be'Yisrael* (Laws of the King in Judaism). Jerusalem: Mossad Harav Kook. (Hebrew)

Feffer, Anshel. 2005. "An Exposure to the South," *Makor Rishon*, Journal (July 22, 2005). (Hebrew)

Feige, Michael. 2009. *Settling in the Hearts: Jewish Fundamentalism in the Occupied Territories*, Detroit: Wayne State University Press.

Feiglin, Moshe. 1998. *Where There Are No Men: The Struggle of the 'Zo Artzeinu' Movement Against the Post-Zionist Collapse*. Jerusalem: Jewish Leadership. (Hebrew)

Felix, Menahem. 1993. "They Don't Mind Padding Their Path to Peace with Our Corpses," *Nekudah* 173. (Hebrew)

Fischer, Shlomo. 2007. *Self-expression and Democracy in Radical Religious Zionist Ideology*. PhD dissertation, Jerusalem: The Hebrew University.

Forum Eretz Moledet. 2008. "Questions and Answers by Rabbi Eliezer Melamed on *Din Rodef*," *Eretz Moledet* (August 11, 2008). (Hebrew)

Friedman, Yoav. 2006. "Religious-Zionist Rabbis: We Will Not Escalate into a Civil War," *Ynet* (June 4, 2006). (Hebrew)

Gabél, Ines. 2011. "The National-Religious Community and the Media: A Love-Hate Relationship," *Israel Studies* 16, 3, pp. 51–72.

Gal, Reuven, and Tamir Liebel (eds.). 2012. *Beetween the Yarmulka and the Beret: Religion, Politics and the Military in Israel*. Ben-Shemen: Modan Publishing House. (Hebrew)

Gal-Or, Naomi. 1990. *The Jewish Underground: Our Terrorism*. Tel Aviv: HaKibutz HaMeuhad. (Hebrew)

Ganz, Chaim (1992). *Philosophical Anarchism and Political Disobedience*. Cambridge, UK: Cambridge University Press.

Ganz, Pazi, and Meital Pines. 2008. *A Trimmed Dream: Gush Katif Youth Hurts, Writes and Yearns*. Jerusalem: Sifriyat Beit-El. (Hebrew)

Garb, Yoni. 2004a. "Young Mafdal Members and the Ideological Roots of Gush Emunim." In *Religious Zionism: The Era of Changes* Asher Cohen and Israel Har'el (eds.) Jerusalem: Bialik Institute, 171–200. (Hebrew)

Garb, Yoni. 2004b. "Messianism, Antinomianism and Power in Religious Zionism: The Case of the 'Jewish Underground.'" In *Religious Zionism: The Era of Changes*, Asher Cohen and Israel Harel (eds.). Jerusalem: Bialik Institute, 323–63. (Hebrew)

Ginat, Gonen. 2006. "Readies with Gonen Ginat," *NRG: Judaism* (May 16, 2006). (Hebrew)

Ginzburgh, Yitzhak (2000). *Kingdom of Israel, Part 2*. Rechovot: Gal Eini. (Hebrew)

Ginsburgh, Yitzhak. (2005). *Kingdom of Israel, Part 3*. Kfar Habad: Gal Eini. (Hebrew)

Ginsburgh, Yitzhak. 2008. "Hayalei Moshe," (Moses' Soldiers), a speech at a *Farbrengen* (Religious get together) (10 Shevat, 5768; January, 2008). (Hebrew)

Ginsburgh, Yitzhak as recollected by Itiel Gil'adi. 2009. "Or leKaf Zayin Heshvan Samech-Tet: Beit HaShalom, Hevron," (On the Eve of 27 Heshvan 5769: The House of Peace in Hebron: a speech at a *Farbrengen* (Religious get together) (27 Heshvan 5769; November, 2008). (Hebrew)

Goldstein, Yossi. 2006. *Rabin: Biography*. Jerusalem and Tel Aviv: Schocken. (Hebrew)

Goren, Shlomo. 1994. "Seruv Pekudah" (Disobeying an Order) *Gilayon Va'ad Rabanei Yesha* 14, 1–2. (Hebrew)

Gorenberg, Gershom. 2006. *The Accidental Empire: Israel and the Birth of the Settlements, 1967–1977*. New York: Times Books.

Great Rabbis. 1980. *Gedolei Tora 'Al Hahzarat Shetahim* (Great Rabbis on Surrendering Lands), Bnei-Berak. (Hebrew)

Greenawalt, Kent, 1987. *Conflicts of Law and Morality*. New York: Oxford University Press.

Greenberg, Mordekhai. 2006. "HaYahas laTo'im," (The Attitude toward the Mistaken), *Kumi Ori* 4, 46–52. (Hebrew)

Greenberg, Mordekhai. 2008. "Kibutz Galuyot," (Ingathering of the Exiles), (an Independence Day Speech in Yeshivat Kerem be'Yavneh). (Hebrew)

Greenfeld, Shoshi. 2006. A Eulogy for her Brother, Yehuda (August 7, 2006). https://www.youtube.com/watch?v=aXOKXrxeJFw. (Hebrew)

Gronich, Zvika. 2015. "Head of Lehava was Recorded: Benzy: Should one Burn Churches? You have a Doubt that one should not?" (May 8, 2015). (Hebrew)

Gross, Zehavit. 2008. "Walking a Tightrope: The Attitude of Religious Zionist Adolescents to the State of Israel after the Disengagement," in Chaim I. Waxman (ed.), *Religious Zionism Post Disengagement: Future Directions*. New York: Yeshiva University Press. 159–88.

Hadid, Diaa. 2015. "Video Shows Israeli Extremists Celebrating Palestinian Child's Death," *The New York Times* (December 24, 2015).

Ha'Etzni, Elyaqim. 1994a. "From Defense Forces to Abandonment Forces," *Nekuda* 175. (Hebrew)

Ha'Etzni, Elyaqim. 1994b. "Civil Disobedience Now," *Nekuda* 180. (Hebrew)

Hagger, Moshe. 2000. "Be'Derekh Meshutefet," (On a Common Path) *Ma'ayanei ha'Yeshuah* (20 Adar, 5770; March, 2010). (Hebrew)

HaLevi, Hayim David. 1976. *'Ase Lekha Rav Responsa* (Accept the views of a rabbi Responsa). Tel Aviv. (Hebrew)

HaLevi, Hayim David. 1987. "Da'at Tora be'Inyanim Mediniyim," (The Torah's Opinion on Political Issues), *Tchumin* 8. (Hebrew)

HaRamati, Yael. 2007. *Orange Boy: Poems of Children from Gush Katif*, Yad Binyamin. (Hebrew)

Harel, Yisrael. 2009. "Golems that Conquered their Creators," *Haaretz* (January 3, 2009). (Hebrew)

Har-noi, Meir. 1994. *The Settlers*. Or-Yehuda: Maariv Book Guild. (Hebrew)

Heads of Mekhinot (Preparatory Institutes), 2004. "Heads' of Mekhinot Letter against Disobedience," *Nana 10 website* (6 Heshvan 5765; October, 2004). (Hebrew)

Hellinger, Moshe. 2002. *The Model of Jewish Democracy Versus the Model of Democratic Judaism in Modern Zionist Orthodox Thought of the 20th Century*, PhD dissertation, Ramat Gan: Bar-Ilan University. (Hebrew)

Hellinger, Moshe. 2005. "Rabbi Isaac Jacob Reines: Founder of Modern Zionist Orthodox Thought," *Jerusalem Studies in Jewish Thought* 18: 349–74. (Hebrew)

Hellinger, Moshe. 2008. "Political Theology in the Thought of the 'Merkaz HaRav' Yeshivah and its Profound Influence on Israeli Politics and Society since 1967," *Totalitarian Movements and Political Religions* 9 (4): 533–55.

Hellinger, Moshe. 2008. "A Clearly Democratic Religious-Zionist Philosophy: The Early Thought of Yeshayahu Leibowitz," *Journal of Jewish Thought and Philosophy*, 6 (2): 253–82.

Henschke, David. 2011. "On the Detachment from Humanity," *Akdamut* 26: 171–85. (Hebrew)

Herriot, Peter. 2009. *Religious Fundamentalism: Global, Local and Personal*. London: Routledge.

Herman, Tamar et al. 2014. *The National-Religious Sector in Israel 2014*. Jerusalem: The Israel Democracy Institute. (Hebrew)

Hirschfeld, Yair. 2000. *Oslo: A Formula for Peace*, Tel Aviv: Am Oved Publishers. (Hebrew)

Hoch, Richard L. 1994. *The Politics of Redemption: Rabbi Tzvi Yehuda ha-Kohen Kook and the Origins of Gush Emunim*. PhD dissertation, University of California, Santa Barbara.

Horowitz, Dan and Moshe Lissak. 1989. *Trouble in Utopia: The Overburdened Polity of Israel*. Albany: State University of New York Press.

Huverman, Haggai. 2004. "A Rabbinic Petition: We Identify with Rabbi Shapira," *HaZofe* (October 17, 2004). (Hebrew)

Inbari, Motti. 2007. "Religious Zionism and the Temple Mount Dilemma: Key Trends," *Israel Studies* 12, 2: 29–47.

Inbari, Motti. 2009. "When Prophecy Fails: The Theology of the Oslo Process— Rabbinical Responses to a Crisis of Faith," *Modern Judaism* 29, 3: 303–25.

Inbari, Motti. 2010. "Messianic Movements and Failed Prophecies in Israel: Five Case Studies," *Nova Religio* 13, 4: 43–60.

Inbari, Motti 2012. *Messianic Religious Zionism Confronts Israeli Territorial Compromises*, New York: Cambridge University Press.

Iserovitch, Hayim. 1996. "The Announcement of the Rabbis for the Land of Israel and the People of Israel." *The Association of Yesha Rabbis Bulletin*, 28. (Hebrew)

Iserovitch, Hayim. 2005. "Weissglass: The Illegal Settlements Will Be Evacuated after the Disengagement," NRG (June 6, 2005). (Hebrew)

Jewish Leadership. 2005. *Clarification of the Duty to Disobey* (2005). Jewish Leadership, January 2005. (Hebrew)

Kaniel, Shlomo. 2004. "The Settlers of the Hill: The Biblical Sabra? A Pilot Study of the Hill Settlers in Judea and Samaria" in: Asher Cohen (ed.), *Religious Zionism: An Era of Change*, 533–58. (Hebrew)

Kapeliouk, Amnon. 1996. *Rabin, un Assassinat Politique: Religion, Nationalisme, Violence en Israël*, Paris: Le Monde éditions.

Karpin, Michael, and Ina Friedman. 1998. *Murder in the Name of God: The Plot to Kill Yitzhak Rabin*, New York: Metropolitan Books.

Kaspit, Ben. 2005. "A Hallucinatory Woodstock," *Ma'ariv* (July 20, 2005). (Hebrew)

Katz, Ya"akov (Ketzale). 2011. "I do not Condemn," *Be'Sheva* (17 December, 2011). (Hebrew)

Kee, Alistair, ed. 1974. *A Reader in Political Theology*. Philadelphia: The Westminster Press.

Knaani, David. 1975. *The Labor Second Aliya and its Attitude toward Religion and Tradition*. Tel Aviv: Sifriat HaPoalim. (Hebrew)

Kopelowitz, Ezra. 2001. "Religious Politics and Israel's Ethnic Democracy," *Israel Studies* 6, 3: 166–90.

Kook, Abraham Isaac HaCohen. 1962. *Iggerot Ha'Ra'AYah* (Letters of Rabbi Kook), vol. 1–2. Jerusalem: Mossad HaRav Kook. (Hebrew)

Kook, Abraham Isaac HaCohen. 1984. *Iggerot Ha'Ra'aAYah* (Letters of Rabbi Kook), vol. 4. Jerusalem: Machon HaRavTzviYehudah. (Hebrew)

Kook, Abraham Isaac HaCohen. 1985. *Orot HaKodesh* (Lights of Holiness), vol. 3, Jerusalem: Mossad HaRav Kook. (Hebrew)

Kook, Abraham Isaac HaCohen. 2015. *Orot* (trans. Bezalel Naor), New Milford: CT; Jerusalem: Maggid Books. (Hebrew)

Kook, Tzvi Yehuda HaCohen. 1967. *Li'Netivot Yisrael* (The Paths of Israel), Jerusalem: Menorah. (Hebrew)

Kook, Tzvi Yehuda HaCohen. 1987. *Le'Hilkhot Zibbur* (Rulings in regard to the Public), Jerusalem: Heikin. (Hebrew)

Kook, Tzvi Yehuda HaCohen. 1995. *Eretz HaTzvi* (The Land of the Deer), (ed., Zalman Melamed). Beit-El: Netivei Or Publishing. (Hebrew)

Kook, Tzvi Yehuda HaCohen. 1998. *Sihot Ha'RaZYaH Le'Sefer Shemot* (Rabbi Kook's Sermons on Exodus), Jerusalem: Makhon HaRavTzviYehudah. (Hebrew)

Lavie, Aviv. 2003. "The Intimidator of the Hills," *Haaretz* (April 8, 2003) (Hebrew)

Lebel, Udi. 2011. " 'Left, Right, Left': Organized Disobedience as a Tool for Shaping The Security Policy During Likud's Governments" in Abraham Diskin (ed.), *From Altalenah to the Present Day—The History of a Political Movement—from Herut to Likud*, Jerusalem: Begin Center and Carmel, 228–54.

Leibowitz, Yeshayahu, 1975. *Judaism, the Jewish people and the State of Israel*. Schocken, Tel Aviv. (Hebrew)

Leibowitz, Yeshayahu. 1987. *On Just About Everything—Talks with Michael Shashar*, Jerusalem: Keter Publishing House. (Hebrew)

Leibowitz, Yeshayahu. 1990. *Law and Morality*. Tel-Aviv: Institute for the study of the labor movement. (Hebrew)

Leibowitz, Yeshayahu. 1995 (1992). "After Kibiyeh," an English translation of "Aharei Kibiyeh," 1953 (168–73), published in Eliezer Goldman (ed.). *Religion, Human Values, and the Jewish State*. Cambridge, MA: Harvard University Press, 185–90.

Leibowitz, Yeshayahu. 1999. *I wanted to ask you Professor Leibowitz*. Jerusalem: Keter Publishing House. (Hebrew)

Levanon, Elyaqim. 2009. "Disobeying Orders from the Right Wing vs. the Left Wing," *Kipa* (October 26, 2009). (Hebrew)

Levanon, Elyaqim. 2010. A Panel Discussing: "How to Avoid a Conflict Between State Laws, the Diplomatic Processes, and Divine Commandments," Third Ramle Conference. *Walla* (April 6, 2010). (Hebrew)

Levinger, Ido, Elhanan Nir, and Dvora Raziel. 2005. *Tzir Kissufim: Tefilot 'al Eretz Yisrael* (Kissufim Route: Prayers for the Land of Israel). Jerusalem. (Hebrew)

Levinson, Chaim. 2015. "Meet the Jewish Extremist Group that Seeks to Violently Topple the State," *Haaretz* (August 7, 2015). (Hebrew)

Levinson, Chaim, and David Barak. *Haaretz* (March 1, 2016). (Hebrew)

Levy, Yagil. (2015). *The Divine Commander: The Theocratization of the Israeli Military.* Tel Aviv: Am Oved Publishers. (Hebrew)

Liebeskind, Kalman. 2010. "Justice Tzvi Tal: I would Have Disobeyed an Order to Evacuate Settlements," *Ma'ariv* (September 8, 2010). (Hebrew)

Liebman, Charles (chapters 2 and 3 with Asher Cohen). 1997. *Religion, Democracy and Israeli Society.* Amsterdam: Harwood Academic Publishers.

Liebman, Charles. S., and Eliezer Don Yehiya. 1983. *Civil Religion in Israel.* Berkeley: University of California Press.

Lijphart, Arend. 1968. *The Politics of Accommodation: Pluralism and Democracy in the Netherlands.* Berkeley; University of California Press.

Lijphart, Arend. 1977. *Democracy in Plural Societies.* New Haven, CT: Yale University Press.

Lior, Dov. 1984. "Gishat ha'Halakha le'Sihot ha'Shalom Bizmaneinu," (The Halakhic Attitude toward Contemporary Peace Talks) *Shevillin* 23, 146–50. (Hebrew)

Lior, Dov. 2002. An Interview with Attorney Shalom Attali, *Sanhedrin* website. (Hebrew)

Lior, Dov. 2004. "Seiruv Pekudah '"l Hiloniyut baTzava," (Disobeying an Order regarding Secularism in the Army) *Yeshiva* website (10 Tamuz, 5764; June, 2004). (Hebrew)

Lior, Dov. 2005–2011. *Dvar Hevron Responsa*, vols. 1–3. Kiryat-Arba: Ha'Machon le'Rabanei Yishuvim. (Hebrew)

Lior, Dov. 2005a. "Is It a Sin for a Soldier to Evacuate Settlements," *Yeshiva* website (12 Adar 1, 5765; March, 2005). (Hebrew)

Lior, Dov. 2005b. "Is It Allowed to Block Roads?" *Yeshiva* website (11 Adar 2, 5765; March, 2005). (Hebrew)

Lior, Dov. 2005c. "Mesirut Nefesh '"l Eretz Yisrael," (Self Sacrifice for the Land of Israel), *Yeshiva* website (10 Iyar 5765; May, 2005). (Hebrew)

Lior, Dov. 2005d. "Thoughts after the Expulsion," *Yeshiva* website (3 Elul 5765; September, 2005). (Hebrew)

Lior, Dov. 2006a. "Confrontations with the Police," *Yeshiva* website (14 Shevat 5766; February, 2006). (Hebrew)

Lior, Dov. 2006b. "Injuring Horses during a Violent Evacuation," *Yeshiva* website (17 Shevat 5766; February, 2996)). (Hebrew)

Lior, Dov. 2006c. "A Response to the Amona Incidents," *Kumi Ori* 4, 10. (Hebrew)

Lior, Dov. 2006d. "Hanikha she'Lo Sharah ha'Tikvah," (Youth Movement Member Refuses to Sing the National Anthem) *Yeshiva* website (29 Adar 5766; March, 2006). (Hebrew)

Lior, Dov. 2006e. "Ha'Hiyuv Lekabel et Simlei ha'Medinah," (The Obligation to Honor the State's Symbols), *Yeshiva* website (4 Iyar 5766; May, 2006). (Hebrew)

Lior, Dov. 2006f. "Zealots for the Name of God," *Kumi Ori* 8, 69. (Hebrew)

Lior, Dov. 2006g. "The War is a Punishment for the Destruction of Parts of the Land of Israel," *Kumi Ori* 9, 20–24. (Hebrew)

Lior, Dov. 2006h. "Milhama 'al HaShem ve'al Meshiho," (A War in God's Name and in the Name of His Messiah), *Kumi Ori* 10, 13–19. (Hebrew)

Lior, Dov. 2007a. "What are Temporal Regulations Compared to Eternal Values," *Kumi Ori* 19, 12–15. (Hebrew)

Lior, Dov. 2007b. "A Leader to the Generation," *Komemiyut* 70 (1 Heshvan, 5768; October, 2007). (Hebrew)

Lior, Dov. 2008a. "It is Forbidden to Hire or Rent Houses to Arabs throughout the Land of Israel," *Eretz Yisrael Shelanu* 20 (Purim 5768; April, 2008). (Hebrew)

Lior, Dov. 2008b. "Kicks of Redemption," *Yeshiva* website (1 Nissan, 5768; April, 2008). (Hebrew)

Lior, Dov. 2009a. "Traffic Rules as a Basis for a Claim for Damages," *The 18th World Annual Congress for Civil Law.* (Hebrew)

Lior, Dov. 2009b. "Becoming a Religious Judge," *Yeshiva* website (30 Kislev, 5769; December, 2008). (Hebrew)

Lior, Dov. 2009c. "The Laws of the State and the *HaTov ve'ha'Meitiv* Blessing," *Yeshiva* website (12 Nissan, 5769; April, 2009). (Hebrew)

Lior, Dov. 2009d. "Mitzvat Yishuv Eretz Yisrael ve'Khibusha," (The Commandment of Settling the Land of Israel and Conquering It) *Yeshiva* website (Iyar, 5769; May, 2009). (Hebrew)

Lior, Dov. 2009e. "Rekhush Goyim be'Pinuyim," (Non-Jews' Property during Evacuations) *Yeshiva website* (22 Sivan, 5769; June, 2009). (Hebrew)

Lior, Dov. 2009f. "Price Tag Policy," *Yeshiva* website (24 Sivan, 5769; June, 2009). (Hebrew)

Lior, Dov. 2009g. "Following the Gaza War," *'Alonei Mamre* 122, 137.

Lior, Dov. 2010a. "Evacuating Settlements," *Yeshiva* website (7 Tevet, 5770; December, 2009). (Hebrew)

Lior, Dov. 2010b. "Sreifat ha'Misgad ve'Hitnatzlut haRabanim," (Torching of the Mosque, and the Rabbinic Apology), *Yeshiva* website (7 Tevet, 5770; December, 2009). (Hebrew)

Lior, Dov. 2010c. "Why to Refrain from Demonstrating against the Destruction from within the Army?), *Yeshiva* website (14 Tevet, 5770; December, 2009). (Hebrew)

Lior, Dov. 2010d. "The State's Halakhic Authority," *Yeshiva* website (6 Nissan, 5770; March, 2010). (Hebrew)

Lior, Dov. 2011. "The Problem of Unrecognized Bedouin Settlements in the Negev in Light of the Halakha," *Fourth Ramle Conference.* (Hebrew)

Lior, Dov, and Daniel Shilo. 2010. *A Letter to Rabbi Eliezer Melamed Following the Arrest of Two of His Students Who Demonstrated against the Evacuation of the Outposts* (27 Kislev, 5770; December, 2009). (Hebrew)

Lorberbaum, Menachem. 2002. *Politics and the Limits of Law: Secularizing the Political in Medieval Jewish Thought.* Palo Alto, CA: Stanford University Press.

Lustick, Ian. 1988. *For the Land and the Lord: Jewish Fundamentalism in Israel*. New York: Council of Foreign Relations.

Lustick, Ian. 1993. "Jewish Fundamentalism and the Israeli-Palestinian Impasse." In *Jewish Fundamentalism in Contemporary Perspective: Religion, Modernity and the Crisis of Modernity*, Lawrence J. Silberstein (ed.). New York: New York University Press, 104–16.

Luz, Ehud. 1988. *Parallels Meet: Religion and Nationalism in the Early Zionist Movement (1882–1904)*. Philadelphia: Jewish Publication Society of America.

Manhigut Yehudit. 2005. *Le'Veirur Hovat Ii haTziyut*, (A Clarification of the Obligation to Disobey) Jerusalem: Manhigut Yehudit. (Hebrew)

Markus, Yoel, 2004. "The Planned Evacuation: 20 Settlements in the Gaza Strip and the West Bank in a Year or Two," *Ha'aretz* (February 2, 2004). (Hebrew)

Marty, Martin. E., and Scott R. Appleby. 1993. "Introduction." In *Fundamentalism and the State: The Fundamentalism Project*, vol. 2, (eds.) Martin E. Marty and R. Scott Appleby. Chicago and London: University of Chicago Press, 1–9.

Mashiach, Amir. 2011. "Halakhic Militancy among Settlers in Judea and Samaria," *Mehkerei Yehudah ve'Shomron* 20: 255–68. (Hebrew)

Meidad, Yisrael. 1994. "By a Tenacious, yet Non-Violent Struggle, We Will Overthrow the Government," *Nekudah* 178. (Hebrew)

Melamed, Eliezer. 1994. "Psak Halakha be'Inyan Seiruv Pekudah," (An Halakhic Ruling Regarding Disobeying a Command) *Yeshiva* website. (Hebrew) http://www.yeshiva.org.il/midrash/shiur.asp?cat=449&id=1978&q

Melamed, Eliezer. 2005a. *Peninei Halachah: The Nation and the Land*. Beracha: Har-Beracha Yeshiva. (Hebrew)

Melamed, Eliezer. 2005b. "A Talk with Leftist Teenagers," *Be'Sheva* (February 10, 2005). (Hebrew)

Melamed, Eliezer. 2005c. "Ha'Derekh Latzet me'ha'Mashber," (The Way Out of the Crisis) *Yeshiva website* (Av 5765; August, 2005). (Hebrew)

Melamed, Eliezer. 2006a. "Amona Responsa," *Yeshiva* website (Shevat 5766). (Hebrew)

Melamed, Eliezer. 2006b. "Lo Mukhanah la'Shir Ha'Tikvah!," (I Refuse to Sing the National Anthem!) *Yeshiva* website (2 Adar 5766; March, 2006)). (Hebrew)

Melamed, Eliezer. 2006c. "Yahaso shel ha'Rav le'Nos'im Bo'arim," (The Rabbi's Attitude toward Burning Issues) *Yeshiva* website (23 Sivan 5766; June, 2006).

Melamed, Eliezer. 2008a. "Establishing Outposts on Private Arab Territories," *Yeshiva* website (5 Adar 1, 5768; February, 2008). (Hebrew)

Melamed, Eliezer. 2008b. "To Praise and not to Denounce," *Arutz 7* (November 13, 2008). (Hebrew)

Melamed, Eliezer. 2009. "Revivim," *Be"heva* (October 29, 2007).

Melamed, Eliezer. 2011. "Pegi'ah be'Aravim ke'Tag Mehir," (Harming Arabs as a Price Tag Attack) *Yeshiva* website (7 Adar 1, 5771; February, 2011). (Hebrew)

Melamed, Zalman. 1998. "People Ask: A Collection of Contemporary Sermons that were Aired between 1993 and 1997." Beit-El: Beit-El Yeshiva. (Hebrew)

Melamed, Zalman. 2003a. "Piskei Halakha be'Nos'im Mediniyim," (Halakhic Rulings in Political Affairs) *Yeshiva* website (4 Shevat 5763; January, 2003). (Hebrew)

Melamed, Zalman. 2003b. "The Anthem and the Flag," *Yeshiva* website (27 Av 5763; August, 2003). (Hebrew)

Melamed, Zalman. 2004a. "Pekudah Menugedet la'Arakhim," (An Order Contrary to Values) *'Arutz 7* (2 Heshvan 5765; October, 2004). (Hebrew)

Melamed, Zalman. 2004b. "Come in Crowds!" *Be'Sheva* (July 15, 2004). (Hebrew)

Melamed, Zalman. 2005a. "Disobeying Orders Strengthens the IDF." *Yeshiva* website (Adar 1, 5765; February, 2005). (Hebrew)

Melamed, Zalman. 2005b. "The IDF is in a Trap," *Yeshiva* website (Sivan 5765; June, 2005). (Hebrew)

Melamed, Zalman. 2005c. "What are the Boundaries of the Struggle?" *Yeshiva* website (7 Tamuz 5765; July, 2005). (Hebrew)

Melamed, Zalman. 2005d. "Zekifut ha'Komah be'Seiruv ha'Pekudah," (Standing Tall While Disobeying Orders) *Yeshiva* website (14 Tamuz 5765; July, 2005). (Hebrew)

Melamed, Zalman. 2005e. "Ha'Gishah ha'Mamlakhtit," (The *Mamlachti* Approach) *Yeshiva* website (27 Tamuz 5765; August, 2005). (Hebrew)

Melamed, Zalman. 2005f. "Be'Inyenei Isur 'Akirat Yishuvim," (Issues Relating to the Prohibition of Uprooting Settlements) *Yeshiva* website. (Hebrew)

Melamed, Eliezer. 2005g. "Responsa on Uprooting," parts 1–3, *Yeshiva* website. (Hebrew)

Melamed Zalman. 2005h. "Torah and Democracy," *Yeshiva website.* (Hebrew)

Melamed, Zalman. 2005i. "Seiruv Pekudah LeKhathilah?" (Disobeying Orders A Priori?) *Yeshiva website* (10 Av 5765; August, 2005). (Hebrew)

Melamed, Zalman. 2005j. "How did Rabbi Weiss Fulfill the Order?" *Yeshiva* website (18 Av 5765; August, 2005). (Hebrew)

Melamed, Zalman. 2005k. "Why is God doing this to us?" *Yeshiva* website (18 Av 5765; August, 2005). (Hebrew)

Melamed, Zalman. 2005l. "Ha'Yahas la'Medinah le'Ahar ha'Gerush," (The Attitude toward the State after the Expulsion) *Yeshiva* website (22 Heshvan 5766; November, 2005). (Hebrew)

Melamed, Zalman. 2006a. "La'Akor 'Atzei Zayit shel 'Aravim?" (To Uproot Arab's Olive Trees?) *Yeshiva* website (3 Tevet 5766; January, 2006). (Hebrew)

Melamed, Zalman. 2006b. "Misdar Boker ve'Shirat ha'Tikvah ba'Yeshiva," (Morning Gathering and Singing the National Anthem in the Yeshiva) *Yeshiva* website (3 Shevat 5766; February, 2006). (Hebrew)

Melamed, Zalman. 2006c. "Megarshei Amona Resha'im?" (Are the Amona Evictors Evil?) *Yeshiva* website (7 Shevat 5766; February, 2006). (Hebrew)

Melamed, Zalman. 2006d. "Eikh Tzarikh le'He'avek 'Al Eretz Yisrael?" (How Should the Battle over The Land of Israel be Conducted?) *Yeshiva* website (8 Shevat 5766; August, 2006). (Hebrew)

Melamed, Zalman. 2006e. "Le'Ma'amaro Shel HaRav Melamed be'Inyan Amona," (Re: Rabbi Melamed's Paper on Amona) *Yeshiva* website (18 Shevat 5766; February, 2006). (Hebrew)

Melamed, Zalman. 2006f. "The Violence in Amona," *Yeshiva* website (21 Shevat 5766; February, 2006). (Hebrew)

Melamed, Zalman. 2006g. "Le'Hakim Ma'ahazim 'al Shetah 'Aravi?" (Is it permitted to Establish Outposts on Arab Property?) *Yeshiva* website (5 Adar 5766; March, 2006). (Hebrew)

Melamed, Zalman. 2006h. "Le'Veirur Darkeinu,' (A Clarification of Our Path) *Yeshiva* website (16 Sivan 5766; June, 2006). (Hebrew)

Melamed, Zalman. 2006i. "Le'Veirur Darkeinu," (A Clarification of Our Path) Part 2, *Yeshiva* website (16 Sivan 5766; June, 2006). (Hebrew)

Melamed, Zalman. 2006j. "There Will be a War over Judea and Samaria," *Yeshiva website* (20 Tamuz 5766; July, 2006). (Hebrew)

Melamed, Zalman. 2008a. "Lo Yikhr'a ve'Lo Yishtahaveh," (We Will Not Kneel or Bow), *Komemiyut* (15 Adar2, 5768; March, 2008). (Hebrew)

Melamed, Zalman. 2008b. "Tikkun 'Het ha'Meraglim,' (Repairing the Sin of the Spies), *Komemiyut* (24 Sivan 5768; June, 2008). (Hebrew)

Melamed, Zalman. 2008c. "Hovat Seiruv Pekudah," (The Obligation to Disobey an Order) *Yeshiva* website (26 Heshvan 5769; November, 2008). (Hebrew)

Melamed, Zalman. 2010. "Ha'Tikkun: Ha'Im Titakhen Leumiyut Beri'ah u'Mussarit u'Mahem Yesodoteyah," (Repairing [*Tikkun*]: Can a Healthy and Moral Nationalism Exist and what are its Foundations) Third Ramle Conference (April 6, 2010). (Hebrew)

Melamed, Zalman. 2011. "Inter-Religious Tension Increases," *Yeshiva* website (27 Tishrei 5772; (October, 2011). (Hebrew)

Melamed, Zalman. 2012. "A Responsa on Price Tag Attacks," *Yeshiva* website. (Hebrew)

Minka-Brand, Hadas, Yuval Zur, and Limoe Nadav. 2006. "'The Wisdom of Command—Between the Tree and the Bird': A Comparative Analysis of Motivating Subordinates during the Task of Disengagement in the Golani Brigade and the Pilot School," *Psikhologia Tzeva'it* (Military Pshychology) 5: 81–146. (Hebrew)

Mozes, Hanan. 2009. "From Religious Zionism to the Post-Modern Religious: Directions and Developments in Religious Zionism since the Assassination of Yitzhak Rabin," PhD dissertation, Bar-Ilan University. (Hebrew)

Mozes, Chanan, Moshe Hellinger, and Jonathan Rynhold. 2014. *Between Legitimate Protest and 'Price Tag' Violence: Religious Zionist Attitudes to a Potential Large-Scale Evacuation of West Bank Settlements.* Ramat Gan: The Argov Center for the Study of Israel and the Jewish People, Bar-Ilan University.

Nahsoni, Kobi. 2011a. "The Chief Rabbis against the Police: A Severe Offence," *Ynet Judaism* (June 27, 2011). (Hebrew)

Nahsoni, Kobi. 2011b. "Rabbis Sherlow and Aviner: Do Not Exit While Women Are Singing," *Ynet Judaism* (September 14, 2011). (Hebrew)

Nakdimon, Shlomo. 1978. *Altalena.* Tel-Aviv: Edanim Publishers and Yedioth Aharonot. (Hebrew)

Naor, Arye. 2001. *Greater Israel: Theology and Policy.* Haifa and Lod: Haifa University Press and Zemora Bitan Publishers. (Hebrew)

National Youth Union and Komemiyut. 2007. "Preparations on the Right: A War on the Outposts," *News First Class* website (October 1, 2007). (Hebrew)

Negbi, Moshe. 2004. *We have become Like Sodom: On the Slope from a Law Abiding Country to a Banana Republic*, Jerusalem: Keter. (Hebrew)

Neuhaus, Richard John. 1986. *The Naked Public Square: Religion and Democracy in America*, 2nd ed. Grand Rapids, MI: William B. Erdiness.

Newman, David. 2010. "From Hitnachalut to Hitnatkut: The Impact of Gush Emunim and the Settlement Movement on Israeli Politics and Society," *Israel Studies 10*, 3, pp. 192–224.

Newsroom website. 2005. "The United Staff for the Land of Israel and the Legal Forum for the Land of Israel Call Not to Block Roads with Burning Tires," *Newsroom: Truth Without Borders* (June 22, 2005). (Hebrew)

Nir, Shaul. 1984. "Revival of the Nation," *Ha'aretz* (November 16, 1984). (Hebrew)

Nir, Tomer. 2011. "Head of Shavei Shomron Yeshiva: We've Exposed a ShaBaK Agent in the Yeshiva," *Srugim* website (December 19, 2011). (Hebrew)

Ovadiah, Moti. 2011. "And I Wish to Thank my Policemen for Allowing me to be here," *Ynet* (June 28, 2011). (Hebrew)

Parliamentary Inquiry. 2006. *Parliamentary Inquiry Committee of the Events that Took Place in Amona*. Interim Report. Chair: MK Yuval Steinitz. (Hebrew)

Pedhazur, Ami, and Arie Perliger. 2009. *Jewish Terrorism in Israel*. New York: Columbia University Press.

Pedahzur, Ami (2012). *The Triumph of Israel's Radical Right*. New York: Oxford University Press.

Peleg, Shmuel (Muli). 1997. *Spreading the Wrath of God*. Tel Aviv: HaKibutz haMeuhad. (Hebrew)

Peleg, Shmuel (Muli). 2003. *If Words Could Kill: The Failure of Israeli Political Discourse*. Jerusalem: Akademon Books. (Hebrew)

Pel'i, Yosef. 2005. "The Prohibition of Taking Part in Evacuating Jews," *Ve'Lo Yinateshu 'Od*, 3. (Hebrew)

Peretz, Rafi. 2010. "New Chief Rabbi of IDF: There is No Place for Disobedience in IDF," *Walla* (January 26, 2010). (Hebrew)

Peri, Yoram. 2005. *Brothers at War: Rabin's Assassination and the Culture War in Israel*. Tel Aviv: Babel. (Hebrew)

Persico, Tomer. 2014. "Twenty Years since the Goldstein's Massacre: On Romantic Neo-Hasidism and Holy Vengeance," *Haaretz* (February 19, 2014). (Hebrew)

Philipott, Daniel, 2007. "Explaining the Political Ambivalence of Religion," *American Political Science Review*, vol. 110, 3: 505–25.

Piekrash, Tuli. 2005. "Sharon's Fingerprints are Present in all Documents Approving the Establishment of Outposts," *HaZofe* (March 9, 2005). (Hebrew)

Pioterkovsky, Shlomo. 2011, "Rabbi Levanon's Students—The Outstanding Platoon," *Be'Sheva* (18 December, 2011). (Hebrew)

Porat, Hanan. 2008. An Interview with Ro'i Sharon, *Ma'ariv* (November 19, 2008). (Hebrew)

Prime Minister's Office, 2004a. "The Corrected Disengagement Plan," *Press Release*. (Hebrew)

Prime Minister's Office, 2004b. "SeLA Administration—Aiding the Gaza and North Samaria Settlers—Begins its Work" *Press Release*, Security Cabinet Decision (September 14, 2004). (Hebrew)

Ra'anan, Zvi. 1980. *Gush Emunim*. Tel Aviv: Hapoalim Library. (Hebrew)

Rabin, Yitzhak. 1996. *The Rabin Memoirs* (with Dov Goldstein, translated by Dov Goldstein). Berkeley: University of California Press.

Rabinowitz, Nahum Eliezer. 1995. "In the Wake of the Rabbinic Ruling Forbidding the Evacuation of IDF Bases in Judea, Samaria and Gaza) *Gilyon Va'ad Rabanei Yesha*, 27, 1–2.

Rahat, Menahem. 2005. "The 20 Commandments," *NRG* (April 6, 2005). (Hebrew)

Ratt, Avi. 2011. "A Litigation is Born—the Finals: Fuad vs. Rabbi Levanon," *Ynet Judaism* (December 15, 2011). (Hebrew)

Ravitzky, Aviezer. 1996. *Messianism, Zionism, and Jewish Religious Radicalism*, Chicago: Chicago University Press.

Ravitzky, Aviezer. 1998. *Religion and State in Jewish Philosophy*. Jerusalem: Israel Democracy Institute. (Hebrew)

Ravitzky, Aviezer. 1999a. "The Messianism of Success in Contemporary Judaism" *The Encyclopedia of Apocalypticism* III: 204–29.

Ravitzky, Aviezer. 1999b. *Freedom Inscribed: Diverse Voices of Jewish Religious Thought*. Tel Aviv: Am Oved. (Hebrew)

Rawls, John, 1971. *A Theory of Justice*, Cambridge, MA: Belknap Press of Harvard University Press.

Raz, Joseph, 1979. *The Authority of Law*. Oxford: Clarendon Press.

Reichner, Elyashiv. 2005. "The Dunes' Youth," *Katif.net* (Tamuz 5765; July, 2005). (Hebrew)

Reinman, Yair. 2004. "Head of the Religious Kibbutz Movement in an Open Letter against Disobedience," unpublished (4 Heshvan, 5765; October, 2004). (Hebrew)

Rimon, Yosef Zvi. 2006. "A Useless Prayer? On the Profound Strengths Revealed during the Expulsion from Gush Katif," in Yitzhak Bart (ed.), *Alumat Or*, Kfar Maimon: Sara Eldar, 40–45. (Hebrew)

Røislien, Hanne Eggen. 2007. "Living with Contradiction: An Examination of the Worldview of the Jewish Settlers in Hebron," *International Journal of Conflict and Violence*, 1, 2: 169–84.

Rosen-Zvi, Yishai. 2007. "Political Radicalism in the Works of Yeshayahu Leibowitz: History, Theology, and Ethics," in: Aviezer Ravitzky (ed.), *Yeshayahu Leibowitz: Between Conservatism and Radicalism*. Jerusalem and Tel Aviv: Van-Leer Institute and HaKibutz haMeuhad, 335–53. (Hebrew)

Rotenberg, Hagit. 2004. "How to Stop the Bulldozer," *Be'Sheva* (June 17, 2004). (Hebrew)

Rotenberg, Hagit. 2007. "On the Frontline," *Be'Sheva* (November 22, 2007). (Hebrew)

Rotenberg, Naftali. 2007. "Service, Disobedience or Rebellion: The Proper Action arising from Moral Duty and Civic Loyalty," in: Aviezer Ravitzky (ed.), *Yeshayahu Leibowitz: Between Conservatism and Radicalism*. Jerusalem and Tel Aviv: Van-Leer Institute and HaKibutz haMeuhad, 366–87. (Hebrew)

Roth, Anat. 2009. "Religious-Zionism in the Test of *Mamlachtiut*: From Kfar-Maimon to Amona," in: Ya'akov Siman-Tov (ed.), *The Disengagement Plan: The Concept and its Collapse*. Jerusalem: Konrad Adenauer Stiftung Israel and The Jerusalem Institute for Israel Studies, 35–70.

Roth, Anat. 2011. *Theories of Fundamentalism Tested against Reality: The Torani Stream of Religious Zionism and Its Struggles against the Disengagement Plan and the Destruction of Houses in Amona*, PhD dissertation. Ramat Gan: Bar-Ilan University. (Hebrew)

Roth, Anat. 2014. *Not at any Cost—From Gush Katif to Amona: The Story behind the Struggle over the Land of Israel*. Tel Aviv: Miskal-Yedioth Ahronot Books and Chemed Books. (Hebrew)

Rubinstein, Amnon. 2000. *From Herzl to Rabin: The Changing Image of Zionism*. New York: Holmes and Meier.

Rubinstein, Danny. 1982. *On the Lord's Side: Gush Emunim*. Tel Aviv: Hakibutz Hameuchad Publishing House. (Hebrew)

Sabato, Shabtai. 2005. "Ha'Emet ve'haShalom Ehavu" (Truth and Peace Embrace), unpublished document. (Hebrew)

Sach, Yaniv. 2005. "Arik's Keeper," *NRG*. (April 26, 2005). (Hebrew)

Sadan, Eli. 2005. *Ne'emanuteinu la'Torah ve'la'Tzava* (Our Loyalty to the Torah and to the Army), Eli: Bnei David. (Hebrew)

Sadan, Eli. 2006. *Le'Hossif Or: Iggeret el ha'No'ar* (To Add Light: A letter to the Youth), Eli: Bnei David. (Hebrew)

Sadan, Eli et al. 2006. *Darkeinu la'Et haZot* (Our Path for this Time) Eli: Bnei David. (Hebrew)

Sadan, Eli. 2012. *Kriat Kivun la'Tzionut ha'Datit* (An Ideological Call to Religious-Zionism), Elie: Bnei David. (Hebrew)

Sagi, Avi. 2003. "From the Land of the Torah to the Land of Israel—From One Broken Dream to Another: A Study of the Crisis in Religious Zionism." In *A Hundred years of Religious Zionism*, vol. 3, (eds.), Avi Sagi and Dov Schwartz. Ramat Gan: Bar-Ilan University Press, 457–74. (Hebrew)

Sagi, Avi. 2010a. "Does Bnei Akiva Still Exist?" *De"ot* 46, 10–14. (Hebrew)

Sagi, Avi. 2010b. "Conscientious Disobedience and Its Status in the Jewish Tradition," in: Moshe Hellinger (ed.), *The Jewish Political Tradition through the Ages: In Memory of Daniel Elazar*. Ramat Gan: Bar-Ilan University Press, 359–89. (Hebrew)

Sagi, Avi, and Dov Schwartz. 2003. "From Pioneering to Torah Study: Another Perspective." In *A Hundred Years of Religious Zionism*, vol. 2, (eds.) Avi Sagi and Dov Schwartz. Ramat Gan: Bar-Ilan University Press, 73–75. (Hebrew)

Salmon, Yosef. 1990. *Religion and Zionism: First Encounters*. Jerusalem: Ha'Sifria ha'Zionit. (Hebrew)

SaMea, H. 2006. "I Seek My Brothers: A True Dialogue between a Father and Daughter," *Olam Katan* (13 Shevat 5766; February, 2006). (Hebrew)

Sasson, Talia. 2004. *Intermediate Opinion Concerning Unauthorized Outposts*, Submitted to Prime Minister Ariel Sharon by Talia Sasson. (Hebrew)

Sasson, Talia (2015). *On The Brink of the Abyss—Is the Triumph of the Settlements the end of Israeli Democracy?* Jerusalem: Keter Books. (Hebrew)

Sarour Moti, and Avi Zontag (eds.), 2004. *Ki "Ai'yin be'Aiyin Yir'u* (They Shall See Eye to Eye). Jerusalem: Yeshivat Har-HaMor. (Hebrew)

Savir, Uri. 1998. *The Process: 1,100 Days That Changed the Middle East.* New York: Random House.

Schiff, Shaul. 2004. "Rabbi Abraham Shapira: It is Forbidden to Lend a Hand to a Racist Transfer of Jews from Gush Katif," *Ha'Zofe* (June 25, 2004). (Hebrew)

Schmitt, Carl. 1985. "Political Theology," in: *Political Theology: Four Chapters on the Concept of Sovereignity*, trans. George Schwab. Chicago: The University of Chicago Press.

Schwartz, Dov. 2000. "Between Time and Eternity: Studies on the Ephemeral Concept of Secularism in Religious Zionist Thought," in: Avi Sagi, Dudi Schwartz, and Yedida Z. Stern (eds.), *Judaism Inside and Out: A Dialogue between Two Worlds.* Jerusalem: Magness Press, 169–81. (Hebrew)

Schwartz, Dov. 2001a. *Challenge and Crisis in Rabbi Kook's Circle.* Tel Aviv: Am Oved. (Hebrew)

Schwartz, Dov. 2001b. "Insights into the Research on Religious-Zionist Thought," *Akdamut* 10: 125–31. (Hebrew)

Schwartz, Dov. 2002. *Faith at the Crossroads.* Leiden: Brill.

Schwartz, Dov. 2008. "Religious Zionism and the Struggle against the Evacuation of Settlements: Theological and Cultural Aspects," in: Chaim I. Waxman (ed.), *Religious Zionism Post-Disengagement: Future Directions.* New York: Yeshiva University Press, 93–117.

Schwartz, Dov. 2009. *Religious Zionism: History and Ideology.* Boston: Academic Studies Press.

Schwartz, Hayim Avihu. 2004. "To Rejoice and Praise despite the Hardships" (A Sermon Given at the Independence Day Celebration), Yeshivat Beit-El, *Yeshiva* website (6 Iyar, 5764; April, 2004). (Hebrew)

Segal, Haggai. 1987. *Dear Brothers: The Story of the Jewish Underground.* Jerusalem: Keter. (Hebrew)

Segal, Haggai. 1999. *Yamit, haSof: Ha'Ma'avak la'Atzirat haNesigah mi'Sinai* (Yamit, the End: The Struggle to Stop the Withdrawal from Sinai). Beit-El: Beit-El Library. (Hebrew)

Segal, Haggai. 2004. "Do We Always Await Orders?" *Be'Sheva* (June 17, 2004). (Hebrew)

Shafat, Gershon (with Zivya Granot). 1995. *Gush Emunim: The Story behind the Scenes.* Beit-El: Beit-El Library. (Hebrew)

Shahor, Naomi. (2015). *The Rabbinate in Judea Samaria and Gaza 1969–2005: Continuity and Change in the History of the Modern Rabbinate in the State of Israel*, PhD thesis. Ramat Gan: Bar-Ilan University. (Hebrew)

Shapira, Avraham. 2005. *Morashah: Kovetz Sihot u'Ma'amarim* (Tradition: A Collection of Sermons and Papers). Jerusalem: Machon HaRavTzviYehuda. (Hebrew)

Shapira, Yehosu'a. "Ki 'Aiyin be'Aiyin Yir'u: Parashat Shelah Lekha" (They Shall See Eye to Eye: *Shelah Lekha* Torah Portion) *Yeshivat Ramat Gan* website. (Hebrew)

Shapira, Yitzchak. 2009. *Torat HaMelech* (The Torah of the King). Yizhar: The Torah Institute, Yeshivat Od Yosef Chai. (Hebrew)

Sharon, Ariel. 2003. A Speech at the 4th Herzliyah Conference (November 18, 2003). (Hebrew)

Sheleg, Yair. 2000. *The New Religious Jews.* Jerusalem: Keter. (Hebrew)

Sheleg, Yair. 2004. "Rabbi Tau's Grayish Disobedience," *Ha'aretz* (September 15, 2004). (Hebrew)

Sheleg, Yair. 2007. *Rule According to the Majority?* Jerusalem: Israel Democracy Institute. (Hebrew)

Sherlow, Yuval. 2010a. *Disengagement Responsa.* Tel Aviv: Miskal. (Hebrew)

Sherlow, Yuval. 2010b. "A Letter to Students in the Yeshiva, its Alumni and its Future Students on the Contemporary Question of Hesder Yeshivot," *Yeshivat Petach Tikvah* website (5 Tevet 5770; December, 2009). (Hebrew)

Sherlow, Yuval. 2011. "Shaliach li'Dvar "veirah ba'Hitnatkut" (Agency in regard to Commiting a Crime during the Disengagement) *Moreshet* website (18 Tishrei 5771; September, 2010). (Hebrew)

Shilo, Emanuel. 2005. "Realistic Religious Zionism," *Be'Sheva* (August 18, 2005). (Hebrew)

Shilo, Emanuel. 2006. "The Spirit of Amona: From the Editor's Table," *Be'Sheva* (February 10, 2006). (Hebrew)

Shragai, Nadav. 2004. "Outpost after Outpost: This is How a Continuous Jewish Settlement is Created in the West Bank," *Ha'aretz* (June 9, 2004). (Hebrew)

Shragai, Nadav. 2005. "During the Evacuation of Yamit: Yehudah Richter Holed Up in the 'Suicide Bunker': Now He's Getting Ready for a Re-Play in Dozens of Settlements," *Ha'aretz* (June 10, 2005). (Hebrew)

Shragai, Nadav. 2007. "They're Fed Up with the State," *Ha'aretz* (January 28, 2007). (Hebrew)

Shragai, Nadav. 2008a. "The New Settler's Policy: 'Price Tag' on every Evacuation by the Army," *Ha'aretz* (March 10, 2008). (Hebrew)

Shragai, Nadav. 2008b. "Rabbi Wolpe in a Gathering against the Evacuation of the 'House of Contention': Today, The Israeli Government is the Enemy of the Jewish Nation and the Land of Israel," *Ha'aretz* (November 17, 2008). (Hebrew)

Shragai, Nadav. 2008c. "Retired District Judge Shtruzman: The High Court Erred in the 'House of Contention' Affair," *Ha'aretz* (November 19, 2008). (Hebrew)

Shragai, Nadav. 2008d. "Evacuation of the 'House of Contention' in Hebron: Why Are the Heads of the Yesha Council Silent?" *Ha'aretz* (December 5, 2008). (Hebrew)

Shochetman, Eliav. 1990–1991. "Hakarat ha'Halakha be'Hukei Medinat Yisrael," (Recognition of Israeli Law in the Eyes of Halakha), *Jewish Law Annual* 16–17: 417–500. (Hebrew)

Shochetman, Eliav. 1995. *Va'Ya'amide'ah le'Ya'akov le'Hok* (And He confirmed it as a Law to Jacob). Jerusalem: Kol Mevaser. (Hebrew)

Singer, Peter. 1973. *Demcracy and Disobedience*. Oxford: Clarendon Press.

Smart, Brian, 1978. "Defining Civil Disobedience," *Inquiry* 21: 249–60.

Smotritch, Bezalel. 2011. "What in the Blazes do we have to do with Shimon Peres?" *Be'Sheva* (December 17, 2011). (Hebrew)

Sprinzak, Ehud. 1981. "Gush Emunim: The Tip of the Iceberg," *The Jerusalem Quaterly*, 21, 28–47.

Sprinzak, Ehud. 1986. *Every Man Whatsoever is Right in his Own Eyes: Illegalism in Israeli Society*. Tel Aviv: Hapoalim. (Hebrew)

Sprinzak, Ehud. 1993. "Three Models of Religious Violence: The Case of Jewish Fundamentalism in Israel." In *Fundamentalism and the State: The Fundamentalist Project*, vol. 2, (eds.), Martin E. Marty and R. Scott Appleby. Chicago and London: University of Chicago Press, 469–90.

Sprinzak, Ehud. 1995. *Between Extra-parliamentary Protest and Terrorism: Political Violence in Israel*. Jerusalem: Jerusalem Institute for Israel Studies. (Hebrew)

Sprinzak, Ehud. 1998. *The Ascendancy of the Religious Right in Israel*. Oxford: Oxford University Press.

Sprinzak, Ehud. 1999. *Brother against Brother: Violence and Extremism in Israeli Politics from Altalena to the Rabin Assassination*. New York: The Free Press.

State Commission of Inquiry. 2010. *State Commission of Inquiry into the Handling of the Evacuees from Gush Katif and Northern Samaria by the Authorized Authorities*. Chair: Justice Eliahu Mazza.

State Inspection Committee, Protocol. 2005a. Protocol No. 200 of the State Inspection Committee (July 11, 2005). (Hebrew)

State Inspection Committee. 2005b. Protocol No. 258 of the State Inspection Committee (December 21, 2005). (Hebrew)

Stern, Yedida Z. 1999. *Pesikat Halakha be'She'elot Tziburiyot* (Halkhic Rulings in Public Matters). Jerusalem: Israel Democracy Institute. (Hebrew)

Stern, Yedida Z. 2000. "Public Leadership as Halakhic Authority," in: Avi Sagi, Dudi Schwartz, and Yedida Z. Stern (eds.) *Judaism Inside and Out: A Dialogue Between Two Worlds*. Jerusalem: Magnes Press, 235–69. (Hebrew)

Stern, Yedida Z. 2004. *State. Law. Halakha*. Section 3: *Religion and State: Halakha's Role*. Jerusalem: Israel Democracy Institute. (Hebrew)

Sternberg, Eran. 2006a. "Flag of Disobedience or Rag of Statehood," *Be'Sheva* (May 21, 2005). (Hebrew)

Sternberg, Eran. 2006b. "First Right wing Objector Prevailed and was Jailed," *Yesha News* (August 15, 2006). (Hebrew)

Tal, Uriel. 1987. *Myth and Reason in Contemporary Judaism*. Tel Aviv: Hapoalim Library and Tel Aviv University. (Hebrew)

Talmon, Jacob Leib. 1985. *Political Messianism: The Romantic Phase*. Boulder, CO: Westview Press (first published at London: Secker and Warburg, 1960).

Tau, Tzvi Yisrael. 2005. *Shu't Emuni be'Noseh Pe'ilut Panim el Panim, Le'Or Me'oraot haSha'a* (Faith-based Responsa on the subject of Face to Face Activities, in Light of Actual Occurrences). NRG. (Hebrew)

Taub, Gadi. 2010. *The Settlers and the Struggle over the Meaning of Zionism*. New Haven, CT: Yale University Press.

Thoreau, Henry David 1993. *Civil Disobedience and other Essays*. Dover Publications.

Trop, Aharon. 2004. "Evacuating Jews is a Sin: An Interview with Rabbi Avraham Shapira," *Be'Sheva* (October 15, 2004). (Hebrew)

Trop, Aharon. 2005. "Ohev et haBeriyot uMekarvan la'Torah" (Loves the People and Brings them Closer to the Torah) *Ma'ayanei haYeshu'ah* (3 Heshvan 5766; November, 2005). (Hebrew)

Trop, Aharon. 2006. "A Loyalty Test," *Be'Sheva* (May 3, 2006). (Hebrew)

Trop, Aharon. 2007. "Tziyut la'Halakha le'Ma'an haTzava" (Obeying the Halakha for the Sake of the Army), *Yeshiva* website (2 Elul 5767; August, 2007). (Hebrew)

Tzachi, Adam. 2005. "Ballad to a New Diaspora," *Tzura* website.

Uman, Yisrael. 2006. "The Attitude toward the Expelled: A National Disgrace," *NRG* (January 22, 2006). (Hebrew)

Unger, Yaron. 2010. "The Limits of Obedience and Disobedience to Military Command." Jerusalem: Knesset Research and Information Center. (Hebrew)

Union of Hesder Yeshivot. 2009. "The Decision of the Gathering of Hesder Yeshivot Rabbis Against Demonstrations within the IDF," *Union of Hesder Yeshivot* website (November 25, 2009). (Hebrew)

Waldman, Eliezer. 2006. "La'Et haZot, 'Am Yisrael Hai uMargish" (At this Time, The Jewish Nation is Alive and Feels) *Yeshiva* website. (Hebrew)

Walzer, Michael et al. 2000. *The Jewish Political Tradition*. Vvl. 1: Authority. New Haven, CT, and London: Yale University Press.

Wasserman, Avraham. 2007. *Morag Harutz: Analogyot Tana'khiyot le'Ahar haGerush miGush Katif umi'Tzfon haShomron* (The Diligent Thresher: Biblical Analogies after the Expulsion from Gush Katif and Northern Samaria), *Yeshiva* website (Tishrei 5767; September–October, 2007).

Waxman, Dov. 2008. "From Controversy to Consensus: Cultural Conflict and the Israeli Debate over Territorial Withdrawal." *Israel Studies*, 13, 2: 73–96.

Weisburd, David. 1989. *Jewish Settler Violence: Deviance as Social Reaction*, University Park: The Pennsylvania State University Press.

Weisburd, David, and Hagit Lernau. 2006. "What Prevented Violence in Jewish Settlements in the Withdrawal from the Gaza Strip: Toward a Perspective of Normative Balance." *Ohio State Journal on Dispute Resolution* 22, 1: 37–82.

Weiss, Efrat, and Shmulik Hadad. 2006. "Settlers Sign an Urgent Petition against Olmert," *Ynet* (August 2, 2006). (Hebrew)

Weiss, Efrat. 2008a. "House of Contention: We will stand as a Bulwark to Prevent Destruction," *Yedi'ot Aharonot* (November 18, 2008). (Hebrew)

Weiss, Efrat. 2008b. "Yesha Council Chairman: Expel Daniela Weiss from Hebron," *Yedi'ot Aharonot* (December 3, 2008). (Hebrew)

Weiss, Erica. 2014. *Conscientious Objectors in Israel—Citizenship, Sacrifice, Trials of Fealty*. Philadelphia: University of Pennsylvania Press.

Weiss, Hillel. 2009. "Israel is no Longer a State," *Ye'udi* website. (Hebrew)

Weiss, Yisrael. 2010. *Straight from my Heart: A Diary of Service*. Tel Aviv: Miskal Books. (Hebrew)

Weissman, Aliza. 1990. *The Evacuation: The Story of the Evacuation of the Settlements in Sinai*. Bet-El: Bet-El Library. (Hebrew)

Weitzen, Shlomo Yosef. 2008. "The Outpost's Agreement," *Yeshiva* website.

Weitzen, Shlomo Yosef. 2009. "Taking Part in 'Price Tag' Attacks," *Yeshiva* website.

Weitzman, Yehoshua. 2005a. "Al haSe'arah be'Inyan Seiruv haPekudah 1" (The Storm over Disobeying Orders 1) *Yeshivat Ma'alot* website (27 Heshvan 5765; November, 2004). (Hebrew)

Weitzman, Yehoshua. 2005b. "Al haSe'arah be'Inyan Seiruv haPekudah 2" (The Storm over Disobeying Orders 1) *Yeshivat Ma'alot* website (19 Kislev 5765; December, 2004). (Hebrew)

Weitzman, Yehoshua. 2005c. "Hirhurim be'Ikvot haMatzav (Tokhnit haHitnatkut)" (Thoughts Regarding the Situation [The Disengagement Plan]) *Yeshivat Ma'a lot website* (25 Kislev 5765; December, 2004). (Hebrew)

Wilcox, Philip C., Jr. 2011. "The Settlers and the Struggle over the Meaning of Zionism." *The Middle East Journal* 65, 1:143–145.

Willian, Yossi. 2008. *Song of the Detatched*. Haifa: Sha'anan College. (Hebrew)

Wolf, Itzik. 2006. "Battle of the Rabbis," *HaZofe* (June 25, 2006). (Hebrew)

Wolpe, Shalom Dov. 2011. "Rabbi Wolpe Responds to Rabbi Yoel Bin-Nun's Letter—Fascinating!" *SOS Israel* website. (Hebrew)

Yaron, Zvi. 1992. *The Philosophy of Rabbi Kook*. English version by Avner Tomaschoff. Jerusalem: Department for Torah Education and Culture in the Diaspora of the World Zionist Organization.

Yifrach, Yehuda. 2014. "The Religious Manifesto behind 'Price Tag': Birth Pains of a New Nation." *NRG*, April 28, 2014. (Hebrew)

Zemach, Mina. 2010. "The Results of the Socio-Political Identity of Israeli Youth" in: Zameret-Kercher, Hagar (ed.), *Both This and That: Identity Contradictions Among Israeli Youth*—The Third Research Study of the Friedrich Ebert Foundation into Changes in National, Cultural and Personal Attitudes. Tel Aviv, Friedrich Ebert Foundation, 28–104. Haksel, Ralph and Natanson, Rubi (publishers) (Hebrew)

Zertal, Idith, and Akiva Eldar. 2007. *Lords of The Land: The War over Israel's Settlements in the Occupied Territories 1967–2007*, (translated by Vivian Eden). New York: Nation Books.

Zik, Adir. 2004. "I Will Lie Down in Front of the Bulldozers," *Be'Sheva* (10 June, 2004). (Hebrew)

Zini, Eliyahu Rahamim. 2005a. "An Evacuation from Gush Katif as a Crime against Humanity," *Open Letter in Yeshivat Or vi'Yeshu'ah* website (4 Av 5765; August, 2005). (Hebrew)

Zini, Eliyahu Rahamim. 2005b. "A Sermon I Delivered on Tuesday, 12 Av, the Day of the Brutal Uprooting from Gush Katif, according to the Orders of the Dictator Who Officiates as Prime Minister of Israel," *Open Letter in Yeshivat Or vi'Yeshu'ah* website. (Hebrew)

Ziv, Yossi. 1995. "Leibowitz and Civil Disobedience," in: Avi Sagi (ed.), *Yeshayahu Leibowitz: '.lamo veHaguto* (His World and Thought). Jerusalem: Keter, 228–37.

Zoldan, Yehuda. 2006. "Gvurah u'Mesirut Nefesh be'Gush Katif" (Heroism and Self-Sacrifice in Gush Katif) in: *Michael li'Yeminekha*. Jerusalem: Mahu't, 73–81.

Index